Ludwig Drums
(Djembe)
0.00
Drums
Hand Claps
PARLOPHONE
45 RPM
TICKET TO RIDE
THE BEATLES
MADE IN GT. BRITAIN
PARLOPHONE
ARDMORE & BEECHWOOD LTD
45-R 4949
MADE IN GT. BRITAIN
LOVE ME DO
(Lennon - McCartney)
THE BEATLES
STRAWBERRY FIELDS FOREVER
Ludwig
THE BEATLES
IF I WERE 21 I'D VOTE FOR RINGO

Web – www.ringostarrandthebeatlesbeat.com
www.beatlesbeat.com

Email – info@ringostarrandthebeatlesbeat.com
info@beatlesbeat.com

Facebook – http://www.facebook.com/ringostarrandthebeatlesbeat

Twitter – @beatlesbeatbook

RINGO STARR
AND
THE BEATLES BEAT

ALEX CAIN AND TERRY McCUSKER

Alex Cain Terry McCusker.

Matador
9 Priory Business Park,
Wistow Road, Kibworth Beauchamp,
Leicestershire. LE8 0RX
Tel: (+44) 116 279 2299
Fax: (+44) 116 279 2277
Email: books@troubador.co.uk
Web: www.troubador.co.uk/matador

ISBN 978 1785899 553
978 0993268410 (eBook-ePub)
978 0993268403 (e-Book-Mobi)
978 0993268427 (e-Book-eReader)

British Library Cataloguing in Publication Data.
A catalogue record for this book is available from the British Library.

Typeset in 11pt Aldine by Troubador Publishing Ltd, Leicester, UK

Matador is an imprint of Troubador Publishing Ltd

Alex dedicates this book to his wonderful wife Joanne for her help and support, to Daniel, Benjamin, and Joseph for subjecting them to constant Beatle music, and to his Mum and Dad for introducing him to the music.

Terry dedicates this book to Tom and Moll, for their endless patience.

CONTENTS

ABOUT THE AUTHORS

Like John Lennon a quarter of a century before him, Alex was born at Oxford Road Maternity Hospital, Liverpool, as the Beatles' latest single *Eleanor Rigby/Yellow Submarine* sat atop the charts. A drummer for many years, he has enjoyed a career in TV sound, most notably working on Channel 4's *Brookside* and *Hollyoaks*, plus numerous productions for BBC, ITV and Independents. He is particularly proud of his contribution to the BBC documentary of another of his heroes, *Dennis Wilson -The Real Beach Boy*.

After leaving school, Terry was lucky enough to be working in the same building that housed the famous Cavern club in Liverpool. Here he was able to observe the birth of Merseybeat, and of course to see - close up - the most famous of all of those bands. Within three years of seeing the Beatles at the Cavern, Terry was himself playing the sweat-clubs of Germany and elsewhere. Working as a freelancer he has played all over Europe, America and the Middle East with many varied bands and artists on stage, screen or radio. Still in demand, he can be seen doing anything from powering along a ten-piece, or merely standing up playing his cocktail kit with a trio in his local pub.

FOREWORD BY DON POWELL

"I first became aware of the Beatles (especially Ringo) when I got their first album *Please Please Me* as a birthday present for my young sister. In those days, when you bought a record, there it was - *NO* cellophane covering. Anyway, I decided to play it for myself before she got it on 'the day'.

I fell in love with it straight away, especially Ringo's style and playing (I was just starting myself and was getting influences from anywhere). Ringo's style (although I didn't really understand it at the time) was *VERY* original, he 'swings' like crazy...... listen to, *There's a Place* and his original style of playing on *Anna* - no one played like that then. The first time I heard *Please Please Me*, I couldn't understand what I thought was 'white noise' over the record. Listening closer, I realised it was Ringo's hi-hats being played slightly open with his right hand stick pattern 'smashing the hats', playing side to side..... I started doing the same straight away, but was told off for playing too loud............ THANK YOU, RINGO!

Ringo also had a 'clumsy' way of doing a drum-fill, which became very infectious and very annoying to us would-be drummers, WHO COULDN'T DO IT LIKE HE COULD......

A VERY UNDERRATED PLAYER, WHO DESERVES MORE CREDIT....... there, I've said it!

From a very big Ringo Starr fan.....

Don Powell..... (Slade)

PS. My sister never did get the LP for her birthday.... she had a 'stick of rock' instead."

St. Paul's Presbyterian Church Youth Club
a*n*n*o*u*n*c*e a Return Visit of
POLYDOR RECORDING
—A*R*T*I*S*T*S—
The BEATLES
on Saturday 10th
March . 1962
in the Church Hall
North Road
also The COUNTRY FOUR with Brian Newman
★ Admittance
By Ticket Only
TICKETS
Five Shillings
From 7-30 p.m.
to 11-30 p.m.
Right of admission reserved

PREFACE

Alex

I've long had the idea of evaluating the percussive element of the Beatles' music, an area that has been touched upon, but seemingly never in isolation. Being born and bred in Liverpool, the Beatles have naturally loomed large in my life. Indeed, at the height of Merseybeat my Dad played drums with the Country Four, sharing the bill[1] with the Beatles.

When my parents purchased the *1967-70* compilation in the early 1970's, my little world literally opened-up before me. While my mates were listening to the last-gasps of Glam-Rock, I was immersing myself in the incredible diversity of songs on the album we all knew as '*Double-Blue*'. However, for me, the drums were 'king'. From the drum-fill soaked opening of *Strawberry Fields Forever*, I was hooked. I wanted to be a drummer.

Fast-forward 40-odd years (gulp!), and I still have my passion for all things 'Fab', with 'new' material and remasters being released year on year. With the release of the *Love* album in 2006, Ringo was hailed as the star of the show, his solid yet inventive drumming knitting the 'mashed-up' segueing and sequencing of Beatles classics perfectly. This perception was reinforced by the release of the remastered Beatles catalogue in 2009, the audio restoration processes revealing a previously unheard depth to the sound of his drums and cymbals, ultimately placing Ringo's intuitive, instinctive drumming to the forefront of the mixes.

What Ringo played provided the template for drummers across the world, the building blocks of modern rock drumming. It wasn't simply *what* Ringo played, it's *how* and *when* he played. Ringo possesses a sensitivity and empathy that enhances each song without dominating. Scratch beneath the surface of the Beatles' musical output, and you will soon discover layers of percussive elements which display just how much care and attention to detail they put into their music. Their exponential level of artistic freedom afforded them this luxury, although as their power grew they never committed to tape anything that was 'sloppy' or not *for the good of the song*.[2] While avoiding the pitfalls of repetition, each single or album had to be better and different than the preceding one, a philosophy that also extended to Ringo's drumming. In light of this, it's remarkable how Ringo was able to adjust to these demands, his drumming sitting perfectly both within *and* around each song, binding it all together as one simple coherent package.

With this book we are also challenging the public *perception* of Ringo Starr, the drummer, which has shifted from idolatry, to mild disdain and indifference, and back to idolatry, with many re-appraisals along the way. Many conversations (especially online) regarding Ringo's drumming turn to the oft repeated John Lennon retort to an enquiry asking if he believed Ringo was 'the best drummer in the world'. Lennon reportedly snapped back - "He's not even the best drummer in the Beatles[3]". This Lennon 'barb' has since been debunked, and holds as much credence as Abraham Lincoln's quote about not believing everything you read on the internet. While researching his *All These Years* series of books, Mark Lewisohn could find no evidence of the quote ever being muttered by Lennon, indeed he discovered it was first attributed to comedian Jasper Carrott in 1983 - some three years after Lennon's death. That such a quote could be taken as a truth betrays a commonly held attitude towards Ringo - that of the goofy 'happy-go-lucky' scruff from the Dingle who got lucky. Eric Morecambe after all, referred to him as "Bongo" - an image reinforced by his portrayal in the *Beatles Cartoon* series ("Uh-hu…yuuuuur…"[4]). It's a fact Ringo was never a 'flash' drummer in the eyes of non musicians (he didn't even 'twirl' his drumsticks), anyone could have done what he did - right? Tellingly, that line of thought is usually uttered by those who don't know a crotchet from a hatchet, certainly never repeated by drummers. Ringo may have been in the

The goofy persona of his cartoon character did little to enhance Ringo's image

right place at the right time, but John, Paul and George were no fools - they were picking up a drummer they considered to be the best in Liverpool. Within 18 months, Ringo would be the most popular Beatle in America. Did Marge Simpson write to John, Paul or George?[5]

Of course Ringo is no Buddy Rich[6], and we have been mindful to caution ourselves that we are dealing with an artist who has no pretensions about his playing. Ringo is first and foremost a Rock and Roll drummer who loves nothing more than getting up on stage and 'bouncing-off' his bandmates. It is that professionalism, vitality and showmanship that undoubtedly contributed so much to the Beatles enduring success.

> "Now everybody seems to have their own opinion
> Of who did this and who did that
> But as for me I don't see how they can remember
> When they weren't where it was at."
>
> **(Paul McCartney, *Early Days*)** [7]

I first met Terry when our paths crossed at Mersey Television in the early 90's, where he was employed as a consultant on the excellent drama series *And the Beat Goes On*, which aired on Channel 4. The series told the tortuous story of a Merseybeat group in the early Sixties. Terry's first-hand knowledge of the period proved invaluable to the production, his sourcing of authentic instruments of the period was especially memorable, as was the ability of the actors who played them - most of the music was recorded live, 'in situ'.

Terry would later re-join Mersey TV on a more permanent basis, handling music clearance for the company's productions, *Brookside*, *Hollyoaks*, and *Grange Hill*. As I was also employed on these shows as a dubbing (re-recording) mixer, I found myself working closely with Terry, and as drummers both susceptible to the charms of importing vintage drums from the States, we struck-up an instant rapport. Many years later, having both left the company (now Lime Pictures), we remained friends, and when I began this project I invited Terry to help out. As Paul McCartney alludes to on the track *Early Days* from his album *New*, I felt it vital to call upon someone who was actually around to witness the incredible musical explosion that was soon to engulf the world. Terry is that rare beast - a drummer who regularly saw the Beatles at the Cavern, and for this book he is able to offer first-hand experiences of seeing both Ringo and Pete Best play with the group. He is also able to provide us with a feel for what it was like to be a drummer during the incredible period that was the 1960's[8] - both the tools available and the constraints within which the musicians performed. What started out as a book by Alex Cain *with* Terry McCusker, became a book by Alex Cain *and* Terry McCusker, and it's all the better for it.

Alex Cain

PREFACE

Terry

I was delighted to be asked to take part in this project by my old chum Alex Cain. We had worked together for Mersey Television on various programmes, he as a dubber, a very skilled and demanding job requiring high concentration levels and an ability to edit and enhance the audio track in conjunction with added effects and music to video footage, and me as general dogsbody. He worked in a dubbing suite situated next door to my 'office' - which in reality was little more than a converted broom cupboard[9].

We found that we had lots of things in common, not only are we both drummers, but we like all kinds of music and in particular the Beatles of whom Alex has an in-depth knowledge. He can deliver devastating one liners, usually with the intention of pricking the balloons of pomposity or aimed at the perversity of inanimate objects. Like me, he is an inveterate giggler with an ability to see the funny side of life and many a day passed where one or both of us was reduced to watery eyed helplessness, retreating to our lairs, bent double with aching ribs.

Working on this project has been a labour of love. Listening to the songs has rekindled memories which have taken me back to my callow (misspent?) youth, and has made me appreciate with a more informed ear the brilliance and genius of four 'layabouts' from Liverpool. Nowadays I can listen to five or six versions of the same Beatles track on an expensive pair of headphones, but they somehow don't compare to the original mono versions which I played on my old 'radiogram'[10] now forlornly standing, mouldy and neglected in my garage along with the original LP's in their tatty old Sellotaped sleeves. Nor does a download compare with buying the latest LP from NEMS, reading the sleeve notes on the bus and willing it to go faster so I could get home, drop the needle in the groove, and crank up the volume.
My earliest memory of Ringo is of nearly being run over unintentionally (I think) outside the Cavern when he did a fast

three-point turn in his turquoise Ford Zephyr - it could have been the more luxurious Zodiac version, but I was too busy jumping out of the way to notice! In those days he sported a beard and a swept back 'Teddy Boy' haircut and I had no idea who he was – somebody told me that he was the drummer with Rory Storm and the Hurricanes. Next time I saw him, the beard had gone and in fact, so had his drums. He had just joined the Beatles and was playing a lunchtime session at the Cavern. His kit hadn't arrived.[11] Ringo worked the first session of the day sitting down playing just a hi-hat, a couple of cymbals and stomping his feet. I was impressed, not only by his rhythm, but also by the courage he showed by going on stage without drums - a sitting duck for all those Pete Best fans who resented the fact that their hero had been sacked a short time before.

For sure, without Ringo, the Beatles wouldn't have been the Beatles we know today - their music would have been very different. One thing we must surely agree on is that their music still sounds 'fab' over four decades after they split, and let's not forget that Ringo was one quarter of that successful band. Indeed, someone once said that the Beatles were greater than the sum of their parts – I couldn't have put it better.

Terry McCusker

PART ONE

How To Use This Book

OVERVIEW

The Songs

The group's worldwide catalogue was largely non-standardised until it was released on CD for the first time in 1987. Until *Sgt. Pepper's Lonely Hearts Club Band* in 1967, when the Beatles were able to negotiate the terms of a new contract with EMI, their releases would differ from territory to territory, with the North American market in particular radically different from the original British releases. The 1987 CD releases globally unified the music, taking the British LP's, adding the US LP version of *Magical Mystery Tour*, and collecting the remaining non-LP singles and EP releases on two CD's, christened *Past Masters Volumes 1 & 2*. With this book, by including the songs present on the *Past Masters* compilations, the reader is able to fire up a CD, Mp3 player, LP, or whatever medium their Beatle music currently resides, and follow each album, track by track.

With this in mind, we have approached the presentation of this book by following the sequence of the group's original *British* releases. While this may not accurately follow the recording dates of the songs, we have included those dates next to each song title. The Beatles were so prolific and regimented in their recording sessions and the subsequent releases from those sessions, that there were very few songs left-over from one session to the next. There are of course exceptions[1], but as those songs are in single figures (and as such are indicated in our text), it has little or no effect upon an appreciation of their musical development.

Where songs were issued on multiple formats (for example a single release also being included on an LP), we have included the song twice. On two occasions (*A Hard Day's Night* and *Eleanor Rigby/Yellow Submarine*) singles were released on the same day as LP's on which they appear. We have included these releases as footnotes to the LP's but have not commented upon them as we have already done so within the LP.

Mono or Stereo?

> "I have always espoused that the Beatles' music needs to be listened to in mono, at least up to the White Album. The only mixes that the band heard and gave their seal of approval to were the mono mixes up to that point."
>
> **Ken Scott, EMI Abbey Road engineer.**

In the 1960's, mono was the dominant audio format. The public largely listened to music on underpowered single-speaker radios[3] and record players. Music in cars nearly always came via a single (under dash) speaker, being nigh-on impossible to appreciate above the rumble of cross-ply tyres on tarmac. Stereo was an emerging and niche listening format, much the same as SACD, HD Audio downloads, and Blu-Ray Audio is today. Mass-market appeal for stereo exploded in the late 1960's, with stereo soon becoming the dominant format.

Until the release of *The Ballad Of John And Yoko* single in 1969, all of the Beatles' singles were issued exclusively in mono. Prior to *Abbey Road*, LP releases were issued in both mono and stereo, with the mono mixes receiving the greater attention from the band, George Martin and his staff. Mono versions of the Beatles' songs are unique and considered by many to be superior to the stereo mixes, as mono mixes 'lock' the sound into a solid, coherent listening experience.

The Beatles began their recording career with a mere 2 tracks to record onto. A year later EMI had installed 4-track machines, with which the Beatles recorded until the introduction of 8-track halfway through the *White Album* sessions in 1968. Because of the limitation of track availability, percussion was often 'dislocated' on the stereo mixes. For example, to create space for other instruments, a cowbell may have been mixed (or 'bounced down') and placed on one track, usually along with, for example, the bass guitar and drums. As a result, the engineer had to have a clear idea how the cowbell would 'sit' in the mix, and adjusted its level accordingly. It was critical to get this correct, and as such, how this sounded in mono was his primary concern. A good example of this is *I Need You* from the *Help!* LP. The cowbell on the mono version sits unobtrusively in the mix, while on the stereo version the cowbell is dominant, clumsily appearing as if the fader was moved up in an almost half-hearted and forgetful fashion.

The limitations of the stereo mixes could also lessen the impact of a song. John Lennon was apparently horrified when he heard the stereo mix of *Revolution*, and quite right he was too. The stereo version lacks the power and urgency of the mono mix, the separation of instruments providing a dislocated listening experience. If the listener is not aware of the volume of his system, the opening bars of the mono version (especially on vinyl) can be rather disturbing!

In compiling this book, we have listened to both mono and stereo versions of the songs, the mono to provide us with an overall picture of how the drums and percussion were intended to 'sit in the mix', the stereo to allow us to utilise the separation of the instruments in order to deconstruct the percussive elements at play. The release of the *Beatles In Mono* vinyl LPs in late 2014 proved to be especially helpful in our appraisal of the mono mixes, and we thoroughly recommend them.

We have written solely about what we hear on the recordings – other works have relied upon and quoted from sources who were recalling events some 30 – 50 years previously. Whilst this "from the horse's mouth" approach may appear preferable, stating Ringo played "this" or "that", when quite clearly he played "the other" is unfortunate.

The Beatles' Studio Practices

During their early studio career, the Beatles would rehearse a song as a group, and when happy with the results, would proceed to make recordings. Each recording is referred to as a *take*, irrespective of these takes being complete or not. Occasionally, portions of different takes would contain stronger performances than others, and would be edited together by making copies of the recordings and splicing the tapes together to produce the illusion of one unified recording. One such example of this is *She Loves You*, where the cuts in the tapes can be detected at [1.21] and [1.28].

As the Beatles' songs and use of the studio expanded, they would perform less as a single unit, basic recordings being made with drums, guitar and/or piano, and perhaps a guide vocal. Bass guitar and other embellishments (percussive, orchestral, or vocal etc.) would then be added to the original take. The recording of *The Beatles* LP heralded a return to group recordings, with this edict providing the basis of the *Get Back* project the following year.[4]

Technicalities

Each song's recording engineer is listed, as this had a bearing upon the overall sound that was captured on tape. George Martin is assumed to be the Producer, unless otherwise stated.

Timings relative to the music are indicated beneath bars, allowing the reader to accurately follow the description or notation of the songs. Regarding notation, as Ringo is a drummer with such a great amount of 'feel', it is pertinent to note it is sometimes impossible to transcribe the subtle nuances of his playing. Ringo played ever so slightly *behind* the beat[5], he would often strike the drum skins milliseconds either side of the natural beat (as indeed 99% of drummers do), and as such this is impossible to accurately represent in notation form. However (occasionally using grace notes) we have attempted to remedy this, presenting Ringo's patterns as accurately as possible.

Notation

The time signature (or *meter*) of each song is stated below the title of each song description, for example -

Day Tripper
Time Signature – *4/4*

Where appropriate, and to unclutter bars, we have occasionally removed rests. Timing will still be obvious due to notes of other instruments occurring where rests have been removed.

Pie Charts

Pie charts display the percussion instruments used by the Beatles on an LP by LP basis. Whilst some songs destined for release as singles were recorded during sessions held chiefly to create the next LP, we felt it better not to include these, as such a small sample is not particularly representative of the group's fondness for a particular instrument at that point in time. One exception is the EP release *Magical Mystery Tour* (in Pt 2), where sessions were held with a standalone release in mind. We have not produced a chart for the *Yellow Submarine* LP, as songs for this release were recorded on an ad-hoc basis, across a period of more than a year, with the last song recorded nearly a year before the release of the LP.

Where the only percussion instruments present are drums, we have displayed this as 'drums'. On the rare occasions there are no drums or percussion (e.g. *Yesterday*), we have displayed this as "none". Where songs have instruments that make-up a set of drums and are played in isolation or form the dominant feature (e.g. the use of brushes on the snare), we have treated them as individual, separate instruments.

Terminology

Regarding *drumming* and *recording* terminology, we have assumed most readers have a basic understanding of such matters. However we have attempted to simplify matters as much as possible, rather than alienate (and bore) readers who have little technical knowledge of the subject. We encourage those readers to refer to the *Glossary* whenever possible.

We have used the term *'miking'* to describe the use of a microphone to record drums. This seems a better route to take than using alternatives such as *'micing'*, *'mic-ing'* or even would you believe, *'microphing'*.

The Beatles often referred to 'bridge' sections of songs as 'middle 8's', regardless of how many bars are actually contained in the bridge. We refer to these passages as either 'bridges' or 'middle 8's'.

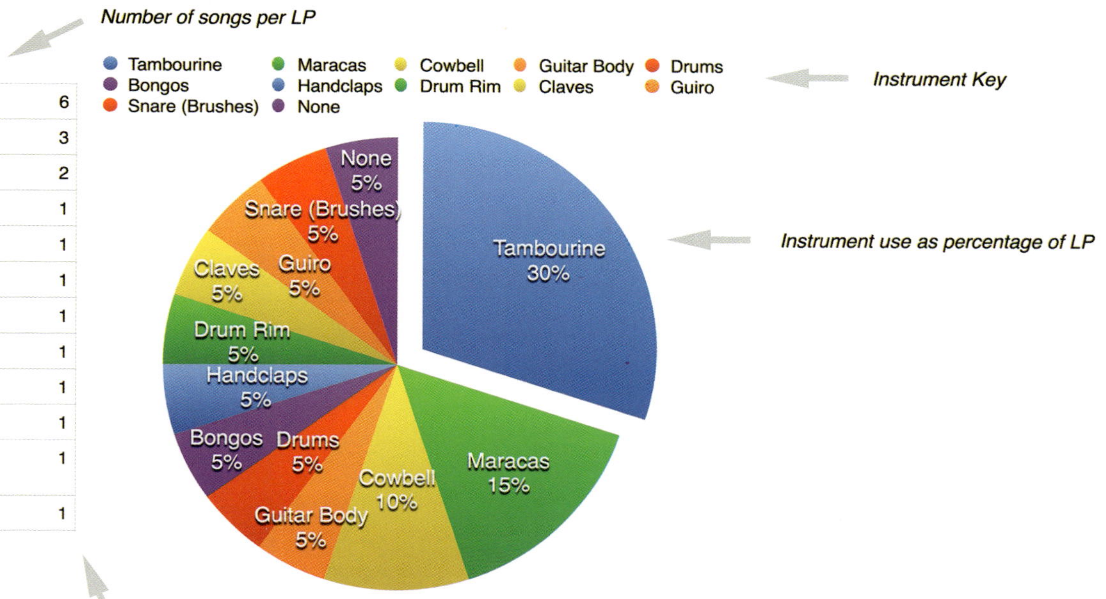

14 Songs

Tambourine	6
Maracas	3
Cowbell	2
Guitar Body	1
Drums	1
Bongos	1
Handclaps	1
Drum Rim	1
Claves	1
Guiro	1
Snare (Brushes)	1
None	1

Instrument name

Number of times instrument is used within LP

Notes

To expand upon certain themes, we have included expanded and extensive notes.

Content

Finally, a quick word for seasoned Beatle fans. There are many pieces of information which may well be considered to be 'common knowledge', but we have included such matters to aid the casual listener and music fan.

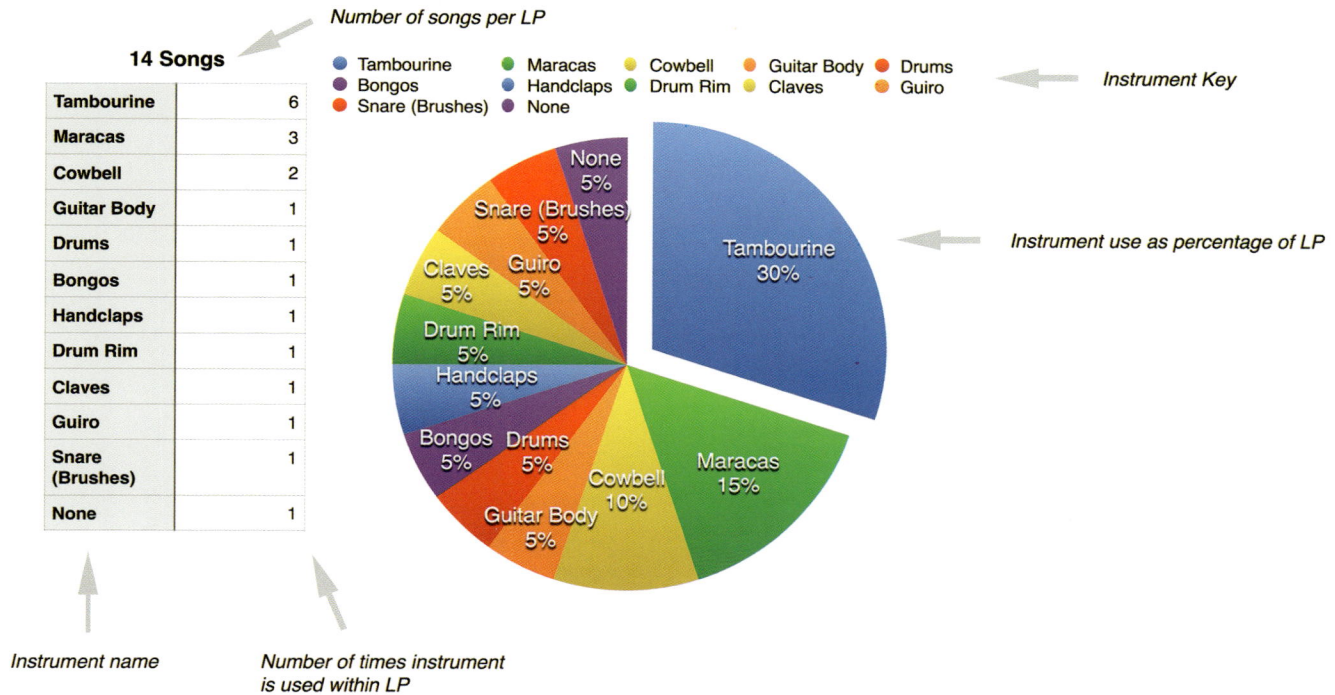

A SHORT GUIDE TO DRUM NOTATION

This book is not intended to be a drum tutor – indeed the subtleties and nuances of Ringo's instinctive drumming make it virtually impossible to transcribe his playing accurately. A case in point is his snare drum work leading to the chorus in *Taxman* – even displaying accents (the symbol >) on the notation is insufficient to translate the feel and human element of his drum strokes. Additionally, a great deal of the (sometimes overdubbed) percussion is buried deep in the mix and is difficult to hear, let alone commit to bars of drum notation. As a result, our transcriptions are entirely our own interpretation of what we are able to hear.

Time Signatures

4/4 is the most used time signature (or meter) in Western music – indeed, for this reason, it is referred to as 'common time'. The bottom number tells you the value of the note, and the top number tells you how many of those there are in the bar. Taking that into account, in the bars below we can see that a bar indicating 3/4 tells us that we should count 3 times per bar: 1,2,3 ….. etc. With a bar of 4/4 we count 1,2,3,4 …. and so on.

You may be forgiven for thinking that all Beatles songs are in this simple 4/4 time, because they are all so easy to sing along to. However, Lennon, McCartney, and Harrison were true wordsmiths, and often found themselves in the position of having to make the music 'fit' the words. Consequently, many well-known songs had multiple time signatures within a few bars of each other – *All You Need Is Love'* and *Here Comes The Sun* being prime examples. It's testament to Ringo's drumming skills that the listener is largely unaware of such changes in meter.

Drum Notation

In the first bar below, we have one whole note, indicating that single note lasts for the duration of the bar – we should therefore count '4' for the length of the bar. The second bar shows that whole note halved, indicating two notes are being played: so we should count '2' for each half note. The third bar contains four 1/4 notes, count '1' for each note, and so on…..The final bar contains 16th notes – we should therefore quickly count 16 times the same length of time we counted the whole note of the first bar.

So, for the purposes of our notation, the bar below (from *Day Tripper* but commonly found on many Pop/Rock songs), displays the most common 1/8th note hi-hat pattern. As these quavers are the lowest notes of value, we can easily deduce where the bass and snare drums are struck.

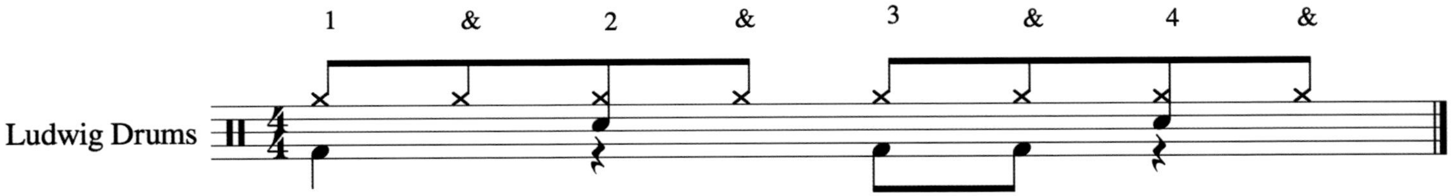

Rests

As we have seen, a note indicates a beat of specific length, conversely, a rest is merely a silence of a certain length. Where no notes are played, rests take their place. However, for the purposes of simplicity (and avoiding the bars looking as if we have swatted a fly upon them), we have removed some rests where their place is indicated by a note or rest on another line. Looking at the previous bar, we are able to accurately place the bass drum and snare without using rests.

Below we have illustrated the commonly used rests. We can see how they relate to each other within bars, and also (in the second example) how they relate to other notes.

Drum and Cymbal Notation Keys

Drum Notation Key

On the facing page, we can see the placement of the instruments commonly used by Ringo, and in the case of the Beatles as a group, percussion. Concerning drums, until late 1968 (with the *White Album* sessions) Ringo used a four-piece drum kit, from that point on the mid tom shown below came into play.

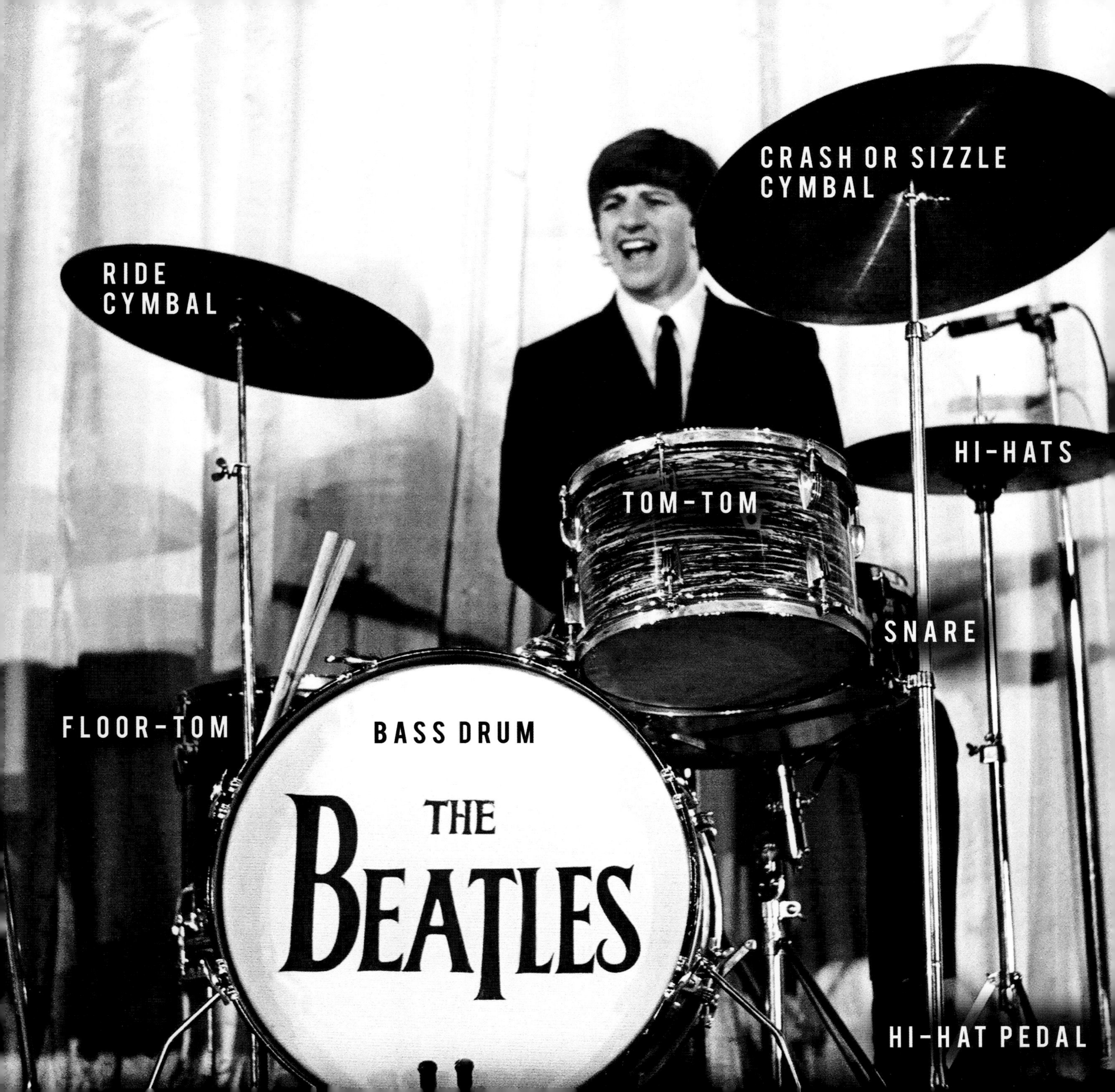
CRASH OR SIZZLE CYMBAL
RIDE CYMBAL
HI-HATS
TOM-TOM
SNARE
FLOOR-TOM
BASS DRUM
THE BEATLES
HI-HAT PEDAL

Drums

Cymbal Notation Key

Perhaps due to having a limited (but for the day perfectly adequate) set-up, Ringo was inventive with his use of cymbals. A typical set-up of the day included hi-hats, ride, and crash cymbals. As there is virtually no documentation as to the type of cymbals Ringo used, we have found it difficult to translate exactly what he was playing. We do however know Ringo used the same 14” Zildjian hi-hats throughout the Beatles’ recording career, but that doesn’t help us a great deal as we know when he is playing hi-hats – after all, a pair of hi-hats are ‘a pair of hi-hats’.

Ringo extensively used a sizzle cymbal (a cymbal with a series of rivets positioned within holes around the cymbal edge, lending unsurprisingly a ‘sizzle’ effect when struck). It seems he used this either as a crash or ride cymbal, to fill the air with a sound he was unable to obtain from his other cymbals. For simplicity, we have notated this use as either ‘ride’ or ‘crash’ cymbals.

A feature of Ringo’s early drumming, is his use of (partially) open or ‘swishy’ hi-hats. Again, this is virtually impossible to transcribe, as drum notation tells us hi-hats are either (fully) open, or closed. Due to this, when Ringo employs his famous ‘swishy’ hi-hats, we treat them as being closed, but often refer to their ‘swishy’ employment.

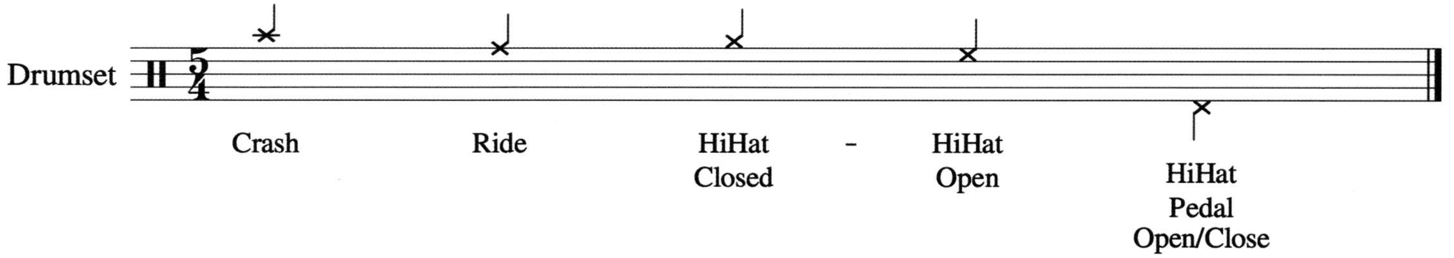

Cymbals

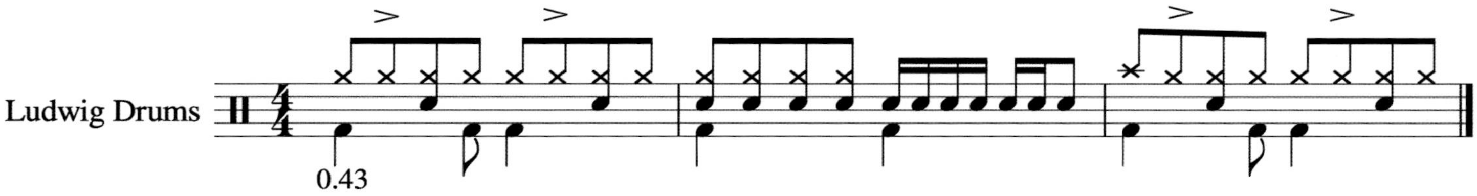

Notation Articulations

Occasionally we have used ‘articulations’ to emphasise aspects of Ringo’s drumming that are difficult to translate to bars of notation.

Accents

In the following bars (from *Nowhere Man*), with the use of accents (the symbol >), we can see Ringo placing emphasis (accenting) the 2nd and 6th hi-hat eighth notes.

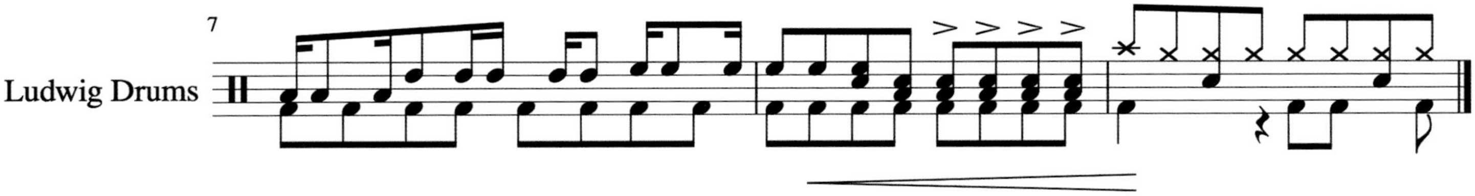

Crescendo

The symbol < beneath a bar, denotes a passage gradually getting louder across it’s denoted length. Here we have a bar of Ringo’s drum solo from *The End,* displaying both crescendo *and* accents working together to create the desired effect.

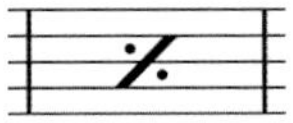

Repeat

The repeat symbol (above) allows us to illustrate repetition without producing cumbersome and extensive notation. Using the example, of *Baby's In Black*, the repetitive bars are shown here -

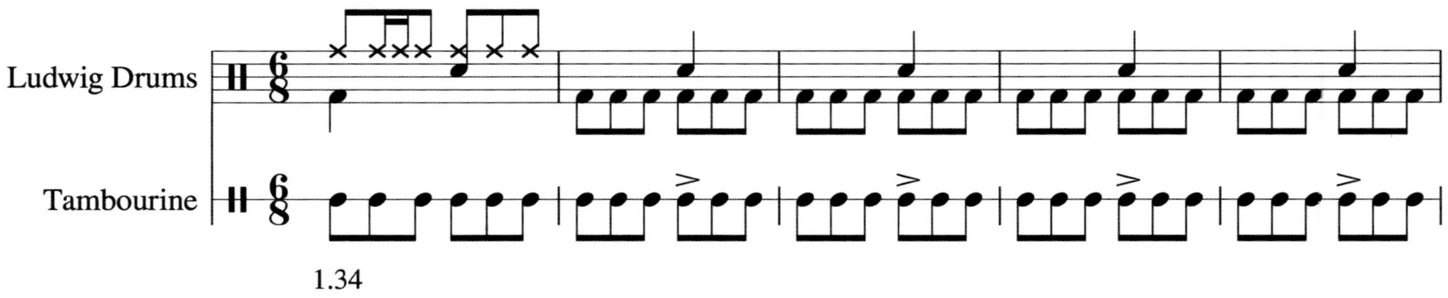

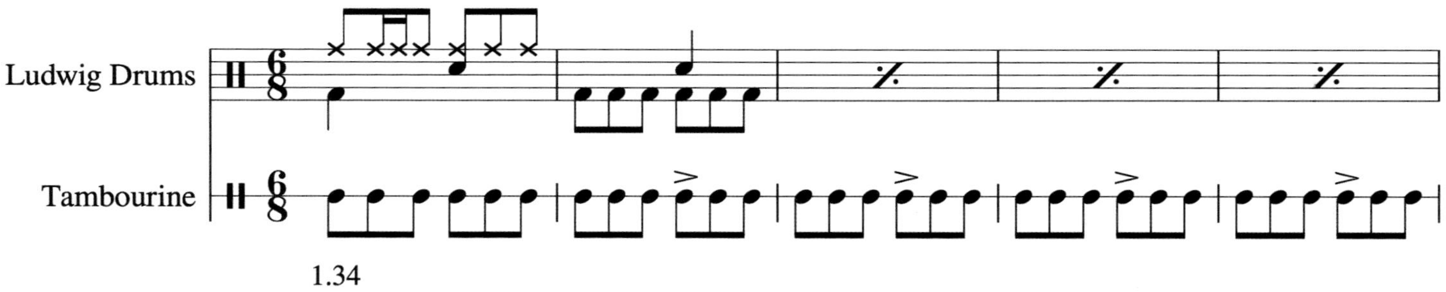

and are simplified and shortened using the repeat symbol in bars 3 to 7.

PART TWO

Merseybeat Memories – Terry's Recollections

THE MERSEY BEAT

1950's/60's Britain was a very different place, life was certainly a lot harder than today. If old black and white photos are examined, it will be seen that most men wore hats and very likely, long overcoats. The reason? Well it was so cold. Without sounding like Monty Python's '*Old Yorkshiremen*[6]', most people lived in draughty old properties, nobody had heard of central heating or double glazing, and carpets were a luxury. Everyone was used to seeing 'Jack Frost' on the inside of their windows.

Houses usually had just one or two fireplaces which burned dirty, smelly coal, and it was nothing for a nine or ten year old to 'lay' the fire ready for the evening by tearing the Liverpool Echo (at that time a broadsheet) into strips, then tying a knot in each one before placing an intricate layer of firewood on top ready for the coal to be skilfully added and set alight. Woe betide you if it wasn't roaring away before your parents got home from work, after all it provided the hot water for the whole house.[7]

The result of coal burning was of course a tremendous amount of smoke emanating from millions of chimneys which in the winter produced SMOG[8] – a mixture of smoke and fog. This noxious mixture managed to see off a great many people, young and old alike, and produce chest complaints in others. Obviously, for a sickly child like Ringo, suffering from tuberculosis, these conditions could have been potentially life threatening, and he was packed off to cleaner air on the other side of the Wirral Peninsula. No wonder he now prefers the more temperate climate of California!

Just after the war and well into the Fifties, rationing was still in force, indeed most children had never seen a banana or pineapple. For a great percentage of people living on the wartime diet, walking everywhere and being active meant they were slim. As a result, unlike today, there was virtually no obesity. On the negative side, Sunday was a dreary and boring day for youngsters. You may get the chance to kick a ball around, but shops were closed and of course there were no computers or television – in fact not many families had even a washing machine or telephone. However, Sunday lunch was the highlight and main meal of the week.[9] This was usually eaten to the sounds of Family Favourites, a request program which joined serving soldiers (mainly from the BAOR or British Forces On the Rhine) to their families at home. Conscription was still compulsory, and the Beatles would have been invited to join the Army if National Service had not ended mere months before Ringo and John's birthdays.

Post-War, Liverpool was struggling. Vast areas of the city had been destroyed by the Luftwaffe, with the resulting blow of loss of life and livelihoods. With the shrinking of Empire and the emergence of the Common Market, Britain now looked towards Europe for its trade. Liverpool faced west rather than east, and this, coupled with the take-off (no pun intended) of air travel, destroyed passenger shipping – a huge blow to the region.

With such a dreary background, how did Liverpool produce a movement which became the centre of popular music in the 60's? After the hardships of the 1950's, conditions were right for this quiet revolution in as much as the country was moving into a new decade and hopefully leaving the memory of war, and basic poverty behind. Prime Minister Harold McMillan was mocked for telling the nation they'd "never had it so good", but with time his words probably rang true. Medical care in the form of the National Health Service had been established, and rationing was a thing of the past. Conscription was coming to an end and there was plenty of work for youngsters, and therefore they had more spending power in their pockets than their peers before them. A new social phenomena had arrived – the *teenager*, and they were soon questioning the old ways. No longer the domain of their elders, they wanted fun and excitement of their own. These *teens* had their own style (gone was the time-honoured fashion of dressing as mini versions of their parents), their own language, and more importantly they had their own music.

Raised on a diet of Country and Folk, with a smattering of Jazz, Liverpool teenagers were already receptive to musical trends, and threw their weight behind the new 'fad' of Skiffle. Simple to busk, the craze inspired teens to hastily form themselves into Skiffle groups. Skiffle soon subsided, and the nation's youngsters returned broom handles, tea-chests and washboards to their mothers, and with it the urge to perform. In Liverpool, groups merely morphed into Rock and Roll outfits. Rock and Roll may have faded somewhat over the following few years, but not up on the Mersey.

The Beatles were then just one of these purveyors of this peculiar brand of music, but it was in Hamburg where they honed and perfected their act. Timing is of course everything, and the Beatles returned from Germany in late 1960 looking like they had come not just from another country – but from another planet. Litherland Town Hall had never witnessed a performance the likes of that on December 27, 1960 when the Beatles made a triumphant return. While current trends back home had mellowed somewhat (with home-grown 'boy next door' acts such as Cliff Richard and Tommy Steele dominating the charts), the Beatles' repertoire had hardened and expanded.

Word quickly spread, and the group were fortunate to procure a base in the city centre (the Cavern) where they could immediately stamp their musical authority on the other bands, the host of office workers at the lunchtime sessions, and also night-time clubbers. Their set-list, not only filled with the sounds of Buddy Holly, Chuck Berry, Elvis and Carl Perkins, but also American Rhythm And Blues artists such as The Miracles and Arthur Alexander. They possessed a rich musical brew which had slowly been fermenting, and their hard rocking act made the heart pound. Also the four of them (a magic number, three not enough, five too many) had totally different personalities that kids could easily identify with. Everybody had their favourite, whether you were male or female. Their style, flair and especially the music they played was very attractive to youngsters who had been brought up on a safe, insipid diet of Dickie Valentine, Michael Holliday, and Jimmy Young.

The Beatles' influence grew rapidly, and in a short time everybody was talking about them. People wanted to look like them (to be attired in black was compulsory) and of course, they spoke, swore and behaved like their audience. Not only that, they had an abundance of stage presence, were genuinely humorous and full of personality. Thousands of guys thought 'I could do that' and immediately went out and bought musical instruments by the ton. It was rumoured that soon there were over a thousand bands on Merseyside in a very short time, seemingly overnight. Fortunately for them they had a large, young audience of like-minded teenagers hungry for this new style of music who filled youth clubs, church halls, and dance halls. Adverts in the local papers of the time displayed literally dozens of venues and functions, all showing live bands, some as many as five or six playing at the same venue in one night.

With this explosion of talent, promoters and agents from around the country descended on Liverpool in droves looking for the 'next big thing' and bands were surprised to find that one weekend they were playing the local hop and the next they were in a strip club in Germany! Whilst other cities had their own small music centres, none were as vibrant or extensive as the Merseybeat scene, and around the country everyone wanted Liverpool bands. And so the message spread.

CHRISTMAS 1963
THE CAVERN — THE HOME OF THE BEATLES

LUNCHTIMES AT THE CAVERN

I had just left school and was working in an old building on the corner of North John Street and Mathew Street (now the 'Hard Day's Night Hotel') when my school chum Brian Harney dragged me down those damp steps for the first time and I discovered lunchtime sessions and the Beatles! At the time I didn't realise just how cool it was to go to a club and hear a live band in your lunch break, we thought that's what everyone did. And how lucky was I that the band was the Beatles? To me they were to become not only inspirational, but aspirational. It was at this point that my life turned from 50's black and white into full blown '60's Technicolor Cinemascope'. And it all started at……

The Cavern

In an unassuming street in the centre of Liverpool can be found perhaps the most famous music club in the world. The buildings that line the street were in fact warehouses (now plush offices and expensive clothes shops) and the area was the site of the old fruit market, with lorries coming in and out by the minute. It was a busy, bustling place. Also with all that smelly, rotten fruit, it certainly wasn't uncommon to spot the odd rat running around, usually heralded by a couple of screaming girls – beehive hairdos waving in the breeze – running to escape the equally frightened rodent.

The Cavern entrance was a virtually unmarked doorway with a short corridor leading to steep steps which led down into the cellar. The 'Cave' was a most unhygienic place and always had problems with sanitation which meant that it had to be sluiced out daily with mops and buckets of disinfectant. This aroma stuck to your clothes and advertised to passers by just where you had spent your lunch hour. To this day if I smell Dettol[10], I am transported back to 1961.

I remember the doorman Paddy, as a large, benign figure, who became more friendly as you got to know him. He stood no messing though, and many is the troublemaker whom he lifted quite literally by the scruff of his neck and the seat of his pants, 'helping' the offender up the stairs before depositing him into the street like a sack of laundry, along with the friendly admonition to "go 'ome, your Mum's got cakes" – or something very similar. On entering, you would immediately notice how dark it was with just a sliver of red light showing at the bottom of the unlit steps – although later on a lit up sign was installed in the stairway for safety's sake.

After a sharp left turn at the bottom and a few more steps down, you came to a table with a red lamp where you produced your membership card (where did mine go?) and paid a pittance of an entrance fee. The aforementioned steps though were narrow, pitched extremely steeply, and very dangerous, definitely not to be attempted after drinking alcohol, although many did, often arriving at the bottom in an undignified dishevelled heap. In fact looking in much the same state as the person whom Paddy had just gently ushered out. This one and only public entrance however was also the exit and therefore posed a serious hazard in the event of a fire. (There was another escape route from the band room where a door led into a narrow corridor which took you out into the street, amps and drums were often brought in this way).[11]

In short, if modern-day Health and Safety legislation was in existence, they would have had the place closed down in a heartbeat. It was no surprise when years later, the council elected to do exactly that and filled the old place in. But that's another story.

Looking back, before Beatlemania took hold, it's strange to think that many times we would go down to the club just after midday to find virtually nobody there apart from the Beatles who may be be rehearsing a number or just walking round having a Pepsi, just chatting to people. Regretfully, I didn't have the nerve to go and talk to the band – even then they were on a higher plane. Anyway, the Cavern was that sort of place, and no I didn't take photos or make tape recordings – I couldn't afford a camera or a tape machine – although my friend Ian Hunter of the Valkyries did take a portable tape down there and recorded a Beatles set. A couple of weeks ago I asked him if he still had it and ruefully he replied that sadly he had recorded over it. Well, he did hear them every week and tape was expensive!

On entering that first time, my ears were assailed by a powerful rendition of Chuck Berry's *Memphis Tennessee*. The heat and noise in the place was tremendous and the smell of hot dogs, onions, disinfectant and damp brought tears to my eyes. I was smitten. It was July 1961 and the Beatles had just returned from Hamburg for the second time (they first played the Cavern in early 1961) and their lunchtime sessions usually alternated with Gerry and the Pacemakers. They were wearing black T shirts (unheard of) and leather trousers (where did they get those from?). I didn't recognise the guitars they were playing. After asking around I found out that they had bought their Rickenbacker and Violin Bass Hofner in Germany, you couldn't get anything like them in run down post-war Britain. All this together with the music they played – I had never heard of the Coasters or Chuck Berry – they looked and sounded…alien. Nothing like those nice Shadows my Mum liked.

One of the guitarists (John Lennon) was leaning back on an old piano looking bored and, horror of horrors, picking his nose, although nobody seemed to mind or even notice! The bass player seemed affable enough and the guitarist on the left didn't say much. The drummer Pete Best was laying down a monumental beat on his old white pearl kit of Premier and the walls throbbed with the sheer ferocity and drive of the bass guitar and bass drum – you could feel it thudding into your stomach. Pete played in a very solid way, not fussy, his kit sounding really powerful which at that time was exactly what the Beatles were all about. Amazingly, in this dump, the place was full of attractive girls, although they all seemed to have eyes for the band, especially that drummer. They adored him, and though they were shouting his name, he just

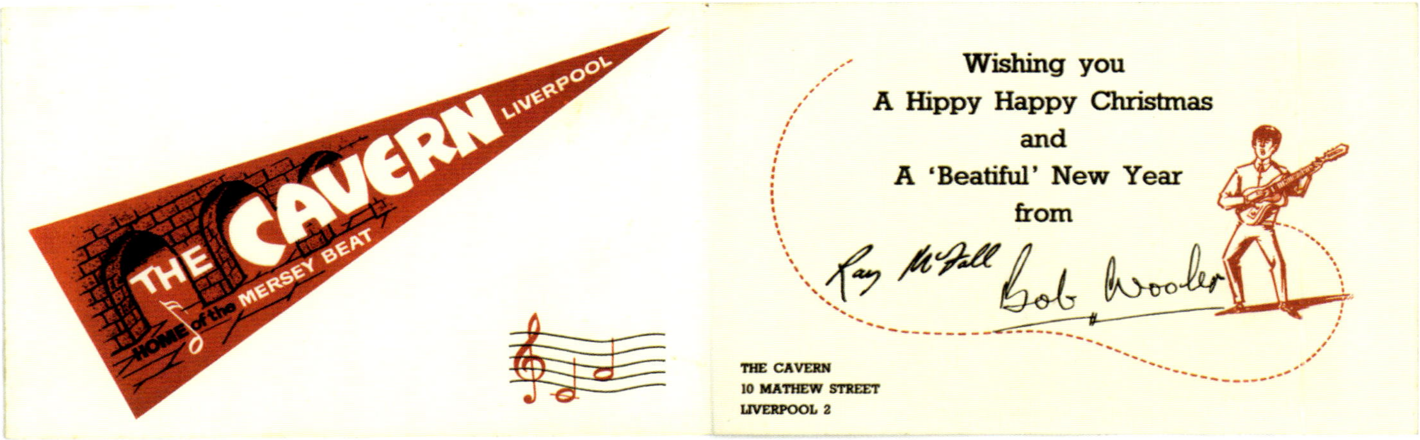

stared stonily back and they would literally go hysterical when he went out front to sing the occasional song (at this point, Paul would take over on drums). All this from a local band who hadn't made a record, been on TV, didn't have a manager, and no one had heard of – how could they fail? Strangely, the guys were impressed with Pete and liked him because not only was he able to hammer his drums hard, but he looked as if he could handle himself as well – you would certainly think twice before you punched him in the eye!

It wasn't long before word got out about 'this band' and Cavernites started asking at the local record store for Beatles records. The proprietor, Brian Epstein, took note of this and took a walk one day across Whitechapel and up into Mathew Street. The girls in the office – who were as alert as Meerkats when it came to the Beatles – informed me of his visit and that the Beatles were 'going to go places'. Brian Epstein saw something in them that impressed – maybe others had, but they didn't have the money or nous to do anything about it – however, Brian wasn't afraid to knock on doors on their behalf. He was debonair, smartly dressed, very organised and well educated. Plus he had experience of theatre and the presentation required to put on a good show. Even though the band were turned down by record companies, he resolutely knocked on other doors until he got a foot in and forced them open. The day he saw them things changed, for all of us.

Over the next few months their local fame grew as more and more people got wind of them and you could see that Liverpool was going to be too small to hold on to them. Whilst us, their true fans were glad to see them making good, a part of us didn't want them to leave and become successful because we knew we wouldn't see the same band again.

And that's just what happened.

After that, I only ever saw the Beatles at one other venue and that was at the Majestic Ballroom in Birkenhead. They had changed, not only in the clothes they wore and their attitude, but they now had a hit record, and with their new image were rapidly on their way to becoming the Beatles that everyone now knows. Still, I treasure my young man's memories of that magical time, when the best live band I have ever seen spread their wings and went on to dazzle the world.

THE
BEATLES
played here for Heswall
Jazz Club three times
in 1962 wearing their
stage suits for the
first time

Pete and the Beatles became the blueprint for my future, and a year or two later I found myself playing a similar kit on the Cavern stage wondering if I sounded the same…probably not. I never did get the chance to ask Cilla Black (formerly the Cavern cloakroom attendant) how she made a mistake by giving my mate Roddy Kelly's mohair overcoat to the wrong person!

HAMBURG

What an experience Germany (and especially Hamburg) was for the young band member in the early sixties. My first impression was how clean and tidy everywhere was. Also how friendly everyone seemed to be towards us, even though Hamburg had suffered grievously at the pounding they had taken from our 'thousand bomber raids' less than twenty years before. Looking back, we must have rubbed shoulders with more than a few ex German servicemen including no doubt a few Nazis, and yet we never experienced any aggravation from that quarter.

For a time we stayed in the same place the Beatles stayed in…the infamous Pacific hotel – the same place, where, it was rumoured that Lennon had urinated on hapless nuns from the hotel balcony[12]. After the club had closed, bands, still full of uppers would decamp to one of the many bars until it closed at maybe four o'clock, and then move to the one just opening next door which would be catering for the commuting businessman who would start their day with a coffee and brandy. On Saturday at closing time, everybody would make their way to the fishmarket which would be buzzing with activity. Restaurants and bars would be doing a roaring trade as would the sellers of fish and smoked eels.

Yet what a culture shock it all was. On our first night, we were taken by one of the other bands to a quiet backwater street called Herbertstrasse, where we were amazed to find dozens of ladies in various shop windows in various stages of undress – you didn't see anything like that in Birkenhead! It was explained to us that prostitution was legal in Germany, and indeed a state run brothel (the Eros centre) was only a few doors away from the Top Ten club. Nowadays in these 'enlightened' times, it is a common enough sight in some parts of Europe, but in those days, it literally stopped us in our tracks. However, I never heard of any of the bands actually visiting these places and paying up, not when there always seemed to be a squad of young ladies who were anxious to polish up their English and show us round their city. Mind you these girls would often be welcoming the new band arrivals whilst waving the old band off. The Reeperbahn though was were it was all at, whether it was a show with two women wrestling in mud, or a Jayne Mansfield lookalike stripper arriving in a black Mercedes with a fully grown Cheetah in the back!

A culture shock indeed.

PART THREE

The Beatles' Drummers

EARLY DAYS

The road that led to Ringo Starr becoming the Beatles drummer was, with one huge exception, a particularly unspectacular route, with the band (like so many groups) acquiring and losing a series of drummers along the way. Like most bands in the early stages of their development, the fledgling Beatles went through a procession of drummers, before settling on a long-term 'sticksman'.

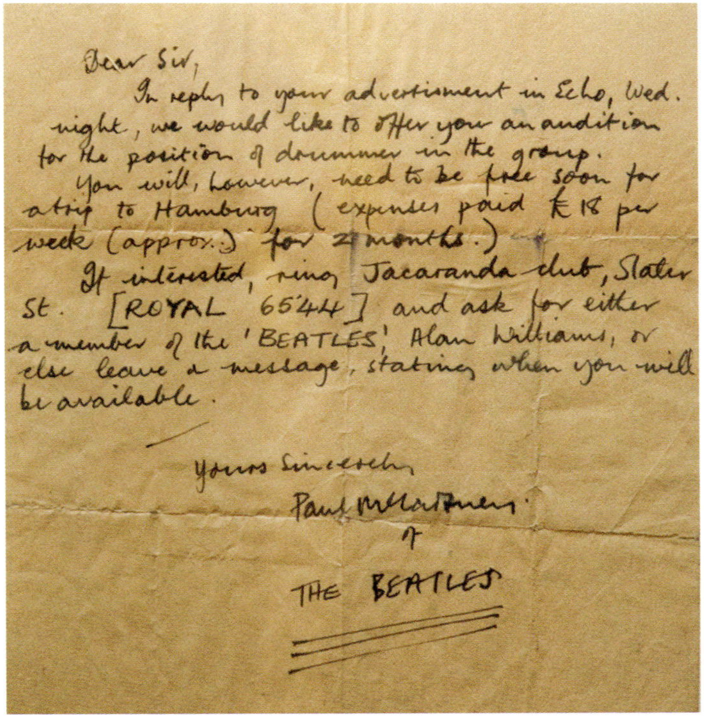

Dear Sir,

In reply to your advertisment in Echo, Wed. night, we would like to offer you an audition for the position of drummer in the group.

You will, however, need to be free soon for a trip to Hamburg (expenses paid £18 per week (approx.) for 2 months.)

If interested, ring Jacaranda club, Slater St. [ROYAL 6544] and ask for either a member of the 'BEATLES', Alan Williams, or else leave a message, stating when you will be available.

Yours sincerely,

Paul McCartney

of

THE BEATLES

Handwritten letter by Paul McCartney inviting an unknown drummer to audition for the Beatles, found inside a book in 2011 at a car boot sale in Bootle, Liverpool.

Colin Hanton

Holding the distinction of being the first 'Beatles drummer', Colin Hanton thumped the skins for Lennon's fledgling skiffle group The Quarrymen. Colin also apparently became the first drummer to come under the critical eye of Paul McCartney, quitting the group soon after the arrival of their new guitarist. After the inclusion of two Quarrymen performances in *The Beatles Anthology*, Hanton reformed the Quarrymen.

Michael McCartney

As strange as it may seem, despite not having a drummer after Colin Hanton's exit, the Quarrymen (or the 'Japage 3' [13]as they now called themselves), had access to a drum kit. Believed to have 'fallen off the back of a lorry' (possibly the Quarrymen's lorry), there suddenly existed within the McCartney household a rudimentary set of drums, of the Dallas 'Gigster' variety. This starter drum set was a cheap and affordable entry into the world of drumming for many a teenager in the Fifties. Mike recently confirmed he was definitely in line to be the next Beatles drummer, and at least on one occasion, he played the drums with John, Paul and George at a rehearsal in the McCartney household on Forthlin Road. Unfortunately, after breaking his arm falling from a tree, with the resulting nerve damage leaving his arm "flapping like a fish", Mike didn't possess the necessary strength in his arm to be considered as Colin's replacement. The drum kit however proved useful for Paul, as like every instrument he turned his hand to, he gained an instant understanding of them, thus becoming a real nuisance for every drummer he subsequently played with. Around this time, Paul was especially proud to master the tom-tom fills in Chuck Berry's *Sweet Little Sixteen,* later showing the reticent Pete Best how to play them.[14]

Tommy Moore

With the chance of an audition and possible tour of Scotland for Impresario Larry Parnes in the offing, the Silver Beatles found themselves drummer-less. However, their sometime manager Allan Williams procured the services of one Tommy Moore, a worker in a Liverpool bottle factory. Seemingly picked-upon by Lennon, and the unfortunate recipient of the loss of teeth in a motor accident, the tour was a disaster for the timid and mild-mannered Moore, who quit the group as soon as he was back home in Liverpool. Or so the story goes.

Anthony Hogan's[15] father was both a colleague and friend of Tommy Moore. Ant recalls – "Tommy worked with my Dad at the Garston Bottle Works (Standard's I think it was called), they were good friends. Tommy left to go to Scotland with the Beatles, and when he returned, my Dad, who was the Union Rep, got him his job back on the fork-lift truck at the factory. Tommy said Stuart Sutcliffe was a lovely lad, and George was a great bloke. John was a cocky idiot and Paul was 'ok', but followed John's lead a lot. He said John and Paul had this importance about themselves – George and Stu were just 'lower' band members to them."

"Tommy said John would always be 'having a go' at Stu, he was cruel to him even though he was his friend. He would make him sit on his own, and Paul and George would just put up with it even though it was clear they did not like it. He said Stu was hopeless on the bass and took a long time to learn anything, and it was really basic stuff he could play. But he was such a nice bloke. Tommy was fed up of John giving Stu 'skits'[16] all of the time, and John was calling Tommy 'old man' and 'gutter-rat' at times, making out Tommy was from the slums. Most of it went over Tommy's head but it riled him that John targeted Stu so much".

"Regarding the Scotland tour, Tommy said they were 'bloody awful', but it was fun as girls were asking for autographs. Then of course came the van crash with the guitar case that hit Tommy on the face, causing him to lose his top teeth. He was sitting waiting for the ambulance and he could hear John saying "He'd better not have ★★★★★★ this up for us!". In hospital Tommy was feeling awful. They came in to see him and John just said "You gotta play". Tommy told him "where to go". John basically tried to pull him from the bed while giving him threats of a beating. The others pulled John away and Tommy said he could see they were all shaken by it, and that they told John Tommy had to stay in hospital. Tommy got fed up and got dressed as by now it was an embarrassing scene on the ward. He played the rest of the dates while all the time John would laugh at the state of Tommy's face. It was then that Tommy decided he would try to get his old job back, and 'sort out' Lennon when he got home".

"When they returned they had one or two bookings, and for the sake of the other lads he agreed to play, but made it clear he would be leaving. However, the friction continued. "They were all eating in a cafe[17] one day after a practice session. John was giving Stu hell and Tommy told him to leave him alone. John got in Tommy's face shouting "what you going to do old man" so Tommy decked him. Of course John jumped back up, and Tommy came off worse before it was broken up. He remembers very well the sly boot that John put into his side as they were pulling him back. "On the last gig Tommy packed away his drums, went up to the lads and shook their hands. When he got to John he punched him to the floor, telling him not to get up or he would really hit him hard. John stayed down and Tommy left.... no longer a (Silver) Beatle".

Despite the friction between Lennon and Moore, the group were not going to let him go easily. "Now one thing for certain is the lads (including John) knew that Tommy was a good drummer, in fact George would later say he was the best drummer they had. Tommy thought the others convinced John they needed him back. A trip to his flat on Smithdown Lane was met with a "★★★★ off" from his girlfriend. They then went to the bottle works and tried to convince him, but he was not interested. It was here my Dad entered the Beatles story. He came to the gate and said "He doesn't want to know, now ★★★★ off!" ".

Although he had trouble with John, Tommy still said that if there was trouble there was nobody you would want by your side more than John. It was his cruel ways Tommy could not stand. He was never bitter about leaving them, saying, "Yes, the money would have been nice", but he was happy for them, and a big fan. He had all their records.

But what of Tommy Moore the drummer? Ant saw Tommy play – "He was an awesome drummer, I had a pair of his sticks until they went missing at a party. Tommy was a 'top bloke', a very quiet man, very laid back. He would do anything for anyone. I was stunned when he told me he had hit Lennon, he was the 'calmer-down' at the pub when rows broke out. But if we are pushed, we all react. It was a very sad time for me when Tommy died, I was just 16, it broke my heart. I loved that guy, I still do. He was like an Uncle to me".

Norman Chapman

Once again without a drummer, while sat in Allan Williams' Jacaranda Club in Slater Street, the Beatles heard a practicing drummer's beats drifting on the wind. Following their ears, they soon found Norman Chapman, who managed 3 engagements before National Service (military draft) removed him from the group's drum throne, and with it, possible world domination.

Johnny 'Hutch' Hutchinson

An imposing and intriguing character, Johnny Hutch was the drummer for The Big Three, who rivalled the Beatles for the position of the greatest live act of the Merseybeat scene. Although he despised them, Hutch stood in for the Beatles on occasion – famously for the late arriving Tommy Moore at the Larry Parnes audition, and bridging the gap between Pete Best's departure and Ringo Starr's arrival. Bill Harry has recently related the late Cilla Black said Brian Epstein wanted Johnny to replace Pete Best ahead of Ringo, but his proposal was vetoed by the group[18].

Right: The Big Three - L-R Brian Griffiths, Johnny Hutchinson, Johnny Gustafson.

PETE BEST

Randolph Peter Best was born in Madras, India, in 1941. Moving to Liverpool at the age of 4, Pete grew up in the suburb of West Derby, some 4 miles east of the city centre. Pete frequented a teenage club along the road from his house on Haymans Green at the Pillar Club, Lowlands. It was here that Pete met George Harrison (who was also 'freelancing' as he called it with his mate Ken Brown in the Les Stewart Quartet). George soon brought his friends John and Paul along to the Pillar Club[19].

As a rival to the Lowlands club, and to entertain the local youths and her offspring, Pete's mother Mona opened the Casbah Coffee Club in the cellar of her substantial home. After helping with the decorating of the new club, and re-using their old name, the drummer-less Quarrymen (with Ken) performed at the opening night of the Casbah in August 1959. Over the coming months, the Quarrymen perfected their act, becoming the Silver Beatles.

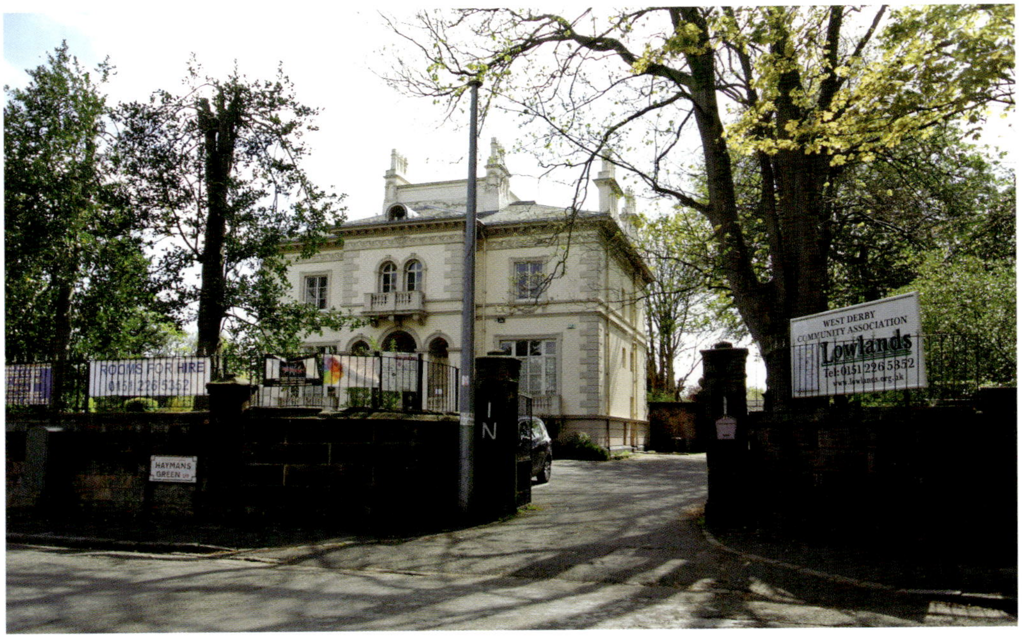

Lowlands, Home of The Pillar Club

8 Haymans Green, home of the Best family and the Casbah Club

A year on from their Casbah debut and still without a regular drummer, the Silver Beatles had secured a long engagement in Hamburg, Germany. In the meantime, after taking a liking to and tinkering with drums at the Casbah, Pete had caught the drumming bug. He had soon formed a group, the Blackjacks, performing a handful of times at the venue. In anticipation of their foreign engagement, and it must be said, desperation (it was made clear they *had* to have a drummer), the Beatles approached Pete to join them. Luckily, the short-lived Blackjacks had disbanded, and Pete was off to Germany.

MERSEY BEAT EXCLUSIVE STORY

BEATLES CHANGE DRUMMER !

Ringo Starr (former drummer with **Rory Storm and the Hurricanes**) has joined **The Beatles**, replacing **Pete Best** on drums. Ringo has admired The Beatles for years and is delighted with his new engagement. Naturally he is tremendously excited about the future.

The Beatles will fly to London to make recordings at E.M.I. Studios. They will be recording numbers that have been specially written for the group, which they have received from their recording manager **George Martin** (Parlophone).

THE BEATLES TO PLAY CHESTER

As a result of the phenomenal Box Office success of The Beatles during their 4-week season of Monday nights at the Plaza Ballroom, St. Helens, the directors of Whetstone Entertainments, controllers of the ballroom, have engaged The Beatles for a series of four Thursday night sessions at the Riverpark Ballroom, Chester, which commenced on 16th August.

SEE THE STAR SHOW with recording artistes
Brian Poole and the Tremilos
* * *
Ian and the
TOWN
LITHER

Clipping from 'Mersey Beat', reporting Pete Bests removal. It is prudent to note the article was written and provided by Brian Epstein, and is therefore a sanitised reporting of events, as clearly Pete's sacking was anything but amicable. *Reproduced here with kind permission of* ***Bill Harry.***

In a 1975 interview, John Lennon was frank about this turn of events -

"The reason he got in the group was because the only way we could get to Hamburg we had to have a drummer. We knew of this guy who was living at his mother's house.... who [sic] had a club in it, and he had a drum kit and we just grabbed him – auditioned him and he could keep one beat going for long enough, so we took him to Germany"[20]

Taking up their residency at the Indra club, it soon became apparent that despite owning a shiny drum kit, being a beginner meant Pete only had a rudimentary grasp of the art of drumming. The simplest means of maintaining a steady beat was by instructing Pete to place the emphasis on his bass drum above all other pieces of his drum kit. The Beatles also developed their own method of timekeeping, as recalled by George Harrison -

"We'd often turn around and stomp on the stage, to keep the tempo going right.... We kept that big heavy four-in-a-bar beat going all night long"[21]

Now armed with a unique and overtly bass drum-heavy sound, over the next two years Pete established himself as the Beatles' drummer, with the group performing at the Casbah many times. Mona also had a large influence, securing further bookings as their stature grew, including amongst others their first engagement at the Cavern Club.

Pete seemed to have that rare commodity – popularity with both boys and girls – the boys with his no-nonsense booming bass drum driven beat, the girls with his brooding good looks. Lifting a tag-line from a Jane Russell movie, Cavern DJ Bob Wooler dubbed Pete as "mean, moody, and magnificent", a description that was appreciated by both sexes.

'Pete Forever! Ringo Never!'

The reasons behind the replacement of Pete Best by Ringo Starr have become clouded by the mists of time and the shadow of betrayal and embarrassment. It appears many circumstances conspired to remove Pete from the group, but what proved to be the catalyst, indeed the excuse for his removal lay at the Beatles' test recording session at Abbey Road on Wednesday June 6th 1962. The recording of *'Love Me Do'* from this session (issued on *The Beatles Anthology Volume 1*) makes painful listening. At this stage of the song's development, *Love Me Do* contained a passage which led the group through a gradual increase and decrease in tempo[22]. With nerves clearly getting the better of all involved, and the drumming edgy and hesitant, Pete soon loses command of his timekeeping, leading the group through passages of erratic meter. Author (and non-drummer) Spencer Leigh comments -

> "Pete Best sounds as though he's banging bin-lids and his drumming goes off on a strange tangent in the middle. If this was all George Martin heard of Pete Best, is it all that surprising that he was sacked?"[23]

Pete's hapless performance may of course have been purely down to nerves and being under-rehearsed, but it led to George Martin's assistant Ron Richards (and ultimately Martin himself) being less than impressed. For John, Paul and George this was the straw that broke the camel's back – for Pete, his days as a Beatle were numbered. George Martin took Brian Epstein to one side and told him of his intent to book a session drummer for future recordings. From today's perspective, this development may appear to be rather a surprising revelation, but in the 1950's and 60's it was commonplace – a performance that was acceptable on stage in a 'live' situation rarely translated well onto tape in a recording studio. Different disciplines were required, and studio time was precious – a record producer could ill afford take, after take, until the drummer nailed his performance. George Martin consistently stated it was never his intention to have Pete Best replaced – visually he saw him as the Beatles' greatest asset.

Speaking to Spencer Leigh on BBC Radio Merseyside in May 2016, guitarist Billy Hatton recalled that while recording with the Fourmost at EMI, George Martin and Engineer Norman Smith had told him what happened with Pete at the Beatles' first session at Abbey Road.

> "It was a combination of George Martin and Brian Epstein. George Martin said "I like the band.... but Brian, the drummer is a little bit... you know.. he knows how to play one style of drums, we need somebody who's a bit more inventive on the drums" – and that was the start of them getting rid of Pete Best". It made Brian think "Should we or shouldn't we?"

> "Ringo was one of the most popular drummers when he was with Rory Storm, and he was a more versatile drummer than Pete, wasn't as nice a man as Pete, but a far more versatile drummer. And one of the main

reasons was purely – if you're going to produce something that you think is hopefully going to be heard all around the world, you want the best product you can get. And Pete wasn't quite up to it."

Crucially though, this was not the first time a record producer had expressed his dissatisfaction with Pete's drumming. A year earlier, in June 1961, renowned producer and orchestra leader Bert Kaempfert had signed up the group as Tony Sheridan's backing band for a recording session in Hamburg, but he was apparently unhappy with Pete Best's drumming. Sheridan later commented -

"Kaempfert suggested Pete not play his bass drum, because he used to get too fast… the tempo was a problem."[24]

Kaempfert not only took a dislike to Pete's drumming – he removed his bass drum and tom-toms, leaving him with just his snare, hi-hat and cymbals. Despite this blow to his ego, Pete manfully played on, with Kaempfert's actions providing us with a neat post-script at the end of this chapter.

It was also in Hamburg that a divide appeared between Pete and the rest of the group. Away from their stage-antics, Pete kept himself to himself, not socialising with John, Paul and Stuart, or their new German 'exi'[25] friends, which included Klaus Voormann -

"Pete was always in the background…..but never hung around with the others when they weren't on stage. Socially, he didn't seem to be one of them at all".[26]

Additionally Pete did not partake in the intake of Preludin[27], an 'upper' drug, available on prescription as a slimming aid. 'Prellies' helped steer the group through their long, exhaustive hours on stage. It appeared an 'us and him' relationship developed between Pete and the rest of the group.

Meanwhile, in Hamburg, while sharing the bill with Rory Storm And The Hurricanes the Beatles established a rapport and bond with their drummer, Ringo Starr. Klaus Voormann again -

"Every time Ringo came near the Beatles it was happiness. I know the three of them discussed changing their drummer while they were in Hamburg, because I heard them….they *always* liked Ringo."[28]

As far as the Beatles' Liverpudlian fans were concerned, Pete's ability as a drummer was never in question. Rock 'n' Roll was still in it's infancy, especially the genre's drumming aspect. There was very little in the way of the external drumming influences we have today, no 'rock giants' such as John Bonham or Keith Moon to inspire and be measured against. What was important to a group was a drummer's ability to start and stop playing at the correct times, while maintaining a steady beat throughout. In this respect, Pete ticked all the right boxes. He became known for the trademark booming 'thud' of his bass drum, which cut through the bass and guitars, driving the songs forward. It's reasonable to say Pete Best's drumming was 'good for the time', adequate enough without being spectacular, just fine for a group from the provinces with no experience on the national stage.

Bobby Thompson of Kingsize Taylor and the Dominoes recalls -

> "Pete was a good drummer but he wasn't as solid as Ringo and he was a little too heavy on the bass drum. All you could hear when Pete played was the bass drum, always four to the bar, but he was very good and I saw no reason for him to be sacked. I preferred Ringo as a drummer but that is a personal preference."[29]

The Beatles and Brian Epstein would have not taken the decision to replace Pete with Ringo lightly, as good drummers were difficult to find, drummers who stick around even more so. If a group found a drummer who liked the other members, the music they played, and was tolerant of any petty politics that might be at play, they'd struck gold. Blessings would be counted, and they'd do their very best to keep hold of him. A massive problem would arise if they wanted to replace their drummer – this would invariably require 'poaching' from another group, bringing with it associated feelings of anger, betrayal and distrust, especially in the "small village" which was (and still is) Liverpool. It was often best to maintain the status quo, despite any reservations you may have about your drummer. It appears that until Ringo sat in with them, the other Beatles weren't aware that (with Pete), their act could be improved upon. With Ringo, the chemistry and the 'fit' was perfect. To the girls from the typing pools though, this didn't matter one jot – their heart-throb was gone, and the new guy, even though they were familiar with him, had better measure up pretty quickly. The first date with Ringo after Pete's dismissal began in uproar, with George Harrison gaining a black-eye courtesy of a Pete Best fan (by all accounts a chap called Bruno from West Derby). But by the end of their act, the audience was aware the chemistry was perfect – it was clear Ringo was the right personality, at the right time, with the right amount of experience and confidence to ease into the drummer's throne with the minimum of fuss and disruption. However, some sources have recently indicated that Ringo was merely the third choice to replace Pete – but refuse to disclose who the other two candidates were. Despite his loathing of the Beatles, Johnny 'Hutch' of The Big 3 would certainly have been on the list, the other choice we will have to leave open to conjecture.

Another possible and plausible contributary factor for Best's dismissal may have been the opportunity to remove his mother Mona from the equation. Even after Brian Epstein had taken over management duties, Mona still exerted a great deal of influence[30], and a degree of inertia and irritation had been created by her ousting by Epstein. In short, she was seen as an itch that couldn't be scratched.

While Pete appears to have been the unfortunate victim of many circumstances, the cumulative effect of three record producers[31] being unhappy with his drumming, plus his quiet nature and penchant for solitude clearly took it's toll. With this in mind it is perhaps pertinent to allow Paul, George and John to share their views on the course of events, courtesy of *The Beatles Anthology* -

Paul McCartney: *'George Martin....was not very pleased with Pete Best. George took us to one side and said 'I'm really unhappy with the drummer. Would you consider changing him?' We said, 'No, we can't!' Can we betray him? No. But our career was on the line'.*

George Harrison: *'To me it was apparent: Pete kept being sick and not showing up for gigs so we would get Ringo to sit in with the band instead, and every time Ringo sat in, it seemed like 'this is it'.*

John Lennon: *'This myth built up over the years that he was great and Paul was jealous of him because he was pretty and all that crap. The reason he got in to the group in the first place was because we had to have a drummer to get to Hamburg. We were always going to dump him when we could find a decent drummer, ...and he looked nice and the girls liked him, so it was all right.'*[32]

Pete Best – Post Beatles

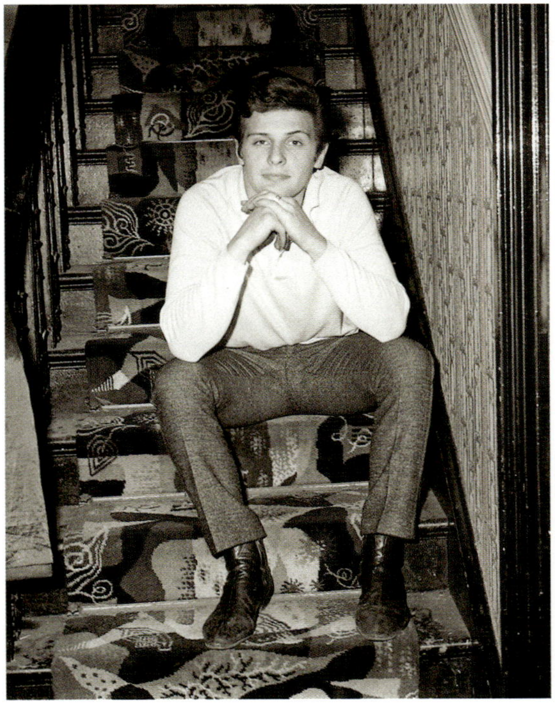

It is worth noting that Pete has maintained his dignity throughout his tribulations, while having to accept the unkind sniping he must have endured over the years. Despite this, he has never resorted to the gutter press to vent his (justifiable) anger and hurt at his denouement. How many of us could have done that?

After being sacked from the Beatles, Pete persevered with drumming, before putting down his sticks in 1968. A series of menial jobs followed, before he successfully pursued a career as a civil servant working in, of all places, a Job Centre. After his retirement, he was coaxed back into drumming, performing at a Beatles convention in the late 1980's. Reforming the Pete Best Band and performing around the world, he once again appears comfortable and proud of his involvement with the Beatles. The release of *The Beatles Anthology* entitled Pete to royalties from his early work with the band which are rumoured to be well over a million pounds.

The Casbah Club is once again open for business, and is proud to be consistently rated as 'Liverpool's number one paid-for tourist attraction', playing host to fans and visiting stars of music, stage and screen. A short distance from the Casbah Club in Hayman's Green lies Everton Football Club's former training ground, Bellefield. Now an up-market housing estate, the site sports two new roads – Pete Best Drive, and Casbah Close, a fitting postscript and honour to the fascinating story of Pete Best.

RINGO STARR

Ringo's Pre-Beatles Life and Career

Ringo's birthplace today, awaiting renovation and adorned with fan graffiti

Ringo Starr was born Richard Starkey on July 7th 1940, at 9 Madryn Street in the working-class area of Dingle, South Liverpool. Soon after, the Starkey family made the short trip across High Park Street to a new home at Admiral Grove. When Richy was three years old, his Mother Elsie divorced his natural Father and married Harry Graves. Richy would remain intensely close to Harry throughout Harry's life.

Richy endured poor health throughout his childhood, with bouts of pleurisy, an appendicitis induced coma, food intolerances, and tuberculosis. As a result, he struggled through school, falling behind academically. Little was expected of him but a life of menial labour. Then at the age of 13, while recuperating from tuberculosis at a hospital 'over the water' in Heswall, Wirral, Ringo 'found' drums.

> "Because a lot of us stayed in bed a long time, they tried to keep us entertained. This woman came and she had a big board with yellow and red marks on it. If she hit the yellow, you'd hit the tambourine; if she hit the red, you'd hit the drum. That was when I got a drum for the first time, and then I wouldn't be in the hospital class band unless I was given the drum after that![33]"

The skiffle craze soon hit Liverpool, and around 1958, Ringo, armed with his first drum kit, co-founded the Eddie Clayton Group. A year later he would join the backing band for a rip-roaring young singer (Rory Storm) and his group The Raving Texans, who would soon become The Hurricanes. With young Richy gaining in stature and popularity, a portion of (the now) Rory Storm and the Hurricanes performance was given over to 'Ringo Starr-Time'. His new nickname was not only given to him due to his penchant for wearing many rings on his fingers, but also to make him appear more exotic to the audience, fulfilling his desire for all things American[34], especially 'Western'.

With Rory and the Hurricane's sharing the bill with the Beatles, close friendships were formed, Ringo occasionally sitting in for the often absent drummer Pete Best. The rest, is indeed history...

10 Admiral Grove –
Richy Starkey's childhood home

Beaming with pride – Harry and Elsie at home, 1C Admiral Grove, 16th February 1964

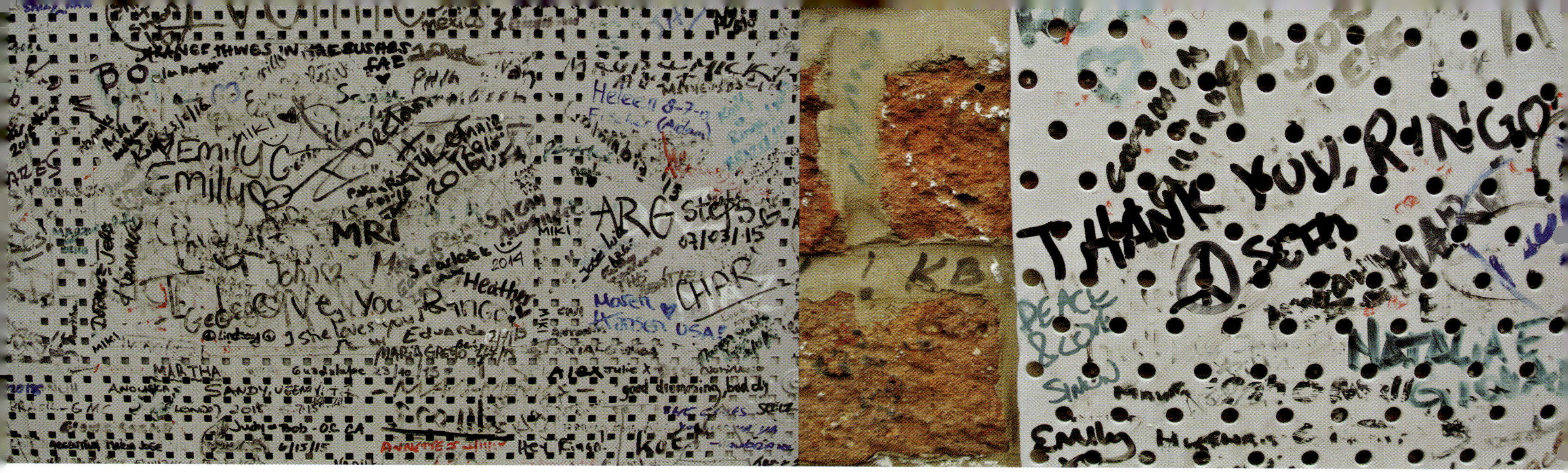

Detail of graffiti on Ringo's Madryn Street birthplace.

The Empress pub at one end of Admiral Grove was featured on the cover of Ringo's first solo LP, 'Sentimental Journey'

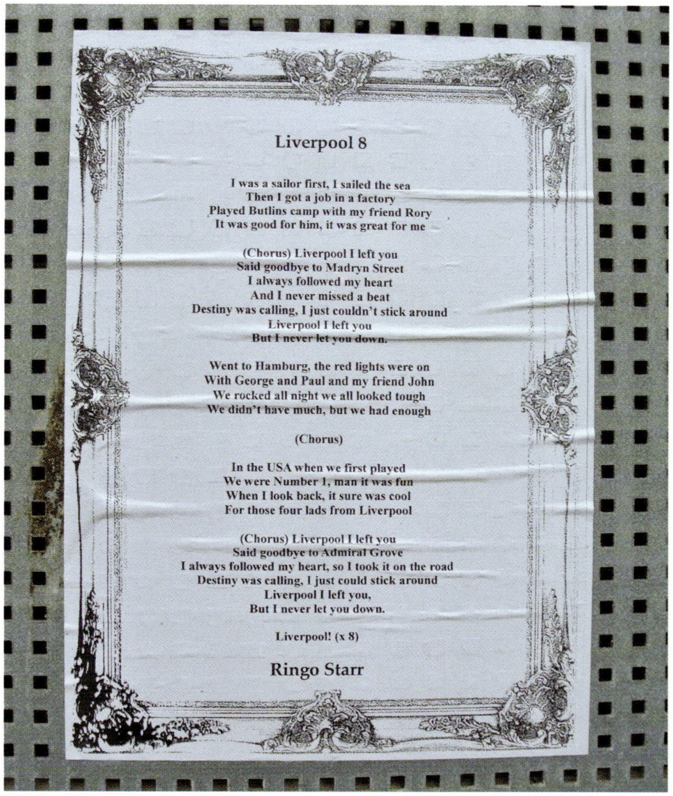
Liverpool 8

I was a sailor first, I sailed the sea
Then I got a job in a factory
Played Butlins camp with my friend Rory
It was good for him, it was great for me

(Chorus) Liverpool I left you
Said goodbye to Madryn Street
I always followed my heart
And I never missed a beat
Destiny was calling, I just couldn't stick around
Liverpool I left you
But I never let you down.

Went to Hamburg, the red lights were on
With George and Paul and my friend John
We rocked all night we all looked tough
We didn't have much, but we had enough

(Chorus)

In the USA when we first played
We were Number 1, man it was fun
When I look back, it sure was cool
For those four lads from Liverpool

(Chorus) Liverpool I left you
Said goodbye to Admiral Grove
I always followed my heart, so I took it on the road
Destiny was calling, I just could stick around
Liverpool I left you,
But I never let you down.

Liverpool! (x 8)

Ringo Starr

Lyrics from Ringo's 2008 song Liverpool 8 adorn a house on Madryn Street

Admiral Grove today

Ringo larking around on stage with Rory Storm and the Hurricanes

THE BEATLES
Ringo Starr made
his official debut here
on 18th August
1962

Above & Left: Although Ringo had performed with the Beatles many times, his first official engagement as a Beatle was at Hulme Hall, Port Sunlight

Ringo's Post-Beatles Life and Career

With the Beatles' break-up ending in such acrimony, it was testament to Ringo's personality and standing that he was the only Beatle to remain close with all of his bandmates in the immediate years following the group's dissolution. While his relationship with McCartney was at the time acutely strained, Ringo played drums on Lennon's *Plastic Ono Band* and Harrison's *All Things Must Pass* LP's. Indeed, there was a desire from the other three to help Ringo be as successful as possible. Perhaps too much of a desire, as during the early 70's Ringo enjoyed the most successful career of all the former Beatles, with 7 consecutive US Top 10 hits to his name, including *It Don't Come Easy* and *Back Off Boogaloo*. His 1973 album *Ringo* is the best of the bunch, with contributions from all 3 former Beatles, plus the likes of Marc Bolan, Elton John, Steve Cropper, and The Band.

On the set of Paul McCartney's 'Give My Regards To Broad Street' (1984). For a short time in the mid 1980's, Ringo played Yamaha drums.

As the 70's advanced, success eluded him, his penchant for partying getting the better of him. His choice of film roles was always questionable, reaching a nadir in 1981 with the release of *Caveman*. However, his participation in *Caveman* proved to be otherwise worthwhile, as he starred opposite former 'Bond Girl' Barbara Bach, whom he married soon after. A series of poor album releases stretched into the 80's, his only success proving to be his narration of the *Thomas The Tank Engine* children's TV Series. In 1998, acknowledging their problems with alcohol, Ringo and Barbara checked into a rehab clinic for a 6 week detox.

With new found energy and purpose, Ringo founded The All-Star Band, with an ever changing line-up including artists such as Dr. John, Billy Preston, Joe Walsh, Levon Helm, and Nils Lofgren. Cleverly turning the spotlight away from himself, Ringo's band members each perform a song or two of their own, ensuring an entertaining and varied concert experience.

Reuniting with George and Paul for *The Beatles Anthology,* Ringo's album releases also saw an upturn in quality and popularity, his *Liverpool 8* album forming the backdrop to his performance on the roof of St. George's Hall at the opening ceremony of Liverpool's induction as European Capital Of Culture in 2008. Ringo's participation was however overshadowed by his comments on the *Jonathan Ross Show*, when he stated there was 'nothing' he missed about his hometown. Ringo also drew criticism that year with his public refusal to sign autographs, many detractors unaware that for years he returned (at his own expense) items he had autographed that had either been requested or sent to him. In his defence, how many of us could have put up with the 50 years of constant attention? After all, the man behind the Ringo mask is still Richy, the drummer from the Dingle.

Ringo performing with his All-Star Band

In 2013 Ringo released a collection of his personal photographs, rather unsurprisingly titled after his 1973 hit *Photograph.* Also that year, an exhibition entitled *Ringo: Peace & Love* was held at the Grammy Museum, Los Angeles. Displaying his drums, clothing and memorabilia, the exhibition drew critical acclaim. Enjoying somewhat of a renaissance, Ringo continues to tour with his All-Star Band.

Former Beatles Fan Club secretary Freda Kelly pays a visit to Ringo and Barbara at the Starkey office in LA, 2015.

At the time of writing, to good reviews, Ringo has released a new album, *Postcards From Paradise*, and has been inducted as a solo artist into the Rock and Roll Hall Of Fame. Why did it take so long?

DRUMMING 'WITH THE BEATLES'

Besides Pete Best and Ringo Starr, there are two other principal drummers in the Beatles story.

Andy White

With a marching band drumming background, Glaswegian Andy White was a prolific and highly regarded session drummer of the 1950's, 60's, and 70's. As Producer George Martin's assistant (Ron Richards) was unhappy with both Pete Best's and Ringo's previous attempts at *Love Me Do,* Andy White was booked for the ensuing remake session. Andy also played on the song's B-Side, *PS I Love You*, and controversially claimed to have also performed the drum part on *Please, Please Me.* In later life, Andy settled in America and became a drum tutor, and courtesy of a student, his car sported a bumper sticker with the legend '*5th Beatle*'. Andy passed away in November 2015.

Jimmie Nicol

On June 3rd 1964, 24 hours prior to departing on their tours of Europe, Hong Kong and Australasia, Ringo dramatically collapsed during a photo-shoot, succumbing to tonsillitis. Rather than cancelling the tours, Brian Epstein sought a replacement drummer. An unpopular decision within the group, at one point Harrison apparently refused point-blank to travel. Calling upon all of his powers of persuasion, Epstein saw to it John, Paul and George agreed to a replacement drummer, and on George Martin's suggestion, Jimmie Nicol was drafted in. The day after a swift 6 song run-through at Abbey Road, Nicol was on tour and onstage, performing admirably and fully entitled to wear the crown of 'Fifth Beatle'. However, Ringo soon recovered, and rejoined the group in Australia on June 15, with Nicol swiftly returning home. Jimmie struggled to cope with his short stint as a Beatle, his fortunes soon taking a downward turn – a year later he was declared bankrupt. His time as a 'jobbing drummer' didn't last, it is believed Jimmie moved into a new direction – property renovation. Believed to still be alive, his whereabouts today are unknown.

At the unveiling of Jimmie Nichol as Ringo's replacement, McCartney, ever the P.R. man, offers an alternative view to that of Lennon and Harrison.

Post Script

Renowned American session drummer Bernard Purdie has claimed he played on 21 early Beatles recordings. According to Purdie, apparently unhappy with the quality of Ringo's drumming, Brian Epstein flew over to New York armed with master tapes of the band's first recording sessions. Purdie claims he was contacted by Epstein, recorded new drum tracks, and was 'paid off' in order to maintain his silence. The problem with this story is the Beatles' early recordings were completed as live performances, with *all* instruments (including drums) recorded together on one track, vocals on the other. It would have been impossible to replace Ringo's drumming, or indeed overlay new drums on top of Ringo's without being able to hear both performances.

Purdie's tale may however possess a grain of truth, as there is evidence a session drummer was booked to 'enhance' Pete Best's drumming on the recordings the Beatles made as Tony Sheridan's backing band in Hamburg two years earlier. Released as a Beatlemania 'cash-in', these tapes suddenly became hot-property. As we have seen, these Hamburg recordings feature Pete Best on half a set of drums, his bass drum and tom-toms having been removed by producer Bert Kaempfert, who was less than pleased with Pete's performances. No wonder Epstein was concerned. It is entirely possible Purdie played over Pete's performance, with only his bass and tom-toms being miked up, giving the impression of a single drummer rather than two playing disparate portions of a set of drums. On the other hand, there is also the small matter of Brian Epstein being in possession of the copyright of the recordings, while also having access to the original master tapes to make overdubbing possible. If Purdie *did* drum on Beatles tracks, the early German Polydor releases provide the only credible source.

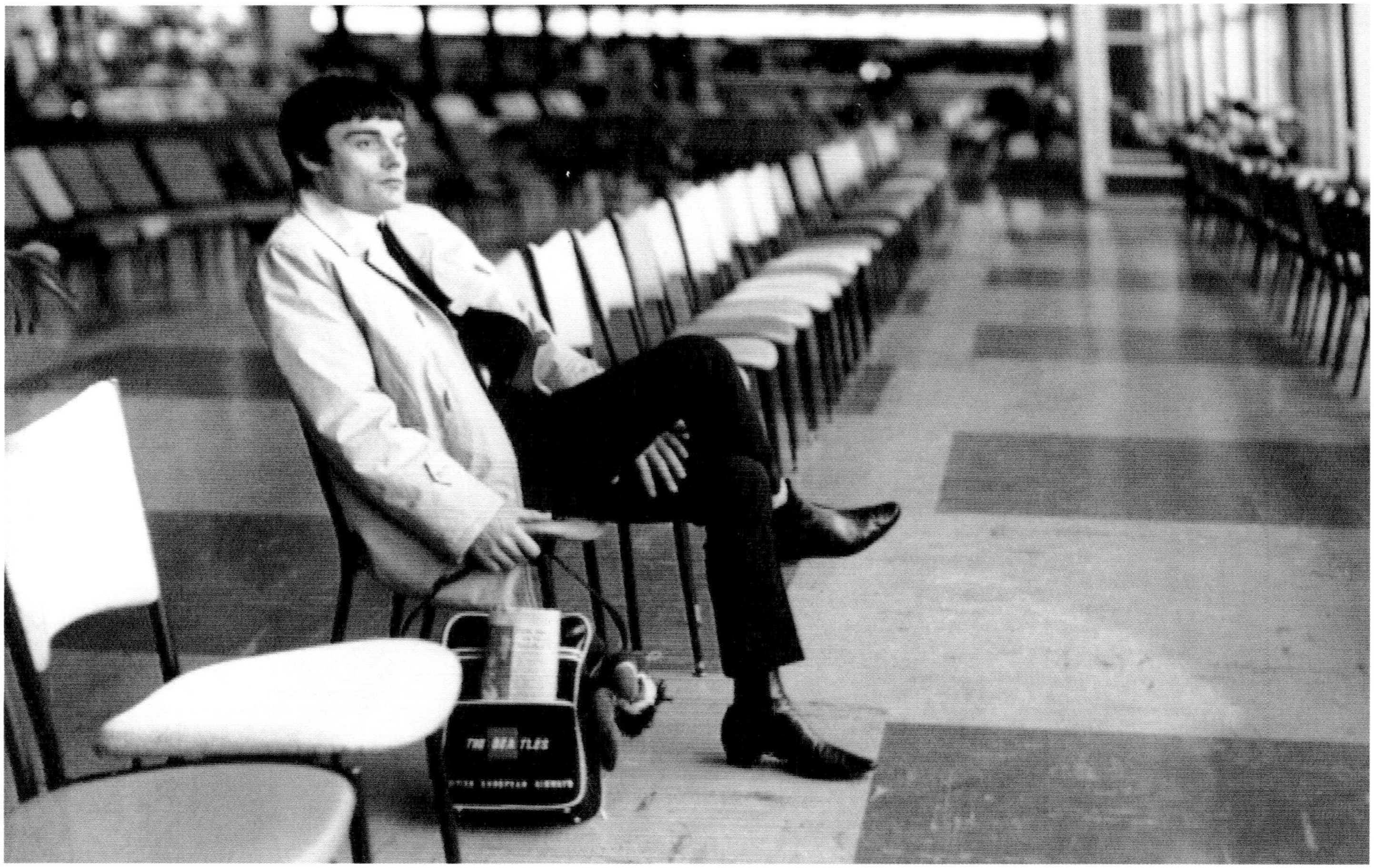

Jimmie Nichol captured in a reflective mood at Essendon Airport, Melbourne, June 15th 1964, his days as a Beatle over

And Finally……

Paul McCartney

As we will see, Ringo was (un)fortunate to have such a talented multi-instrumentalist alongside him. Picking up sticks when the McCartney's somehow acquired a set of drums around 1960, Paul soon proved a capable time-keeper. Ever the perfectionist and full of percussive invention, he was constantly offering rhythmic suggestions, much to Pete Best's chagrin, and Ringo's easy-going acceptance. Paul has played drums on many recordings throughout his career, the stand-out performances coming on his *Band On The Run* and self-titled albums, *McCartney* and *McCartney II*.

PART FOUR

Ringo Starr – Drummer

RINGO'S DRUMMING STYLE

"What struck me about them was that they had a fantastic drummer.. He was swinging like ****. Just incredible"[35]

Klaus Voorman recalling Ringo playing with Rory Storm and The Hurricanes in Hamburg.

"As all the other drummers say, he just is something so special. When he's playing behind you, you see these other bands, they're looking around at the drummer, like, is he going to speed up, is he going to slow down? You don't have to look with Ringo."

Paul McCartney at Ringo's induction into the Rock And Roll Hall Of Fame, April 2015.

Background

One must wonder how much an influence Ringo's lack of schooling due to his ill-health had upon his drumming? Tellingly, when starting out, Ringo only had a few drum lessons (perhaps just the one?), and is on the whole self-taught. Perhaps if he had experienced a regular education he may have had more of an inclination to commit to a more disciplined regime of learning to play the drums? Sure, as a result his drumming is at times 'limited', but unlike the child who had his 'bad habits' coached out of him, he managed to turn this to his advantage. It's this naivety that occasionally sets him apart from other drummers of his time, a great deal of his drumming with the Beatles is purely instinctive – having a good musical ear, he plays *exactly* what is required by the song at *exactly* the right time.

Ringo is also a "social drummer", in that he doesn't like to practice his drumming (alone), he'd much rather have the 'buzz' of playing with other musicians rather than solo. This goes back to his first attempts at playing a drum kit up in his bedroom at Admiral Grove – and after being on the wrong end of the neighbour's wrath, he logically said to himself, "Right, I'll have to find me a band". Again, this approach and desire led him to become an accomplished live performer, a drummer who could be required to start playing, maintain a rock-solid beat without error, and stop at the correct time – qualities which eventually led John, Paul, and George to his door. In other words, Ringo became that rare thing – a reliable "busker" who could drop into any band and do a great job.

Like all musicians, influences are magically aligned with one's own personality and background to produce a distinctive style. Ringo was fortunate to begin playing drums at the time of fresh and exciting youth music of the mid to late 1950's to early 1960's. The sense of joy, excitement and passion that leapt from the stylus of those Rock and Roll records was exhilarating, with the bandmates and session men behind the names breaking new ground with every release. Of course Ringo wouldn't have been aware of the names of these drummers, let alone that more often than not, the same drummer played on many of his favourite hits. Take Earl Palmer. Earl lent his considerable skills to all the major hits of Little Richard, Larry Williams, Sam Cooke, Fats Domino, Eddie Cochran, and Lloyd Price – many of which were later recorded by the Beatles. Jerry Allison's groundbreaking use of much more than his drums to enhance Buddy Holly's songs proved inspirational too, as did the emerging talent of Hal Blaine, whose work with Phil Spector was equally as important.

Technique

What makes Ringo's playing so original and identifiable? Most of what defines Ringo's drumming style can be explained by the fact that he is left-handed, but plays his drums as a right-handed player. This has led to an almost unique approach to playing the drums. A right-handed drummer playing a right-handed drum kit would lead around the drums with his right hand, however Ringo instinctively leads with his left, producing a highly unusual and distinctive style. As a result, the Beatles recordings would benefit from incredibly smooth transitions between verses and choruses, with Ringo creating a percussive 'gap' between his movement from hi-hat or cymbal to his drums.

> "It's like one of those mad accidents, you can't learn it. I was left-handed, my Grandmother didn't like that, she made me go right-handed…. and so I have a right-handed kit, but I'm a left-handed player. All my fills, they don't come in fast, there's always a break 'cos I have to get this (left) hand ready…..
>
> Everybody was saying "Wow! I'm a genius!" but all I was trying to do was play…..backwards." [36]

Due to this unconventional approach, Ringo would also occasionally strike the crash cymbal on his left side with his left-hand, commonplace today, but less so in the 1960's. This ambidextrous approach also built up his strength in both arms, wrists, and hands, and led to him effortlessly carrying off such blistering work as the matched-stroke fills evident on recordings such as *Not A Second Time* and *Old Brown Shoe*.

Perhaps born out of the need for the drums to cut through the raucous smoke-filled atmosphere of the pubs and clubs in Liverpool and Hamburg, Ringo employed two techniques. Firstly, it was his use of the 'matched grip' that afforded Ringo the luxury of creating a powerful backbeat on the snare drum. The matched grip (in Rock drumming now the common method of holding sticks) involves the holding of both drum sticks, with the palms of the hand both facing the drum skin. Ringo's use of the matched grip was revolutionary for the time, and as he was the most visually available drummer of his era, his dismissal of the conventional grip favoured by drummers reared upon the military and jazz styles of previous eras placed him a step away from all that was stuffy and uncool in the world of drumming. That's not to say Ringo was unique in that respect, but it was this image of him up on his drum riser, pounding out the beat with his hands both facing down that proved inspirational to thousands of would-be drummers around the world, many of whom would in time become household names themselves.

Secondly, the famous 'Ringo swish' was a technique he perfected and made his own, having the effect of filling out the sound of the band by making his kit sound bigger. Furthermore, he had a unique way of playing the open hi-hat by moving his right hand laterally from left to right rather than up and down, something we hadn't seen a drummer do before. He achieved this by using his foot to keep the hi-hat cymbals ever so slightly apart, and striking the top cymbal so that it hit the bottom cymbal, thereby making an open 'swishing' sound. The hi-hats were closed tightly only when the song determined it, for example going into the bridge or possibly a chorus, at which point his foot would instinctively move down while he played the hi hat in the 'normal' operating position. A fantastic example of this is *I Won't Be Long* from *With The Beatles* – notice how the hi-hats are snapped shut at the onset of the middle 8 [0.40] & [1.22].

Allied to both of these traits, was Ringo's use of the now commonplace practice of playing the bass drum pedal with the ball of the foot and the heel raised, rather than the traditional manner drummers played with their foot flat on the pedal. This was largely brought about by the fashion of wearing Cuban-heel boots[37], or what naturally became known as 'Beatle Boots'. This meant that you had to play with your toe as your foot couldn't be flat on the footboard, resulting in more power being transmitted to the beater striking the bass drum.

Of course, in respect of these drumming techniques, Ringo was not alone, indeed Pete Best was known for his distinctive, pounding bass drum, while Johnny 'Hutch' of The Big Three was similarly feted for his thunderous solidity, all contributing to the birth and rise of 'Beat Music'.

Ringo's 'Feel'

A word that constantly crops-up when discussing Ringo's drumming is 'feel' – that seemingly indefinable, almost mystical quality that cannot be taught? But where does this 'feel' originate? Musical 'feel' is the ability to breathe life into a song or a piece of music. Some people never have this and their performances remain 'wooden'. A lot depends on technique. In Liverpool and Hamburg Ringo had a fairly wide experience of playing with other types of musicians and here he learnt to use his ears and his own ability allowed him to listen to the message and emotions in each song and thus transfer these emotions to the audience. By the time he stood-in with the Beatles, taking the place of a poorly Pete Best, he had these qualities in abundance, and immediately everything 'clicked' within the group.

"Behind us we had this guy we'd never played with before, and I remember the moment when he started to play – I think it was Ray Charles', "What'd I Say," and most of the drummers couldn't nail the drum part. It was a little difficult to do, but Ringo nailed it. Yeah — Ringo nailed it! And I remember the moment, standing there and looking at John and then looking at George, and the look on our faces was like, **** you. What is this? And that was the moment, that was the beginning, really, of the Beatles."

Paul McCartney at Ringo's induction into the Rock And Roll Hall Of Fame, April 2015.

Over the years as Ringo's drumming skills improved, so did his musical expression, and that upward curve is evident on his later recordings in the studio.

But how does this 'feel' translate into the studio? Why do so many classic Pop and Rock songs possess 'feel', and are revered to this day? The majority of recordings made by the Beatles were constructed from group performances in the early days, to a basic backing track with drums or at the very least an element of percussion such as a tambourine. If necessary, edits were made by combining different but lengthy sections of various takes, but crucially these edits were few and far between, and retained many bars of music. These performances may not be perfectly 'in time', but across the length of the track the listener is unaware of any very slight changes in tempo, and the overall song is constructed from live performances which possess the 'feeling' or atmosphere of musicians enjoying playing together.

With the introduction and widespread use of Digital Audio Workstations (DAW's) such as Pro Tools in the early 1990's, it no longer became necessary to record a song in one piece (or smaller pieces) from start to finish. Suddenly, it was possible to record to a click track, and, by using a computer, copy and paste a small section (or even an individual bar) of music to create a single, complete performance. It may be considered a generalisation, but it rings true that Pop music today lacks the 'feel' of the music of earlier times, largely due to producers being content finding a bar or two of a drum and bass track, and copying and pasting those bars throughout the length of the song. As this drum track originated on a drum machine, with the bass track often sequenced, and the vocal usually processed through tuning and quantising software in order to never stray from the beat and maintain 'perfect' tuning throughout, we are left with the removal of the human element and the sense of 'feel' from the listening experience.

Dependability

Many of the early Beatles releases were subject to extensive edits – the piecing together of different takes – or in numerous cases the 'tagging-on' of edit-pieces – the addition of separately recorded sections (usually endings) to the body of the main acceptable take. It's testament to Ringo's 'internal clock' that he was able to recall the exact tempo of a performance, even after a couple of minutes of chatter had elapsed. Ringo *was* capable of keeping perfect time, but he was also the master of creating the illusion of perfect timekeeping. Occasionally he would also quite deliberately alter the timing of a performance, be it in the studio or more commonly, a live performance. Rather like gently tapping your foot on a car's accelerator (gas) pedal, he would allow the music to shift tempo backwards and forwards, *ever so slightly,* as and when the song required it. This can be quite some feat to achieve, the trick is to make the listener (or more importantly your fellow musicians) blissfully unaware of what has happened, but wondering just what has happened! When recently asked if he could pass on one piece of advice to any young, aspiring drummers, Ringo offered – "Speed up during the guitar solo!" – surely a piece of tongue in cheek advice?

The Beatles play to a packed out Seattle Centre during their second tour of the USA, 21 August 1964. Quite how Ringo was expected to project his drums to the back of the auditorium is mind-boggling when compared to the thumping mega-watt amplification of today

Adaptability

What also sets Ringo apart from his contemporaries is how he was able to adapt to the changing musical landscape around him. Whilst playing the pubs and clubs of Liverpool, Ringo had to learn to alter his style to suit his surroundings. One engagement may be a vast, expansive venue such as the Tower Ballroom in New Brighton, where he would have to employ a heavy-handed approach in order for his drums to be heard at the rear of the venue (drums weren't miked-up in those days), the next may be a relatively small room such as Knotty Ash Village Hall, where he would have employed a lighter touch for fear of overwhelming his bandmates and deafening the audience. The experience of these differing approaches to his playing would stand him in good stead when he found himself within the confines of the recording studio.

Within an incredibly short period of time, Ringo's job description altered radically – after all, the journey from *I Want To Hold Your Hand* to *Strawberry Fields Forever* was a mere 3 years. Ringo was able to negotiate the transition from 'beat' drummer to all-round percussionist in such a ludicrously scant period of time. In a late 1964 interview[38], among the more predictable names such as Bob Dylan, the Supremes, and James Brown, Ringo lists jazz exponents and experimentalists Chico Hamilton and Yusef Lateef amongst his current favourite artists. It was this broad-minded approach towards other musical genres that enabled Ringo adapt to the rapidly changing songwriting landscape of his bandmates. One grain of truth in Lennon's supposed disparaging quote, is that Ringo was not the only competent drummer in the Beatles – he was fortunate (as were John and George) in that the group possessed perhaps the most gifted and accomplished multi-instrumentalist of their age. Paul McCartney was, and is, not only adept with a pair of drumsticks, but he has a powerful musical imagination, which enabled him to get the best out of Ringo by encouraging him to improve. If you compare the early Ringo to the later one, you can see how much he succeeded. Additionally, both John and George had imaginative percussive minds, by all accounts they were quite 'nifty' with percussion instruments and were always pushing Ringo to re-imagine and replicate what in their minds they felt their songs required. Because they played lead, rhythm, bass and drums, each Beatle was also adept in picking up each other's instruments when they saw fit. There didn't appear to be an 'Eh! that's my job..' attitude – a rarity within bands. Territorial marking was always the thing. It's also fair to say Ringo knew his place within the group – but that the other members, always protective and grateful, recognised his unique and incredible contribution to their overall sound.

The greatest testament to Ringo's drumming came from perhaps an unlikely source. Mark Lewisohn's exhaustive exploration of the Beatles' recordings *(The Complete Beatles Recording Sessions)* discovered that in the band's eight-year recording lifespan Ringo was responsible for less than a dozen song 'break-downs' in the studio, a mere fraction of those made by each of the other Beatles – a quite remarkable feat

PART FIVE

The Instruments

THE ANATOMY OF THE DRUM KIT

The Evolution Of The Drum Kit

The drum kit that we are familiar with today is derived from an arrangement of percussion instruments produced in the 1920's and 30's, a time when drummers required more than one or two drums and cymbals in order to keep time for the burgeoning dance and jazz bands. However, the important development occurred at the end of the 19th Century, with the invention of the bass drum pedal. This proved an invaluable tool for drummers, freeing up one of their hands, thus allowing the use of further percussion instruments with which to embellish their time-keeping.

In its simplest form, these early drum kits consisted of a bass drum (with pedal), the ubiquitous snare drum, a cymbal which was usually suspended on a boom arm attached to the bass drum, and possibly a 'low-boy' – a pair of small cymbals mounted on and operated by a foot pedal. As the bass drum retained the dimensions of a chest-mounted marching bass, over time these cumbersome drums took on a deeper and less taller form, the portability of which proved popular.

Manufacturers of drums soon appeared, some developing their marching band drums into drum kits. With this explosion of interest, the hi-hat pedal was introduced, along with smaller drums (tom-toms), again mounted on the bass drum. Wooden blocks and cowbells made an appearance, popular with Latin and Jazz drummers. Drums were now also able to be tuned, and often double-headed. Post-War, the arrangement of the drum kit we know today was complete, primed for the Rock And Roll explosion of the following decade.

The Rock And Roll Drum Kit

By the time Ringo had his hands on his first set of drums, Rock And Roll drumming saw time-keeping emphasis placed strongly on the combination of hi-hat/snare/bass, or ride cymbal/snare/bass. There was little accenting or punctuation of the snare and bass drum as in Jazz, Big Band or Swing – simplicity was the key to the stark, no-nonsense nature of Rock And Roll. Eight beats in the bar dominated the hi-hats or cymbals, the bass drum settled on no more than four, with the snare drum providing the strong backbeat.

RINGO'S DRUMS

"He's very fussy about his drums, you know? They loom large in his legend."

George Harrison, "A Hard Day's Night"

Like most drummers, Ringo started playing drums with a motley selection of second-hand stuff - in short, anything he could get his hands on. Starting out, he made do with a huge marching-band bass drum, with which he could do little more than bash out the most basic of rhythms. On a Christmas visit back home to London, Richy's Step-Dad Harry purchased a set of 1930's dance band drums, struggling alone all the way back to Lime Street Station. While perhaps not up to the demands of a youthful Dingle battering, they were obviously good enough to get young Richy started, because he was soon playing with the in demand and popular Eddie Clayton Skiffle Group.

Ringo's first cymbals were probably nondescript 'bits of old metal' such as Krut, Ajax, and perhaps the odd Zyn - the Zyn '5-Star' cymbals being superior but more expensive. In the early Sixties there wasn't much of a selection of cymbals to choose from, with Zildjians famously working out at around '£1 per inch' - a 20 inch cymbal would cost you approximately £20 - or the equivalent of two weeks wages! No small wonder then, that the crash/ride hybrid cymbal was so popular - why have the expense of two cymbals when with one you could cover both bases?[39]

But perhaps the greatest danger using the bus to travel to and from bookings was the constant threat of a beating from territorial gangs of 'Teddy Boys' (or 'Teds'), and more importantly the probable theft of your precious and expensive instruments. In his early days of skiffle with The Eddie Clayton Band, the group were set-upon after a booking at Broadway Conservative Club, a location a couple of long bus journeys away from their Dingle homes. Eddie was relieved of his newly acquired guitar, and as a consequence Ringo ensured he would only take the bare minimum of his kit to bookings. This usually involved taking his snare drum, cymbal, stands, brushes and/or sticks - basically the maximum he could carry while enacting a quick getaway.

Initially, as Richy would not have had a car, the default alternative was public transport.

Drums and buses didn't mix well, because you invariably required a conductor who was willing to stop the bus long enough for you to throw your gear in the void 'under the stairs' - that's if he agreed to take you in the first place, especially if you were unfortunate enough to own one of those huge, old bass drums rescued from the nearest defunct orchestra pit. It is said that Gretsch produced the smaller 20 inch bass drum due requests for a drum that would fit on the back seat of a New York cab. Elvin Jones is said to have utilised an 18" bass drum for just this reason.[40]

Ringo's Drum Kits

Ajax Edgeware 'Black Elegance' Kit

Sizes unverified, but likely to be -
20 x 15 Bass Drum
12 x 10 Tom
16 x 18 Floor Tom
*Dimensions in inches

On 23rd of April 1958, for the sum of £57 (£68 on hire-purchase), Ringo bought his first real set of drums, a 'Black Elegance' Ajax Edgware kit from Frank Hessy's shop in the centre of Liverpool.

Ringo with Rory and the Hurricanes and his Ajax Edgeware drums at the Tower Ballroom, New Brighton

These birch plywood drums would have been a huge upgrade for Richy, and his drumming would have quickly improved. Ringo's drumming career took a new direction when he joined Rory Storm and the Hurricanes, and with the group's increasing popularity came regular bookings, including seasons in Hamburg, Germany. As a result, over the next two years or so his Edgeware drums would have taken a real battering, leading to the necessary and inevitable purchase of a new set of drums.

Premier Mahogany 'Duroplastic' Kit

Ringo's Rogers Swiv O Matic tom mount

In the September of 1960, Ringo purchased a Premier drum-set in the 'Mahogany Duroplastic' finish. This was a controlled, functional kit and featured on many of the Beatles' early recordings, essentially those releases prior to the *She Loves You* single.

Ringo's Premier drums were essentially sourced from the Premier '58' set, with a 16" x 16" floor floor tom from the Premier '55' range.

14 x 4 Snare drum.
12 x 8 Tom.
16 x 16 Tom.
20 x 14 Bass drum.
*Dimensions in inches

Ringo was also fond of the Rogers 'Swiv O Matic' tom-tom mount on his bass drums, choosing to use this ahead of the pre-installed but clumsy Ludwig Consolette Rail. Sounding somewhat like a Wallace and Gromit invention, the Swiv-O-Matic system was considered a popular upgrade and offered greater flexibility and durability than its Ludwig and Premier counterparts.

Ringo also owned a pair of Premier Bongoes in matching Mahogany plastic wrap.

The Premier 58 set in Mahogany Duroplastic finish.

Premier
RINGO

Ringo's Ludwig Love Affair

Ringo Starr PLAYS··· Ludwig most famous name on drums

Ringo's Premier kit didn't last long, and by the time of the Beatles' recording sessions in late 1962 and early 1963, they do look particularly battered and bruised. By spring 1963, with increasing visibility due to the Beatles' chart and touring successes, Ringo's Premier drums needed replacing, and accompanied by Brian Epstein on a visit to Drum City[41] in London, he clapped eyes on a stunning Ludwig Downbeat set in the Black Oyster Pearl finish. It was love at first sight.

> "I was in London, I was playing Premier at the time....an English make, really heavy, but anyway I loved anything American. We went past this instrument store and they had this kit. I said "Oh great!...look at this kit! I just loved this kit. As I buy this kit the guy goes to rip off the Ludwig sign, I say "No! No! No! You've got to leave that on - it's American!" That's how it started - I just loved the look of the kit, it was American, and it sounded great - I play them to this day."[42]

However, Brian Epstein was unhappy with the bass drum logo staying put, fearing people would believe Ludwig to be the name of the group. Shop owner Ivor Arbiter suggested placing the group's name below the Ludwig logo, and quickly sketched the now iconic 'dropped - T' Beatles logo. Given the Epstein nod of approval, sign-writer Eddie Stokes completed the transition from sketch to finished article. On May 12th 1963 the drums were despatched to Ringo at ATV Studios in Birmingham, making their debut on the set of the *Thank Your Lucky Stars* TV show.

At a stroke, drummers soon desired a Ludwig kit, but at a cost of 275 guineas (nearly £300), it was out of sight when you earned a measly £10 a week. The reason imported drums were so expensive was because in 1950's impoverished Britain, the government was desperate to drag the country back on its feet after six years of a war that had drained it of resources. In an attempt to get British factories up and running again, strict tariffs were placed on many imported goods. A complete ban on American made musical instruments was lifted in 1957, although a high-purchase tax remained. Consequently, that exotic kit of Ludwig or Gretsch that you desperately wanted (all the top American drummers had them) cost over twice as much as the home produced kits. Paradoxically, Jerry Allison of The Crickets (perhaps for similar reasons to us Brits lusting after the exotic) played a white set of English Premier drums[43].

Why did we Brits hanker after these exotic kits? Well, not only did they look the absolute business glistening under stage lights, compared to ancient 'three drum' collections which were begged or borrowed. They had a magnificent, powerful sound and really 'projected', seemingly without using much muscle power. The 'Luddys' seemed to have more attack to them, perhaps due to the choice of wood or thickness of the shells, which were a 'ply sandwich' of Mahogany/Poplar/Mahogany. Then again, maybe this was also because the Premiers had solid, beautiful 'diamond' chrome, die cast hoops which some said 'choked' the sound somewhat. The Ludwig 'triple flange hoops' were made of lighter pressed steel, which had the advantage of having rims which curve outwards and made rim-shots much easier. Even today, engineers like the old Ludwig kits because, as one recently said, 'They provide a lovely mid-range which records beautifully'.

The Beatles first US tv performance on CBS's Ed Sullivan Show on 9th February 1964 led to a massive upturn in the fortunes of the Ludwig Drum Company.

"It's a personal choice, but I feel Avedis (Zildjian) is the best cymbal."
Ringo Starr

"We were a small business at the time the Beatles came in, and then we found ourselves with a 93,000 cymbal back-order, just because of Ringo Starr."
Armand Zildjian

Over the years the amount of sales generated by Ringo must have put quite a smile on the faces of the Ludwig (and Zildjian) families, with William F. Ludwig II joking that the Beatles' appearance on the Ed Sullivan Show was 'the show that launched a thousand orders'. It is said the Ludwig factory was thrown into a three-shift production the very next day, such was the demand for drum kits "like Ringo plays."

In 1964, to mark Ringo's impact on raising the profile (and profits) of the company, William F. Ludwig II presented Ringo with a gold-plated Ludwig Supersensitive snare drum.

"I have never known a drummer more widely acclaimed and publicised than you, Ringo Starr… On behalf of the employees and management of the Ludwig Drum Company, I would like to thank you for choosing our instruments and for the major role you are playing in the music world today."

The Oyster Black Pearl Wrap

Unlike other finishes (such as plain or sparkles) due to the random placement of the wrap onto the drum, no two Oyster Pearl covered drums are identical, leading to easy identification of Ringo's Ludwig drums

Ringo's choice of Oyster Black Pearl wrap proved to be inspired when considering the visual impact of the kit. Although not as vibrant and stark as other finishes offered by Ludwig (Silver and Champagne Sparkle wraps come to mind), Oyster Black Pearl nevertheless provided a strong on-stage presence and focal point without dominating proceedings. Considering the Beatles' public performances were almost exclusively filmed and photographed in black and white, we have been left with a set of visuals of a drum kit wonderfully integrated with it's surroundings. Didn't it just look fantastic on black and white TV sets?

How different would the Beatles' image have been had Ringo chosen a different finish?

Ludwig
PEARL FINISHES
Ludwig pearl finishes are the product of one of the world's leading chemical manufacturers. They are the finest finishes available and will add extra life and lasting beauty to your drums. The hard surface will not scratch, peel or chip. Ludwig now offers the new Multi-Sparkle® pearl, combining any two of the 6 sparkling finishes. Multi-Sparkle® pearl is another Ludwig quality feature available at no extra cost. When ordering—specify outer color first, inner color second.
Black Diamond Pearl
Sparkling Green Pearl
Oyster Blue Pearl
Sparkling Blue Pearl
Sky Blue Pearl
Sparkling Silver Pearl
Oyster Black Pearl
Sparkling Gold Pearl
White Marine Pearl
Sparkling Red Pearl
Sparkling Burgundy Pearl
Sparkling Pink Champagne
Ludwig . . .
NO. 1 CHOICE OF TOP PROFESSIONAL DRUMMERS AROUND THE WORLD!
SOL GUBIN
COLIN BAILEY
. . . including such top groups like Ramsey Lewis, the Beatles, The Yardbirds, The Rolling Stones, Manfred Mann, Gerry and the Pacemakers, Freddie and the Dreamers, The Kinks, Sam the Sham and the Pharoahs, Gary Lewis and the Playboys and Herman's Hermits among others.
JOE MORELLO
Ludwig most famous name on drums
1728 No. Damen Ave.
Chicago, Illinois 60647
ED THIGPEN
ROY HAYNES
DALE ANDERSON
HUBERT ANDERSON
DANNY BARCELONA
RINGO STARR
PERCY PRICE
NORM CHRISTIAN
KENNY CLARE
RED HOLT
FRANK HUDEC
JO JONES
GARY COLEMAN
SANDY NELSON
LARRY ROSEN
ALVIN STOLLER
and many many more

A composite collection of Ringo's Ludwig drums on display at Bloomingdale's Dept store, New York, 2014

Two Ludwig Downbeat Kits

Oyster Black Pearl wrap.
14 x 5.5 Jazz Festival Snare drum.
12 x 8 Tom.
14 x 14 Tom.
20 x 14 Bass drum.
* Dimensions in inches

Originally introduced by Ludwig in 1959, the Downbeat kit was the smaller baby brother of the more popular Super Classic Ludwig kit. Aimed at the Jazz player and those drummers seeking a set of drums which offered greater portability, the Downbeat soon became popular amongst mainstream drummers.

SPARKLING PINK CHAMPAGNE PEARL ILLUSTRATED

THE "DOWNBEAT" OUTFIT

A modern, compact outfit featuring the latest in drum sizes with 4" x 14" snare, 14" x 20" bass, 8" x 12" and 14" x 14" tom toms. Ideal for the progressive drummer playing "one-nighters." Incorporates all of Ludwig's top quality features including: triple flanged hoops, shell mount holders and spurs, flat base stands and the great blue "Speed-Master" pedal.

Available in choice of pearl or lacquer finishes.

	Nickel	*Chrome*
No. 988L—"DOWNBEAT" Outfit, choice of lacquer colors, less cymbals	$335.00	$367.50
No. 988P—"DOWNBEAT" Outfit, choice of pearl, less cymbals	389.50	421.00

Federal Excise Tax Extra

Following list is in pearl finish:

	Nickel
1—No. 906P—4" x 14" "Downbeat" snare drum	$ 64.00
1—No. 920P—14" x 20" Classic Bass drum	114.00
1—No. 942P—8" x 12" Classic tom tom	62.50
1—No. 948P—14" x 14" tom tom with legs mounted	85.00
1—No. 782 —Shell mount tom tom holder	12.00
1—No. 1372—Shell mount cymbal holder	6.50
1—No. 1400—Floor stand cymbal holder	9.95
1—No. 1363—Flat base snare drum stand	9.95
1—No. 1121—High hat sock cymbal stand	19.50
1—No. 133 —Cow bell holder	1.75
1—No. 129 —5" Clear tone cow bell	2.25
1—No. 205 —Blue Speed-Master pedal	18.00
1 pr.—No. 1305—Shell mount folding spurs	4.50
1 pr.—No. 191 —Red rubber wire brushes	1.80
1 pr.—No. 11A —Morello model sticks	1.00
Total	$412.70

Page 22

Its smaller sizes suited the diminutive Ringo as it was easier to 'move around' the kit, and by his own admission made him appear bigger in the process! Despite the small dimensions of the drums, it was and still is a very hard hitting, powerful outfit. The smaller toms really cut through and provide a solid exciting sound, just check out Ringo laying into his Downbeat at the 1964 Washington gig.

Two Ludwig Super Classic Kits

Oyster Black Pearl wrap.
14 x 5.5 Jazz Festival Snare drum.
13 x 9 Tom.
16 x 16 Tom.
22 x 14 Bass drum.
* Dimensions in inches

Ringo's personal favourite, the Super Classic appeared on the Beatles recordings from mid 1964 to late 1968. With sizes larger than the Downbeat, the Super Classic offered greater tuning opportunities, from Jazz to Heavy Rock, and was admired and used by Ludwig endorsees such as Joe Morello and John Bonham.

Ludwig Hollywood Kit

Maple finish
12 x 8 Tom.
13 x 9 Tom.
16 x 16 Tom.
22 x 14 Bass drum.
* Dimensions in inches

Purchased around December 1968 by George Harrison for use in the upcoming *Get Back* project.[44] Perhaps to provide continuity to the Beatle sound, Ringo chose to maintain use of his Jazz Festival snare drum rather than the now more commonly supplied metallic Ludwig Supraphonic snare. An alternative view is that his Hollywood kit was supplied without a snare drum.

THE LUDWIG HOLLYWOOD
...the latest in "Twin" tom tom design

Ludwig's advance design and creative imagination has developed the ideal outfit for today's modern "Rock" drummer. The HOLLYWOOD features the new all-angle retracting double tom tom holder that provides complete angle and height adjustment and allows use of mixed tom tom sizes. The popular Supra-Phonic 400 all-metal snare drum and the famous 201 Speed King pedal are standard. Three different tom tom sizes (8" x 12", 9" x 13", 16" x 16") provide a wide variety of tonal changes and modern effects.

No. 983-1PC—HOLLYWOOD OUTFIT. Choice of pearl finish, chrome, WITHOUT CYMBALS $568.00

Recommended PAISTE-Formula 602 CYMBALS for HOLLYWOOD OUTFIT

2 No. 714HH—14" Matched for Hi-Hat @ $31.50 each .... $ 63.00
1 No. 718TC—18" Thin Crash 47.00
1 No. 720MR—20" Medium Ride 58.00
TOTAL VALUE, Cymbals $168.00

No. 226—Set of 4 PAISTE-Formula 602 CYMBALS, as above, special price $160.00

No. 983-1PCX—HOLLYWOOD OUTFIT. Choice of pearl finish, WITH PAISTE CYMBALS listed above, special combination price $728.00

Outfit includes:		Chrome
1	No. 400—5" x 14" All-Metal Snare	$ 92.50
1	No. 922PC—14" x 22" Bass Drum, pearl	138.50
1	No. 942PC—8" x 12" Tom Tom, pearl	71.00
1	No. 944PC—9" x 13" Tom Tom, pearl	73.00
1	No. 958PC—16" x 16" Tom Tom, pearl	187.00
1	No. 781-1—Retracting Double Tom Tom Holder	20.00
1	No. 1123-1—Hi-Hat Pedal Stand	24.00
1	No. 1363—Flat Base Snare Drum Stand	14.00
2	No. 1400—Floor Stand Cymbal Holder	24.00
1	No. 201—Speed King Pedal	25.00
1 pr.	No. 1305C—Folding Spurs	7.00
1 pr.	No. 193—Wire Brushes	2.50
1 pr.	No. 8A—Orchestra Model Sticks	1.50
	TOTAL VALUE, Drums and Accessories	$600.00

Sparkling Gold Pearl Illustrated

The Ludwig Speed King Bass Drum Pedal

With a history dating back to 1937, the Ludwig Speed King bass drum pedal is still considered by many drummers as THE bass drum pedal. Easily serviceable with the simplest of dual-compression spring mechanisms, a metal link between the footplate and a felt beater, the pedal provides the drummer with that greatest of qualities - the 'bounce-back' of the beater from the drum skin, allowing for greater timing, dexterity and power.

Terry's Jazz Festival Snare

The Jazz Festival Snare

Featured on the majority of the Beatles' recordings, Ringo always favoured the Jazz Festival wooden snare as opposed to the Supraphonic 400 metal snare from the Ludwig range. It was even purloined by Paul McCartney for his 1970 solo album McCartney.

Ringo's Jazz Festival has stayed with him throughout his career, and has been dubbed "The World's Most Famous Snare Drum

PERCUSSION

213 Songs	
Drums	67
Handclaps	38
Tambourine	70
Maracas	31
Cowbell	13
Bongos	12
Congas	5
None	6
Bass Drum	4
Brushes	3
Claves	3
Hi-Hat	3
Timpani	3
Finger Cymbals	3
Indian Percussion	3
Drum (Tom)	2
Packing Case	2
Guitar Body	2
Rim-Taps	2
Guiro	2
Chimes	2
Hand Bell	2
Stick-Taps	1
African Drum	1
Thigh Slaps	1
Matchbox	1
Book Cover	1
Finger Clicks	1
Shaker	1
Chocalho	1
Anvil	1
Snare	1
Foot Tapping	1
Cymbal	1

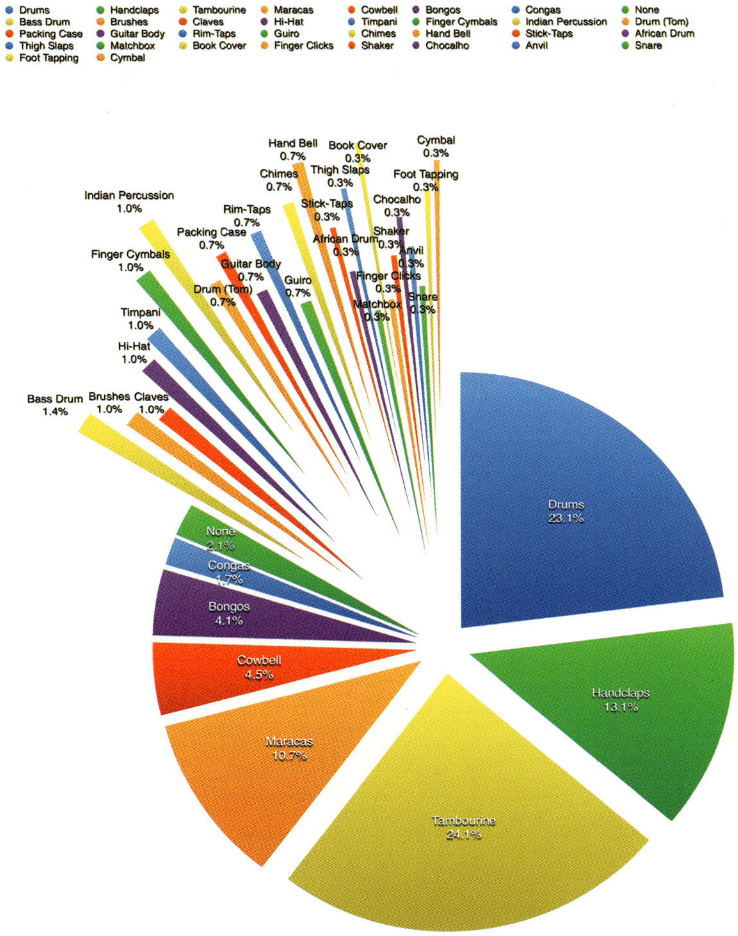

Above we see the breakdown of the Beatles' inventive and imaginative use of percussion derived from all of their songs. Throughout their recording career, the Beatles understood the importance of percussion in helping to shape the presentation of their music. From the spontaneity and simplicity of the handclaps on their first LP (*Please Please Me*) to the orchestral pounding of timpani on their last (Abbey Road), the group were keen to explore the enhancement of their songs with the use of a variety of percussion instruments.

Act Naturally

Perhaps surprisingly, nearly a quarter of the group's output contains nothing more than the use of a set of drums. If we analyse this further, this figure is somewhat skewed by the nature of the recording of the *Please Please Me* and *Let It Be* albums. *Please Please Me*, recorded in a single day, saw the need to commit songs to tape with the minimum of overdubbing, while the 'back to basics' edict of *Let It Be* saw the Beatles shun the use of overdubs. As a result, 9 songs of 14 (*Please Please Me)* and 10 of 12 (*Let It Be*) have no percussion other than Ringo's drum kit.

All Together Now

The simplest and quickest percussive embellishment dates from the formative days of nursery school – the use of one's body. Next to drums, the Beatles favoured handclaps. Imagine *I Want To Hold Your Hand, Eight Days A Week,* or *Here Comes The Sun* without the subliminal drive and hook of handclaps? By contrast, one would think the Beatles would have utilised that other great use of the body – the finger-click (or finger-snap). In fact, the group chose to use finger-clicks just once in their career – during the final verse

and chorus of *Here, There And Everywhere* from *Revolver.* Why eschew such an immediate and effective percussive ploy? From their early performances around the pubs and clubs of Liverpool, the Beatles were keen to avoid what they considered musical clichés – one such example being a performance of Elvis Presley's *Are You Lonesome Tonight,* halted mid-flow by John Lennon, who was less than impressed with Paul McCartney's rapidly descending into parody spoken-word section of the song. This attitude of 'cliché-avoidance' remained with them, and finger-clicks certainly fall into that category, especially from a 1960's perspective. One only has to click a finger and thumb on the second and fourth beats of a bar to be transported into Sinatra territory. By contrast, handclaps were a popular choice, usually recorded as a group, with anybody in the studio at that particular time roped-in for 'clapping duty'.

Any Time At All – The Tambourine

Drawing inspiration from the tambourine-heavy sounds of Motown and the Beach Boys, the tambourine formed an increasingly prominent role in the development of the presentation of the Beatles' music. This instrument, which has been around for over two thousand years and used in many cultures, found its way onto 58 of their 213 tracks. Consisting of a circle of wood or metal, with jingles or 'zils' spaced around its perimeter, an animal skin drawn tightly over the surface and secured around the edge. This instrument can be played like a drum, using fingers, palm, or knuckles, and when used expertly, the effect can be truly stunning. The Beatles' tambourines were fashioned from wood, and late in their careers tambourines without skins were employed. To protect fingers and thumbs, tea-towels were occasionally utilised around the rim. Today, all sorts of variations of the Tambourine are manufactured, mainly using modern plastics which allow more ergonomically friendly shapes to be achieved, giving not only better balance but also having the benefit of being less fatiguing. The Beatles weren't experts in the field, but possessing a natural feel for the music, each could be relied upon to pick one up in the studio and 'help out'. Where for instance would *We Can Work It Out* be without the insistent, alluring, magical sounds providing that driving '16's' feel which binds the fabric of the song together?

Illustrated below, we can clearly see the Beatles penchant for the tambourine increase and peak at the release of *Rubber Soul* in late 1965. This is heightened by the issuing of two singles either side of *Rubber Soul, Day Tripper/We Can Work It Out,* and *Paperback Writer/Rain*. All four songs heavily feature dominant and driving tambourine, prominently presented in the mix.

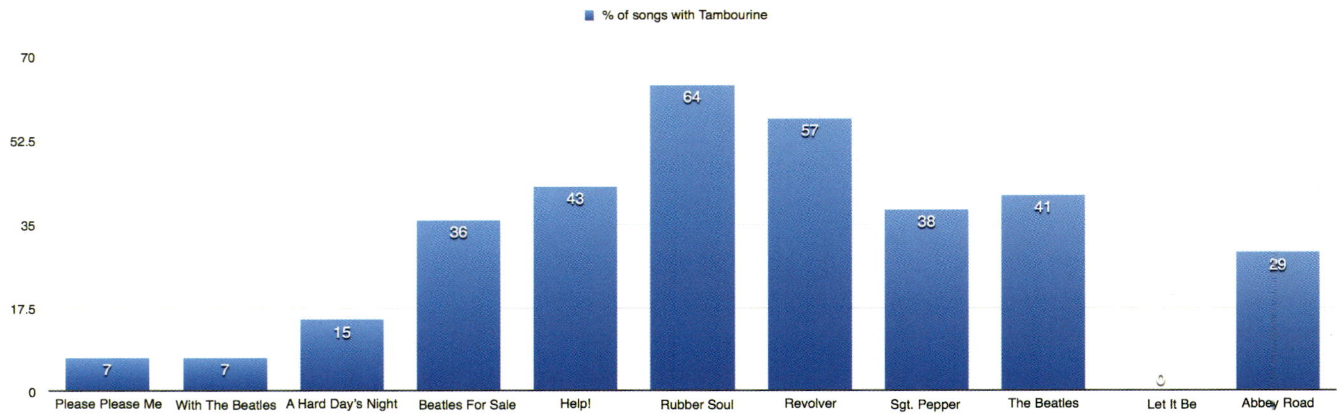

Shake It Up, Baby, Now

While not unique, the use of maracas and shakers (with occasional exotic variants) added another dimension. Whether providing rhythmical tension (*I Want To Tell You*) or a '4 in the bar' constant (*The Night Before*), maracas and shakers were placed at the forefront of the mix. Combined with tambourine, they provided a heady mix of movement, snaking their way around each other. Try to imagine how less an impact the descending chords of *You've Got To Hide Your Love Away* would make without tambourine and maracas. The use of 'hurried' percussion brings us to bongos and congas. Bongos saw prominence in early recordings, adding a hurried touch to songs such as *A Hard Day's Night* or *You're Going To Lose That Girl,* with occasional later reappearances throughout their catalogue. Congas however, chiefly came into use around the time of the *Sgt. Pepper* sessions (1966-7), and remained a popular choice until the group's final recordings (*Abbey Road*).

A staple of American rhythm and blues records, the cowbell was used to maintain a constant, driving beat, usually on straight ahead, no-nonsense 'rockers' such as *You Can't Do That* or *Dizzy Miss Lizzy.* Like congas, the cowbell remained a popular choice, however towards the latter stages of the Beatles career, it's use was tempered somewhat, usually conservatively mixed, gently fleshing-out the musical landscape.

Perhaps the most unique aspect of the Beatles' use of percussion was their eagerness to utilise seemingly anything at their disposal to achieve the required effect. Sometimes the simplest of objects would suffice – the backs of acoustic guitars, drumsticks tapped together, packing cases, even the closely-miked tapping of a book.

The fact the Beatles used over thirty different types of percussion to enhance and compliment their recordings, and that they managed to achieve this with the listener been largely unaware of such devices, is testament to their genius, allied to the skill and professionalism of the recording staff at EMI.

PART SIX

The Studio Environment

RECORDING RINGO'S DRUMS

A drum kit isn't a single instrument, but rather a collection of disparate instruments, the sounds ranging from the deep 'thud' of a bass drum to a high end 'ping' of a cymbal. Each one of these sound characteristics demands attention and a degree of skill when recording it. In the 1960's, many sound engineers had very little idea of how to go about recording a drum kit, sadly there are still more than a few around today who can't, such is the skill required.

Drum Skins

The key to recording drums in the Sixties (and today for that matter) is the understanding of the physical make-up of drum skins, also referred to as 'heads'. In the early 1960's, plastic drumheads were just coming into general use – previously calf skin (vellum) was used. Plastic skins were a huge improvement on the animal skins which used to get sloppy in the heat of a club, and very tight when you packed them into a sub-zero van late at night. Consequently you were constantly spending precious time tuning and detuning the skins. They were also expensive to buy as each hide had to be soaked and then 'lapped' (placed on a wooden hoop) by someone with the expertise to do so. Plastic heads eliminated all these problems and left the drummer with time to do more important things like going to the bar, and hopefully getting to know an attractive member of the audience.

Nowadays, the drummer has the luxury of being able to pick from a vast range of drum heads which will give him the sound he is looking for before he goes into the studio. This cornucopia of heads includes different weights and thicknesses, some with reinforcing patches on top of, underneath and around the perimeter of the head. Some heads have a rough coating, some are smooth, some even have small holes around the edge. They are all designed to give the player the sound he is looking for – all have their supporters and long may they reign. Ringo though wouldn't have had this choice, instead perhaps having just one or two types to choose from.

'Damping' or 'Muffling' Drums

One (of many) problems was how to 'kill' the resonance or 'ring' that a drum throws out when hit forcibly by a drum stick. This 'ring' is of course the vehicle that determines whether or not the sound gets to the back of the room, or simply crawls to the front of the stage and falls off. Ringo would have been used to playing drums that weren't miked-up in the early days, and would have developed the skills necessary to 'throw' an acoustic kit past the noise created by the amplifiers.

However, in a studio, this sound is not welcome, so other steps have to be taken by the engineer. His first job would be to 'dampen' the drum sound down, and even though some drum manufacturers included an internal 'muffler' or 'damper', they proved largely ineffectual. The engineer would sometimes employ a tea-towel, but more often or not use tissue or cigarette packets taped to the drum heads. This had the effect of not only destroying the sound the drummer was used to hearing, but made the head feel lifeless and 'like playing on a badly stuffed sofa[45]'. Duly satisfied, the engineer would make his way back to the control room leaving the drummer ruefully surveying his pride and joy and wondering why the toms he spent so much time and money on now sound like the unwelcome knock of a bailiff on his front door.[46]

Progressive Techniques

The EMI engineers worked hard over the years to improve Ringo's drum sound. As the Beatles progressively pushed back the boundaries, so would the engineering team. EMI's strict rules on recording determined the sound of the Beatles' early recordings, and were ruthlessly enforced. In the early 1960's, rock'n'roll was still the new kid on the block, with classical recordings still making up the bulk of Abbey Road's output. The physical layout, and manner in which orchestras performed dictated how the recording engineers approached their task, with regimented microphone placement the order of the day. Engineers would have to take into account the dynamic range of classical music, quiet passages of music often being followed by incredibly loud ones. A band such as the Beatles however, presented a different challenge. Recording a song with such power as possessed by *Twist And Shout* would have placed stresses upon the microphones of the day, especially when placed closely to drums and amplifiers, and would have been seen as potentially damaging to the equipment. The powers that be certainly weren't ready to allow four scruffs from the provinces any close contact with their sensitive equipment. As a result, the microphones were positioned at what was considered a 'safe distance' from the drums – laughable by the close-miking techniques in use by the end of the Beatles career.

The engineering team would incrementally experiment with the recording of Ringo's drums. On early Beatles' recordings, Ringo's drums were treated to a bass drum microphone (positioned a regulatory 2 foot away), with an overhead microphone a foot or so above his head, hoping to capture the other drums and cymbals as best they could. By the time of *Sgt. Pepper*, the bass drum microphone was positioned right up against the drum head, and was joined not only by one overhead, (this time positioned more forward and closer), but also another a couple of inches above the floor tom, one below the mounted tom, and finally one positioned above the snare and hi-hats. Occasionally, to achieve the desired effect, the front head of the bass drum would be removed, and stuffed with sound deadening materials[47]. The placement of such materials in the bass drum would eliminate the 'ring' or resonance of the drum, producing a dull thud which would give the engineers greater control of the sound through compression and equalisation. The bottom heads of the toms were also occasionally removed, further reducing the 'ring' of the drum, and therefore requiring less damping of the top skin. To deal with the close proximity of the microphone placement, compressors were utilised – devices which would control the level of the audio signal by reducing the dynamic range (the difference between the loudest and quietest passages) of the audio signal from the microphones. Abbey Road used Fairchild compressors almost exclusively on Ringo's drums, and when coupled with the distinctive and powerful Ludwig sound, created magical sounds that everyone wanted to emulate.

It was this interaction between the demands made by the artist, and the reaction of the recording engineers to those demands that constantly pushed back the boundaries, enhancing the finished product that we know and love today.

EMI ABBEY ROAD PRODUCERS AND ENGINEERS

George Martin in control, EMI Abbey Road

The Beatles' relationship with EMI Abbey Road Studios was often much different than the one widely portrayed today. As their fame, wealth and worth to EMI grew, the Beatles were more or less given free-rein to bend the previously strict studio timetables in place at Abbey Road, with late night sessions becoming the norm. However, the cautious approach of the studio management towards technological advances was particularly frustrating for the group. On the rare occasions Abbey Road was already booked, the Beatles would decamp to rival studios, where they revelled in the latest hi-tech recording equipment and surroundings, such as 8-track machines, allowing them potentially more creativity with which to work their magic. Sometimes the grass really was greener.

Eventually, it appears John Lennon and George Harrison in particular found the Abbey Road environment stifling – heralding the construction of a new studio in the basement of their Apple HQ in Savile Row. Ever the sentimentalist, Paul McCartney still retains a fondness for Abbey Road, and occasionally still records at the studio. Perhaps if Lennon and Harrison were still alive, they would possess similar emotions?

The Beatles' Producers

The record producer of the 1960's would be in overall control of the sessions – including budgeting, the booking of musicians, liaising with the record company, and offering advice and encouragement to the artist – in short, providing direction and 'shaping' the overall sound of the finished music.

Sir George Martin

Born in 1926, Sir George is the most successful British record producer, and is widely credited as the 'Fifth Beatle'. However, it's fair to say that it was his close relationship with his engineers that shaped the Beatles sound, and guided them through their musical development. Classically trained on piano and oboe, George Martin wore his Producer's hat superbly, taking on the mantle of mentor rather than an all-out Father-figure. The ill-feeling that pervaded the *White Album* sessions proved to be the tipping point for Martin, and he decided to take a break from proceedings (see 'Chris Thomas' below). Martin returned for the ill-fated *Get Back* sessions, and was coaxed back for the group's final album, *Abbey Road*, as long as the sessions were on his terms, recording in the manner of days gone by.

Chris Thomas

Being born in 1947 and as result a good few years younger than all four Beatles, Chris is a classically trained violinist and pianist. After having a fledgling career as a pop musician, Chris decided to pursue a recording career. Having been George Martin's assistant for only a matter of months, upon returning from holiday, he was greeted with a short note from his Boss -

> *'Dear Chris, Hope you had a nice holiday. I'm off on mine now. Make yourself available to the Beatles.'*

Thrown into the middle of the *White Album* sessions, Chris won the group over, and contributed piano and harpsichord to at least 3, and possibly 6 tracks on the album, the most notable being Mellotron on *The Continuing Story of Bungalow Bill*, and harpsichord on *Piggies*. Chris went on to produce and mix albums for amongst others Pink Floyd, The Sex Pistols, The Pretenders, Elton John, U2 and Pulp.

Phil Spector

Brought in by Lennon and Harrison to make a silk purse out of the sow's ear that were the *Get Back* sessions, legendary (even by the late Sixties) Producer Phil Spector is perhaps best remembered for his schmaltzy treatment of McCartney's *The Long And Winding Road*. For what was slated as a 'back to basics' album, Spector heavily edited some tracks and gave the album a glossy touch that was lacking from the original tapes. He went on to produce successful solo albums for Lennon and Harrison, before falling out with Lennon while recording his *Rock 'n' Roll* album, at one point famously disappearing with the master tapes. Never short of controversy, Spector is currently serving a prison sentence for second-degree murder.

The Beatles' Engineers

The Beatles benefited greatly from the 'in-house' talent at their disposal. New, young engineers had a strict but rapid career progression at Abbey Road. Most started work in the Tape Library, where they became familiar with tape formats, labelling protocol, etc, the perfect education for preparing for life as the next step-up – into the studio environment as assistant engineer. Sometimes referred to as 2nd engineer, this job would involve operating the tape machines, labelling, compiling album tapes from individual masters, and making sure recordings were actually made to tape. Assistants were more or less tied to their chair in front of the tape machine – under no circumstances were they allowed to touch the mixing console, microphones or other studio ephemera. Progression would then be made outside of the recording studio environment to the post of mastering engineer (or cutter), whose duties involved the transfer of the completed, mixed tapes to disc. 'Cutting' was an extremely important and responsible job, if a little solitary. Back into the studio, next on the ladder was the position of (balance) engineer, who's responsibilities would (unsurprisingly) include balancing the recordings through the mixing console before they were committed to tape. Engineers would also be responsible for duties such as microphone placement, adding of compression and contributing to the final mixes.

Norman Smith

> *'A great gentleman, an incredible engineer. Completely forgotten, unfortunately. He was the one, as far as I'm concerned, that started the Beatles on their sonic road to what they got to. He changed the sound on each individual album. He had very specific ideas of how he wanted to change each one.'* – Ken Scott.[48]

Born in 1923 in Edmonton, England, Norman (or 'Normal' as he was christened by John Lennon), engineered the group's output from *Love Me Do* through to *Rubber Soul*. Smith was largely responsible for the 'open' sound of the group's early recordings, attempting to capture their live sound as accurately as possible. Promoted to Producer, Smith went on to produce Pink Floyd's early output (with Syd Barrett), while also having major chart success in his own right as 'Hurricane Smith'. Norman passed away in 2008, aged 85.

Geoff Emerick

Born in London in 1946, Geoff Emerick arguably added the greatest creative input to the Beatles' sound. Possessing a love of recorded sound, with the help of his school Careers Officer, Geoff secured an interview with EMI at Abbey Road. Within weeks he was in place at Abbey Road, and present at the Beatles' first recording session. In 1966 he was promoted to engineer, and whilst working on the *Revolver* sessions, his impact was immediate. Emerick worked on most of the Beatles' sessions until, during the *White Album* recordings, he couldn't take any more of the acrimony and bitterness that pervaded, and refused to work with the group. He was however persuaded to return as engineer for the *Abbey Road* recordings, completing the team for one 'last hurrah'. Particularly enamoured of Paul McCartney's dedication to his art, Geoff would engineer many of his albums from the 1970's and 80's, most notably *Band On The Run*, for which (along with *Abbey Road* and *Sgt. Pepper*) he was awarded a Grammy for 'Best Engineered Album'.

Ken Scott

A Londoner born in 1947, Ken served his time at Abbey Road from 1964 before becoming engineer in late 1967. His first work as engineer with the Beatles was on the *Magical Mystery Tour* sessions – he later engineered many of the Beatles' hit singles, including *"Hey Jude"*, as well as the vast majority of the *White Album*. Ken left EMI in 1969, and enjoyed an incredibly successful career, producing legendary albums by amongst others David Bowie, Elton John, Supertramp, Devo, Duran Duran, and the Mahavishnu Orchestra. Having published his memoirs (the excellent, self-effacing *Abbey Road to Ziggy Stardust*), Ken is still actively recording and producing.

Glyn Johns

Having the distinction of being the first freelance recording engineer in the UK, Johns was Paul McCartney's choice to handle the *Get Back* sessions due in part to his film industry union membership allowing him access to Twickenham Studios. The 'Glyn Johns drum microphone technique' has become legendary, and is simplicity itself. Utilising 4 microphones, namely two closely placed near bass and snare drums, and two positioned overhead, directed and equidistant from the snare. These overhead microphones are panned left and right, with the bass and snare locked to the centre of the mix. The result is a wide, expansive drum sound, which also packs a punch from the bass and snare, a technique employed by Johns for Led Zeppelin's John Bonham.

Ken Townsend

As studio technical manager, Ken Townsend worked on the Beatles' recordings from 1965-7, and was responsible for creating the technique of 'Artificial Double-Tracking', the process by which a second vocal was created from a single track by varying the delay of the vocal, thus negating the need for the artist having to record a second performance.

Phil McDonald

Phil engineered Beatles' sessions towards the end of their career, and left EMI to work for Apple, also engineering many solo Beatles recordings.

PART SEVEN

Andy White & The Beatles Beat?

LOVE ME DO, LOVE ME DON'T?

"When the Beatles signed to EMI in 1962 they recorded *Love Me Do* twice at the company's studios at Abbey Road in London. On September 4th, the song was recorded featuring Ringo Starr on drums. A week later, on September 11th, George Martin produced another version of the song, which this time featured a session drummer, Andy White, and with Ringo playing tambourine".

- From the sleeve-notes of the 1982 12" single release of *Love Me Do*.

The above sleeve-notes offer a simplistic view of a series of events which were to become a source of much confusion and subterfuge – with the relative merits of three drummers taking centre stage. Having secured a 'contract[49]' with EMI's Parlophone label, a June session was booked.

June 6 1962 – Artist Test at EMI Recording Studios (Abbey Road)

With Pete Best in tow, the Beatles' first EMI session was either (depending upon varying memories) an 'artist test' or a straightforward session designed to produce a tangible end product. As we have seen (in Part 6, Chapter 2 – Pete Best), the session was a disaster for Pete – his 'skip beat' proving particularly calamitous. After reviewing the recordings and enjoying the Beatles' company, George Martin decided to arrange a further session, this time to record two songs for a single release. There was however, one caveat – George Martin saw Pete Best's looks as perhaps the group's greatest visual asset, but not his drumming – a session drummer would be hired for future recordings. The writing was clearly on the wall for Pete.

Tuesday September 4 1962 – Recording: *How Do You Do It? / Love Me Do.*

Not believing any of their compositions to be strong enough for their upcoming single, at Ron Richard's suggestion, George Martin selected 'Tin Pan Alley'[50] composer Mitch Murray's *How Do You Do It* as the group's first '45'. Despite resenting the song, the Beatles (with new drummer Ringo Starr) had rehearsed and arranged *How Do You Do It* to suit their particular style of playing. Six songs were auditioned/rehearsed, including five original compositions (one being a fledgling slower version of John's *Please Please Me*, in the style of Roy Orbison). The rehearsal was once again a disaster for the Beatles' drummer. Perhaps overly nervous, and keen to impress after Pete Best's rejection by George Martin and Ron Richards, during the rehearsal of *Please Please Me*, Ringo had a rush of blood to the head.

> "I was playing the bass drum and the hi-hat, and I had a tambourine in one hand and a maraca in the other, and I was hitting the cymbals as well …… trying to play all the instruments at once".[51]

Once again, at the crucial moment, the Beatles' drummer had come unstuck, and his card was marked.

After much rehearsal and discussion, *Love Me Do* was selected as the flip-side. The Beatles begrudgingly recorded *How Do You Do It*, turning in a workmanlike yet professional performance. However, *Love Me Do* took an eternity to record, perhaps due to the song (like *How Do You Do It*) being laid to tape in two passes – instrumental backing first, followed by vocals[52]. As a result, the session over-ran. *Love Me Do* took 15 takes to record, requiring a lot of editing to create the final coherent version. According to Engineer Norman Smith, perhaps picking up on George Martin's displeasure with the rhythm section, and thereby deflecting criticism away from his bass playing, Paul McCartney also wasn't satisfied with Ringo's performance, feeling

> *'It could be better. He didn't make too good a job of it.'* [53]

Ringo's drumming couldn't have been that bad, however, as it was this version from 4th September that was released as the Beatles' first single. Additionally, what is not clear is that if George Martin was unhappy with Pete Best's drumming on the previous session in June, why was a session drummer not hired for this session as intimated to Brian Epstein?

Tuesday September 11 1962 – Recording: *PS I Love You / Love Me Do / Please Please Me.*

Love Me Do was now being recorded for the third time, and such a luxury could not be tolerated, especially as this session was to last no longer than one and three-quarter hours, half the time usually allowed. The song had to be recorded professionally and swiftly. This time, Richards and Martin were taking no chances – he had booked session drummer Andy White to take Ringo's place. White was one of the country's top drummers, and he was well aware of the demands and constraints of the recording studio environment. A session musician would have to be able to perform perfectly and precisely with discipline, control and without error. Ringo however, was a different animal, the studio being alien to him. As far as Ron Richards and George Martin were concerned, Ringo was susceptible to a deadly trap a studio virgin could fall into, namely the dreaded 'red light syndrome'. The new recruit appears calm and collected, until suddenly the studio red light flashes on, and a voice from the control room booms – 'RECORDING!'.

All of a sudden, bowels churn, you break into a cold sweat, your mouth is dry and miraculously, your sticks turn to rubber. After all, this could be your one big chance and now you are about to ruin it for everyone. You just freeze. Some people never get to grips with this phenomenon. With a session man behind the kit, Richards knew he could rely on White to lay down the drum track with minimum fuss, and maximum results. And so it proved, White earning his £5.15s session fee with consummate ease.

> Speaking in 2012, Andy recalls – "It was a really enjoyable experience," and what impressed me was they were doing some really good stuff, but it was all their own stuff and was really new".
>
> "Everything else at the time was a copy of music from the States, which was very successful, but they were doing something new and you could tell it was something different and very special. But I didn't know just how special it would become." [54]

The remake of *Love Me Do* was completed with Ringo playing alongside White on tambourine, and this is the easiest way to distinguish which version has Andy White on drums. It certainly has a punchier feel to it than Ringo's version, due to the fact the rest of the band were more familiar with the song and had probably rehearsed it in preparation for their third attempt at recording it. There is a more confident, professional presentation, due mainly to the added luxury of a tambourine, naturally missing from the Ringo version. The Andy White version was included on the *Please Please Me* LP, and from the issue of the *Beatles Hits* EP was to be the official version for all future releases – the master tape of Ringo's version was either destroyed, or more likely recorded over. Future releases of the Ringo version (from a 1982 anniversary release onwards) were taken from a pristine copy of an original single.

The recording of *Please Please Me* is where the 11th September session begins to get interesting regarding the rhythmical aspect of the Beatles' songs. Speaking of the Beatles' unusual approach to recording, White recalled,

> "They didn't use any written music, and what I had to do was play the routines with them to get an idea what they wanted before we could even start recording."

While not being entirely alien to Andy White, this approach wasn't that common either. Musical notation of the songs to be recorded was usually provided to the session musicians. This less than professional approach of the Beatles would form the basis of Ringo's recording career with the Beatles – his translation and interpretation of their ideas of what the rhythm track of the song should be.

At the 11th September session, The Beatles with Andy White recorded three songs, *Love Me Do*, *PS I Love You*, and at George Martin's behest, a faster version of *Please Please Me*. This version of *Please Please Me* (with White on drums) was believed to have been erased, but resurfaced in 1995 on the Beatles Anthology. According to White, he fashioned the structure of what was to become *Please Please Me* – the trademark drum patterns and the 1/16th note snare fills. On *PS I Love You,* again White plays drums, while at Ron Richard's request, Ringo played maracas throughout.

"Ringo didn't play drums at all that evening," said Richards in 1988.[55]

Ringo has never forgotten, indeed never forgiven George Martin -

> "George didn't want to take any more chances and I was caught in the middle. I was devastated that George Martin had his doubts about me. I came down ready to roll and heard, 'We've got a professional drummer.' He has apologised several times since, has old George, but it was devastating — I hated the bugger for years; I still don't let him off the hook!" [56]

Monday November 26 1962 – Recording: *Please Please Me / Ask Me Why*

Flush from modest yet impressives chart success with *Love Me Do*, the Beatles arrived at Abbey Road to record the follow-up to *Love Me Do*, and this time Ringo was apparently entrusted with the job of laying down the beat on the Beatles' recordings. There was no session drummer booked – the 'Session Fees & Expenses' sheet for Andy White clearly shows no entry for Abbey Road on 26th November. If George Martin wanted to re-record *Please Please Me*, why not rebook Andy White? However, in a recent interview[57], White claimed it is his drumming that features on this version of *Please Please Me* -

> "From the drum sound I can tell that I was on it, because it was a vastly different sound to Ringo's drum-set at that time. This was before he got the Ludwig kit. Each drummer gets an individual sound, first of all by the way they tune the drums and then by the way they play the drums."[58]

Geoff Emerick recalls[59] Ringo jumping on the kit to perform *Please Please Me* at the end of the 11th September session. Most observers have interpreted this as meaning they recorded a version with Ringo, or at worst, this story is a fabrication to deflect attention away from the fact that Andy White – not Ringo – played on *Please Please Me* in addition to *Love Me Do*.

Another viewpoint comes from an article commissioned by Bill Harry for his *'Merseybeat'* newspaper. Documenting the November 26 1962 session, freelance journalist Alan Smith crucially reported -

"Drummer Ringo Starr had just cause to be pleased with himself after the session. During the recording of the Beatles' last disc, George Martin wanted him to do some intricate drumming effects. He was naturally nervous – it was the first time he'd recorded, unlike the rest of the boys – and it took quite a bit of time. On this occasion he had the confidence to perform without worrying."[60]

Whilst being somewhat inaccurate in describing the session as being the first time Ringo had recorded, here is clear, documented evidence that Ringo, not Andy White performed on the November 26th version of *Please, Please Me.*

An EMI publicity shot for the release of 'Love Me Do'

IN CONCLUSION

Love Me Do

The sedentary pace of *Love Me Do* calls for an equally pedestrian and repetitive drum pattern. This laid-back feel leaves the song with an exposed or open sound, and as a result the finger is clearly pointed towards the drummer. Unfortunately there is really no other pattern that will improve matters, a busier pattern would be too fussy for the song, and after all, three different drummers played essentially the same pattern on the three different recordings. Due to this, from a technical viewpoint, the recording of *Love Me Do* appears to have been somewhat problematic, with session Engineer Norman Smith later commenting -

> 'It was a real headache trying to get a (good) drum sound, and when you listen to the record now you can hardly hear the drums at all.'[61]

Indeed, the drums are buried in the mix of both versions, Andy White's bass drum is more precise, due to the more confident approach by the seasoned professional. Ringo's bass drum appears to have been equalised ('eq'd') out of the mix in an attempt to hide the hesitant, lacklustre performance. The addition of tambourine (played by Ringo alongside Andy White) lends power and urgency lacking from Ringo's version.

Another factor to consider when appraising the two versions is the tempo of each recording. Andy White's version is marginally faster, clocking in at approximately 148 beats per minute, with Ringo's version idling slightly at 144 beats per minute. Such a small increase may not appear to alter matters, but here it lifts the Andy White version above Ringo's, the perception of confidence reinforced by the increase in tempo.

Below we have the first 2 bars of both versions of *Love Me Do,* Ringo's version first, Andy White's second. Besides the obvious addition of tambourine (mirroring the snare), Andy White cleverly shifts the bass drum pattern across the two bars, and further towards the busier snare drum beats of the second bar. This provides a sense of urgency absent from Ringo's tentative version, and when allied to the increased tempo and the added tambourine, gives the sort of polished and professional result George Martin and his staff were after all along.

Love Me Do – Ringo Starr September 4 version.

Love Me Do – Andy White version with Ringo Starr on tambourine. 11th September version.

Please Please Me – Andy White Or Ringo Starr?

As we have seen, the details of the recording of *Please Please Me* have become somewhat clouded in the mists of time, chiefly due to the Beatles' first recording sessions being nothing short of a muddled mess, lacking the usual disciplined organisation of a recording company of the day. As a result, Andy White's claim that he is the drummer on the track has never been definitively proven, but also not disproven.

The September 11 Recording.

This first version, an acetate copy of which was unearthed for the *Beatles Anthology,* is an early 'run through' of the song. Raw in confidence and execution, this is clearly a song that requires more work. In particular, the drum fills are hurried and erratic – one example at [1.07] sounds like a suitcase falling down a flight of stairs – odd for a seasoned and respected session man like Andy White, but not unusual for such an early take. Instantly we are aware this is not Ringo, neither in style or execution, nor the sound of the drum kit. The ride cymbal work possesses more of a 'jazz' feel than Ringo's no-nonsense approach. The sound of the drums are more open, closer to Andy White's Ludwig kit than Ringo's 'tighter' Premier drums. It is documented that during this session further takes were recorded[62], but none survived – or did they? It is entirely possible a further recording featuring Andy White on drums was indeed issued as the Beatles' second single. If so, why schedule a further session to re-record the song? As we have seen, when Ringo's earlier recording of *Love Me Do* was released as a single in favour of Andy White's re-recording, EMI were capable of errors or misjudgements.

The November 26 Recording

This later version is a natural, stronger progression of the earlier recording – we hear a different approach in terms of style and delivery. Gone are the hurried yet hesitant fills, replaced by similar but stronger patterns, clearly mimicking but refining the drum track of the earlier recording. Emphasis is placed on the first beat of the bar – a slight accent or 'push' coinciding with a bass drum beat, which is lacking from the September 11th version. As this session took place between the recording of the Andy White *Love Me Do* version and the *Please Please Me* LP, it is difficult to compare the sound of the drums. The *Please Please Me* LP session was designed to emulate the Beatles' live sound, and as such, microphone placement reflected this. A far easier comparison to make is the drum sound of the subsequent recordings from the *From Me To You/Thank You Girl* session. From this we can deduce the drums from the single release of *Please Please Me* sound closer to those of *From Me To You* than Andy White's *Love Me Do*.

Andy White has a lifetime of experience at the very top of the drumming tree – he instinctively knows the sound of his drums, the style and feel of his drumming. However, while we don't doubt his sincerity, live performances of *Please Please Me* (subsequently released on the *Live At The BBC* and *Bootleg Recordings, 1963* albums) show Ringo absolutely nailing the drum part. Solid and forceful, there isn't an ounce of hesitancy or weakness evident. If he could do it live, why not in the studio?

PART EIGHT

The Music

1. Love Me Do / P.S. I Love You

Single – Released October 5 1962
Engineer – *Norman Smith*

Love Me Do

Time Signature – 4/4
Recorded – September 4 1962
Drums, Handclaps – *Ringo Starr*
Handclaps – *Paul McCartney, George Harrison, John Lennon*

Despite all the 'hoo-ha' of who-played-what on *Love Me Do,* Ringo definitely performs on the gentler tambourine-less single version. It may not contain the punch of the Andy White album version, but it undeniably possesses more charm.

Premier Drums

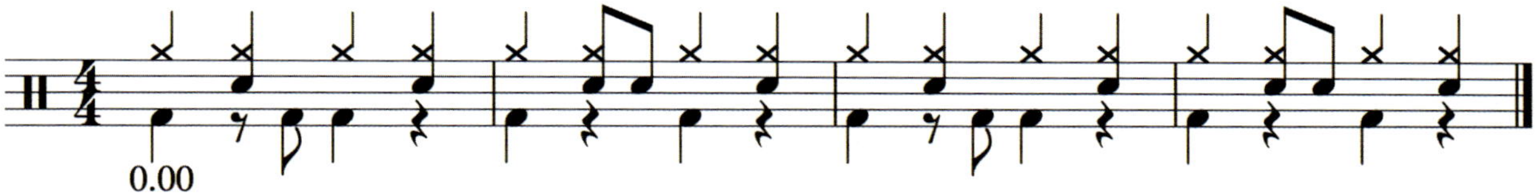

0.00

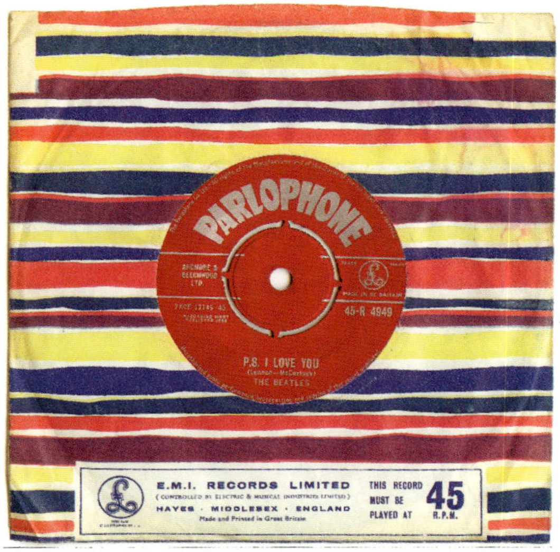

A snapshot of time, the nervousness and trepidation (especially from Paul's faltering vocal) creeps from the speakers. Ringo sounds like he is feeling his way through the song – his confidence increasing with every bar. *Love Me Do* still possesses a hangover from the Pete Best EMI audition version – Lennon can't help but get carried away during the last few bars of the harmonica solo – Ringo doing his best to keep the tempo in check. A taster of things to come – to add urgency and depth, handclaps are introduced over the solo, conservatively placed on the 2nd and 4th beats of the bar.

P.S. I Love You

Time Signature – 4/4
Recorded – September 11 1962
Drums – *Andy White*
Maracas – *Ringo Starr*

The B-Side does not feature Ringo on drums – he is relegated to maracas – what must have been going through his mind? It has been documented there are no drums played on this track, that Andy White instead plays bongos, as it was felt drums weren't suitable for the song. However, while it is difficult to detect a drum track, Andy White plays a credible but not very Beatle-like busy Latin beat on cross-stick snare-rim. Ringo's maracas fill out the otherwise barren percussive landscape, pushing the snare clicks along.

2. Please Please Me / Ask Me Why

Single – Released January 11 1963
Engineer – *Norman Smith*

Please Please Me

Time Signature – 4/4
Recorded – November 26 1962
Drums – *Ringo Starr*

The big break-through song, and despite who does or doesn't play drums on *Please Please Me*, what *is* a fact is the song features a drum part of great (for the day) invention. Taking inspiration from Latin percussion, the Andy White derived drumming features clearly defined patterns – sheer energy and joy leaps out at the listener. Illustrated here with a bar of the preceding verse, great use is made of the space left by the striking of the crash cymbal, allowing the vocal track emphasis.

Premier Drums

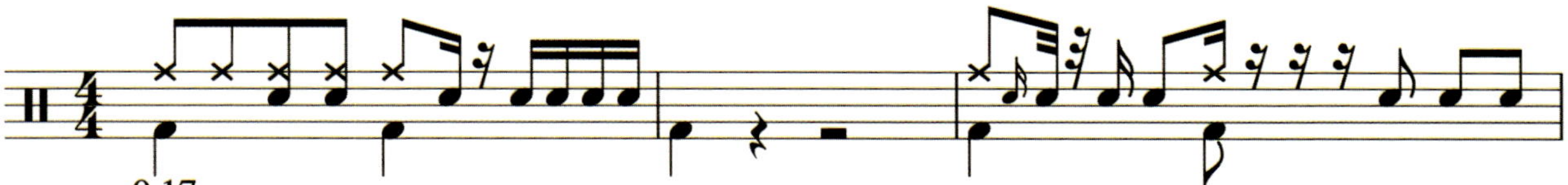

0.17

Here, the robust but simple rhythm works perfectly with Paul's busy bass part, emphasising the vocal phrasing of Lennon's 'Come On, Come On' with some inventive snare work. The song's finale – and a suave ending to boot – features four 16th note fills on snare, used to great effect.

Premier Drums

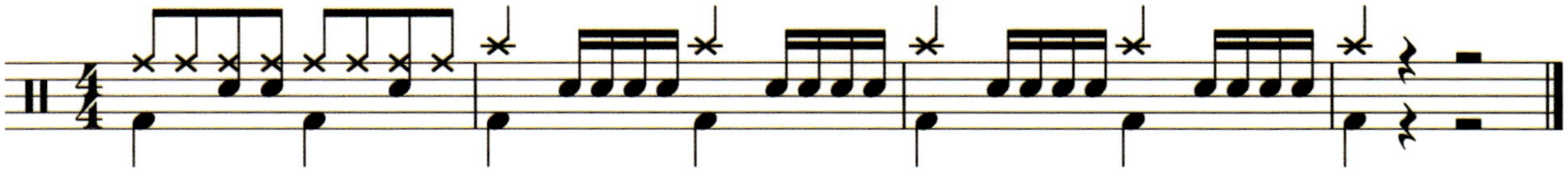

1.47

Ask Me Why

Time Signature – 4/4
Recorded – November 26 1962
Drums – *Ringo Starr*

Perhaps taking a leaf from Andy White's '1,2,3, & 4' cross-stick snare performance on *PS I Love You*, Ringo offers a similar 'cha cha cha' style beat, his snare rim-clicks are busier and more prominent on the bridge, adding urgency. The main difference this time being the structure and slower pace of the song allowing the luxury of the odd drum fill to link sections of the song together. Unusually for Ringo, the fills (at [1.02] & [2.01]) begin with a bass drum/cymbal crash, followed by a swift fill from top tom to floor tom.

3. Please Please Me

LP – Released March 22 1963

Engineer – *Norman Smith*

All Songs Recorded February 11 1963, unless otherwise stated.

14 Songs

Drums	9
Handclaps	2
Maracas	1
Stick-Taps	1
Drums (Brushes)	1
Tambourine	1

Tambourine is played by Ringo in the Andy White version of *Love Me Do.*

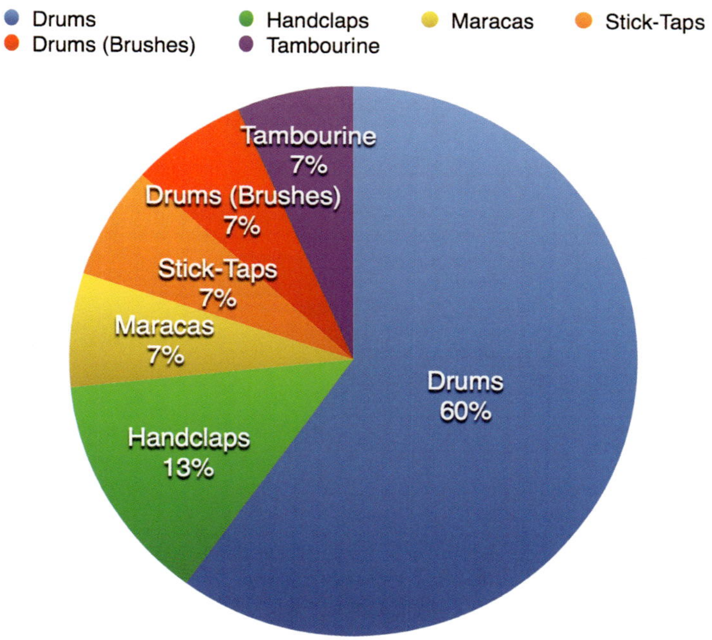

Side One

I Saw Her Standing There
Misery
Anna (Go To Him)
Chains
Boys
Ask Me Why
Please Please Me

Side Two

Love Me Do [Album Version]
P.S. I Love You
Baby It's You
Do You Want To Know A Secret
A Taste Of Honey
There's A Place
Twist And Shout

Famously recorded in 3 relentless sessions[63] totalling 9 hours and 45 minutes, and featuring no less than 8 self-penned songs (highly unusual for the day), *Please Please Me* burst on to the British pop scene like no other debut. Producer George Martin's belief in his act was such that he had faith in them to provide enough material of genuine quality amongst the standard allotted 14 tracks – his original idea being to record the group live at the Cavern Club.

Instead, the pick of the Beatles current live act was selected to be recorded live at Abbey Road Studio 2. With minimal percussive overdubs, Engineer Norman Smith attempted to reproduce their live sound by placing microphones farther away from the instruments than was the studio norm. This allowed the room ambience and sound reflections to contribute to the sound of the finished product. The instruments were recorded on one track of the 2 track BTR recorders, vocals on the other. Present on the vocal track is mic overspill from the instruments, not a problem when both tracks were mixed together in Mono, but on the Stereo mix the effect was disconcerting. To get around this, at the mix-down the Stereo version was treated with echo, to help 'bind' the 2 tracks together. Some prefer this separation, believing the Stereo mix gives the greater impression of the Beatles' live sound.

A testament to Ringo's timekeeping, most tracks on *Please Please Me* were subject to ingenious editing, for example take 1 of *I Saw Her Standing There* features on the album, yet has the count-in from take 9. Such a small session time, coupled with the limitations of 2-track recording, placed restrictions upon percussion overdubs. Simple handclaps enhance 2 songs, drumstick tapping another. Maracas were added to the previously recorded *PS I Love You*.

As Don Powell alludes to in his Foreword, Ringo's drum sound (so brilliantly captured here by Norman Smith) allied with his style of playing was revolutionary. Nobody played drums like this – the energy and power of the infectious beat, the 'swishy' hi-hats and cymbals that filled the air, a potent mix that has endured and still inspires more than 50 years later.

I Saw Her Standing There

Time Signature – 4/4
Drums, Handclaps – *Ringo Starr*
Handclaps – *Paul McCartney, George Harrison, John Lennon*

Bursting out of the traps, with Paul McCartney's somewhat nervous and cheeky count-in, Ringo's enthusiastic drumming starts the *Please Please Me* album off in style. Paul's bass plays a busy "8 in the bar", with Ringo belting the same rhythm out on closed hi-hats throughout. The solid 4/4 beat is employed with verve, and liberally punctuated with snare fills at every available opportunity, 'snapped' triplets preceding verses and the vocal repetition of the finale. The drums have a rawness lacking in many songs of the day, the nervous energy and sheer joy lifting proceedings to a different level. Overdubbed off-beat handclaps are placed over the snare beats 'beefing up' the snare.

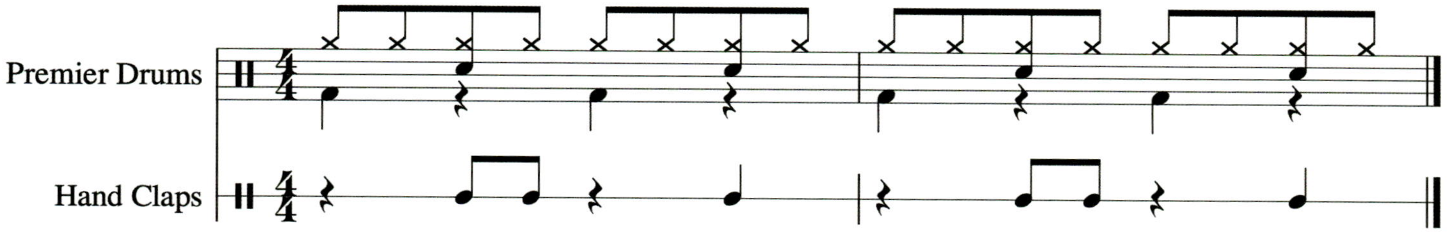

The bass drum, recorded at a low level, appears negligible in the mix, and as a result we have displayed Ringo playing on the first and third beats in the bar. Live performances saw Ringo treat his bass drum part with far less discipline, playfully accenting his bass drum at every opportunity. The forthright nature of the studio version serves the song well – although Ringo displays just the right amount of restraint by reining-in the enthusiasm of his bandmates, especially during the guitar solo.

The drum sound, while representative of its position across the whole album, is particularly high-frequency heavy (compare the bass drum's lack of prominence with that of *Boys*), and may have as much to do with microphone placement as much as George Martin's initial wariness of Ringo's loose bass drum patterns *(see Love Me Do).*

Misery

Time Signature – *4/4*
Drums – *Ringo Starr*

Ringo employs a plodding, lethargic beat, emphasising the lyrical tone of the song. Hi-hats are once again prominent, although this time tightly closed, providing a bed for the stabbed rhythm guitar work. The bass drum, locked to Paul's bass, is accented at [1.21], providing a bridge to the final chorus, nailing the feel and giving the vocals plenty of room to breathe. The drums (especially the hi-hats) get progressively louder as Ringo loosens up and the song develops, he's enjoying himself on this easy to play number.

Anna (Go To Him)

Time Signature – 4/4
Drums – *Ringo Starr*

The predominant beat here displays a great feel for the emotion of the song, (playing individually across bass/snare/and open & closed hi-hats), echoing the broken relationship of the protagonist perfectly. Here are the first 4 bars, displaying an open (or 'choked') hi-hat.

This pattern however, is directly lifted from the Arthur Alexander original, and would provide the template for a popular feature of Ringo's repertoire – similar patterns reappearing on *All I've Got To Do (With The Beatles)*, and *In My Life (Rubber Soul)*[64]. Returning to the music, the snare fill [1.28] mimics the fall into despair of John's vocal delivery. Notice the squeaky bass drum pedal throughout?

Chains

Time Signature – 4/4
Drums – *Ringo Starr*

One of the Cavern Club fan's favourites – with Ringo employing a simple yet jaunty medium-tempo shuffle, motoring the song along at a fair pace. The snare is 'locked' with the guitars, Paul's bass doing much of the rhythm work. At [1.06] and [1.41], Ringo plays ever-so disjointed matched strokes on snare and hi-hat, and as the song reaches it's conclusion, he opens his hi-hats, filling the sound out to great effect.

Boys

Time Signature – 4/4
Drums – *Ringo Starr*

It's 'Ringo Starr-Time', as we are transported back to the sweaty bars and clubs of Liverpool and Hamburg, where groups were expected to play almost continuously for 4 or 5 hours a night. As a result, the drummer was expected to sing because the main vocalists in the band usually lost their voices after a couple of days, although they did come back stronger than ever after a day or two. Here Ringo gets to do his party-piece and in the process gets to show the 'versatility' of the band.

Ringo had mastered the art of simultaneous high energy drumming and singing, so it was no surprise he elected to record his vocal whilst laying down the music track with his band mates. He easily carried it off while performing live, so why would he want to do it any different when it came to committing the song to tape? Well, technically, recording drums is difficult enough (especially so in 1963), and recording the vocals at the same time presented the engineers with the potential of the drums 'leaking' onto the overhead vocal microphone. They seem to have got around this problem by isolating the drums from the other instruments, and placing them along with the vocals (including backing vocals) on a track of their own, the bass and guitars on the other. Luckily, this would add a pronounced edge to the finished product, in particular Ringo's fine vocal performance.

With a heavy '8 in the bar' ride cymbal, there's busy interplay between bass drum and snare -

Notice how prominent and 'clean in the mix' are the snare and ride cymbal compared to the other recordings on *Please Please Me*. Hats-off to Norman Smith!

Ask Me Why

Time Signature – 4/4
Recorded – November 26 1962
Drums – *Ringo Starr*

Previously issued as the B-side of *Please Please Me,* and most definitely featuring Ringo on drums.

Please Please Me

Time Signature – 4/4
Recorded – November 26 1962
Drums – *Ringo Starr*

Issued as the Beatles' 2nd single, February 1963 saw this track make number 1 in the hallowed New Musical Express chart. The mix presented on the stereo version of the LP is actually a composite of mono and stereo versions. It appears that either no harmonica overdub was made for the stereo version, or more likely was lost from the end of the original master reel (later recorded over), so when creating the stereo mix, rather than re-record the harmonica, the mono master was overdubbed onto the vocal (right) channel. This was mostly satisfactorily achieved, but at certain points (most notably from 1.45 onwards[65]) the rather clumsy edits prove jarring, the two drum tracks, though identical, slightly out of sync. Otherwise, the drums on both mixes are identical.

Love Me Do

Time Signature – 4/4
Recorded – September 4 1962
Drums, Tambourine, Handclaps – *Ringo Starr*
Handclaps – *Paul McCartney, George Harrison, John Lennon*

Presented on *Please Please Me* in glorious mono, is the Andy White (with Ringo on tambourine) version of *Love Me Do*. Whether by design or accident, the tambourine lends a punch and energy to a song that can sound lethargic without it.

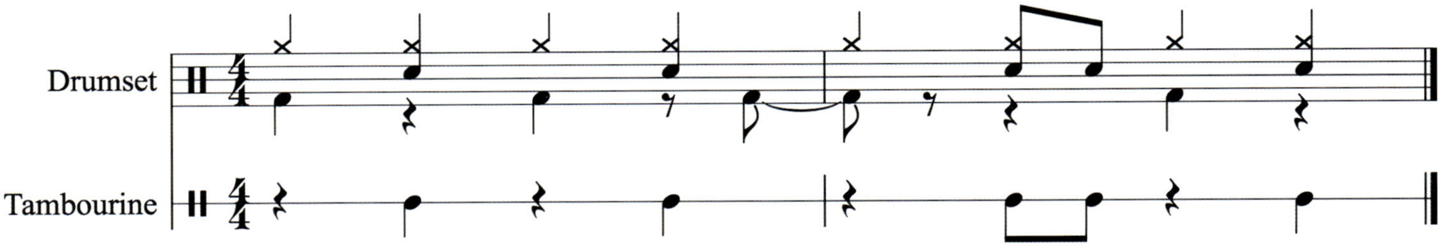

P.S. I Love You

Time Signature – 4/4
Recorded – September 11 1962
Drums – *Andy White*
Maracas – *Ringo Starr*

The B-side of *Love Me Do*, *PS I Love You* again features Andy White on drums. A disgruntled Ringo begrudgingly shakes maracas in the style of a shamed naughty schoolboy, a situation which must have been truly disheartening for the new recruit. However, the maracas fill out the otherwise barren percussive landscape, pushing the snare clicks along.

Baby It's You

Time Signature – 4/4
Drums – *Ringo Starr*

Soulful, tender, sympathetic drumming allows the song to reach its emotional peaks and troughs, especially on the build-up to the chorus. On the solo, Ringo slightly speeds up, but pulls back in time for the returning verse. The bass and drums are locked in a groove throughout, with a 'pushed' bass drum beat on the '2 and' beat of the bar displaying great empathy between the rhythm section, the sparse bass drum treatment clearly illustrated here -

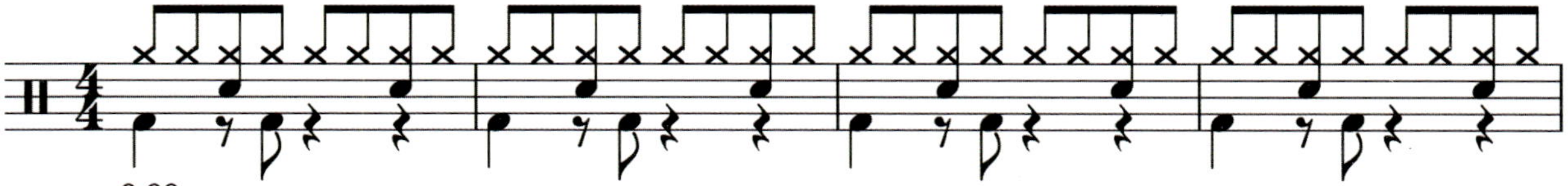

Do You Want To Know A Secret

Time Signature – 4/4
Drums, Drumstick Tapping – *Ringo Starr*

Simple patterns dominate, although at [0.38], [1.04], and [1.43] Ringo employs a solo bass drum beat to bridge the verses, and the fade out. A device favoured by Lennon, as evidenced on *One After 909* found on *The Beatles Bootleg Recordings 1963*. Here, when Ringo declines to play this pattern, John admonishes him – *'What are yer doin'? 'Yer out of yer mind? – do the bum.bum.bum….'*

George Martin brings his experience to the table, with overdubbed drumsticks beaten together and drowned in echo feature on the bridge at [1.08], presumably to add a moment of reflection, and also enliven a necessary but unimaginative portion of the song?

A Taste Of Honey

Time Signature – 3/4
Drums (Brushes) – *Ringo Starr*

Ringo displays his versatility, with competent and relaxed 3/4 snare drum brush playing, a style while being far removed from rock n roll, he would have been well aware of from the dance halls of Liverpool. Here however, he is merely mimicking the Lenny Welch original, save for a change in tempo to a 'shuffle' feel [0.43] and [1.32] giving the song impulsion without feeling forced, echoing the urgent nature of the lyrics, the use of hi-hats heightening the drama. The importance of the brush work to the song is given by it's prominence in the mix.

There's A Place

Time Signature – 4/4
Drums – *Ringo Starr*

Although *There's A Place* displays urgent and hurried drumming by Ringo, he manages to keep things clean, tidy and simple – he was never on an ego trip and his playing here shows that he always played 'for the song'. Using his bass drum and snare, he punctuates and enhances the phonetics of the vocal within the first few bars (bar 3 below).

Interestingly, a similar method is employed throughout the verses, with a bass drum and hi-hat triplet combination revealing the singer's place is actually in his mind, best illustrated here by the 2nd bar below.

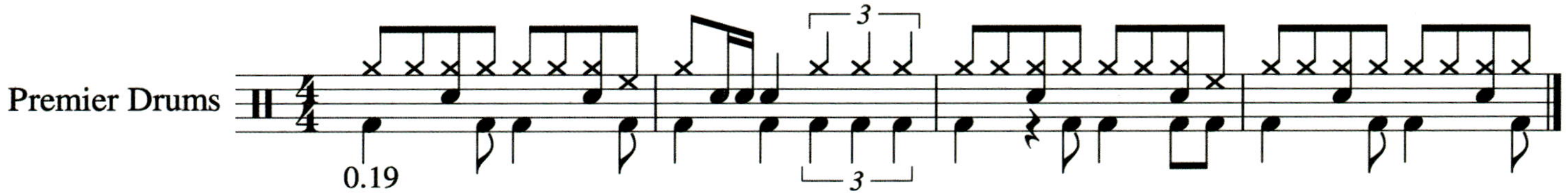

Undoubtedly, *There's A Place* would have made a brilliant last track on the album, if it were not for…….

Twist and Shout

Time Signature – 4/4
Drums – *Ringo Starr*

With such an outstanding interpretation of the Isley Brothers *Twist and Shout,* it's easy to forget the immense pressure the Beatles found themselves under when recording the final song of the session. With the clock ticking (a mere 15 minutes of studio time was remaining), John's cold-ridden sore throat on the edge of collapse, and needing to complete one more track for the album, there was no margin for error. All their stage experience and discipline came to the fore, as they completed the song in one take (a second take was attempted but broke-down as John's vocal faltered).

Simultaneously relaxed yet powerful, determined and faultless drumming binds the individual performances together, driving the song forward. Unusually, Ringo enters the fray with double-handed snare work rather than his right hand on hi-hat or ride cymbal. Blistering, fluid fills abound, spectacularly filling the studio[66] without once disturbing the rhythm [0.22], [0.36], [0.51] and [1.50]. The trade-off between guitars and drums throughout is superb, with Ringo's playing not hindering the efforts of the three vocalists. The switch from ride cymbal to hi-hats on the solo reverses the norm, allowing the build-up and power of the drums to help the song reach a climax at the end of the solo.

Ringo builds the track during the *'shake it, shake it'* section by playing '8's' on the bass drum, snare, and ride cymbal (bars 1, 3, & 5 below), emphasising the vocal line without overwhelming it.

Running down towards the end of the song, we can see how the three different patterns knit together, Ringo skillfully manoeuvring the song towards it's climax. Triumphant triplets finish the song (and the album) off in style. What a day's work!

4. From Me To You / Thank You Girl

Single – Released April 12 1963

Engineer – *Norman Smith*

If there is a combination of songs that display Ringo's Premier kit in all it's … 'glory', it's the two contained on either side of this single. The drums sound thin and weak compared to the larger, more open sound of his Ludwig set. Despite Norman Smith creating even greater separation by placing the vocal microphones further away from the drums, this isolation only served to 'tighten' the sound of Ringo's kit. This is not a criticism of Smith's work (it is worth comparing this single to the preceding *Please Please Me* album with it's wide, echo-drenched sound[67]), rather his technique here displays the limitations of Ringo's Premier kit.

From Me To You

Time Signature – 4/4

Recorded – March 5 1963

Drums – *Ringo Starr*

From Me To You is notable for some hurried snare and tom fills, Ringo enjoying a new found sense of freedom and expression in the studio absent from his earlier performances. Despite this, he keeps his bass drum tightly in sync with McCartney's booming bass. Tightly shut high-hats pin down the middle 8, loosening up on the build up to the snare-fill resolution.

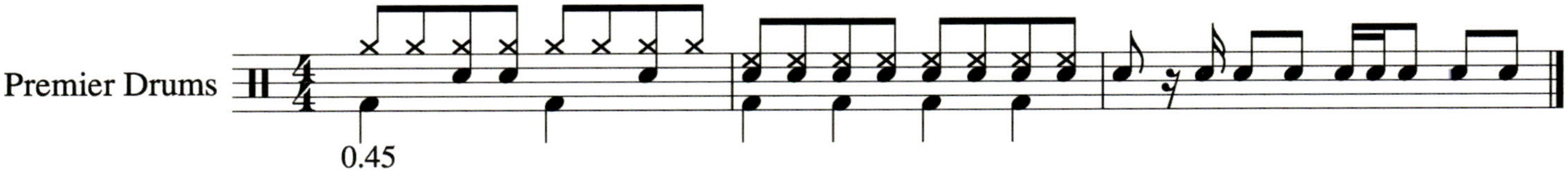

Thank You Girl

Time Signature – 4/4
Recorded – March 5 1963
Drums – *Ringo Starr*

Ringo plays in much the same style on the flip-side of this single with controlled, tight drumming, especially on his drum fills at the end of the song [1.44] and [1.51]. *Thank You Girl* was a work in progress and as evidenced on *The Beatles Bootleg Recordings 1963,* Ringo hadn't quite mastered or developed these fills. As a consequence, the end sequence [1.37] was re-recorded and edited on to the best available complete take. Taking six takes to complete, the tagged-on ending of *Thank You Girl* displays tight snare (and the second time around) tom movements.

Recording the From Me To You/Thank You Girl single, March 5 1963

5. She Loves You / I'll Get You

Single – Released August 20 1963

Engineer – *Norman Smith*

She Loves You and *I'll Get You* are the first Beatles recordings to be adorned and enhanced by Ringo's new Ludwig Super Classic kit – and what an impact it makes. This single is also notable for a change in the techniques involved in capturing the sound of Ringo's drums. Perhaps inspired by the sight of Ringo's new kit, or more likely, the incredibly vital sound it produced, Engineer Norman Smith changed the overhead microphone (to a Coles 4038), giving the kit a more precise sound than previously captured. Additionally, Smith moved the vocal microphones further away from the drums, thereby decreasing the amount of overspill between the different instruments.

Adding to these 'tweaks', he also fed the signals from the drums and bass guitar into separate compressors. Previously each had been channeled into a single compressor, the combined instruments becoming a single, unified signal which would then be output to tape. The signal *now* being laid down would therefore possess 'punch' and definition. These modifications created the effect of depth and power[68] to Ringo's new kit, adding a new dimension to the Beatles sound. This setup would form the basis of the Beatles' drum sound until further experimentation by Norman's successor, Geoff Emerick, in 1966.

Like many recordings of this period in the Beatles career, the final mix of *She Loves You* was subject to edits, however for various reasons they are far more noticeable than other releases. *She Loves You* appears to have been the subject of various equalisation (eq) alterations throughout the session, and when coupled with the greater frequency range of compact disc over 1960's vinyl, the edit points are quite clearly enhanced. The more noticeable edits appear at [1.15] and [1.22], Ringo's 'swishy' hi-hats 'dropping-out' at those points.

She Loves You

Time Signature – 4/4
Recorded – July 1 1963
Drums – *Ringo Starr*

With *She Loves You,* the Beatles (and no doubt George Martin) had clearly thought through the drum patterns, they possess a structure and power that demands attention, Starr executing his moves to perfection. Recorded at a session rudely interrupted by screaming fans rushing into Abbey Road, the excitement and energy created translated to the performance and positively leaps at the listener, grabbing attention and demanding to be heard. Has there been a greater attention-grabbing opening few bars than this? Kicking off with the simple but effective floor tom fill – illustrating purpose and intent -

Swiftly moving on to floor tom/snare/bass drum on the introduction (and subsequent choruses), we soon hear those famous 'swishy' hi-hats dominate[69], swaying comfortably above the pounding bass drum. If anything, the busy patterns *look* impressive when performed live – so much energy adding appeal to the Beatles' live performances.

I'll Get You

Time Signature – 4/4
Recorded – July 1 1963
Drums, Handclaps – *Ringo Starr*
Handclaps – *Paul McCartney, George Harrison, John Lennon*

With the bulk of their 5 hour session devoted to *She Loves You*, the B-Side was afforded little time. As befits a 'rush job', *I'll Get You* features a workmanlike performance by Ringo, he's driving the bus here, no more, no less. He does however attempt to liven things up with a bit of inventive bass drum playing now and then. Off-beat handclaps feature on the opening bars as the only overdub on the track. Due to the more sedate pace and volume, the drums appear more closely miked than *She Loves You*, and while hi-hats dominate, the snare and bass drum have a depth not usually heard on early Beatles recordings. Despite previously having recorded Ludwig drums, perhaps the engineers were familiarising themselves with Ringo's handling of his new kit, achieving the right balance with the rest of the group's instruments?

The Beatles' love of American R&B reached a peak on 'With the Beatles', with 5 of the 14 tracks covers of Stateside black music artists

6. With The Beatles

LP – Released November 22, 1963
Engineer – *Norman Smith*

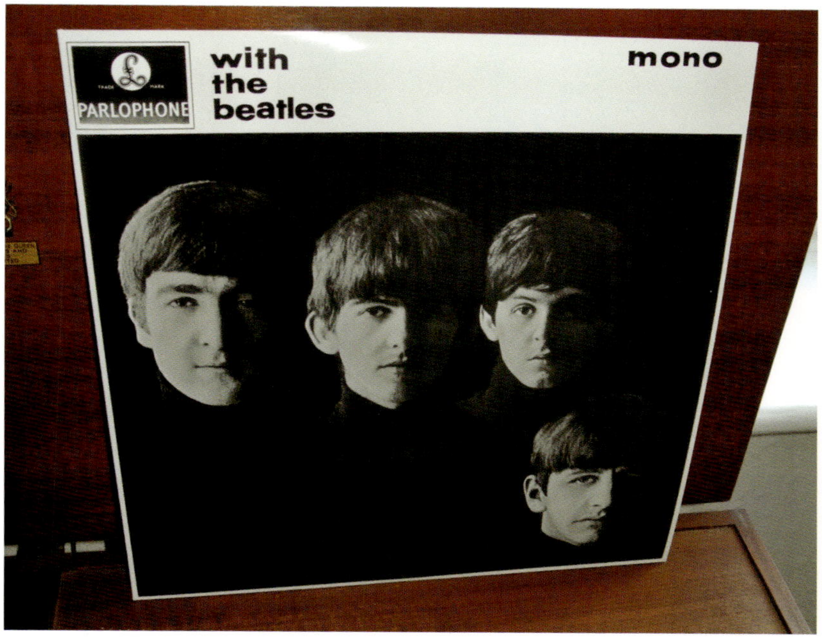

Side One
It Won't Be Long
All I've Got To Do
All My Loving
Don't Bother Me
Little Child
Till There Was You
Please Mister Postman

Side Two
Roll Over Beethoven
Hold Me Tight
You Really Got A Hold On Me
I Wanna Be Your Man
Devil In Her Heart
Not A Second Time
Money (That's What I Want)

Due to the Beatles touring commitments, and in stark contrast to their single-date sessions for the *Please Please Me* LP, recording of their follow-up album would involve multiple sessions. With advance orders in excess of 500,000, it would have been perhaps understandable had the group eased-off and enjoyed some of their new-found fame. Not in the slightest.

14 Songs

Drums	8
Handclaps	3
African Drum	1
Tambourine	1
Claves	1
Bongos	1
Hi-Hat	1
Maracas	1

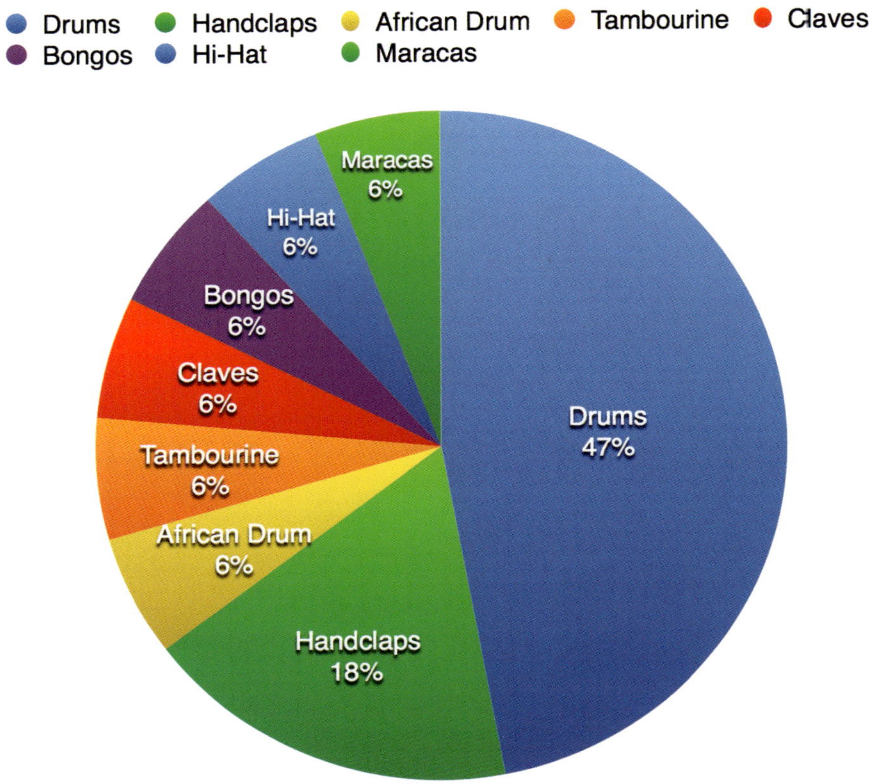

Like it's predecessor, *With The Beatles* has a strong Rhythm & Blues feel (*Please Mr. Postman*) coupled with some hard-rocking Beat music (*I Wanna Be Your Man, Little Child*) , and the contrasting lighter mainstream moments (*Til There Was You*). A veteran of the club circuit, Ringo easily deals with the varying musical styles. Save for the expansive *Don't Bother Me,* percussion overdubs were limited to the now-standard handclaps and the odd dashing of maracas and bongos.

Although featuring six non-original tracks, the album was notable for not containing any previously issued material – namely, single releases. Such was the group's proficiency, their next single release *(I Want To Hold Your Hand / This Boy)* was issued exactly a week later. Again, both titles do not feature on *With The Beatles*. Astonishing by today's standards.

It Won't Be Long

Time Signature – 4/4
Recorded – July 30 1963
Drums – Ringo Starr

A joyous Smokey Robinson & The Miracles inspired album opener, Ringo is clearly relishing playing his new set of Ludwig drums. Straightforward and forthright drumming dominates, in particular featuring a pattern much beloved of the era, Ringo and the Beatles no exception[70]. Rather than play a simple beat with the snare on the 2nd beat of the bar, it was popular in the day to also place a snare beat on the '2 and' beat, as shown here -

A simple but highly effective device, used to 'fill-out' the drums, especially effective when attempting to flood a venue with sound, this pattern appears regularly throughout the Beatles' early recording career. Open hi-hats on the middle 8 and chorus, closed on the verses, Ringo places the emphasis on the vocal, while sixteenth note dominated snare fills flesh out the song between choruses and verses. Unusually, Ringo declines the opportunity of a snare fill between the last verse and chorus, maintaining his disciplined drumming throughout.

All I've Got To Do

Time Signature – 4/4
Recorded – September 11 1963
Drums – Ringo Starr

An understated early Lennon ballad, featuring some wonderfully controlled and soulful drumming from Ringo. Recalling the staccato interplay of hi-hat/snare/bass of *Anna* from *Please Please Me, All I've Got To Do* is punctuated by a straight 4/4 beat on the chorus and middle 8.

Note how Ringo punctuates the bridge with four accented beats on his bass drum, literally 'pushing' the song along – playing with such force the bass drum is very close to distortion[71].

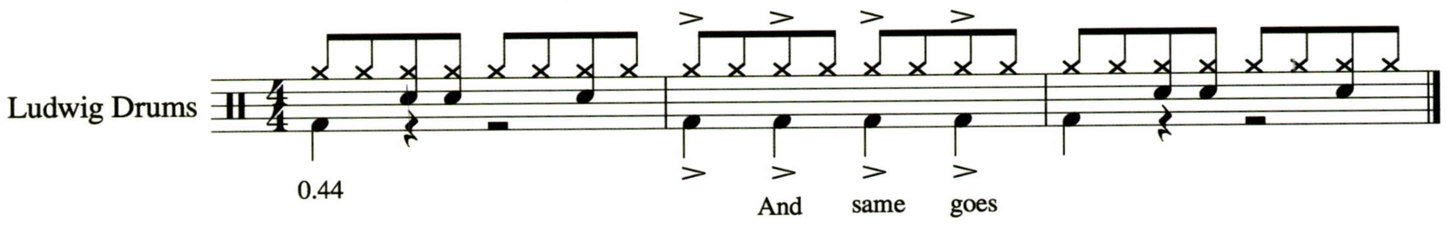

Evident on *All I've Got To Do* is our old friend, the squeaky bass drum pedal. It is possible (but unlikely) Ringo was still using his trusty Premier pedal,[72] as any drummer (including both Authors) who graduated to the Ludwig Speed King[73] from the basic and unforgiving Premier alternative would attest to. Ringo's Ludwig drum kit had by now been engaged for around five months of constant touring and recording, and if Ludwig Speed Kings are not given a shot of lubrication every now and again, they complain loudly, even after such a relatively short spell of time.

All My Loving

Time Signature – 4/4
Recorded – July 30 1963
Drums – Ringo Starr

For many in America, *All My Loving* recalls their first sight of the Beatles, with Ringo sat atop his Ludwig kit on the Ed Sullivan show on 9th February 1964. Like many Lennon/McCartney compositions of the period, *All My Loving* begins as if in mid-flow, the immediacy of the hook taking us by surprise, and once more Ringo proves he's ahead of the game, effortlessly swinging his way through the verses.

Resisting the temptation to allow the song to 'swing' too much, Ringo forces the song along, utilising that fine line between a 'jazzy' swing and a rock beat. Ringo often used this shuffle feel, with a heavy emphasis on his 'swishy' open hi-hats. On stage, if the tempo was counted in too fast, he had the option of utilising 4 in the bar hi-hats, playing this way wouldn't be too hard on the wrists and importantly, the tempo wouldn't drop.

The drums, in particular the snare, briskly move the song along, and are employed in a trade-off with John's rhythm guitar work, perhaps inspired by The Crystals' recent hit *Da Doo Ron Ron*?

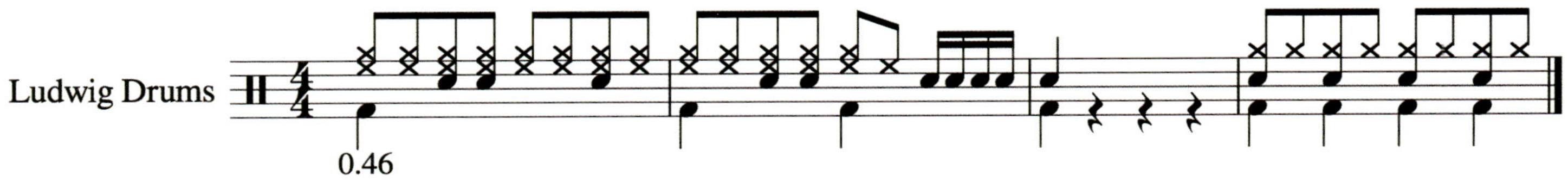

A plodding bass drum is surrounded by the snare on beats 2 & 4, doubling up on the chorus, Ringo plays four in the bar on bass and snare (bar 4), breaking away from the shuffle feel he uses elsewhere in the song, and providing a measure of urgency.

Post-Script

An alternative pressing[74] of *All My Loving* which features a five beat count in by Ringo on his hi-hat cymbals, giving us an indication of the working practices of the Beatles at that point in time. Counting-in just the first five beats, Ringo leaves the sixth beat silent – ensuring his hi-hat doesn't spill over the incoming vocal introduction. A technique surely suggested by George Martin or Norman Smith?

Don't Bother Me

Time Signature – 4/4
Recorded – September 12 1963
Drums, African Drum – Ringo Starr
Tambourine – John Lennon
Claves – Paul McCartney

This recording of George's first composition for the group was the Beatles' second attempt at the song, their perseverance rewarded by the unusually liberal use of percussion, necessitated by the sparse arrangement. The forthright nature of the drumming and dominant rhythmical patterns of the guitars lend the song a hollow, repetitive sound. The stop/start nature of the rhythm and the barren repetition of the song is however rescued by inventive percussive overdubbing, with John on tambourine, Ringo on an African drum (djembe), and Paul on wood block. This unusual arrangement drew comment on Tony Barrow's album sleeve-notes, and while his layman's description of the use of a "loose-skinned Arabian bongo" is somewhat wide of the mark, the observation of Ringo "pound(ing) out the on-beat percussive drive" is perceptive enough. The tambourine on the constant 2 & 4 beats of the bar, allows the wood block to be placed around them in a playfully erratic nature -

Ringo mimics the 'pushed' rhythm by accenting the bass drum on the play-out. Already, with only one album and a handful of singles behind them, the Beatles show they are prepared to use percussion[75] as a means of enlivening and enhancing their songs.

Recording 'Don't Bother Me', George lays down his vocal, while the other Beatles concentrate on percussion, John on the tambourine, Ringo on the African drum (djembe), and Paul on wood block.

Little Child

Time Signature – 4/4
Recorded – October 3 1963
Drums – Ringo Starr

A piece of raucous Liverpudlian 'chat-up', originally conceived as Ringo's vocal contribution to the album, *Little Child*[76] sees him providing a solid if unspectacular backbeat, punctuated by George Martin's piano. The rocking style of the backing behind the harmonica solo is straight from their stage act, the snare and accented bass drum trading thumping blows in perhaps Ringo's most raucous recorded drumming display yet, before returning to a rigid structure for the final verse and chorus -

Till There Was You

Time Signature – 4/4
Recorded – July 18 & 30 1963
Bongos, Hi-Hat – Ringo Starr

Bongos and a single hi-hat beat played with the foot provide the backing on this gentle ballad. The rather random bongos are played in a functional manner, providing a pseudo-Latin feel and are arguably too fussily prominent in the mix. A popular ballad and a mainstay of the Beatles' early stage performances, Ringo would tackle the bongo pattern on a combination of bass drum, small tom, and snare, with the snare-wires disengaged.

Please Mr. Postman

Time Signature – 4/4
Recorded – July 30 1963
Drums – *Ringo Starr*
Handclaps – *Ringo Starr, Paul McCartney, George Harrison, John Lennon*

If ever a song personifies the Beatles' then current fascination with American Rhythm and Blues, it is *Please Mister Postman,* taking The Marvelettes' 1961 hit, and making it their own. Opening with a bass and snare drum beat dominant on the 1st and 2nd beats of the bar, this is further interspersed with rhythm guitars chopping along with the snare on the 3rd & 4th beats of the bar.

Ringo's drumming is so soulful here – listen how at [0.23], rather than using a drum fill to bring in the first verse, he opts for an accented single stroke bass drum beat, swiftly pursued by three snare strokes. Following on from a delightfully sloppy snare fill [0.38], Ringo plays a controlled fill at [1.09], thus setting up the second portion of the song. This simple yet effective handiwork perfectly complements the relatively busy contributions of the other Beatles both instrumentally and vocally – one of Ringo's great strengths. Off-beat handclaps round off the track – an especially powerful device when used in isolation with the drums and vocals at [1.54] & [2.09].

Roll Over Beethoven

Time Signature – 4/4
Recorded – July 30 1963
Drums, Handclaps – *Ringo Starr*
Handclaps – *Paul McCartney, George Harrison, John Lennon*

Unusually, Ringo employs a more straightforward 4/4 beat for the verses, rather than the pattern he employed throughout live versions of this song (see *It Won't Be Long*). The handclaps supply the urgency on this studio recording, dominant and providing a constant beat. Open hi-hats dominate the verses, replaced on the middle 8 bars by some nifty work on the snare, easing us towards the guitar solo. Notice how the handclaps provide power and purpose, mimicking the bar chords of John's rhythm guitar.

Hold Me Tight

Time Signature – 4/4
Recorded – September 12 1963
Drums, Handclaps – *Ringo Starr*
Handclaps – *Paul McCartney, George Harrison, John Lennon*

Cunningly sequenced by George Martin, we hear the continuation of the handclap/rhythm guitar combination from *Roll Over Beethoven*. First attempted during the sessions for the *Please Please Me* LP, *Hold Me Tight* was remade from take 20 – the final version here being an edit of takes 26 and 29. Take 21 was released on *The Beatles Bootleg recordings 1963*, however take 20 (the first of the remakes) sees Paul instructing Ringo to try out a four-beat rhythm on his floor-tom, before feeling it sounded too much like *Running Bear*, Johnny Preston's 1959 hit song. Some interesting track sequencing here, with simple 4 in the bar handclaps again providing urgency throughout the song, placed on the off-beat at the end of each bar in the middle 8. This section is also noticeable for some superb floor tom work from Ringo, using the power of his new drums. Notice how the handclaps sit with both the bass drum and open hi-hats?

Ironically, this is pretty much the beat that *Running Bear* is based upon – a simple enough pattern, but a degree of dexterity is needed to retain fluidity. Ringo finds his way back to the hi-hats on the verse/chorus with thunderous tom fills at [1.10]

and [1.51]. The bass drum, unusually lightly recorded compared to other tracks on the album, is accented around the 'hold' & 'tight' of the vocal. A much maligned 'album filler', mainly due to the occasionally flat vocal from McCartney, it's fair to say the song is saved by the Little Richard *Lucille*-style chugging rhythm guitars, drums and handclaps, culminating in the 'train arriving at the station'-like ending.

You Really Got A Hold On Me

Time Signature – 4/4
Recorded – July 18 1963
Drums – *Ringo Starr*

Ringo nails the groove of this Tamla label classic, tight drumming and a heartfelt snare backbeat providing the basis for an adventurous cover of the Smokey Robinson original. Again, his Ludwig kit really shines on this track, providing much of the 'feel' here. The drums benefit from the still evident distant microphone techniques as they thunder around the studio, especially at [1.47], where we hear an ear splitting snare fill. There's a fine-line between clumsy timing and 'feel', with the Beatles seemingly having difficulty recording the final section at [2.52]. Proving especially troublesome to perfect, a further take of this section was spliced to an earlier recording. Indeed at [2.35] there is a hint of a mis-placed beat, or quite possibly poor tape edit?

I Wanna Be Your Man

Time Signature – 4/4
Recorded – September 12 1963
Drums – *Ringo Starr*

Ringo's vocal contribution on *With The Beatles* (and many a live show-stopper) is still being performed by him today, such is the song's popularity and longevity. He's always looked comfortable and proud performing it, and rightly so, the song also providing the Rolling Stones with one of their major early hits. At the group's first concert in America at the Washington Coliseum, Ringo performed the song like a man possessed, thumping hell out of the diminutive, un-miked Ludwig Downbeat kit – it's his moment and he's grabbing it with both hands. Hi-hats swishing, bass drum thudding, this is Beat music at it's best – a simple repetitive, pounding, energetic beat, driven along by Ringo at a furious pace. Witness the bridges at [0.29] to the second verse, at [0.59] to the solo, and at [1.43] to the fade-out. Random handclaps appear on the vocal track before the solo from [0.45] and from [1.19]. In contrast to the recording of *Boys (*from *Please Please Me*), Ringo's vocal was placed on a separate track (with a later overdubbed 2nd vocal), his drums separated and placed with the other instruments. Despite Lennon's later indifference to this track, it remained a staple of their live set, being performed well into their last concerts in 1966.

Ringo performs 'I Wanna Be Your Man' at the Washington Coliseum, February 11th 1964

Devil In Her Heart

Time Signature – 4/4
Recorded – July 18 1963
Drums, Maracas – *Ringo Starr*

Always on the look-out for quality songs to perform and make their own[77], here the Beatles smooth their way through this otherwise obscure B-Side by US girl-group the Donays. Drums to the fore from the off, with a simple snare to bass drum fill which is unimaginatively repeated throughout (bars 1 and 5) and also at the hackneyed ending. Although open hi-hats dominate, the song was deemed to require the overdubbing of maracas (albeit nervous and hesitant) from the second bar onwards. A basic off-beat snare pattern bestrides the track.

Not A Second Time

Time Signature – 4/4
Recorded – September 11 1963
Drums – *Ringo Starr*

Ringo's drumming is often overlooked on this belter of a Lennon song, and is quite possibly his most inventive work on *With The Beatles*. After a Ringo-less introduction, a strong and closely-miked bass drum and off-beat snare dominate, the drums sounding particularly distorted throughout. Ringo's powerful use of accented snare around the bass drum is particularly inspiring – clearly he doesn't have to structure the drum patterns in this manner, yet the song benefits greatly from this device. *Not A Second Time* is most noticeable for Ringo's quite brilliant use of matched-stroke drum fills – at [0.43], [1.03], & [1.50]). Matched-strokes fills are just that – striking a drum, or drums, simultaneously with both hands, giving the beat a 'fatter' more powerful sound than would be possible individually. Here they are – the 2 bars before and after the piano solo, and at the introduction to the play-out -

Ringo performs these fills with panache – it would have been easier and more conventional to strike the snare first and then the tom, but here he shows real flair, executing the fills with purpose and power – quite brilliantly lifting the song above its station. Snare punctuations weave around the vocal, the fade-out featuring a truly inventive moment – the snare/hi-hat interplay around Lennon's impassioned pleas of "no, no, no, no, no…" [1.58].

Money

Time Signature – 4/4
Recorded – July 18 & 30 1963
Drums – *Ringo Starr*

A crowd-pleasing song from their live set[78], Ringo plays (almost) exclusively on his floor tom, snare and bass, pounding out a compulsive and unforgiving no-nonsense rhythm, the piano solo embellished with handclaps. Early verses have some lovely hi-hat timekeeping as he concentrates the beat on his floor tom. Only at 1.59 does he move his right hand from floor-tom to ride cymbal, closing the track by repeating the four beats to the bar of the floor-tom on his bass drum, urgently bringing the song and the album to an uncompromising and breathtaking conclusion.

Cleverly upping the urgency towards the finale, Ringo employs 8 in-the-bar bass drum beats -

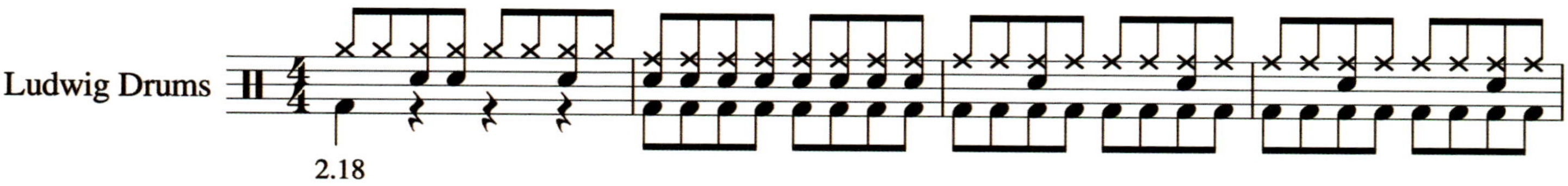

A stripped down version (minus George Martin's overdubbed piano) was released on *The Beatles Bootleg Recordings 1963*, revealing the power and subtlety of Ringo's playing, his floor tom work particularly enhanced.

Gentle-giant Roadie Mal Evans makes Ringo's Ludwig Downbeat drums appear Lilliputian

7. I Want To Hold Your Hand / This Boy

Single – Released November 29 1963

Engineer – *Norman Smith*

I Want To Hold Your Hand

Time Signature – 4/4

Recorded – October 17 1963

Drums, Handclaps – *Ringo Starr*

Handclaps – *Paul McCartney, George Harrison, John Lennon*

I Want To Hold Your Hand – the song that seduced America, and again we have well defined rhythmical patterns, simply oozing diversity and panache. The stark nature of the opening bars demands attention, open hi-hats dominating. Having seen fit to embellish *I'll Get You* and most of *With The Beatles* with off-beat handclaps, they again feature heavily. Prominently mixed, the handclaps form an integral part of the song's success – providing a hook in which to reel-in the listening public.

The bridge [0.50] features tightly closed hi-hats, heightening their impact when open again at [1.02], raucously leading into the chorus. Era-defining matched-stroke fills again feature on snare/tom/floor tom [0.20], saving the best for last at [2.06]. Having earlier played them straight, they take us by surprise, occurring ever so slightly behind the beat – splendid stuff!

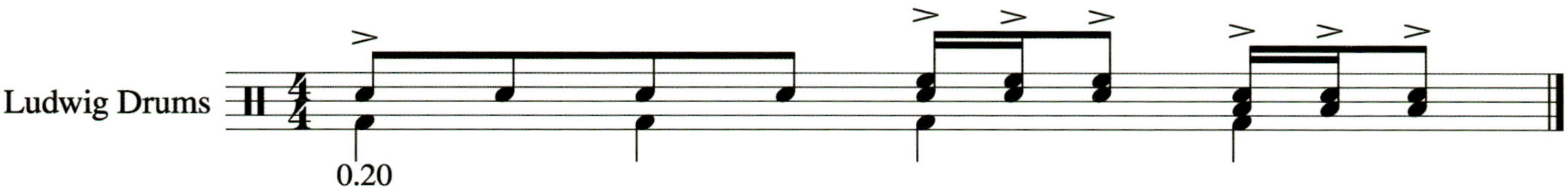

This Boy

Time Signature – 12/8

Recorded – October 17 1963

Drums – *Ringo Starr*

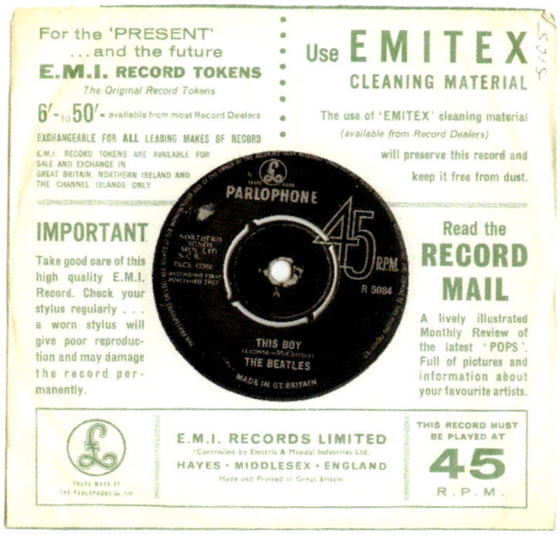

This Boy is unusual in that it features Ringo on brushes – he briskly busks on his hi-hats, filling out the introduction and verses with variations on this theme -

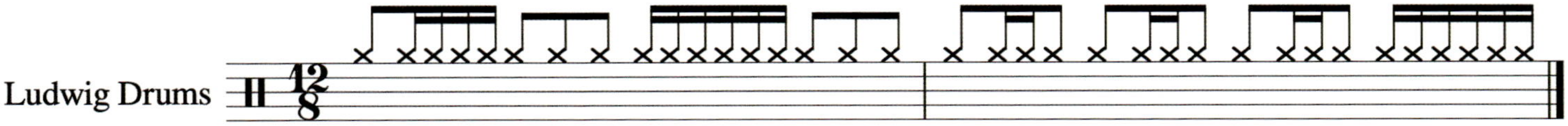

On the lead-in to the middle 8, Ringo accents the hi-hats before moving into normal bass/snare/hi-hat territory, a solid structure underscoring Lennon's impassioned vocal. Accented hi-hats again lead-up to the fade [1.52]. A very novel, innovative approach.

8. Can't Buy Me Love / You Can't Do That

Single – Released March 16 1964

Engineer – *Norman Smith*

Can't Buy Me Love

Time Signature – 4/4

Recorded – January 29 1964

Drums – *Ringo Starr*

Hi-Hat Overdub – *Norman Smith*

Opening toms make way for some sloppy yet powerful back-beat drumming, perfectly complementing the laid-back feel of the song. Ringo tends to play harder on the choruses and guitar solo, placing emphasis on these passages, providing a harder edge where necessary, again with snare drum and hi-hats dominating. An interesting footnote to *Can't Buy Me Love* is the fact it was recorded in Paris during the Beatles' first French visit. When the tape arrived at Abbey Road for mixing, it was discovered that due to an error in the French studio, the tape had been creased, and as a result Ringo's hi-hats had lost a great deal of their definition and presence. According to Geoff Emerick, due to Ringo's lack of availability (he was away filming *A Hard Day's Night*), Norman Smith overdubbed hi-hats on to the track. A session fee was paid to 'a drummer' that day, which backs up this version of events, although singer Helen Shapiro (who was at Abbey road recording that day) remembers Ringo overdubbing the hi-hats, a practice she recalls being commonplace. If Smith did indeed play, as seems likely, he did an excellent job of emulating Ringo's distinctive hi-hat style.

Incidentally, a similar calamity befell *Jet* from Paul McCartney's 1973 album *Band On The Run*, with Engineer Geoff Emerick managing to rescue the recording by adding top-end equalisation to the mix.

You Can't Do That

Time Signature – 4/4
Recorded – February 25 1964
Drums, Bongos – *Ringo Starr*
Cowbell – *Paul McCartney*

A song largely influenced by Lennon's love of American Rhythm and Blues artist Wilson Pickett[79], and although possessing a busy and full track mainly due to Ringo's half-open hi-hats, *You Can't Do That* features liberal use of overdubbed cowbell (Paul) and bongos (Ringo).

The punctuation between snare and bass drum (2nd bar above) at the end of the chorus is particularly inspired, cleverly emphasising the vocal *'told you before'* by stressing the '4 and' beats of the bar. Equally inventive are the last few bars of the song, the drums and percussion dropping out just when you expect them to close the song.

Note – being buried in the mix and difficult to hear, the bongos illustrated above are an approximation of Ringo's varied, busking style throughout the song.

The Beatles recorded 'Can't Buy Me Love' during their concert season at the Olympia Theatre, Paris, January 1964

9. Long Tall Sally

EP – Released June 19 1963

Engineer – *Norman Smith*

Side One	Side Two
Long Tall Sally	Slow Down
I Call Your Name	Matchbox

With the LP release of music from the new Beatles movie not scheduled for another month, and the March release of *Can't Buy Me Love* a distant memory in the 'here today, gone tomorrow' world of 1960's pop, there had to be a new Beatles release – and quick. Extended Play records were a popular format (especially in still austere Britain) – enabling the cash-strapped record buying public access to songs not usually found as singles or popular album tracks. The Beatles were no exception, with their fifth UK EP release *Long Tall Sally* being the first to feature songs unreleased in the home market (two having been released as album tracks Stateside). Here, three of their personal stage favourites were presented along with a Lennon composition *I Call Your Name*, originally recorded by NEMS stablemate Billy J. Kramer.

Long Tall Sally

Time Signature – 4/4

Recorded – March 1 1964

Drums – *Ringo Starr*

A simply astonishing track, even more so as the Beatles' version of Little Richard's *Long Tall Sally* was recorded in one take – thereby equalling their feat on *Twist And Shout*. They didn't even bother with a second attempt, they knew they'd got it in one. It's a blistering performance from all concerned – Paul's vocal, John and George's twin guitar solos, even George Martin on piano puts in a great turn. As for Ringo, he never lets up from his forthright and solid beat, his punctuation on snare and bass drum tight and precise. Ringo treads that narrow path between a shuffle and straight '8's' as he saves his best for last – terrific triplet movements[80] between snare, tom and cymbal. The sample presented here is a sample from [1.40] onwards -

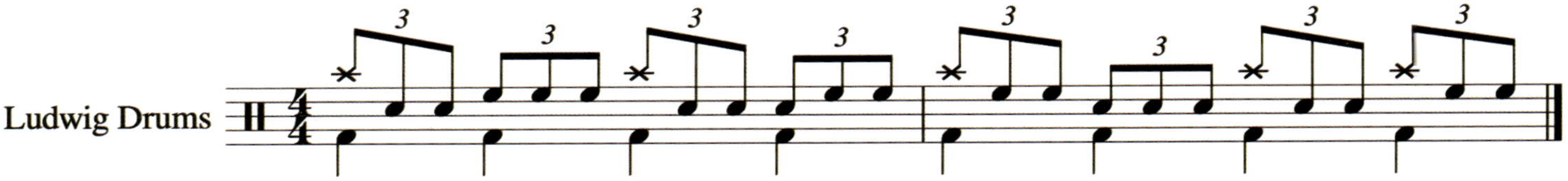

I Call Your Name

Time Signature – 4/4
Recorded – March 1 1964
Drums, Cowbell – *Ringo Starr*

A workmanlike 4/4 beat from Ringo, enlivened by seamlessly moving in and out of a great shuffle beat on the (for the day) experimental swinging 'ska' section at [1.08]. The emphasis on the tightly tuned snare, with the cowbell cleverly dropping out of the mix, notice how the perceived tempo change is achieved by the switch from eighth to accented quarter note (opening) hi-hats. Four-in-the-bar snare beats (bar 3) ease the transition.

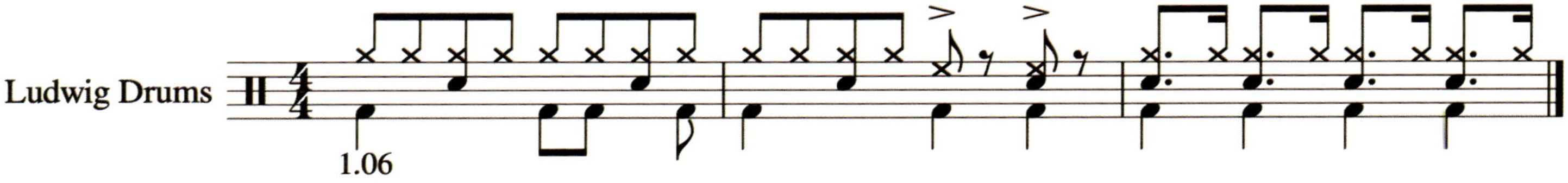

The return to a straight 4/4 almost a mirror image of the move into the ska section – an unexpected but welcome variation from the norm.

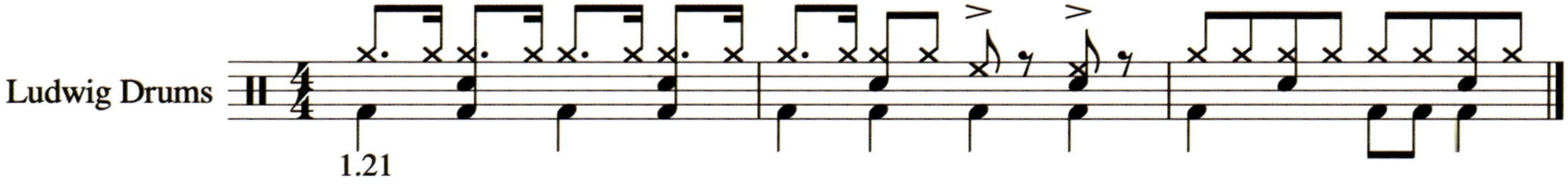

Slow Down

Time Signature – 4/4
Recorded – June 1 1964
Drums – *Ringo Starr*

As with all the tracks on the EP, a great open drum sound sees Ringo with his head down, ploughing-through on swishy hi-hats.

Machine-gun snare and tom fills at relevant points between verse and chorus, the best utilising quadruplets on snare, then tom at [2.26] -

and playing 'against the beat' with triplets at [2.43] -

Matchbox

Time Signature – 4/4
Recorded – June 1 1964
Drums – *Ringo Starr*

With the song's composer and performer Carl Perkins present at the session, Ringo must surely have been apprehensive about his performance here. If he was it doesn't show as he leads us through a Rockabilly shuffle with perfection. Playing constantly on bass drum, snare and ride cymbal without interruption (save for the ending), perhaps to create a smoother transition from the guitar introduction, the Beatles saw fit to overdub 4-in the bar handclaps.

10. A Hard Day's Night

LP – Released July 10, 1964

Engineer – *Norman Smith*

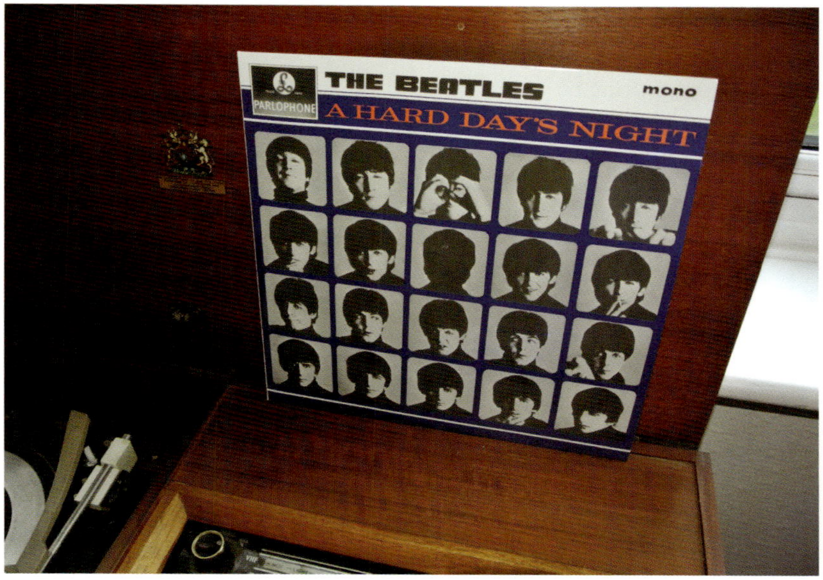

Side One

A Hard Day's Night
I Should Have Known Better
If I Fell
I'm Happy Just To Dance With You
And I Love Her
Tell Me Why
Can't Buy Me Love

Side Two

Any Time At All
I'll Cry Instead
Things We Said Today
When I Get Home
You Can't Do That
I'll Be Back

13 Songs

Drums	6
Cowbell	2
Bongos	3
Tambourine	2
Claves	1
Hi-Hat	1
Drum	1

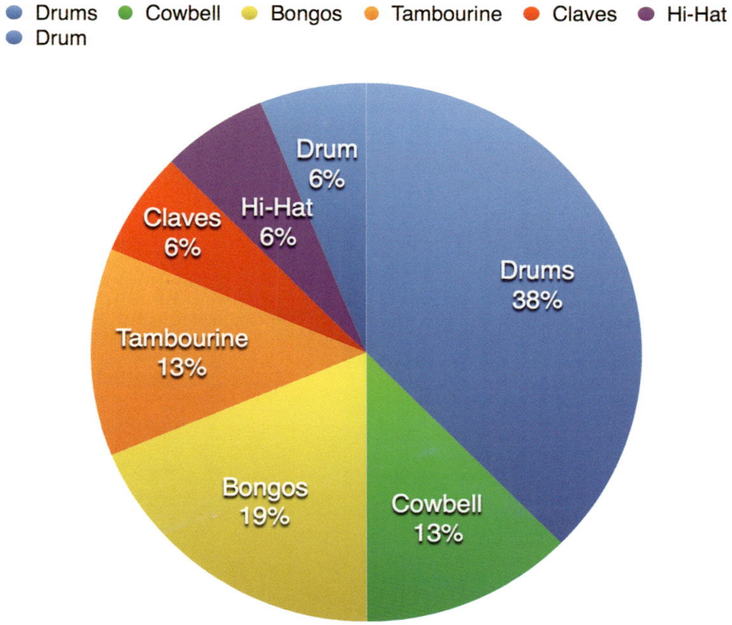

A Hard Day's Night sees Ringo in the full-flow of Beatlemania, assured of his place in the Group, sure of the Abbey Road surroundings, and with any lingering doubt by George Martin as to his abilities behind him. He plays with confidence, and finds himself branching out into other areas of percussion not heard previously on the group's recordings.

A Hard Day's Night

Time Signature – 4/4
Recorded – April 16 1964
Drums, Cowbell – *Ringo Starr*
Bongos – *Norman Smith*

Ringo employs a solid 4/4 beat throughout, supplemented by somewhat erratic bongos, which, alongside a cowbell on the middle 8, makes the rhythm track a little cluttered. It's worth noting Geoff Emerick's observation [81]'Ringo seemed especially 'on' that morning, attacking his drums with a ferocity I hadn't seen or heard before'. Maybe he'd taken to bed early with a cup of cocoa the night before? Ringo apparently had trouble mastering the overdubbed bongos, the task was given to Norman Smith who performs admirably. As can occasionally happen, perhaps he'd played just that bit *too hard*, and was a little de-sensitised to the different demands of bongo playing? Or perhaps he was just too 'on'? Emerick also recalls how (with John & Paul's backing vocals) Ringo played bongos and cowbell, 'together at the same time, on a single track'. Obviously to play cowbell and bongos at the same time would be some feat!

I Should Have Known Better

Time Signature – 4/4
Recorded – February 25 & 26 1964
Drums – *Ringo Starr*
Cowbell? – *Ringo Starr?*

In the movie, *I Should Have Known Better* is 'performed' in a train carriage, an apt setting as once again, a no-nonsense 4/4 beat is employed, moving the song along without a break. More prominent on the mono mix, an acoustic rhythm guitar is pronounced on the first and second beats of the bar of the first five bars, providing another constant, helping to move the song along, and more prominent on the mono mix, a cowbell is detectable on the first two beats of the introduction, probably played by Ringo.

If I Fell

Time Signature – 4/4
Recorded – February 27 1964
Drums – *Ringo Starr*

In the *A Hard Day's Night* movie, we are fortunate that Director Dick Lester heavily featured Ringo by focusing the group's TV studio rehearsal of *If I Fell* around him, for once allowing the camera to linger on the drummer and his kit for longer than usually afforded. Picking up the beat after an accented snare/hi-hat introduction, we have another simple 4/4 beat, once again letting the song breathe. Snare drum cross-stick work dominates from the hurried and punctuated drum intro, repeated only on the return from the middle 8's.

I'm Happy Just To Dance With You

Time Signature – 4/4
Recorded – March 1 1964
Drums, Tom Tom – *Ringo Starr*

After the straight 4/4 monotony of the first three tracks of *the LP,* Ringo is allowed the luxury of accenting the song played both live on bass drum (the choruses and first and last bars of the song), and an overdubbed tom-tom on the 1st and & 4th eighth notes of the bar on the verses. The resulting effect is a terrifically tight performance.

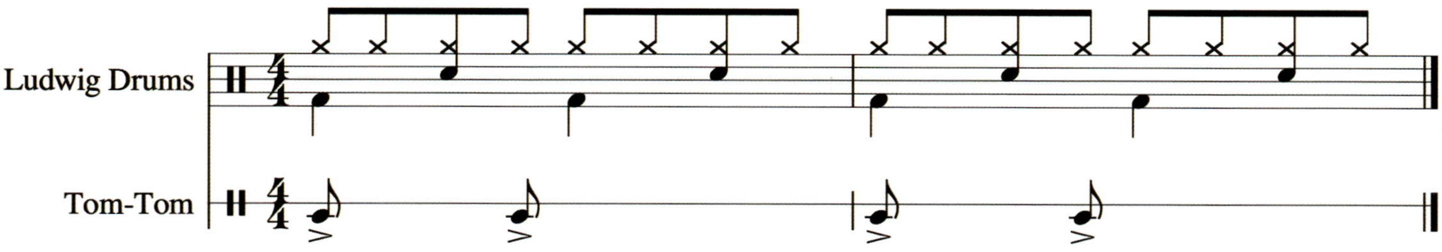

There is some confusion as to the type of drum played here, some claiming it is "a loose Arabian drum", although this line of thought appears to have been lifted from Tony Barrow's sleeve-notes on the rear of *With The Beatles*, where he writes of the use of such a drum on *Don't Bother Me*. To our ears it simply appears to be a loosely tuned (slackened-off) tom-tom, perhaps played with the butt-end of a drumstick to give a deeper sound, perhaps Ringo's 13" drum from his Ludwig kit?

And I Love Her

Time Signature – 4/4
Recorded – February 25, 26 & 27 1964
Bongos, Claves, Hi-Hat – *Ringo Starr*

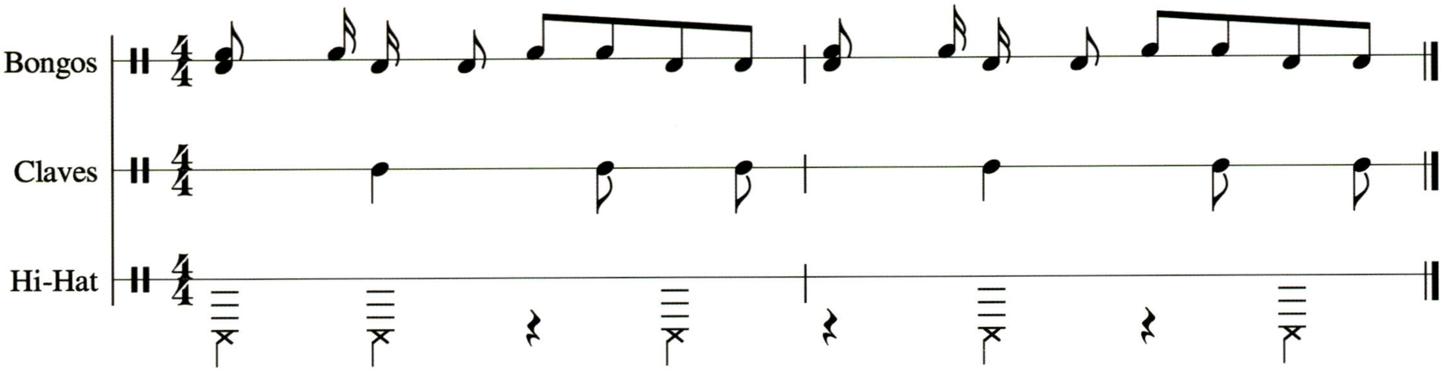

After twice unsuccessfully attempting this beautiful McCartney ballad on his Ludwig kit, Ringo kept things simple, with liberal use of bongos throughout and subtle timekeeping with his hi-hat pedal. Claves are also simultaneously employed, recorded well and played with great effect. The result is a tender treatment, allowing McCartney's smooth vocal and Harrison's languid guitar hook to showcase the melodic nature of the song.

Recorded two days earlier, Take 2 (below) sees simple tom-tom and hi-hat work, before launching into a standard 4/4 hi-hat/snare/bass beat, wisely ditched in favour of the lighter touch of bongos, claves and hi-hat.

Tell Me Why

Time Signature – 4/4
Recorded – 27 February 1964
Drums – *Ringo Starr*

From the very start, Ringo's tumbling drum fill (from snare / to tom / to crash cymbal) sets the upbeat tone of this rocker, belying the nature of the laid back 4/4 drumming.

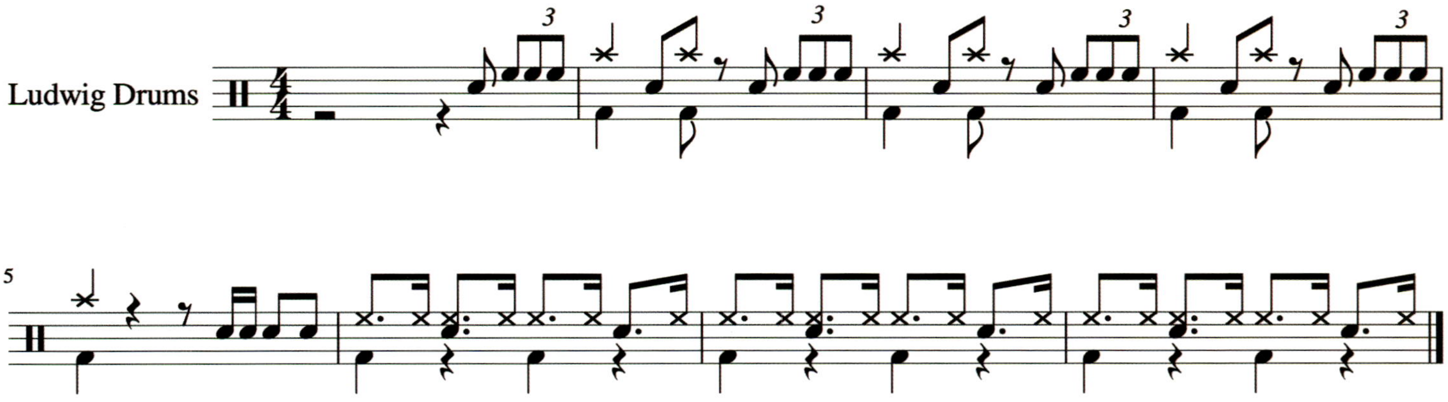

The song is most noticeable for the faultless triplets across snare and toms at [1.41]. Other drummers may have been tempted to execute a simple snare to tom fill – not so Ringo. The sheer power he draws out of his snare and floor tom is breathtaking.

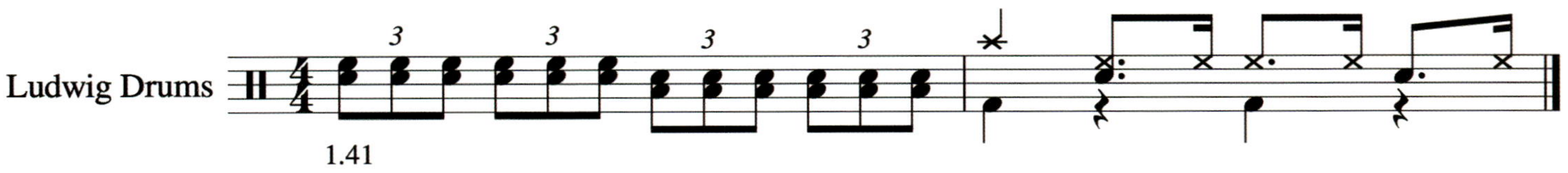

Can't Buy Me Love

Time Signature – 4/4
Recorded – January 29 1964
Drums – *Ringo Starr*
Hi-Hat Overdub – *Norman Smith*

Released as a single some 4 months prior to the *A Hard Day's Night* album, and featuring heavily in the film, this laid-back rocker features some equally slack drumming from Ringo.

Any Time At All

Time Signature – 4/4
Recorded – June 2 1964
Drums – *Ringo Starr*

A single, startling snare stroke heralds the opening of Side 2 of the LP, followed by hurried snare beats in the second bar.

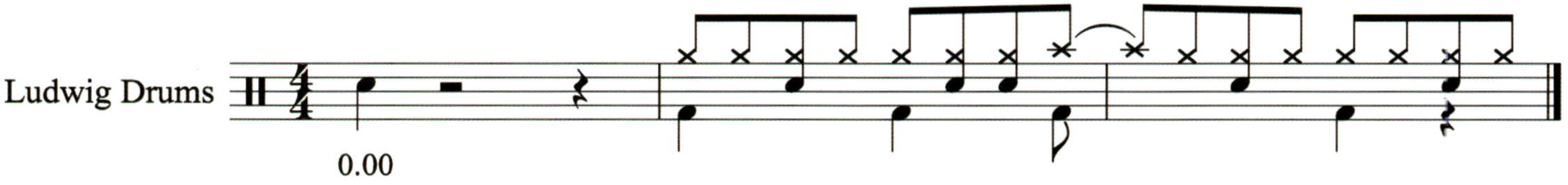

The device is repeated as this combination again punctuates the chorus.

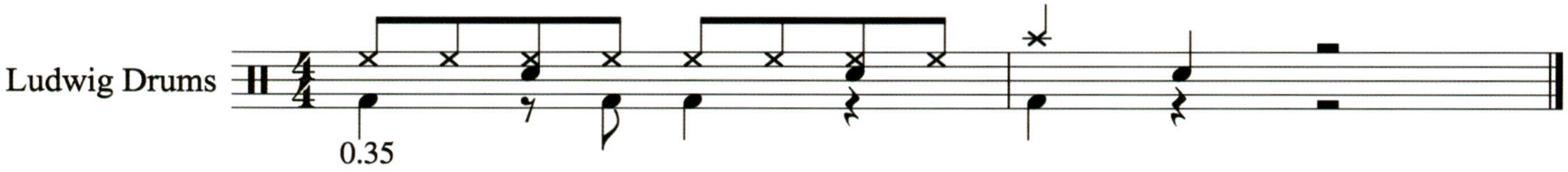

Providing a solid ‘boom, boom-boom’ on his bass drum, again playing slightly harder (but not faster) during the solo, allowing Harrison’s 12 string Rickenbacker and George Martin’s piano to dominate. Like the approach to the chorus, the song’s ending reverses it’s opening, being cut short rhythmically by the crack of the snare drum. The guitar takes the part of a cymbal to close the song, pointing the way to their new musical directions.

I’ll Cry Instead

Time Signature – 4/4
Recorded – June 1 1964
Drums – *Ringo Starr*
Tambourine – *John Lennon*

Unusually, this Country & Western inspired track was recorded in two sections (later to be spliced together), and it’s probably for this reason tambourines dominate the mix, smoothing out the edits and distracting the listener by providing a constant beat. Playing on the second beat of every other bar, the drums take a back seat, relegated low down in the mix.

Things We Said Today

Time Signature – 4/4
Recorded – June 2 1964
Drums, Tambourine – *Ringo Starr*

This McCartney romantic ballad sees Ringo employing one of the oldest tricks in the book – closed hi-hats on verses, 'rockin'-out' open hi-hats on the middle 8/chorus. This time the middle 8 and play-out is further enhanced by tambourine (the play-out on the second beat of the bar). Most of the percussive element of the remainder of the song is provided by the rhythm guitars, chiefly on the intro and play-out. The recording of *Things We Said Today* marks the use of dampening Ringo's snare with a cloth or tea-towel for possibly the first time, the result a pleasing 'thwack' which compliments the acoustic feel of the recording.

When I Get Home

Time Signature – 4/4
Recorded – June 2 1964
Drums – *Ringo Starr*

Quintessential Ringo – open 'swishy' hi-hats and cymbals to the fore – snare bolstered by floor-tom, you can almost feel his drums and cymbals crashing off the studio walls, leaking onto the other instrument mikes.

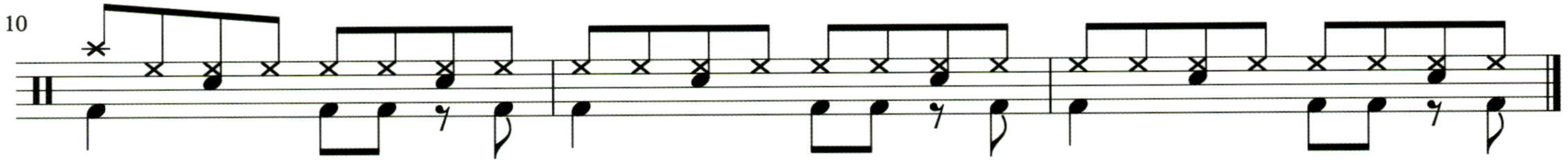

Snare and guitars trade-off on the bridge between chorus and verse (bar 9), as is the norm with the structure of many Beatles songs of this period. Again, Lennon's rhythm guitar provides much of the percussive feel.

You Can't Do That

Time Signature – 4/4
Recorded – February 25 1964
Drums, Bongos – *Ringo Starr*
Cowbell – *Paul McCartney*

Previously released as the B – Side of *Can't Buy Me Love.*

I'll Be Back

Time Signature – 4/4
Recorded – June 1 1964
Drums – *Ringo Starr*

The album closer, *I'll Be Back* is especially noticeable for it's unusual opening, perhaps a nod to the song's earlier conception being rooted in 6/8 time? Lennon found it impossible to sing and play in that time signature, and it was soon abandoned in favour of a more conventional 4/4. As with so much of the songs on *A Hard Day's Night*, Ringo provides a solid back-beat, a counter-point to the percussive flamenco style guitars. Subtle accented bass drum punctuates the song throughout.

A Hard Day's Night / Things We Said Today

Single – (Released July 10 1964)
Engineer – *Norman Smith*

Issued as a chart-topping single on the same day as the A Hard Day's Night LP, on which both tracks feature.

11. I Feel Fine / She's A Woman

Single – Released November 23 1964
Engineer – *Norman Smith*

I Feel Fine

Time Signature – 4/4
Recorded – October 18 1964
Drums – *Ringo Starr*

> *"The drumming is basically what we used to think of as What'd I'd Say* (by Ray Charles) *drumming. There was a style of drumming on What'd I Say which is a sort of Latin R&B that Ray Charles's drummer Milt Turner played on the original record and we used to love it. One of the big clinching factors about Ringo as the drummer in the band was that he could really play that so well."*
> **Paul McCartney**[82]

As we move to the end of 1964, we see more studio experimentation from the group. *I Feel Fine* possesses the (in)famous opening bars of guitar feedback – yet it's the prominence of the drum pattern that's arguably the striking feature here.

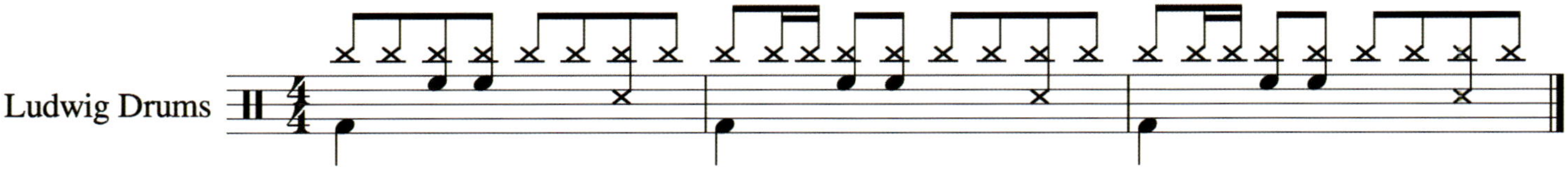

By late 1964, the Beatles were afforded more time to develop their songs in the studio – from basic strumming/working-out to final product. The drum parts were no different – they would evolve. Utilising his snare more freely than usual, takes 1-6 see Ringo developing his drum part, feeling his way, getting to learn what is best to play for the song. Take 6 is not vastly different than take 1, but it is played with more purpose and confidence. Crucially though, it wasn't 'right' for the song. That's why the drum pattern changed (probably from Paul's suggestion) to what we know and love today, with the movement from tom to cross-stick snare and interplay between drums and ride cymbal bell. This was not a massive shift from the earlier takes, as Ringo is essentially playing the same pattern, but with greater fluidity than the 'stuttering' pattern of simply staying on the snare, allowing time to trade-off (and be more inventive with) the bell of the ride cymbal.

Perhaps to extend the song further, the guitar solo is extended with a 4 bar guitar break, Ringo re-introducing the song with an offbeat feel between snare and a combination of bass drum and floor tom -

As for live performances, probably due to having to play harder to make the drums heard, Ringo made subtle changes to his drum part, simplifying the pattern and occasionally substituting the cross-stick snare for a full-bodied stroke.

She's A Woman

Time Signature – 4/4
Recorded – October 8 1964
Drums, Chocalho – *Ringo Starr*

She's A Woman is distinctive in that although it possesses an incredibly sparse arrangement, this remains hidden by a strong drum and percussion track. With a chocalho (a type of 'shaker' hailing from Portugal) to the fore, providing a harsher sound than maracas, the hi-hats are somewhat buried in the mix. With Lennon's chopping rhythm guitar placed on top of the snare, no backing vocals, no Harrison present until his overdubbed guitar, and only the addition of piano to come, the emphasis falls on Ringo to provide purpose and drive – he has to bring the components together by providing unity. This is achieved with busy 8th note hi-hats in the verses, open '8's' hi-hats on choruses, and a no-nonsense yet lively bass drum pattern.

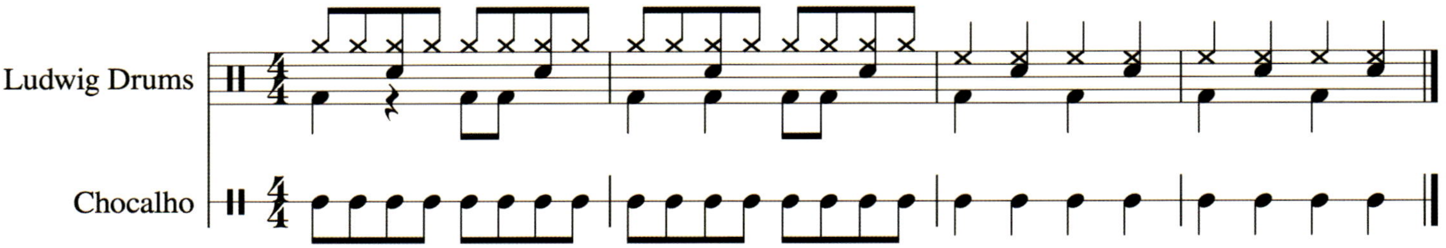

1.12

McCartney's rolling bass provides much of the rhythmic variety here, along with the '8-in the bar' chocalho, although Ringo does his best by using the bass drum to mimic the phonetics of the vocal throughout.

It is also worth noting that the "choppy" guitar slashes at the start of the track are placed on the 2nd and 4th beats in the bar, not as usual on the 1st and 3rd beats. If the drummer doesn't hear the guitarist's count-in (if he bothers to do one!), the drums would most probably enter at the wrong time, creating much mirth and merriment amongst band members, a red-faced drummer, and confusion amongst the audience! Interesting then, that when performed live, Ringo joined the introductory bars of guitar with the following -

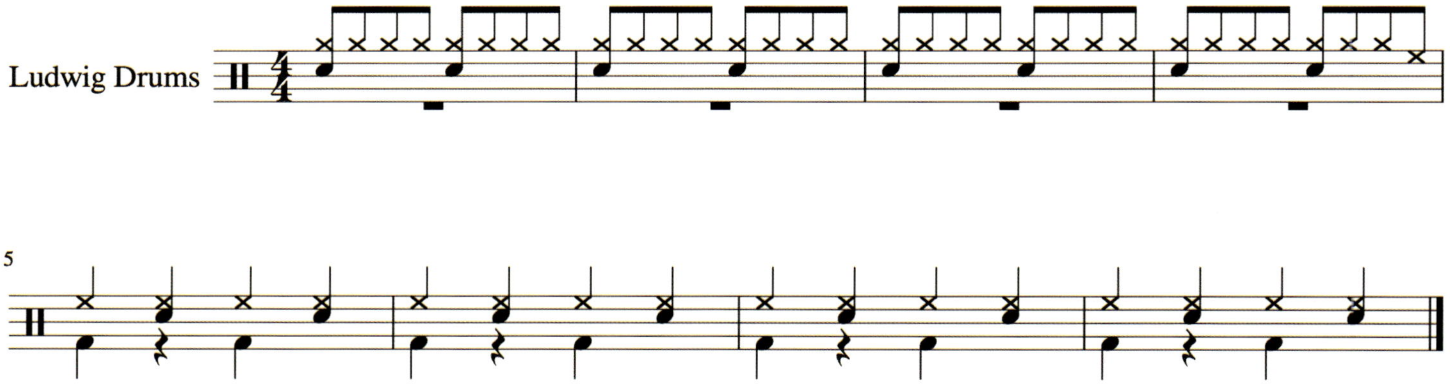

12. Beatles For Sale

LP – Released December 4 1964

Engineer – *Norman Smith*

Side One

No Reply
I'm A Loser
Baby's In Black
Rock And Roll Music
I'll Follow The Sun
Mr. Moonlight
Kansas City/Hey, Hey, Hey, Hey

Side Two

Eight Days A Week
Words Of Love
Honey Don't
Every Little Thing
I Don't Want To Spoil The Party
What You're Doing
Everybody's Trying To Be My Baby

14 Songs

Tambourine	5
Handclaps	4
Drums	2
Packing Case	2
Bass Drum	1
Drum	1
Timpani	1
Thigh Slaps	1

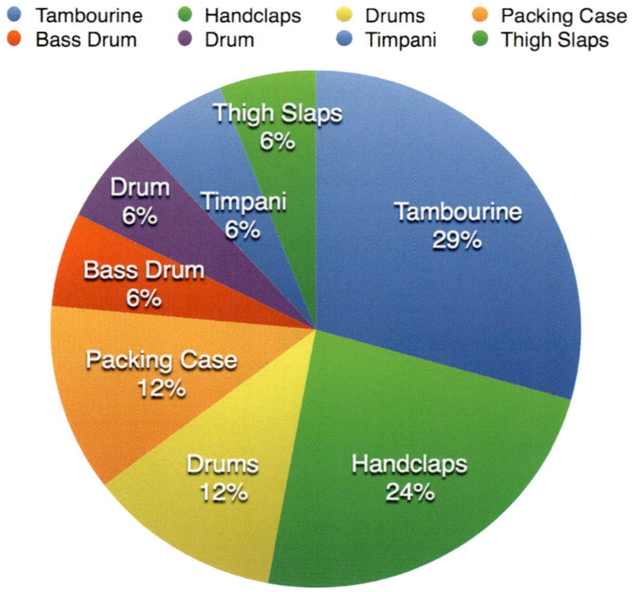

'We didn't want to fall into the Supremes trap where they all sounded similar, so we were always keen on having varied instrumentation. Ringo couldn't keep changing his drum kit, but he could change his snare, tap a cardboard box or slap his knees.'[83]

With another Christmas release looming, and extensive tours underway, the Beatles recorded their new album whenever possible between performances. Such was the demand for new material, they were only able to call upon 8 original compositions, the remaining 6 tracks lifted from their (now increasingly distant) Cavern era set-list. Percussion-wise, despite such haste there's a large amount of improvisation and experimentation on show, from simple thigh slaps to expansive timpani.

No Reply

Time Signature – 4/4
Recorded – 30 September 1964
Drums, Bass Drum, Handclaps – *Ringo Starr*
Handclaps – *Paul McCartney, George Harrison, John Lennon*

Featuring a pseudo Bossa-Nova beat on the verses, there is a neat use of light and shade as Ringo performs cross-stick snare (sounding suspiciously dampened with a tea-towel) with particular restraint and discipline throughout this short [2.15] album opener. Bass drum is negligible, with the merest of touches on beat three in the second bar, and certainly after that. Indeed the bass drum is detectable only by our old friend, the squeaky bass pedal footplate mechanism. If this is the case and Ringo *is* playing bass drum, it is highly unusual for him to not play the faux Bossa-Nova rhythm with hi-hats.

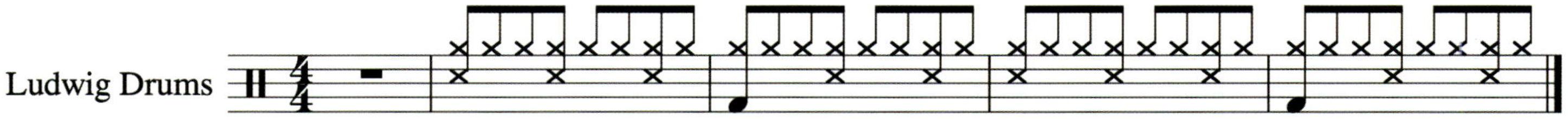

With this in mind, it seems to be the case that Ringo is showing restraint – deliberately keeping the bass drum and hi-hat levels low in the initial opening bars, to heighten their impact in the chorus?

The stereo mix of *No Reply* has Ringo's live performance in the left channel, while in the right channel we can hear on each chorus, Ringo's overdubbed bass drum and crash cymbal strokes (bars 2-5 below).

Worthy of mention is the muting of the cymbal by quickly grabbing it to stop it resonating, and therefore bleeding over into the next passage of the song. Unusually for the strict standard employed by the Abbey Road staff, it appears they neglected to edit out or correct an ever so tentatively mis-timed bass drum beat at [2.02]. However the mono mix shows no such error – the dislocation is caused by the overdub being placed on one side of the stereo mix, appearing 'out of time' to the listener.

Energetic '4 in the bar' handclaps are performed by all four Beatles in the middle 8 section, with the bass drum matching the hi-hat beat for beat, before the song returns to its Bossa-Nova origins. This has the effect of driving along the rhythm and powering-up the feel, a trick which the band often used.

1.02

I'm A Loser

Time Signature – 4/4
Recorded – August 14 1964
Drums, Tambourine – *Ringo Starr*

Brisk shuffle drumming from Ringo on this Lennon Country-Rock flavoured track. A precursor to 'Help!' whose simultaneous double handed fills between verse and chorus are here taken by an accented bass drum, a feature throughout the song. Ringo's kit is deliberately mixed low, determined by its position as recorded live. Despite this, *I'm A Loser* features a strong snare back-beat and prominent tambourine in the chorus. Hi-hats and cymbals are highest in the mix, although they appear more prominent in the mono version. They vie with the rhythm guitar for dominance in the verses, the guitar solo featuring a 'full-on' ride cymbal. A hint of urgency is offered by hurried bass drum on the transition from verse to chorus.

Baby's In Black

Time Signature – 6/8
Recorded – August 11 1964
Drums, Tambourine – *Ringo Starr*

An effortless 'waltz-feel' workout by Ringo, with a great 6/8 feel on his ride cymbal, *Baby's In Black* proved a popular part of the Beatles' live act throughout 1965. An interesting exercise in keeping a languid and potentially limp beat alive, Ringo employs simple, solid, patterns. Along with a lively and fluid bass drum, we hear the utilisation of 'swing – style' 16th notes on his ride cymbal (bars 1 & 9 below) to provide much of the energy. Ringo almost can't help himself as he breaks his discipline at [1.30] by bringing forward a snare beat. Overdubbed tambourine sloppily emphasises the vocal (introduced in the first bar below), enhancing the final passages of the song.

Rock And Roll Music

Time Signature – 4/4
Recorded – 18 October 1964
Drums – *Ringo Starr*

Lacking enough original material for the new album, the Beatles raided their old set-list[84], this time presenting a stroll through this Chuck Berry standard. Staying on hi-hats throughout (save for the final middle 8 at [1.56] when he adds a bit of sparkle by utilising the bell of his ride cymbal), it's standard-fare for Ringo, walking the fine line between a shuffle and 'straight 8's', a great groove. The Beatles recorded this several times, the tempo differing slightly on each version.

I'll Follow The Sun

Time Signature – 4/4
Recorded – 18 October 1964
Thigh Slaps – *Ringo Starr*

An interesting exercise for Ringo, as he echoes Jerry Allison of The Cricket's work on Buddy Holly's *Everyday* by slapping his thighs with the palms of his hands. In order to provide more depth and less of a 'slap', this overdub had the bottom frequency range enhanced. Great stuff.

Mr. Moonlight

Time Signature – 4/4
Recorded – August 14 1964
Drums, Unknown Drum – *Ringo Starr*

Derided by many as being the most unloved Beatles track, Mr. Moonlight highlights the lack of original material at hand for *Beatles For Sale*. There is some conjecture over just who is playing drums and (if any) percussion. Due to the somewhat misleading sleeve-notes, it does appear to have become written in stone that George is playing a kind of 'African drum', with Ringo on 'percussion'. It is possible George is playing the African drum first heard on *Don't Bother Me* from *With The Beatles*, topping and tailing each chorus with a single strike for good measure. Listening to the stereo mix, the right channel has the overdubbed drum, sounding exactly like the drum being struck in the left channel by Ringo. It is apparent this drum is simply Ringo's 13 inch tom-tom, the top skin slackened-off with perhaps the bottom skin removed – giving us the deep, resonant 'thud', almost comedic in it's prominence in the mix. Elsewhere, to our ears it's simply a case of Ringo lightly tapping out a Rhumba-style rhythm on his kit, the toms and snare (without the wires engaged), possibly dampened with tea-towels. The 'give-aways' to this being the return of our old friend the squeaky bass drum pedal throughout (see *Words Of Love*, recorded at the same session, October 18 1964), coupled with the deftly played footwork on the hi-hat, prominent at [0.30]-[0.33] and over the organ solo. Not to mention this approach perfectly mirrors the drum pattern found on the Dr. Feelgood & The Interns original.

Kansas City/Hey Hey Hey Hey

Time Signature – 4/4
Recorded – 18 October 1964
Drums, Handclaps – *Ringo Starr*
Handclaps – *Paul McCartney, George Harrison, John Lennon*

Another former Cavern Club crowd favourite, and once again Ringo forms the bedrock on which the other Beatles (and George Martin on piano) strut their stuff on this Little Richard medley. After the opening triplet-driven matched grip patterns on snare and floor tom (illustrated below), a superbly executed ride cymbal shuffle beat dominates, enhanced by the addition of multiple handclaps from the final flourish at [1.58]. A perfectly executed triplet snare/bass drum flam at [1.12] is subtly mimicked but not repeated by just a single snare stroke at [1.35]. Very rarely does Ringo play the same thing twice, even on a song as simple as this.

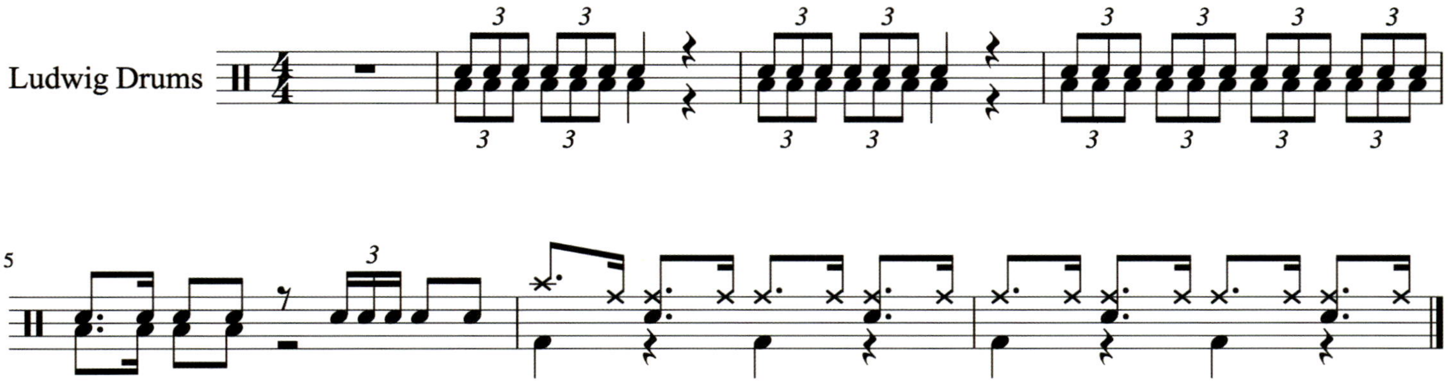

Eight Days A Week

Time Signature – 4/4

Recorded – 18 October 1964

Drums, Handclaps – *Ringo Starr*

Handclaps – *Paul McCartney, George Harrison, John Lennon*

Unusually, *Eight Days A Week* contains the same accented triplet 4-bar fade-in and fade-out, played on overdubbed and dampened floor tom -

An additional cymbal crash /bass drum combination placed at the song's conclusion, elsewhere swishy hi-hats and handclaps dominate one of the most percussive and free-flowing Beatles tracks to date. Possessing an almost 'pushed' shuffle feel, a stifled tom flam [0.27] heralds the hook of the song's title before making way for strong 8th note handclaps. The songs 'hook' however, is the '& 4' handclaps, neatly filling the gaps between the vocal phrasing of the chorus -

The bridge below illustrates the simplicity of the drum part – understated and underplayed, a sympathetic treatment which lets the song flow, even allowing for the interruption of the 'hanging' vocal interlude (bars 3 & 4).

Alex – Whilst working on the *Brookside*[85] sound dub, I was lucky enough to work closely with Director Jeremy Summers, who's TV & Film credits reads like a 'whose-who' of the golden age of British entertainment. Amongst his work, he directed the movie *Ferry Across The Mersey*, featuring Gerry And The Pacemakers, stablemates of the Beatles from Brian Epstein's NEMS Enterprises.

Jeremy told me he was present when Gerry Marsden and the group were recording tracks for the film at Abbey Road. George Martin was producing, and on this occasion, he was late for the session. Jeremy recalled this was unusual as George Martin was the ultimate professional, he was never late, especially for his recording sessions. Time marched on, to the extent that the group were rehearsed, and ready to record. Eventually the studio door burst open and in marched Mr. Martin, looking flustered and worse for wear. He apologised to Jeremy, the engineers, and of course Gerry and his expectant Pacemakers. "Sorry everyone – that bloody McCartney! – he phones me in the early hours of the morning – "George! George! I'm in a nightclub, I've got a great idea for a song, get a pen and paper and write this down in case I forget!". "What was it?" someone asked. "Oh, I don't know", said George, "Something about 'eight days a week'[86]."

Words Of Love

Time Signature – 4/4
Recorded – 18 October 1964
Drums , Packing Case, Handclaps – *Ringo Starr*
Handclaps – *Paul McCartney, George Harrison, John Lennon*

Beatles For Sale already features one Buddy Holly influence (see *I'll Follow The Sun*), now it's time for a full blown homage to their hero. Following the original version closely, when played in a loop it's noticeable just how much the song slows down over it's course, this tempo change occurring across the 16 bar instrumental break. Such an error may have been due to time constraints – *Words Of Love* was clearly recorded in a hurry – the last of the seven songs recorded in the nine hour session on October 18 1964. Of course this tempo change may also be the result of splicing together Takes 2 & 3 to produce the finished product.

Derek Taylor's sleeve-notes claim Ringo plays a packing case on this track, perhaps added as a homage to another Holly track, *Not Fade Away*? Although it does appear to be in addition to a dampened snare, the tapping of the case provides a gentle percussive element. Handclaps are treated with equalisation, this time enhancing the mid-bottom range.

Honey Don't

Time Signature – 4/4
Recorded – 26 October 1964
Drums, Tambourine – *Ringo Starr*

Time to hit the Rockabilly trail with this Carl Perkins favourite. Ringo's drums are AWOL, only the snare and hi-hats are audible here, the sparse arrangement is fleshed out with a prominent tambourine on the 2nd & 4th beats, the acoustic guitars providing much of the rhythm. The instinctive cry *'Rock on George, for Ringo one time!'* harks back to the on-stage banter of their early days.

Every Little Thing

Time Signature – 4/4
Recorded – 29/30 September 1964
Drums, Timpani – *Ringo Starr*

Every Little Thing is a defining point in the Beatles' recording history – the use of timpani by Ringo on the chorus marks the first use of an orchestral percussion instrument in a Beatles song. Joined by Paul on piano, and John on the guitar intro, Ringo overdubbed simple accented high and low timpani strokes onto the 4th track of the EMITAPE on September 30 1964. An interesting aspect of the drum track is the busy 8 beats in the bar bass drum on the chorus, picking the song up from it's pedestrian introduction.

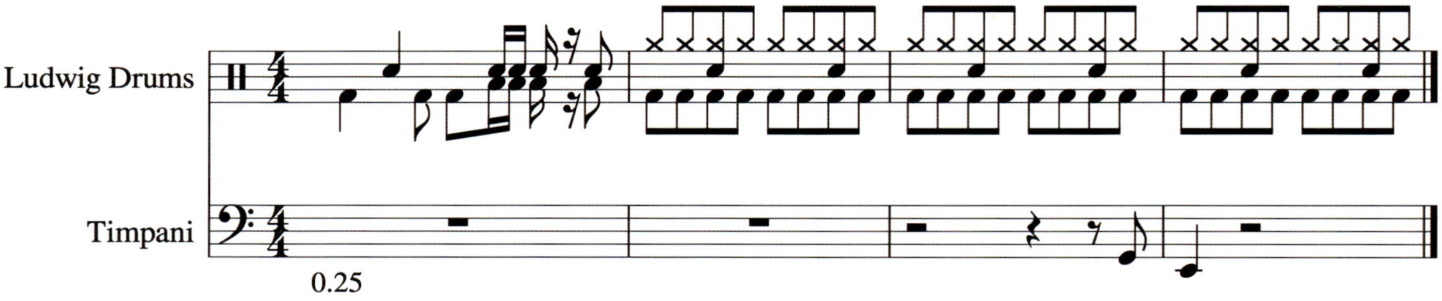

I Don't Want To Spoil The Party

Time Signature – 4/4
Recorded – 29 September 1964
Drums, Tambourine, Packing Case/Guitar Body – *Ringo Starr*

A Country rocker originally written for Ringo to perform, *I Don't Want To Spoil The Party* is driven by energetic drumming, the pace picked up further by tambourine and (possibly) packing cases or an acoustic guitar body on the middle 8 sections [0.52] & [1.48]. The drums appear to be faded *into* the mix, rather than naturally starting with the song. Although barely detectable (especially on the verses), the recording is notable for a change in the bass drum microphone – from this point on, an AKG 020 would be the 'go-to' bass drum microphone at Beatles sessions.

What You're Doing

Time Signature – 4/4
Recorded – 29/30 September 1964
Drums – *Ringo Starr*

Perhaps taking inspiration from The Ronettes track *Be My Baby*, *What You're Doing* opens with Ringo somewhat mimicking the feel of famed American session drummer Hal Blaine's[87] iconic opening snare and bass drum fill.

Save for reprising this pattern prior to the coda, this McCartney-led 4 bar drum pattern is unusually not repeated, Ringo instead opting for a straight 4/4 on bass, snare and hi-hats, evidenced on earlier takes. Slowly becoming standard practice, a tea towel dampens the snare. The solid delivery of the drums, coupled with the songs' similarity to *Rubber Soul's Drive My Car* and *The Word* saw *What You're Doing* form the basis of a medley on the 2006 *Love* album. The 2009 Remasters also saw *What You're Doing* shine like no other – the natural reverb of Studio 2 is brought to the fore here.

Everybody's Trying To Be My Baby

Time Signature – 4/4
Recorded – 18 October 1964
Drums – *Ringo Starr*
Tambourine – *John Lennon*

Another Cavern and Hamburg favourite, another Carl Perkins cover – and much of the same as we heard on *Honey Don't*. However the drum track has more prominence this time, along with tambourine, the reverb drenched vocals and clean guitar licks from George. Here Ringo lets the lead guitar take centre stage, perhaps aware that his tightly tuned snare may prove too dominant, his bass and cymbal stabs are muted by comparison. He let's rip on the false ending though, showing off his tight, snappy snare work to great effect. A lazily played 8 in the bar tambourine backs up the snare throughout.

13. Ticket To Ride / Yes It Is

Single – Released April 9 1965
Engineer – *Norman Smith*

Ticket To Ride

Time Signature – 4/4
Recorded – February 15 1965
Drums, Tambourine, Handclaps – *Ringo Starr*

One of Ringo's most lauded tracks, *Ticket To Ride* provides a feast of drumming invention and originality. Drawing heavily upon the new breed of 'Rock' as purveyed by the likes of The Who and the Yardbirds, *Ticket To Ride* sounded unlike any record yet released. At the heart of the song is Ringo's magnificent drum pattern, embellished with a refreshing variety of tom fills and no-nonsense tambourine. The drum pattern, apparently suggested by McCartney, sees the snare falling on the 2nd and '3 and' beats of the bar, with the tom on the '4 and' beat. Alongside the prominent placement of tambourine from the off – on the 2nd and 4th beats – we have Harrison's Duane Eddy style downward guitar strokes, providing a percussive constant while lending the song a stark syncopation.

The final verse sees added urgency and fluidity provided by a variation on the main pattern heard earlier, with the snare falling along with the tambourine on beats 2 and 4.

Muted off-beat handclaps on the play-out mimic the main drum pattern of the song, the tambourine injecting urgency. Also worthy of mention, Ringo plays his snare and tom with *both* hands, adding another layer of depth to an already

atmospheric soundscape. Frequently played live by the Beatles, it's difficult to make the drums sound as full as the recording, it takes strength, discipline and confidence, and Ringo carried it off with customary ease.

Yes It Is

Time Signature – 12/8
Recorded – February 16 1965
Drums, Tambourine – *Ringo Starr*

In contrast to its 'busy' A-Side, the 12/8 time *Yes It Is* sees Lennon in a tender mood. Drawing on the earlier *This Boy*, this time Ringo is less busy, opting instead for a laid-back approach, with gently struck hi-hat and bass drum buried behind the prominent overdubbed choked hi-hats, which coincide with cross-stick snare.

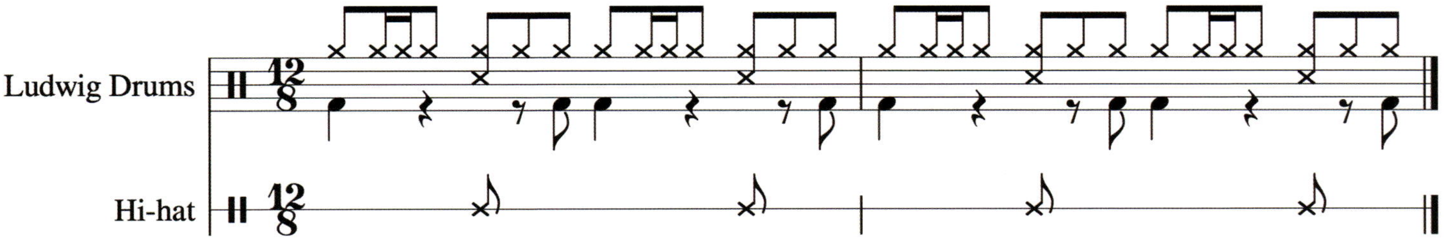

Much of the rhythmic urgency is provided by John's busily strummed acoustic guitar, George once again 'pushing the envelope' by providing a dreamy counterpoint with his innovative volume/tone pedal, enhancing the pervading somnambulistic air.

14. Beatles VI [US Release]

LP – Released June 14 1965
Engineer – *Norman Smith*

Bad Boy

Time Signature – 4/4
Recorded – May 10 1965
Drums, Tambourine – *Ringo Starr*

Requiring two more songs for a new US Capitol LP, *Bad Boy* was hastily committed to tape at the same session as another Larry Williams cover[88] (*Dizzy Miss Lizzy*), but remained unreleased in the UK until it's inclusion on the following year's LP *A Collection Of Beatles Oldies…But Goldies,* surely serving as an enticement for completists only.

The track itself? A workmanlike run through of an old favourite, notable for some nifty 'tommy-gun' style snare work. While Ringo's cymbal shines, the tambourine perhaps sits too high in the mix?

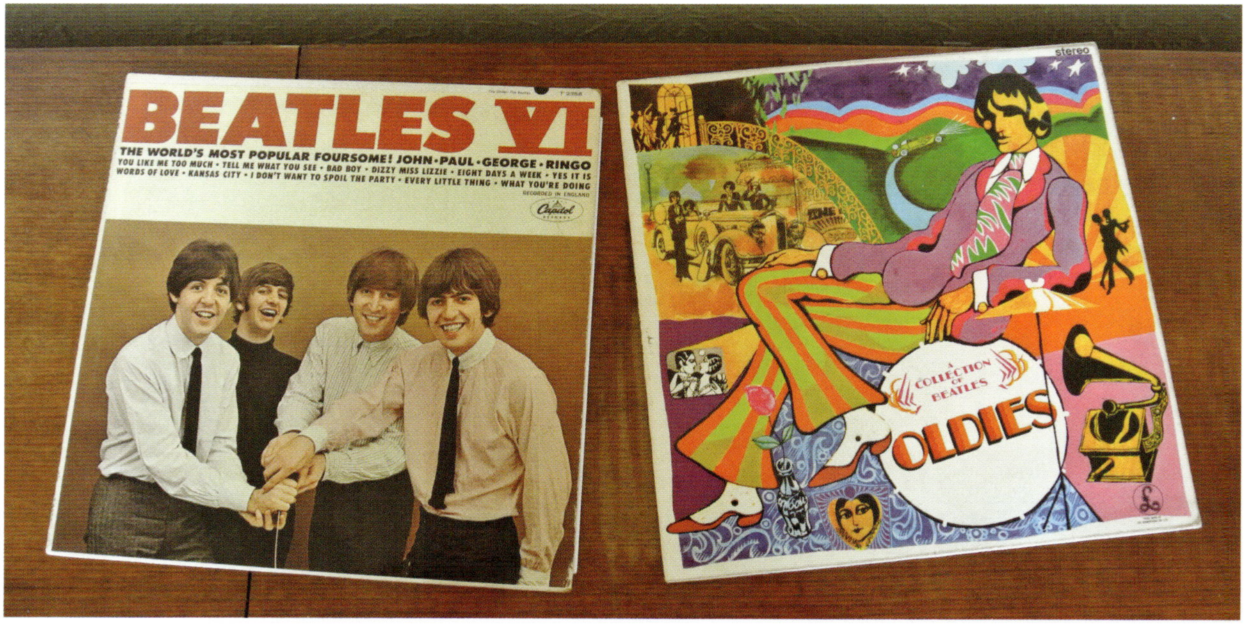

15. Help! / I'm Down

Single – Released July 19 1965

Engineer – *Norman Smith*

Help!

Time Signature – 4/4

Recorded – April 13 1965

Drums, Tambourine – *Ringo Starr*

On paper, there's nothing spectacular about the drum patterns in *Help!*, what is impressive is that Ringo effortlessly executes them with swagger, discipline and panache. Luckily, due to the song's appearance in the opening sequence of the film of the same name, we can see him in full 'devil may care' flow. Opening the song, he keeps time with his left hand on the hi-hats, striking bass drum and crash cymbal (with his right) before introducing the first verse with a trademark tom roll. Solid, accented simultaneous strokes on snare and tom provide a further bridge between verse and chorus (bar 2 below).

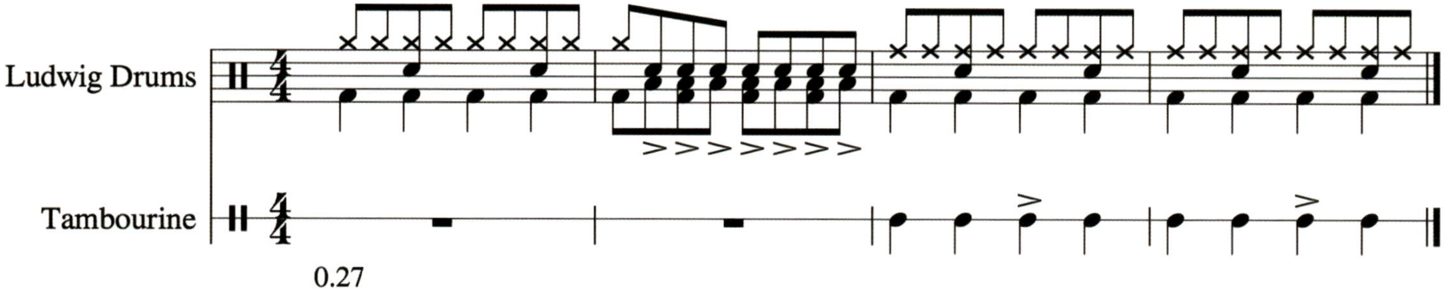

Ringo keeps the song moving with slightly heavier touches on the ride cymbal – tambourine embellishments on the chorus giving the song an even bigger boost. The final verse sees Ringo strike the bell of his ride cymbal on the first beat of every other bar, picking up the pace on bass and snare (over-dubbed tambourine on the first beat of the bar mimicking the effect), re-introducing the chorus with those trademark matched-strokes.

Due to George having difficulty retaining fluidity with the last few bars of the bridge between chorus and verse, George or John (or both?) keep time by striking the palm of a hand on an acoustic guitar, an essential device in the days before click-tracks. The guitar part was later overdubbed by George (when he had the time to practice and perfect it!) but the guitar knocks are still present on the track, due in no part to the absence of drums or percussion.

I'm Down

Time Signature – 4/4

Recorded – June 14 1965

Drums, Bongos – *Ringo Starr*

The B-Side of *Help!*, *I'm Down* features sharp snare punctuations and cymbal-grabs from Starr, with some wonderful Motown-style snare/tom/snare rolls thrown in for good measure. The open sound of his kit is a joy, adding to the excitement of the recording, especially Take 1 found on *Anthology 2*. Mixed progressively louder, busy bongos keep the chorus's moving along, becoming almost dominant over the drums. On the play out, the bongos mimic the vocal intonation. Regarding the raucous vocal, it's incredible to think McCartney recorded *Yesterday* after this!

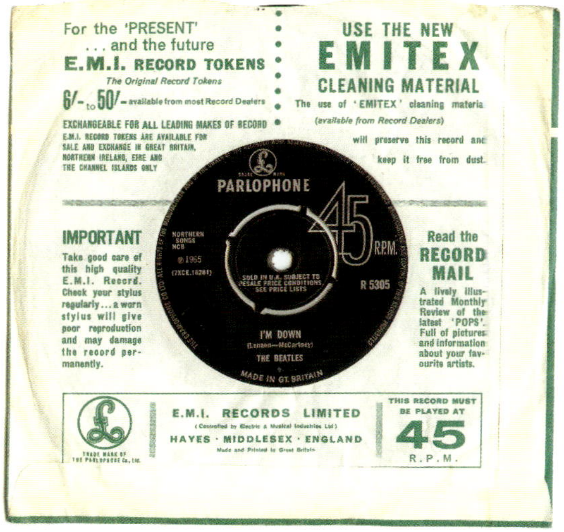

16. Help!

LP – Released August 6, 1965
Engineer – *Norman Smith*

Side One

Help!
The Night Before
You've Got To Hide Your Love Away
I Need You
Another Girl
You're Going To Lose That Girl
Ticket To Ride

Side Two

Act Naturally
It's Only Love
You Like Me Too Much
Tell Me What You See
I've Just Seen A Face
Yesterday
Dizzy Miss Lizzy

14 Songs

Tambourine	6
Maracas	3
Cowbell	2
Guitar Body	1
Drums	1
Bongos	1
Handclaps	1
Drum Rim	1
Claves	1
Guiro	1
Snare (Brushes)	1
None	1

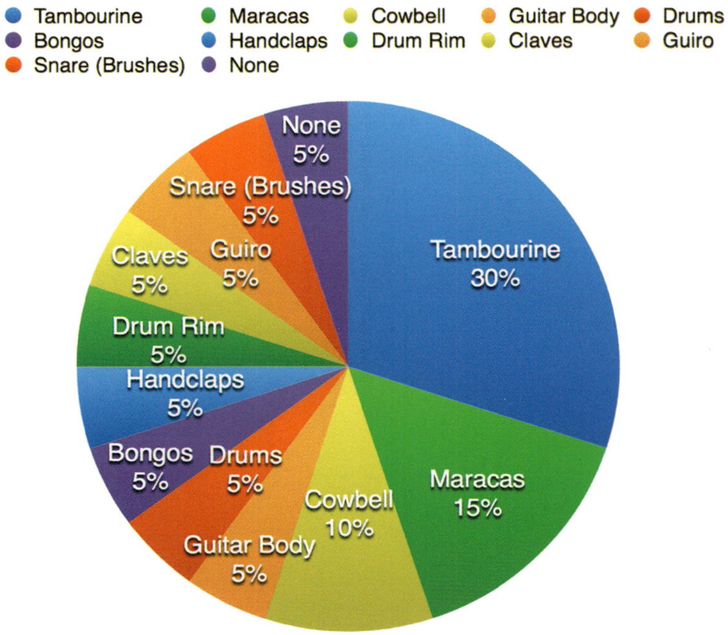

The glamorous life of a rock star – filming Help! on Salisbury Plain

With the group's workload showing no sign of waning, their second film commitment meant recording of the next album would be a long drawn-out affair (February – June). As a result there is a greater diversity of material evident on *Help!* than ever before, Ringo performing to order with his usual casual dependability.

Help!

Time Signature – 4/4
Recorded – April 13 1965 Drums, Tambourine – Ringo Starr

Released as a single some 3 weeks previously, Help! is a superb example of Ringo's trademark time-keeping solidity.

The Night Before

Time Signature – 4/4
Recorded – February 17 1965
Drums, Maracas – *Ringo Starr*

An underrated soulful ballad from McCartney, and thanks to George Martin's sequencing *The Night Before* keeps the pace moving along nicely. With liberal use of his ride cymbal, Ringo accents his bass drum on the last bars of the introductory passage. The middle 8 section is embellished by maracas (filling the space taken by the ride cymbal) with nifty movement from tom to snare (reprising the Latin feel of *I Feel Fine)*.

You've Got To Hide Your Love Away

Time Signature – 4/4
Recorded – February 18 1965
Tambourine, Maracas – *Ringo Starr*

This gentle 'waltz' is actually triplets contained within a 4/4 structure. More prominent on the mono mix of the album, Ringo keeps time with brushes on his snare and features tambourine from the second verse onwards, maracas on the chorus, the development outlined here -

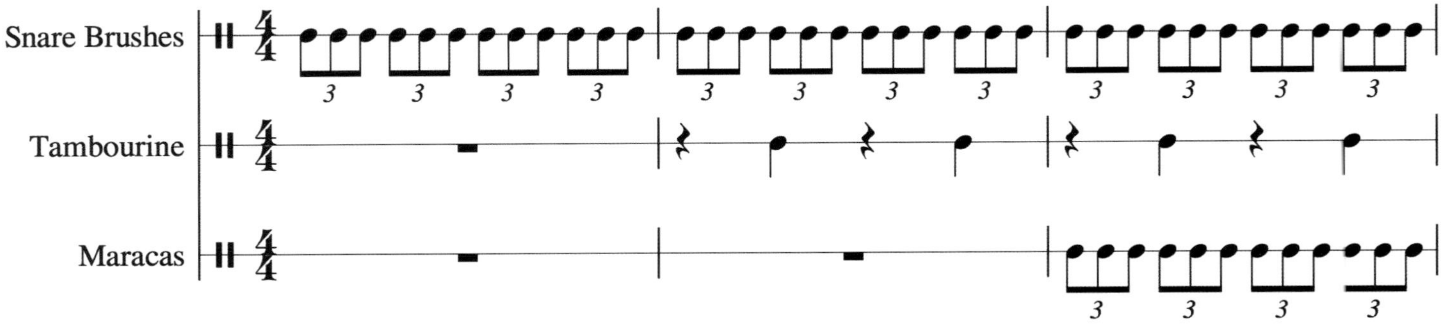

Moving to the closing flute solo, we hear swift use of the maracas, hastening the close of the song -

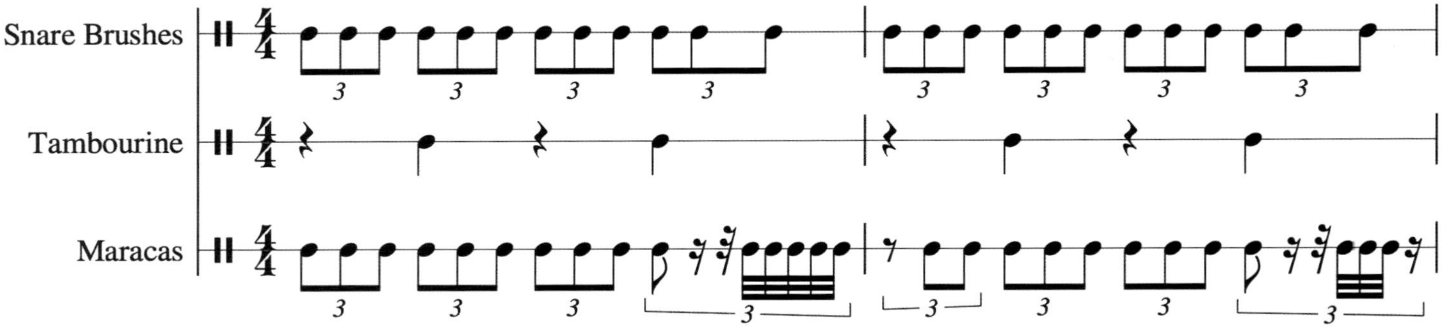

1.46

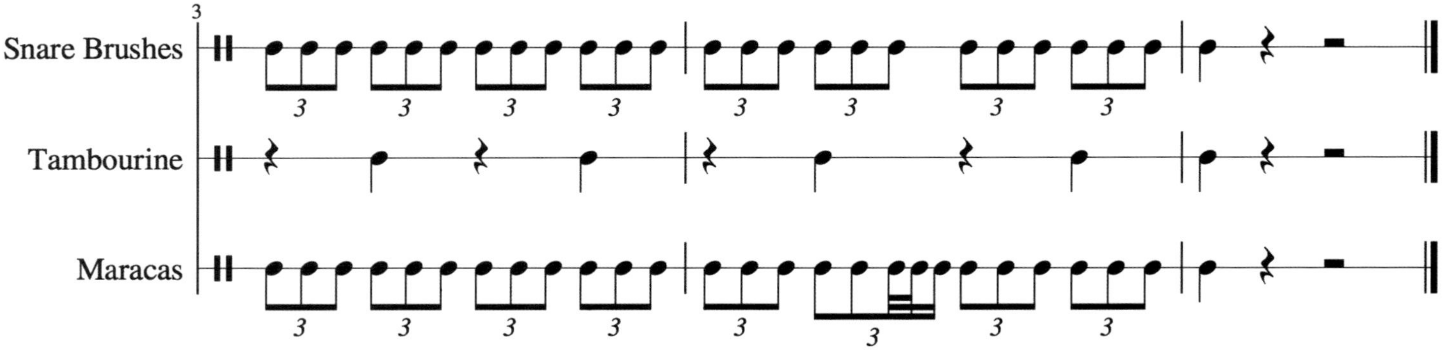

I Need You

Time Signature – 4/4
Recorded – February 15/16 1965
Drums, Guitar Body, Cowbell – *Ringo Starr*

Ringo's drums are buried in the mix here, the rhythm track building with Ringo's overdubbed freestyle playing on the back of an acoustic guitar, vying for dominance with his drums and John's snare overdub. Straightforward, the pattern never alters its course throughout the songs 2.28 duration, moving along swiftly, but with restraint. The cowbell (playing 'straight 4's') on the middle 8 section is somewhat prominent and disjointed in the stereo Mix.

Another Girl

Time Signature – 4/4
Recorded – February 15/16 1965
Drums – *Ringo Starr*

Starr's drums and McCartney's bass are tightly played together here, swinging their way throughout the song – Ringo punctuating the end of each line with accented beats on his bass drum and snare, occasionally removing snare beats for good measure (bar 4 below).

The snare and bass drum mimic the rolling nature of the bass guitar and the consonants of the lyrics, Ringo grabbing the cymbal at the resolution of each verse. In the song's sequence within the movie, Ringo can also be seen playing hi-hats on some sections, giving away the thought of a possible overdubbing of the rather prominent ride cymbal?

You're Going To Lose That Girl

Time Signature – 4/4
Recorded – February 19 1965
Drums, Bongos – *Ringo Starr*

One of the Beatles' classier offerings, *You're Going To Lose That Girl* is nevertheless noticeable for the (somewhat) busily overdubbed bongos throughout. Perfectly placed in the Mono mix, disjointed in the Stereo, the bongos fall into a staccato resolution over the last few bars of the song. Despite this, Ringo is in an otherwise relaxed mood, save for his speeding up and accented bass drum prior to the guitar solo (that old trick again!).

Ticket To Ride

Time Signature – 4/4
Recorded – February 15 1965
Drums, Tambourine, Handclaps – *Ringo Starr*

Previously issued as a single on April 9, and here rounding off side 1 of the original LP.

Act Naturally

Time Signature – 4/4
Recorded – June 17 1965
Drums, Drumstick / Snare Rim Tapping – *Ringo Starr*

After the drama of *Ticket To Ride*, we return back to Earth with another slice of Country & Western showcasing from Ringo. Reprising his pattern from *Help!*, and with an almost 2/4 country feel, he strides through the song with his usual understated panache. Overdubbed drumsticks on the snare rim add a sense of urgency.

It's Only Love

Time Signature – 4/4
Recorded – June 15 1965
Drums, Tambourine – *Ringo Starr*

Here Ringo reprises his earlier accented snare/hi-hat/bass drum pattern (see'*Anna* from *Please Please Me*), this time using snare cross-sticking to give a Latin feel to the track. A busy tambourine beefs up the chorus and lightens the mood. Amazingly, the song checks out at only [1.56].

You Like Me Too Much

Time Signature – 4/4
Recorded – February 17 1965
Drums, Tambourine – *Ringo Starr*

Again a similar pattern to *Help!* and *Act Naturally*, straddling the fine line between 'straight 8's' and a shuffle feel which Ringo again performs admirably. Some well-timed snare fills bring in the verses and middle 8, which is again, along with the chorus, embellished with a dominant tambourine.

Tell Me What You See

Time Signature – 4/4
Recorded – February 18 1965
Drums, Tambourine, Claves – *Ringo Starr*
Guiro – *Paul McCartney*

A lovely percussive element here, a straight 4/4 beat marvellously enhanced by Paul on closely miked guiro, with Ringo on tambourine and claves (1st bar above). The star of the show however is Ringo's superbly recorded tightly-tuned snare

Ringo doing his utmost to maintain his calm while acting naturally during a scene from Help!

drum, which, when coupled with the almost distorted bass drum, resolves the transition between chorus and verse in explosive fashion (bars 2 & 3). The bass drum also neatly follows McCartney's bass to good effect.

I've Just Seen A Face

Time Signature – 4/4
Recorded – June 14 1965
Brushes on Snare, Maracas – *Ringo Starr*

Accented brushes on snare provide a hectic pace to this country flavoured song. Maracas enhance the chorus and acoustic guitar solo.

Yesterday

Time Signature – 4/4
Recorded – June 14 1965

Quite possibly the only Beatles recording not to feature a single percussive element, it's therefore likely Ringo was in the canteen?[89]

Dizzy Miss Lizzy

Time Signature – 4/4
Recorded – May 10 1965
Drums, Cowbell – *Ringo Starr*

It's easy to dismiss this Larry Williams cover as an album filler, taking the track count to the requisite 14, as along with another Larry Williams song *Bad Boy*[90], it was recorded at the behest of Capitol Records to flesh-out another album for the US market. However, it's an important milestone in the Beatle's recording history – this was the last rock 'n' roll standard from their Hamburg days they would commit to tape. *Dizzy Miss Lizzy* is a blistering-paced ride through the Beatles' past – in future they would conjure enough of their own material for their albums.

Ignoring Earl Palmer's superb snare drum shuffle[91] from the 1958 original, like other Merseybeat drummers Ringo commits himself to a straight 4/4 beat. Along with the persistent use of his crash/ride cymbal, Ringo plays precise shotgun snare fills between verses, the obligatory cowbell driving the song along. Perhaps due to the song being inherently powerful yet simple to play, the Beatles thought enough of *Dizzy Miss Lizzy* to consistently include it in their live set, as did John with his 1969 *Plastic Ono Band* performance[92] at the Toronto Rock 'n' Roll Festival.

17. Day Tripper / We Can Work It

Single – Released December 3 1965
Engineer – *Norman Smith*

Day Tripper

Time Signature – 4/4
Recorded – October 16 1965
Drums, Tambourine – *Ringo Starr*

One half of a great double A-Side single, *Day Tripper* is notable for predictable yet well executed single-tom rolls, and some quite inventive snare work from Ringo. Driven by high in the mix tambourine, the repetitive drum pattern of the chorus is broken-up and enlivened by some lovely touches on the snare that are sneaked-in to the beat at [0.40] and [2.11], as illustrated below.

Tambourine creates tension ahead of the tom-rolls that herald each verse. The play-out is a joy, Ringo revelling in the chance to disrupt the flow [2.34] and [2.41], alternating with the resurrected tom rolls from earlier, the best of which is saved from the obscurity of the fade-out [2.47].

We Can Work It Out

Time Signature – 4/4
Recorded – October 20/29 1965
Drums – *Ringo Starr*
Tambourine – *George Harrison or Ringo Starr*[93]

We Can Work It Out has the distinction of possessing one of the most striking pieces of time-altering trickery only the Beatles could unwittingly conjure up. The perceived change in meter of the bridge occurs without the listener being aware of such a change – all without a hiccup. Utilising triplets, the song slips seamlessly into a 3/4 feel contained within a 4/4 structure[94], rather than moving to a strict, jarring change from 4/4 to 3/4. Once underway, the triplets (a bass drum/ cymbal crash combination followed by two tambourine beats), are reminiscent of Bavarian oompah, tumbling towards a sharp return to the 4/4 feel, bringing the protagonist's views back into focus. A device aided by Starr's reading and handling of the situation.

6
3
3
9
3
3
13

RUBBER
SOUL

18. Rubber Soul

LP – Released December 3 1965

Engineer – *Norman Smith*

14 Songs

Tambourine	9
Maracas	3
Drums	3
Cowbell	1
Bass Drum	1
Finger Cymbals	1
Hi-Hat	1
Drums (Brushes)	1
Matchbox	1

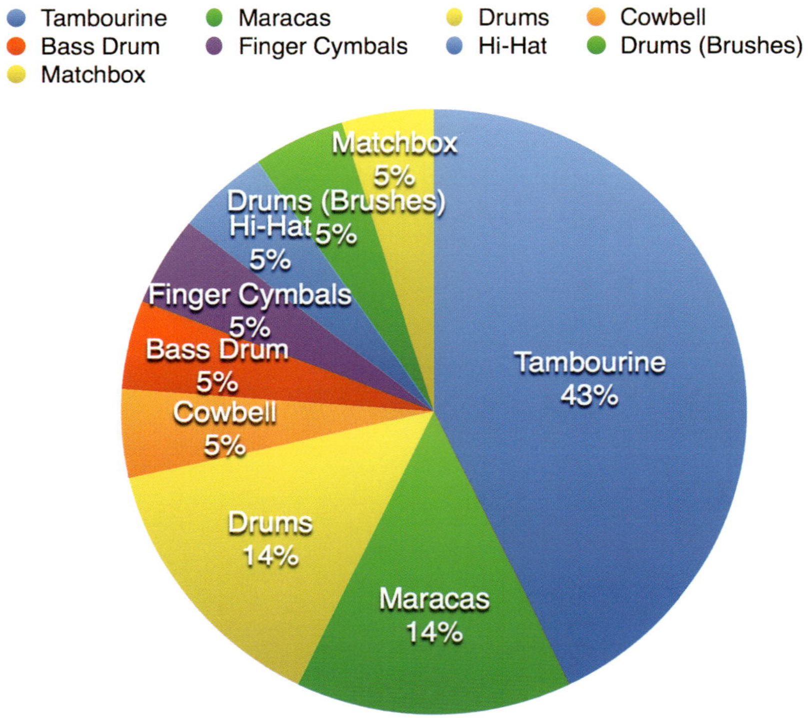

Side One

Drive My Car
Norwegian Wood (This Bird Has Flown)
You Won't See Me
Nowhere Man
Think For Yourself
The Word
Michelle

Side Two

What Goes On
Girl
I'm Looking Through You
In My Life
Wait
If I Needed Someone
Run For Your Life

Having enjoyed (and endured) a hectic 2 years, it was obvious the Beatles were no 'flash in the pan' and were a force to be reckoned with for a good few years to come. With this growth in their stock, EMI allowed the group the flexibility of spending more time in the studio. *Rubber Soul* was recorded in sessions across an unprecedented 4 weeks, the first time a Beatles album was afforded the luxury of not having to be fitted in around other projects. The Beatles had always had one eye across the Atlantic for inspiration, and latterly had become influenced by the burgeoning Memphis Blues & Soul scene, especially those artists on the Stax[95] label. Indeed, during the *Rubber Soul* sessions they recorded a Booker T & the MG's style instrumental. The uninspiring *12 Bar Instrumental* lay on the shelf until its eventual release on the *Anthology* series. It was under this influence that Ringo returned to a more soulful feel on *Rubber Soul*. Additionally, his Ludwig kit was more closely miked, giving a fuller, much more rounded sound.

By the end of 1965, it had become clear the Beatles saw their live performances as literally a sideshow, merely contractual obligations and a chance to 'count the beans'. With the release of *Rubber Soul*, their focus had switched to the studio as a means of presenting their art. Ringo has stated that *Rubber Soul* is the album where things 'started to get interesting', as the band began their transition from mop-tops to Rock Svengalis.

George Martin's 1987 remix of *Rubber Soul* delivered a more expansive sound, due to an increase in reverb over the original 1965 stereo versions (which thankfully can be found on the Mono Remasters box set). This went against the original plan for *Rubber Soul* as, before work commenced on the album, it was agreed by the Beatles, George Martin, and Norman Smith that the new album should possess less reverb (either natural or added at the mixing stage). As a result, Ringo's Ludwig kit appeared to benefit from closer microphone placement, with a more controlled sound evident. In particular the bass drum and toms sound deeper and richer, being more prominent in the mix. The opposite can be said of the cymbals, with less 'swish and wash' and more precision. Complimenting and enhancing the new approach, Ringo continued using the tight top snare skin employed on *Help!*.

Drive My Car

Time Signature – 9/8, 4/4
Recorded – October 13 1965
Drums, Tambourine, Cowbell – *Ringo Starr*

Drive My Car has a most confusing introduction – the opening bar of the guitar introduction occurring in common time (4/4), followed by a bar of 9/8, before settling into the robust 4/4 meter of the song. As the sole instrument present in these two bars is lead guitar, the seemingly off-beat timing proves disconcerting and jarring. It's likely the opening guitar break was an after-thought – a means to introduce the song in a dramatic fashion, with little concern for the resulting time signatures. Ringo would have to have coped with placing his own introduction, providing a bridge between the guitar and main body of the song. Due to the 9/8 timing, his fill is dramatic in it's execution – alternating between tom and snare, tumbling towards the next bar. Is Ringo going to make it, is he going to come in on time? Thankfully he does, and after a smooth yet reticent sweep across the bars, we soon find ourselves back in the familiar territory of common (4/4) time.

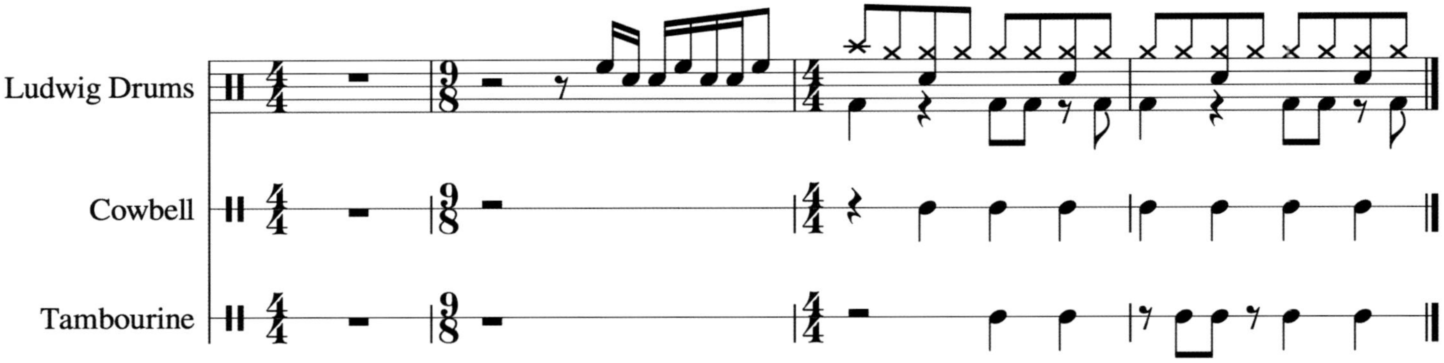

With Paul and George's guitars snaking their way around the vocals, Ringo's drums (especially his tightly tuned snare drum) are prominent in the mix, cutting through and binding the track together. The (in)famous interplay between snare and bass drum that bridges the verses to the chorus [0.16], [1.06], [1.22] provides a touch of drama. A high in the mix tambourine embellishes and mimics that interplay, providing back to the vocal *'Beep-beep, beep-beep, yeah!'* (illustrated below). A cowbell provides some continuity, ever present save for the above instrumental break at the end of the chorus.

Norwegian Wood (This Bird Has Flown)

Time Signature – 12/8
Recorded – October 12/21 1965
Bass Drum, Tambourine, Finger Cymbals – *Ringo Starr*

Take 1 of *Norwegian Wood* sees Ringo playing a bass drum/ride cymbal pattern with finger cymbals, progressing by adding snare on the verses for a heavier touch.

This was seemingly deemed too 'busy' an arrangement for the song, Ringo's drums abandoned in favour of a sparse arrangement of bass drum, finger cymbals and tambourine, allied to an increase in tempo.

However, there also developed an accented (off-beat) bass drum, enhancing the bridge between the vocals. The starkness of the first bridge [0.31], illustrated here -

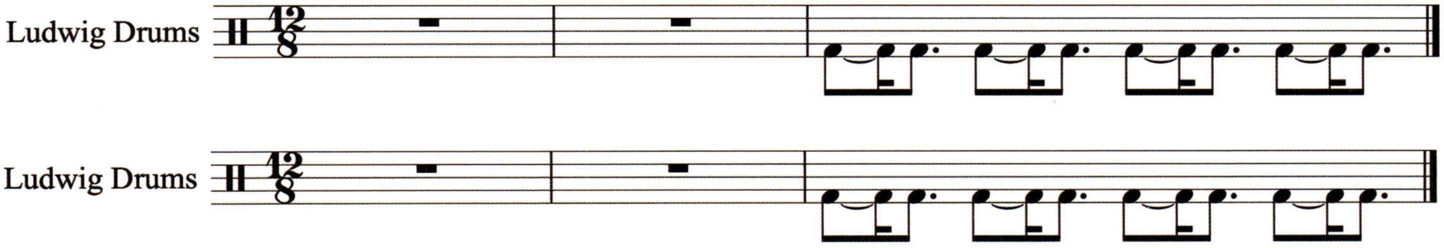

The second bridge, occurring after the sitar solo is greatly enhanced, not only by the addition of finger cymbals, but also the busier bass drum from Take 1.

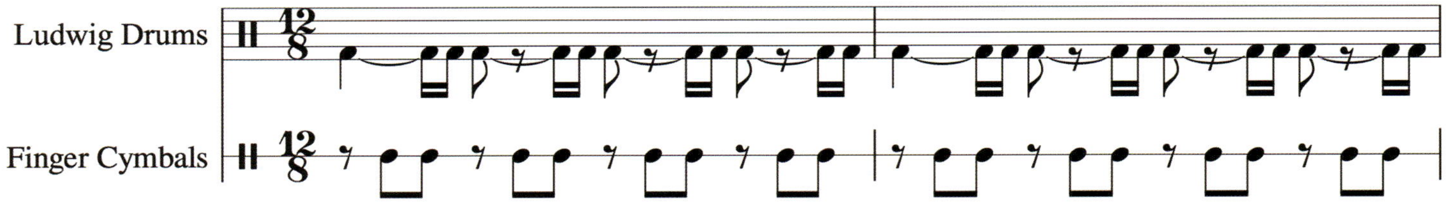

1.19

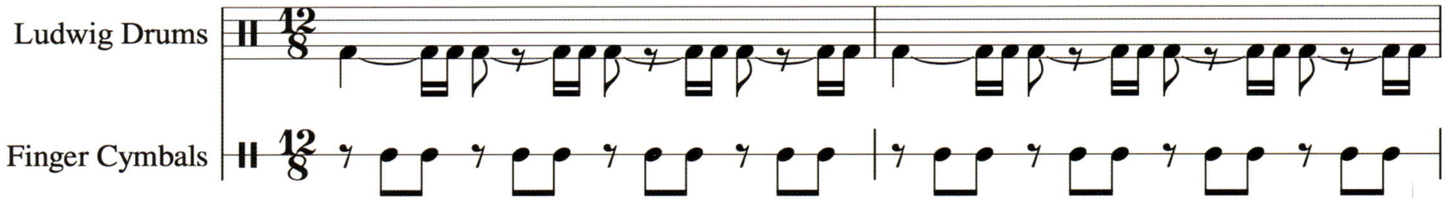

You Won't See Me

Time Signature – 4/4
Recorded – November 11 1963
Drums, Tambourine, Hi-Hat – *Ringo Starr*

There appears to have been a degree of experimentation with the recording of Ringo's drums on *You Won't See Me.* They certainly sound different to the other songs on *Rubber Soul*, leading to the possibility of extra microphones being employed, his kit also seems to have benefitted from closer microphone placement. Another possibility is the use of a different compressor, although such an event didn't occur until the *Revolver* sessions the following year. The sessions for *Rubber Soul* would be Norman Smith's last for the Beatles. Was he using this time to experiment with equipment, trying out new ideas? Possible, but unlikely. Along with *Girl*, *I'm Looking Through You*, *'Wait'* (a left over song from the *Help* sessions), *You Won't See Me* was recorded at a 13 hour deadline-busting session. Hardly the time for experimentation? A more likely scenario is the probable acceptance of a quickly recorded drum track, necessitating in the overdubbing of a hi-hat part due to poor microphone placement burying the hi-hats and enhancing the drums?

Regarding the music, a startling opening bar on crash cymbal and bass drum, followed by sharp tambourine beats sets the tone.

A hurried second bar sees Ringo swiftly moving around his toms in tandem with the snare, before settling on the main beat of the song – a simple 4/4 beat with the overdubbed hi-hat triplets (illustrated on bars 3 and 4). At [0.26] and [1.40], we hear mistakes with the overdubbed hi-hats – they end too late, overlapping and clashing with the timing of the drum track. Despite this, the overall effect is one of movement and busyness, the tom-fills occurring at precisely the correct moments, a great example of Ringo's drumming being sympathetic to the song. More prominent on the mono mix, we have spontaneous off-beat handclaps (probably by Paul) on the vocal track of the playout. Also of note, is Ringo's switch to '4 in the bar' and later off-beat improvised overdubbed hi-hats, perhaps born out of boredom, or an instruction to embellish the play out?

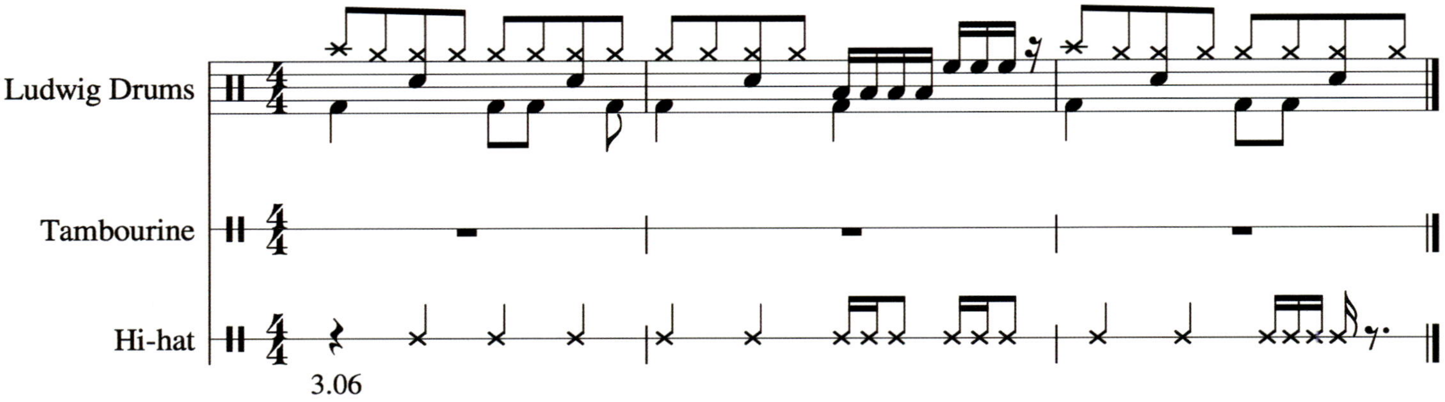

Nowhere Man

Time Signature – 4/4

Recorded – October 21/22 1965

Drums – *Ringo Starr*

Alongside an overly busy bass guitar part, Ringo again wisely offers a simple restrained 4/4 beat, sleepily ambling along allowing the guitars to shine and that busy bass to provide the drive. Despite this, Ringo cleverly manages to liven up such a simple pattern by way of accented hi-hats, on the beat before the snare stroke.

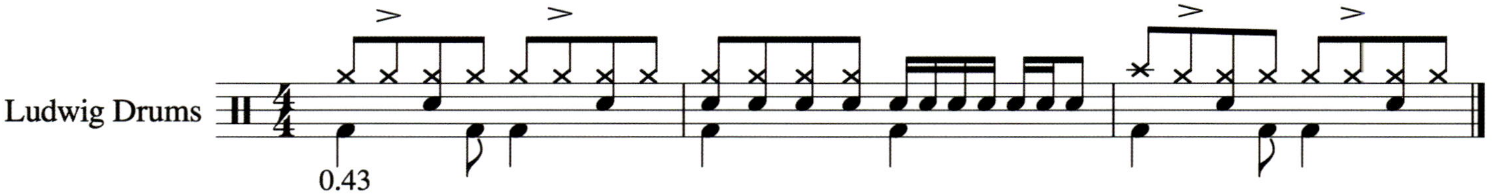

An uncharacteristic snare roll precedes the first chorus and subsequent verses and choruses, with an unintentional snare rim-shot following the buzz-snare roll into the guitar solo [0.48]. Another occurs at [1.34], after a characteristically sloppy (but effective) fill between snare and tom. This is the only time in the song such a fill occurs and was probably purely instinctive, it's non-appearance in subsequent passages was probably a wise move?

Think For Yourself
Time Signature – 4/4
Recorded – November 8 1965
Drums, Maracas – *Ringo Starr*
Tambourine – *John Lennon?*[96]

The percussion and drum track is particularly well thought-out here. After a strong guitar intro, Ringo introduces the verse with off-beat accents on this (rapidly improving) Harrison track.

There is simple snare/bass interplay during the verses (with the snare dismissing the expected second beat in the bar, instead falling on the 4th). An interesting exercise in using percussion as punctuation, McCartney's unusual fuzz bass [played over his usual Hofner] gives a sharper, harsher sound to the track compared to the previous silky sounds of *Nowhere Man*, with rhythm guitar providing the constant throughout. Heavily accented maracas and tambourine provide a colourful contrast, especially in the chorus's, illustrated here -

195

Inventive drum fills punctuate, with flams and sixteenth snare beats scattered liberally over the basic track.

The Word

Time Signature – 4/4
Recorded – November 10 1965
Drums, Maracas – *Ringo Starr*

Continuing the off-beat feel of *Think For Yourself*, *The Word* contains some blistering fills from Ringo, ranging from strong snare [0.22 – 0.24], to some less than crisp snare/tom work [2.22 & 2.33] – the best of the bunch arriving at [1.24 – 1.26]. The 'musical joke' at [1.56], where Ringo opts for simple bass drum accents rather than fills provides a moment of light relief – or perhaps he flunked it, thinking better of the fill he was going to play?

Ringo precedes most of these fills by opening his hi-hats, leaving a beat empty before striking a drum – a great device for adding a touch of 'feel', and one which was rapidly becoming a Beatle trademark. Providing continuity from the previous track (*Think For Yourself*) maracas provide a '16's' feel and urgency on the verses by playing around the off-beat guitar and the hard driving 4's feel on hi hats. The effect builds a sense of tension by busily playing over the last bars of the chorus.

Michelle

Time Signature – 4/4
Recorded – November 3 1965
Drums – *Ringo Starr*

Once again, Ringo plays a simple 4/4 beat on bass/cross-stick snare/hi-hats, perfectly complimenting the tender nature of the song. The bass drum playing around the starkly strummed acoustic guitars is particularly notable [0.45].

What Goes On

Time Signature – 4/4
Recorded – November 4 1965
Drums – *Ringo Starr*

The formula now well established for Ringo's cameo vocal turn – following on from *Help's Act Naturally* (Country-Rock, 1st track, Side 2), this track could also have easily slotted into *Beatles For Sale*. His country shuffle beat with prominent hi-hats (trading off with Harrison's superb Carl Perkins/Chet Atkins Guitar) never waivers, save for the usual Starr trait of speeding-up over the guitar solo. Playing with that intensity without skipping a beat is pretty impressive stuff. His first songwriting credit to boot – even if he contributed only 'around 5 words'!

Girl

Time Signature – 4/4
Recorded – November 11 1963
Drums (with Brushes) – *Ringo Starr*

Almost mirroring his work on Michelle, this time brushes replace sticks, possibly allowing a degree of flexibility with which to strike cymbals and snare. Indeed, the brush phrases on cymbal brings an urgency to proceedings. Verses almost solely feature dual brush work on the snare, the bass drum buried deep in the mix (compare with the bass drum on *Michelle*). Cymbal snatches feature on the guitar bridge [2.00], the corresponding bridges leading to the chorus [1.29] featuring no cymbal work at all, allowing the vocal to flow.

I'm Looking Through You

Time Signature – 4/4
Recorded – October 24, November 6/11 1965
Drums, Tambourine, Matchbox – *Ringo Starr*

Dissatisfied with 3 previous attempts at the song, the final version is noticeable for the use of Ringo's bass drum and snare, possibly deliberately played as rim-shots[97]. Version 1 begins with hurried handclaps -

The remake version officially released sees the busy handclaps replaced by, of all things, Ringo tapping on a matchbox!

As has become the norm, there is a 'high in the mix' tambourine (played by George), employed to hasten salient points throughout the song – at the end of verses, throughout the bridge, and the play-out. Regarding rim-shots, consistently striking rim and skin at precisely the same time can be a difficult device to employ, especially when played with restraint as on *I'm Looking Through You*. Ringo has a few near-misses but manages to hold it together, until completely miscuing a rim shot at [1.57].

As an aside, (and displayed on the album sleeve-notes), Ringo plays Hammond organ on the chorus, although the instrument sounds more like a Vox Continental organ.

In My Life

Time Signature – 4/4
Recorded – October 18/22 1965
Drums, Tambourine – *Ringo Starr*

Revisiting former glories, Starr (probably again under the direction of Lennon) opts for a similar hi-hat/snare/bass drum interplay to *Anna* and *All I've Got To Do*. Here is the pattern, presented as the first 2 bars of drums after the guitar introduction -

The most noticeable element of Ringo's playing on *In My Life* is how closely miked, high in the mix and harsh his drums sound for such a tender song. A little more room ambience may have been tempting but this would have been against the grain of the 'dry mix' diktat laid down for the album. As is the norm, the mono mix eliminates the harshness of the stereo versions.

Featured here from the final bar of the solo, are the last bars of In My Life, illustrating the diversity of Ringo's playing, plus the addition of tambourine to enhance the occasional sparse arrangement.

Wait

Time Signature – 4/4
Recorded – June 17/ November 11 1965
Drums, Tambourine, Maracas – *Ringo Starr*

Despite spending more time in the studio, and also producing the next single (*Day Tripper/We Can Work It Out*), *Rubber Soul* was short of the required 14 track sequence. Left over from the previous Help sessions, *Wait* provided the album with the balance of 7 tracks per side. Ringo's kit evidently displays different microphone placement than on the rest of the album, and perhaps to make it bed-in with the more recent tracks on *Rubber Soul*, overdubbed tambourine and maracas dominate, whilst his drums are buried deep in the mix.

Otherwise, the track is notable for some precise, thunderous tom fills from Ringo, especially when introducing the chorus at [0.10], [0.32], [1.07] and [1.42], exploding from open hi-hats to tom. On the final middle 8 section at [1.16], we hear a matched snare and floor tom tapping out the tension, racked up by an almost overpowering tambourine. Also on display is some nice interplay between ride cymbal and tambourine on the verse, evident from the start of the track and subsequently repeated throughout.

ebay

Packing Slip

This is not an invoice

Deliver to

Jack Monaghan
47 Ravenscliffe Drive
Glasgow, East Renfrewshire G46 7qs
UK

Message to jmon5698

Thanks for ordering Ringo Starr And The Beatles Beat. Please like our Facebook page - https://www.facebook.com/ringostarrandthebeatlesbeat/ follow us on Twitter (@beatlesbeatbook) and Instagram (beatlesbeatbook) and visit www.beatlesbeat.com.

Ringo Starr And The Beatles Beat / Ringo's White Album (Deluxe) Book Bundle (123697236987)	Price: £50.00, Qty: 1	**£50.00**
	Subtotal:	**£50.00**
	Postage and packaging:	**£4.70**
	Total:	£54.70

If I Needed Someone

Time Signature – 4/4
Recorded – October 16/18 1965
Drums, Tambourine – *Ringo Starr*

Recorded live with just vocals and tambourine overdubbed, the rhythm track plods along in unspectacular 4/4 fashion, Ringo expanding his sound to include his ride cymbal on the middle 8 section and guitar solo. Matched strokes on snare and hi-hat are played over the title vocal, but are absent at [2.02], heralding the end of the song. It's subtle touches like this that display the influence the extra studio time had upon the Beatles' final product.

Run For Your Life

Time Signature – 4/4
Recorded – October 12 1965
Drums, Tambourine – *Ringo Starr*

Enlivened and embellished with the now ubiquitous tambourine (played accented and '8 in the bar'), *Run For Your Life* is a lesson in repetition without variation – save for the two bar guitar introduction, the remaining bars[98] of drums and percussion are identical.

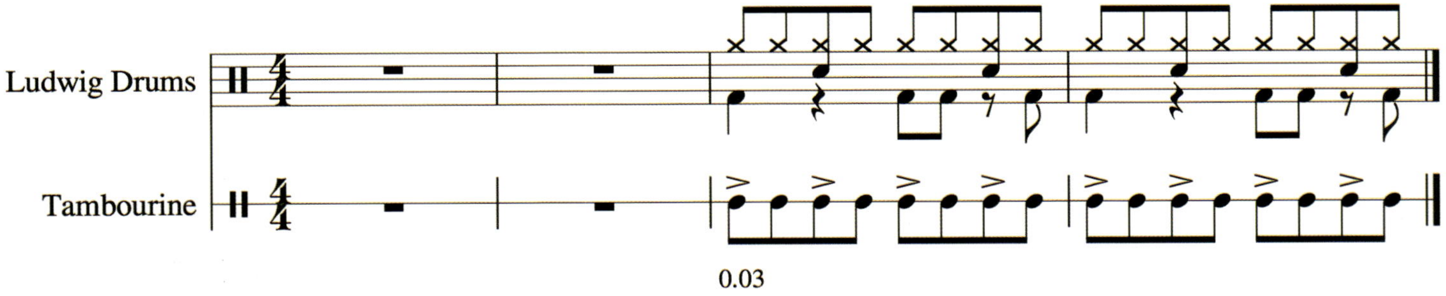

With the lyrical content and feel shamelessly lifted from Elvis Presley's *Baby Let's Play House*, Ringo revisits *What Goes On,* playing a typically restrained Rockabilly shuffle, although played in a much looser fashion this time. Despite this, while being reminiscent of *Can't Buy Me Love,* the guitar solo passage does not display the loose rocking style of the earlier song, opting for a more even, controlled approach typical of *Rubber Soul*. Occasionally, monotony works.

19. Paperback Writer / Rain

Single – Released June 10 1966

Engineer – *Geoff Emerick*

This superb single sees the Beatles swiftly moving towards their most experimental phase, with tape-speed variations, speaker cabinets used as microphones, plus backwards tape effects all adding up to a most spectacular single release. Coincidentally, by mid-1966 the Pop world was moving towards a heavier, 'rockier' feel. Perhaps aware of this, *Paperback Writer* and *Rain* combined this approach with greater studio experimentation. The sessions for this single and the subsequent *Revolver* album saw a change in the *sound* of Ringo's drums, which had been progressing with every release in terms of microphone placement and prominence in the mix of their records. This took a leap forward with the promotion of Geoff Emerick from 2nd engineer (the glorified title for tape operator) to engineer. Geoff's attitude seems to have been firmly in the 'rules are there to be broken' camp – this was the Beatles after all. With this attitude in mind, he broke almost every rule in the Abbey Road engineer's rule book. Microphones were moved closer to the drums (with the bass drum sound benefitting the most), and where necessary, the front skin of the bass drum and bottom skins of the toms were removed. This stronger signal from the drums was then fed through Fairchild 600 valve compressors and limiters, providing power, purpose and punch.

These innovations placed a greater emphasis on Ringo's drums, in that they could be heard with an increasing degree of clarity and separation – no more were they a part of a 'muddy' rhythm track. As a result, Ringo was placed centre-stage, he was not merely providing the backbeat, his drums were pushed to the forefront of the Beatles' sound.

Paperback Writer

Time Signature – 4/4
Recorded – April 13/14 1965
Drums, Tambourine – *Ringo Starr*

The 4 bars above provide a snapshot of the drum track, illustrating the busy, repetitive tambourine (echoing the overdubbed hi-hat work of *You Won't See Me)* plus snare and tom fills that reintroduce the verses. We hear Ringo in forthright mood, providing the platform for Paul's pumped up bass part. In more ways than one, this is *Day Tripper* Pt 2 – yet *Paperback Writer* benefits from a heavier, more modern sounding drum kit, particularly the heavier bass drum. The bass guitar in particular provides much of the rhythmical quality, the drum track providing a repetitively solid bass. Perhaps Ringo was saving himself for the B-Side?

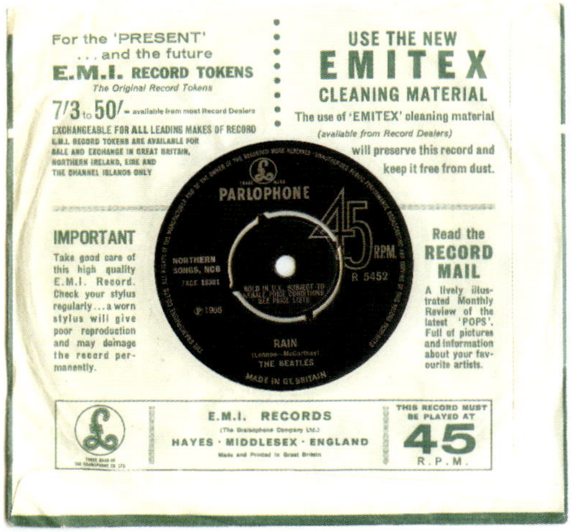

Rain

Time Signature – 4/4
Recorded – April 14/16 1966
Drums, Tambourine – *Ringo Starr*

> "I think I just played amazing. I was into the snare and the hi-hat. I think it was the first time I used this trick of starting a break by hitting the hi-hat first instead of going directly to a drum off the hi-hat."
> *Ringo Starr* [99]

To achieve the 'trippy' feel required, *Rain* was performed at a quicker tempo, the tape consequently slowed down on playback. There also appears to have been a degree of tomfoolery regarding the control of the tape varispeed – the song appears to speed-up and slow down throughout, although as we will see this may not have all been due to surreptitious knob twiddling.

Ringo's performance here is quite unique and remarkable, busily attacking his kit from the get-go, with fills every few bars as the pleasure takes. Prominent tambourine (simultaneously overdubbed with the backing vocals), plays on the 4 beats of the introduction, then beats 2 and 4 until the final 2 verses, thus keeping a constant focal point around which the drums move. The 17 bars below represent the first 32 seconds of the song, introduced by the sharp attention-grabbing sixteenth note snare pattern, setting the tone for what follows. Everything here is purely instinctive – of particular note throughout is the movement between hi-hat and snare, (exemplified at [0.16] – bar 9 below), rather than moving from snare to tom as he had moments before.

Ludwig Drums
Tambourine
5
9
13

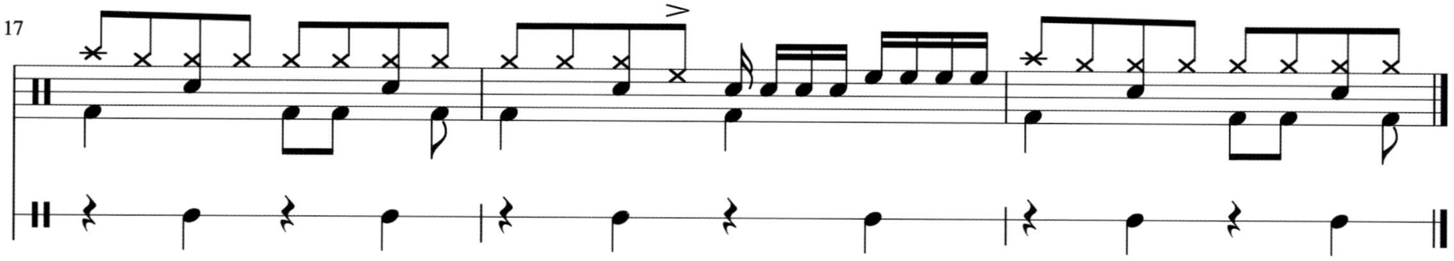

Near the end of the second verse, we return to the subject of erratic time keeping[100] alluded to earlier – namely the insertion of a 'cheeky' 2/4 bar at 0.44. Whether this was by accident or design we'll probably never know, but it certainly adds a twist to proceedings. Coupled with John's elongated vocal, we are transported through a passage of uncertainty, with Ringo doing his best to navigate us safely.

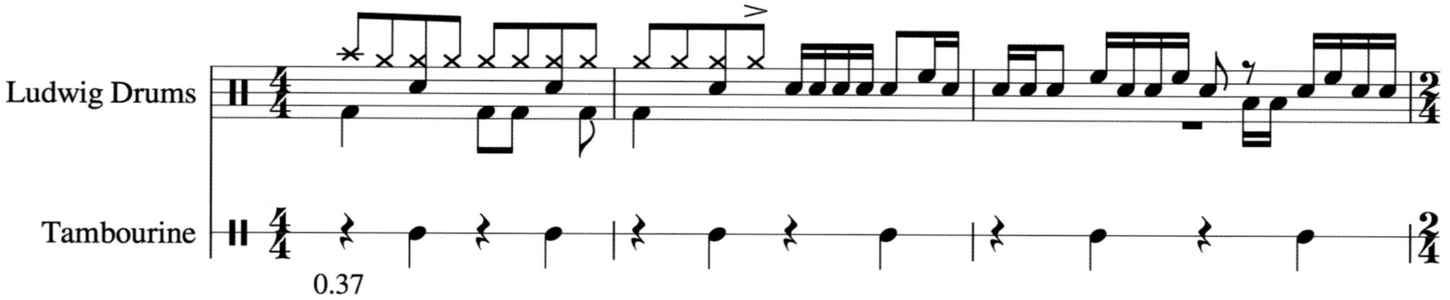

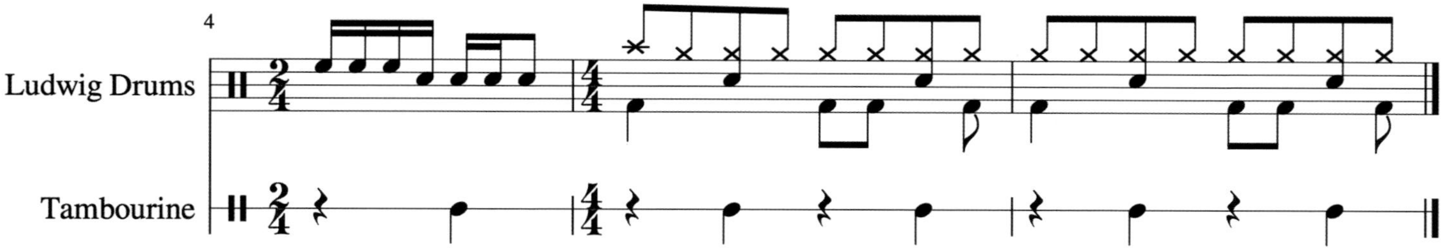

The much lauded interaction between bass guitar and drums at [2.24] below, is truly innovative, as is the dramatically syncopated fill and melodious bass that bring it cascading back in wonderfully.

So, yet another fantastic single release, and a foretaste of what was to shortly follow on *Revolver*.

20. Revolver

LP – Released August 5 1966

Engineer – *Geoff Emerick*

14 Songs

Tambourine	8
Handclaps	3
Maracas	2
Cowbell	1
Drums	1
Tabla	1
Finger Clicks	1
Bass Drum	1
Shaker	1
None	1

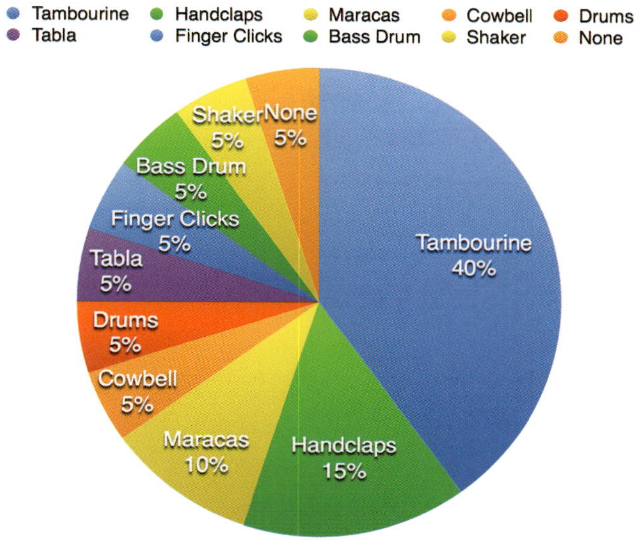

Side One

Taxman
Eleanor Rigby
I'm Only Sleeping
Love You To
Here, There And Everywhere
Yellow Submarine
She Said She Said

Side Two

Good Day Sunshine
And Your Bird Can Sing
For No One
Doctor Robert
I Want To Tell You
Got To Get You Into My Life
Tomorrow Never Knows

Revolver was more than just a continuation of the themes explored on *Rubber Soul*, it was a massive leap forward in the Beatles' development as songwriters and musicians. As the album was being released, the group were due to embark on their final US tour, where they would perform songs far removed from what they were now creating in the studio. If ever there was a time to announce their arrival as a studio based group, it was now.

Like George Martin previously, Abbey Road's engineers became the conduit through which the Beatles' rapidly expanding musical minds would be channelled[101]. As we have seen with the sonic improvisation and experimentation on the *Paperback Writer / Rain* single, the end result was a more powerful yet controlled sound, making it possible to achieve such truly groundbreaking, thunderous sounds as heard on *Tomorrow Never Knows* and *She Said, She Said,* set against the tender tom-tom strokes of *Here, There And Everywhere*.

Taxman

Time Signature – 4/4
Recorded – April 20/21/22, May 16 1966
Drums, Tambourine, Cowbell – *Ringo Starr*

This brilliantly bitter opener from George, protesting about the high level of tax being levied on high earners such as the Beatles, required a harsher, nastier sound. With this in mind, Ringo keeps things simple yet solid, the fluidity of 8 in the bar hi-hats or cymbals entirely absent from the verses. Bass and snare drums in tandem with the stark rhythm strokes of the guitars provide the backbone for McCartney's busy bass. In contrast to the erratic rhythm of the first four bars (not including the faux count-in), the fifth bar begins with two stark quarter notes – simultaneously played on bass and crash cymbal, then bass drum, snare and crash cymbal, serving as a hint to the following "*Tax-man*" vocal of the chorus.

Snare fills precede the repeating heavy cymbal crashes which dominate and punctuate the end of every 4th bar of the verses, ride cymbal being employed on the chorus. This pattern dominates, and is soon joined by cowbell and tambourine, building intermittently, being mixed in and out as the song progresses -

The mono and stereo mixes of *Revolver* contain many subtle differences, once such example being the placement of the cowbell in *Taxman*. The example above is taken from the mono mix, however, the cowbell appears later in the stereo version -

Regardless of how they are mixed, the cowbell and tambourine augment what potentially may have been a sparse drum track, in particular the tambourine beefs up the guitar solo (played by Paul) perfectly. It is prudent to note how much looser the tuning and closer the miking of the snare is compared to previous albums.

Eleanor Rigby

Time Signature – 4/4
Recorded – April 28/29, June 6 1966

The song that inspired a Liverpool housewife[102] to exclaim "How did four scruffs from round here come up with that?" How indeed? Despite the obvious lack of drums on *Eleanor Rigby*, George Martin's score possesses a strong rhythm, the strings are not slushy, but crisp and choppy. Note the Bernard Hermann *Psycho*-esque sharp jabs of the strings keeping time, providing a superb '4's & 8's' feel, punctuating the stark lyrics perfectly.

I'm Only Sleeping

Time Signature – 4/4
Recorded – April 27/29, May 5/6 1966
Drums – *Ringo Starr*

Despite the harsher acoustic and percussive treatment of earlier takes[103] (*Anthology 2*), the finished version has a much softer, lighter feel, in part to the prominence of the ride cymbal and snare. A laid-back nonchalant feel in the great Ringo fashion of playing ever so slightly *behind* the beat. With the dominant created illusion of space, single and double strokes on the ride cymbals round off the chorus [1.09] and [1.58], simple tom fills providing the bridge [1.23] and [2.11] to the verse. The steady drum groove displays the Beatles moving ever deeper into experimental territory. Float upstream indeed.

Love You To

Time Signature – 4/4
Recorded – April 11/13 1966
Tambourine – *Ringo Starr*
Tabla – Anil Bhagwat

Percussive duties were handled by Anil Bhagwat improvising on tabla, with Ringo supplying simple tambourine time-keeping. The shock of such a departure from the norm must have been difficult to comprehend for Beatles fans (with the probable exception of those in the Indian Sub-Continent, of course).

Here, There, and Everywhere

Time Signature – 4/4
Recorded – June 14/16/17 1966
Drums, Finger Clicks – *Ringo Starr*
Finger-Clicks – *Paul McCartney, George Harrison, John Lennon*

A sympathetic, tender treatment by Starr, perfectly complimenting the nature of the song which is McCartney's personal favourite of his own compositions. After an interesting expositional first two bars in 9/8 and 7/8, deft touches on the tom usher in the first verse. This treatment is mirrored throughout, with the addition of a similarly gentle crash cymbal at pertinent points.

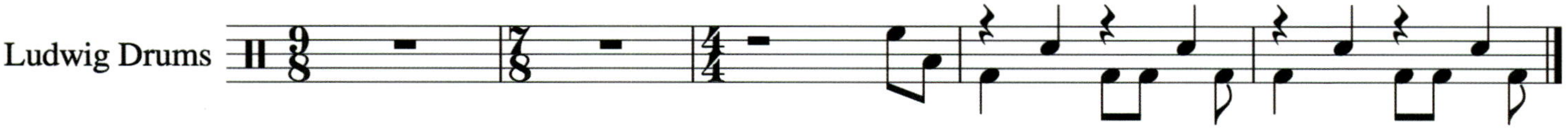

To achieve such control over his drums and cymbals, Ringo employed a combination of both sticks (for the drums) and overdubbed brushes (for the cymbals), the cymbal strokes in particular requiring too much reserve and finesse for sticks to have been employed. Making their solitary appearance on a Beatles recording, finger-clicks (playing 2 and 4 in the bar) play over the snare on the final chorus. Notice how the finger clicks are presented differently in the mono and stereo mixes, the mono version here displaying the care and attention deserving of the song -

The stereo mix however, displays a clumsiness that is usually indicative of the lack of involvement by any of the Beatles, yet both mono and stereo mixes were completed on Tuesday June 21st 1966, with the group in attendance. The finger clicks within the stereo mix appear and disappear seemingly due to an engineer fading up that particular track too early, perhaps realising his mistake, quickly dropping and again raising the fader?

Yellow Submarine

Time Signature – 4/4
Recorded – May 26, June 1 1966
Drums – *Ringo Starr*
Bass Drum – *Mal Evans*

What is there to say about *Yellow Submarine,* a song almost every child born since the Sixties has been nurtured on, and which still divides opinion? Ringo's famous back-beat enlivens the chorus, driving it along by means of a forceful bass drum. From the final chorus [2.03] to the fade-out, trusted roadie Mal Evans donned a marching bass drum, and led the procession of session guests (including Marianne Faithfull and Brian Jones) around Studio 2, thumping the drum as he went. Stamping feet weave in and out of the mix, although in fact the sound was achieved by placing coal in boxes, and moving them back and forth.

She Said, She Said

Time Signature – 4/4, 3/4
Recorded – June 21 1966
Drums, Shaker – *Ringo Starr*

Over the preceding year or so, the likes of Keith Moon of the Who, and the many proponents of the burgeoning Blues and formative psychedelic scenes had 'upped the drumming game', so to speak. It was no longer deemed acceptable to lay down a simple beat for the other musicians to weave their magic upon. It's also entirely plausible Ringo may have felt the need to be more adventurous on this track, as there are only three Beatles present – Harrison taking over bass guitar duties from the absent and apparently grumpy McCartney. As a result, the solid and unadventurous bass lines offer little in the way of rhythmical quality. And so we have fantastic, blistering drumming from Ringo, all the more impressive when the song could easily have been played as a straight 4/4 rocker (save for the 3/4 on the middle 8), with the occasional fill.

None of that here, with Ringo displaying some of his finest work, possibly topping his earlier work on *Rain?* Mirroring *Taxman*, it's this lack of hi-hats on the main body of the song that enable Ringo to launch himself into his fills, his hesitant snare work as he moves around his kit [0.08, bar 5 below] and [0.30] are inspired, and perfectly sets-up his heavy cymbal crashes.

As mentioned, the middle 8 sections utilise a simple beat, with hi-hats employed for the only time in the song. The transition from 4/4 time to 3/4 [0.57] and [1.39] is seamless, as is the shift to the hurried bars of the fade [2.20] with heavily struck cymbal.

One of the quirks of *She Said She Said* is the fact that once again the Beatles fell short of the requisite 14 tracks for the new album. Considered by some fans to be their finest 'Rock' offering, it's nothing short of incredible what the group could conjure up at short notice, under such pressure, with only 3 members present.

Good Day Sunshine

Time Signature – 4/4, 3/4, 5/5
Recorded – June 8/9 1966
Drums, Tambourine, Handclaps – *Ringo Starr*
Handclaps – *Paul McCartney, George Harrison, John Lennon*

On first hearing, this is essentially a simple drum track, however it does contain fairly complex elements, for example the chorus alternates between 3/4 and 5/4 bars. *Good Day Sunshine* is perhaps the finest example of what was expected of Ringo at this stage of his career as a Beatle. Due to the rather sparse arrangement and slow tempo, it was obviously deemed necessary to bolster the backing track with as much percussion as possible. Ringo laid down the basic simple drum beat along with the other Beatles, adding cymbal, snare and rim-clicks the following day. All four Beatles contributed handclaps, with an extra tambourine thrown in for good measure. The best way to hear this sequence of recordings, and to differentiate between them, is to listen to the ubiquitous stereo mix. Simply put, the overdubs are placed on the right hand channel, the earlier basic recording on the left. The bars below illustrate the gradual development of percussion on the track, best typified by the chorus. The first 2 bars here show the basic track of drums as laid down by Ringo on Wednesday June 8 1966. Tambourine again makes an appearance, perhaps played by John or George, as there appears to be only one guitar present?

Next we have the following day's addition [by Ringo] of bass drum and crash cymbal.

Finally, the complete percussion track with contributions from all four Beatles.

Due in part to the clumsy mixing limitations of the day, the resulting stereo mix is occasionally a slightly jarring mishmash of rhythm, however to the untrained ear the song flows along nicely, especially the case when listening in mono. Whilst it is not impossible to play these rhythms together live, it does however take a fair degree of dexterity to achieve. At the point where the overdubs kick-in on the chorus, play the single snare beat with one hand, using the other to accent the cymbal crashes in tandem with the bass drum.

And Your Bird Can Sing

Time Signature – 4/4
Recorded – April 20/26 1966
Drums, Tambourine, Handclaps – *Ringo Starr*
Handclaps – *Paul McCartney, George Harrison, John Lennon*

Ditching the busier '8 in the bar' hi-hat feel (bar one above) of earlier takes in favour of a '4 in the bar' (bar two), along with the twin-guitar lead, McCartney's busy bass again provides most of the energy. Overdubs (again in the right channel) include improvised tambourine throughout, open and closing hi-hats and handclaps on the bridge [0.36], off-beat on the first dual guitar solo [0.51].

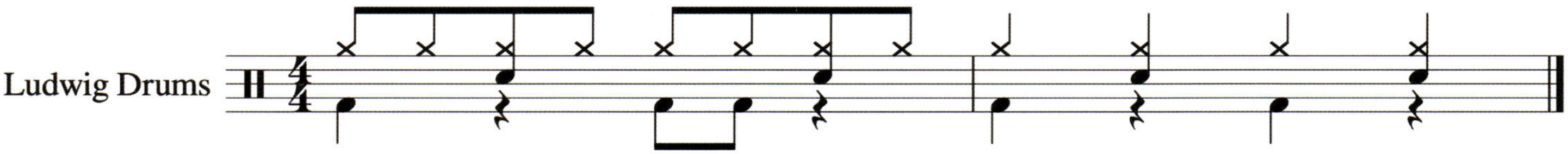

Of note is the placing of the tambourine on the first and third beats of the final passage of the repeated guitar break, providing a counterpoint to the guitar stabs.

For No One

Time Signature – 4/4
Recorded – May 9/16/19 1966
Drums, Tambourine – *Ringo Starr*

After the exuberance of *And Your Bird Can Sing*, Ringo again plays a subtle, understated pattern, which is so low in the mix, it is barely detectable. Like *Good Day Sunshine* the drums and percussion appear in the right channel of the stereo mix.

In stark contrast to the completed version, earlier takes see Ringo deftly but boldly playing bass drum, snare and ride cymbal -

This was soon replaced by the progression illustrated below.

After the 8 bar first verse, Ringo changes direction, utilising an open hi-hat to fill the gaps between snare strokes.

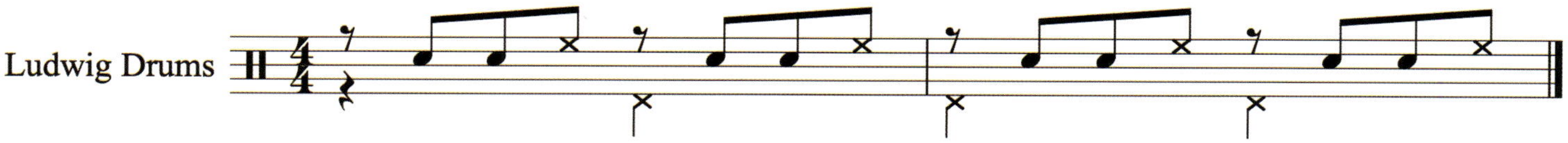

For the chorus, it appears McCartney settled for a variation on both patterns, perhaps placing the earlier full drum kit performance (or a subsequent recording) underneath a variant on the preceding verses. There is a twist though, this time the open hi-hat falls with the snare, reinforcing the purposeful accented tambourine.

However, the percussive contribution is non intrusive, supporting Paul's lovelorn lyric and the mournful French horn solo beautifully, perfectly swaying around the melody of the vocals, and bonding to the forthright piano.

Dr. Robert

Time Signature – 4/4
Recorded – April 17/19 1965
Drums – *Ringo Starr*
Maracas – *George Harrison*

Playing a simple beat on snare and bass embellished with the usual 'dry' maracas overdub (this time from Harrison), Ringo's ace up the sleeve is again keeping things simple, allowing the song to flow and negotiating the many chord changes throughout. The only concession is the busy bass drum pattern, which snakes around McCartney's bass line with ease.

I Want To Tell You

Time Signature – 4/4
Recorded – June 2/3 1966
Drums, Handclaps – *Ringo Starr*
Handclaps – *Paul McCartney, George Harrison, John Lennon*
Tambourine, Maracas – *John Lennon*

Unusually beginning with a (distantly mixed) single snare beat set within the framework of Harrison's guitar riff, Ringo allows the bass to provide much of the percussive urgency, whilst his bass drum is negligible (on the stereo mix). The snare is joined early on by single tambourine taps and a shaking maraca, announcing the vocal at [0.11], mimicked at [0.33], [0.53], [1.29] and [2.04]. With simple tom rolls linking verses, he lets fly with alternating snare/tom beats after the bridge linking the chorus, the ferocity of the attack coming as quite a shock after the subtlety of the preceding fills [1.09] and [1.45].

The tambourine[104] patterns prove interesting, with single beats up until the middle 8 passages, where they are played on the first, and then first and second beats at [0.57] and [1.33]. From the final verse we have strong multiple handclaps [1.48], with random tambourine on the play-out, leading the song to it's wailing conclusion. There is a possible mixing error in the stereo mix at [0.36], a rogue handclap quickly being pulled-out?

Got To Get You Into My Life

Time Signature – 4/4
Recorded – April 7/8/11, May 18, June 17/20 1966
Drums, Tambourine – *Ringo Starr*

A great example of Ringo's (and the Beatles) 'less is more' attitude to drums. It is worth comparing the original version with that of Cliff Bennett & the Rebel Rouser's contemporary hit cover version – Mick Burt's more upfront drumming may be technically superior and a damn sight more exciting (especially live), but it can also prove somewhat 'over-egged'. The Beatles' version has the drums taking a back-seat, a clue to this laid-back approach is in the mono version, where the drums sit low in the mix, the song being driven along by overdubbed tambourine and the closely miked brass section. Perhaps it is the simplistic hi-hat counting, but on the Stereo Mix, Ringo's fills that precede the 2nd verse [0.33] and top and tail the chorus [1.01] and [1.40] seem tame and timid by comparison, but by way of contrast bind the track together to great effect on the mono mix. A sense of urgency after the superb guitar bridge [1.49] seems to wake Ringo from his slumber, his hesitant off-beat snare work [2.01] and more adventurous tom fills [2.08] [2.19] and [2.23] livening up the play-out.

Tomorrow Never Knows
Time Signature – 4/4
Recorded – April 6/7/22 1966
Drums, Tambourine – *Ringo Starr*

Pre-dating the use of drum loops by some 20 years, *Tomorrow Never Knows* pushes Ringo and his drum kit to the forefront of the mix. The relentless, repetitive pattern, played with such feel and solidity by Starr, is taken to a different level by Geoff Emerick's groundbreaking engineering – the close microphone technique, the removal of the bottom skins and slackened-off tuning of Ringo's drums combining to provide a sonic depth hitherto absent from the record collections of the buying public. Add to this the employment of an almost overloaded signal and heavy compression, and the effect we are left with is truly mesmerising.

As a work in progress, Take 1 of *Tomorrow Never Knows*[105] possesses a less striking drum pattern, with none of the driving tom-tom work of the final release. By comparison, the toms are replaced by sixteenth note ride cymbal, plus, bringing a halt to the rhythm, simultaneous snare strikes, illustrated below -

Tomorrow Never Knows sees Ringo utilising his ambidextrous ability to the full. By maintaining right – handed constant eighth notes on the ride cymbal, he draws powerful sixteenth note beats from the tom-tom with his left hand. With this approach Ringo is able to draw more sound from his cymbal than he would otherwise have been able to if he had struck the tom-tom with each hand, keeping the track awash with sound.

Here we have the simple, repetitive drum track, with the tambourine patterns deliberately providing variety throughout as the song progresses -

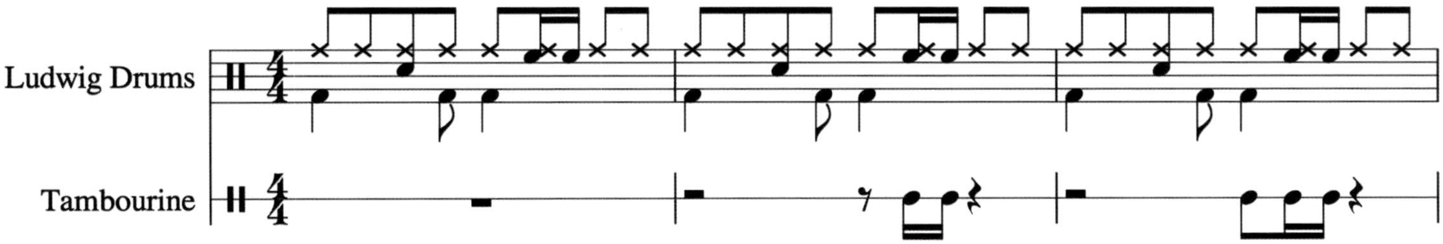

For many, *Tomorrow Never Knows* proved to be a polarising moment, you were either 'with it' or not. Ask Don Draper[106].

Eleanor Rigby/Yellow Submarine
Single – Released August 5 1966
Engineer – *Geoff Emerick*

This double A-side single, released on the same day as Revolver, is unique in that it is the only original Beatles single not to feature a performance on a conventional drum kit.

21. Strawberry Fields Forever / Penny Lane

Single – Released February 17 1967

Engineer – *Geoff Emerick/Dave Harries*

In May 1966 the Beach Boys released their new album *Pet Sounds*. This jewel of creativity was not lost on the Beatles and it certainly had some bearing when, in November 1966 they moved into the studio to start recording their next album[107], which was to be intended to be a reminiscent look at the group's early life in Liverpool. Allied to this, the band came off the road for good in August 1966, their concert at Candlestick Park proving to be their last. A direct consequence of the Beatles spending more time in the studio was the increased length of time between releases. There would soon be a six month gap between the last single (*Eleanor Rigby/Yellow Submarine*) and the next, and with a new album some time away, the already completed songs *Strawberry Fields Forever* and *Penny Lane* were plucked from the new project[108]. And what a shock it was too – a brand new direction, not only in sound, but in image, with moustaches very much in evidence.

Strawberry Fields Forever

Time Signature – 4/4, 2/4, 3/4
Recorded – 24/28/29 November, December 21/22, 1966
Drums – *Ringo Starr*
Bongos – *John Lennon*
Maracas – *George Harrison, Terry Doran*
Tambourine – *Mal Evans*
Guiro – *Neil Aspinall*

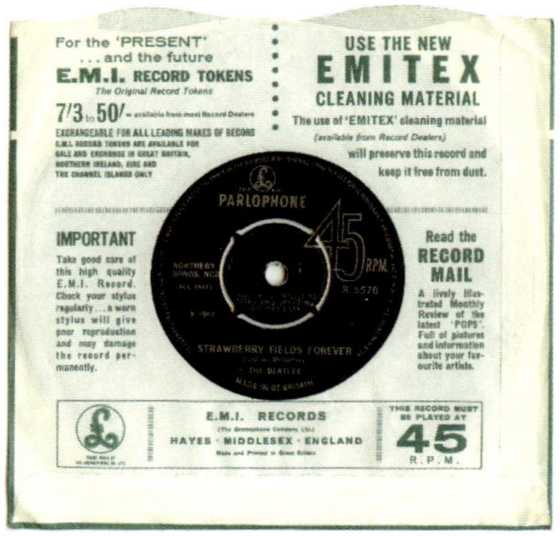

With *Strawberry Fields Forever* we hear the Beatles (and arguably the EMI staff) reaching the peak of their creative powers, and with Ringo very much to the fore, he proves he's not just along for the ride. Fresh from the sonic innovations of the Revolver sessions, *Strawberry Fields Forever* benefits greatly from Geoff Emerick's tweaking of (and experimentation with) Ringo's drum kit.

However, all is not as it may appear. With Emerick and Martin not yet present at Abbey Road, the impatient, waiting Beatles were keen to record. After he had set the microphones, Technical Engineer Dave Harries risked the wrath of George Martin by both engineering and producing the start of the session. Emerick was less than impressed with Harries' recording of Ringo's cymbals, singling out the prominence of treble, or 'top-end'. However, it is perhaps this quality that makes the drum track shine, the cymbals providing a counterpoint to the close-miking of the toms, giving the track a richness and depth that serve to enhance the impact of George Martin's string score. Ringo's fills display a weight and touch purely sympathetic to the song. Which is just as well – as Ringo (probably under instruction) declines to fill-out the song with the usual steady beat – hi-hats are entirely absent, relying upon bass and snare drums to keep time. Unusual for a Beatles record (of any period), tambourine (here played by Mal Evans[109]) is largely absent – instead we have maracas, prominent in the mix from the start, taking the place usually reserved for hi-hats.

After the Mellotron 'flute' introduction from Paul, drums enter the fray with a nice loose fill over two bars, before moving into a solid snare and bass drum beat. These rich, languid fills punctuate throughout, the interplay between toms and snare [0.14] and [1.43] particularly notable. As hinted at the song's introduction (below), just when you thought the song was settling into a straight 4/4 measure, the meter is dictated by the evocative lyrics (bars 11-14 below) -

The completed release of 'Strawberry Fields Forever' is a composite of two versions differing in tempo cleverly masked not only by Geoff Emerick's quite brilliant edit [0.59 – across "go-ing to"], but also Ringo's hurried drum fill. When coupled with a variation in tape speed, the change in tempo adds to the deception perfectly.

Additionally for good measure, at [2.11], in the absence of drums or percussion, and providing the rhythm and purpose, George Martin introduces Lennon's current 'flavour of the month' – the recording of a cymbal-strike looped and played backwards. At [2.32] we have the addition of overdubbed and accented snare, beefing-up the already busy drum track.

Ringo's bass drum punctuation of the chorus (bars 13 and 14 above) is mirrored by floor tom at the songs finale, preceding the lengthy instrumental coda. With the 'kitchen sink' philosophy typical of the Beatle use of percussion during this period, Ringo is given licence to add as much colour as possible, a task made all the easier by multiple overdubs by the Beatles and their entourage. With more than a little help from his friends, we hear a busy 16th note dampened bass drum (or turned on its side floor-tom) overdubbed during the choruses and the fade in/out -

3
Ludwig Drums
Maracas
Tom Toms
Tambourine
Snare Drum
Tap
6
Ludwig Drums
Maracas
Tom Toms
Tambourine
Snare Drum
Tap

The extraordinary play-out features tambourines, timpani, maracas, bongos, backwards-cymbal tapes, but alas, no detectable kitchen sink. Incredible stuff. As above, presented here are the prominent instruments, namely maracas, tambourine, and tom-tom.

A game-changing song, no doubt.

On the cusp of Hippiedom – Ringo pictured at home, January 1967

Penny Lane

Time Signature – 4/4
Recorded – December 29/30, 1966. January 4-6, 9-10, 12,17, 1967.
Engineer – *Geoff Emerick*
Drums, Tambourine, Handclaps – *Ringo Starr*
Handclaps – *Paul McCartney, George Harrison, John Lennon*
Congas – *John Lennon*
Handbell – *George Harrison?*[110]

A complete contrast to the performance on the flip-side, *Penny Lane* sees Ringo keep it simple once again – providing a solid, yet lazy back-beat on this McCartney dominated piece (the track features just these 2 Beatles on instrumentation – Lennon contributes backing vocals and handclaps, the latter seemingly Harrison's only contribution). The key to understanding the percussive track on *Penny Lane* is the process that was taken while recording. McCartney began by layering the piano track, which then saw the addition of tambourine. The drum track arrived later, the tambourine presumably to provide a constant for the earlier instrumental recordings.

As a result, Penny Lane is an excellent example of Paul McCartney's percussive song construction, laid-out thus:

Intro – Lightly struck opening and closing hi-hats keep time on the 2nd beat of the bar. A hint of hi-hat time keeping, seemingly obscured by the piano.

Verse – Introduced by a snare/tom fill (0.17), a simple snare beat followed by a return to the hi-hats of the opening bars. A laid-back, simplistic solo snare, until returning to the open/closed hi-hats -

Ludwig Drums

0.13

Chorus – Simplicity itself – bass and snare drum. At [0.45], the drum track is given more prominence by being increased in the mix.

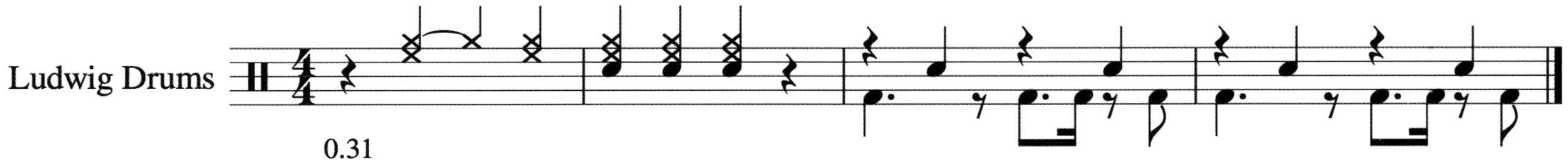

Verse – Tambourine joins the snare, with the relaxed open hi-hat and fill of the introduction. Linking the bridge to the conga embellished trumpet solo [1.08] is a double – triplet hand bell, one of the last overdubs on the track -

Throughout the remainder of the song, the perception of pace and purpose is maintained, with busier bass drum than earlier, but still only accompanied by snare. However, there is a hint[111] of the snare being possibly enhanced with a corresponding beat on the floor tom?

We soon return to the solo snare and tambourine [1.42], before a sense of drama is added by the snare's replacement at [1.49] with the open hi-hat motif we saw earlier. Curiously, perhaps to maintain a flow, McCartney places a single, stray tambourine beat in the mix [2.16].

More forceful drumming (again brought to the front of the mix) sees us to the resolution, the final flourish of ride cymbal.

All of this occurs with the listener being largely unaware of the subtle differences in each passage, especially in the still largely mono world of 1967.

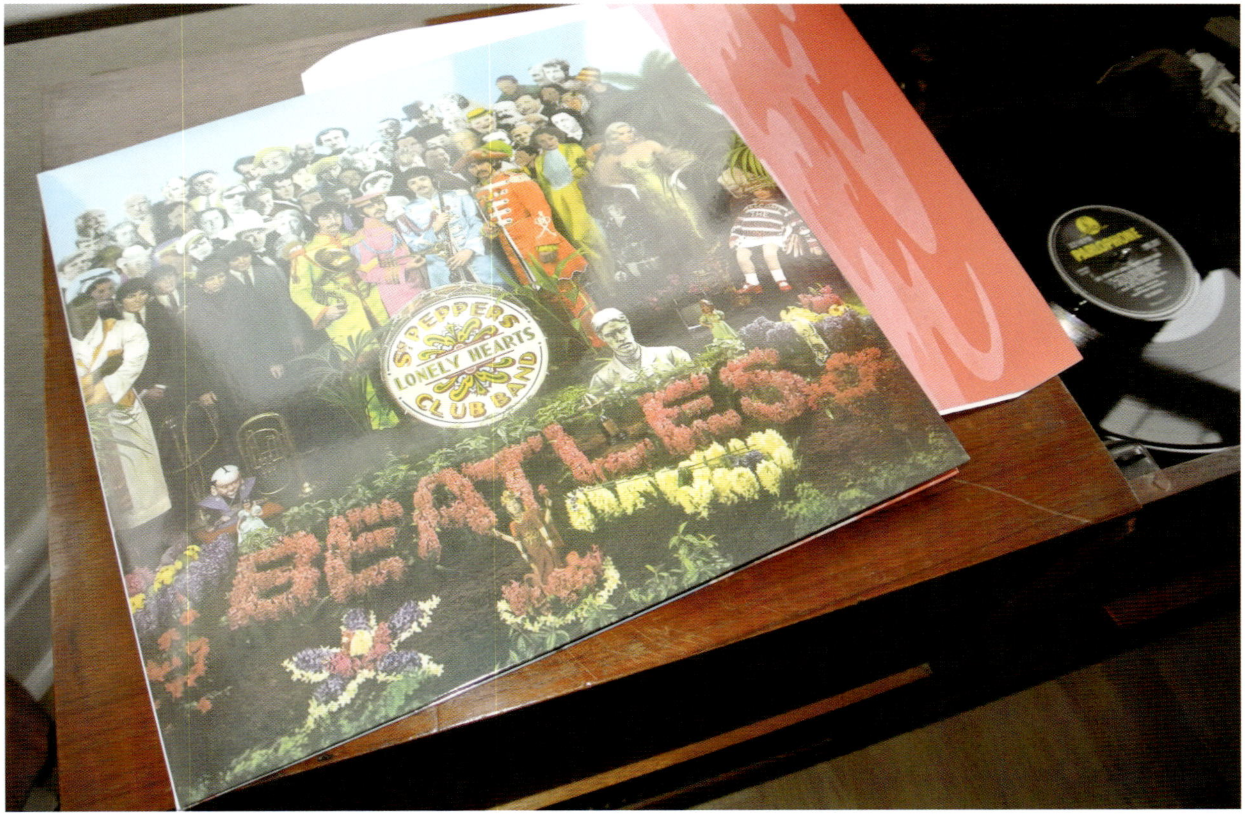

22. Sgt. Pepper's Lonely Hearts Club Band

LP – Released June 1 1967

Engineers – *Geoff Emerick, Adrian Ibbetson, Malcolm Addey, Ken Townsend*

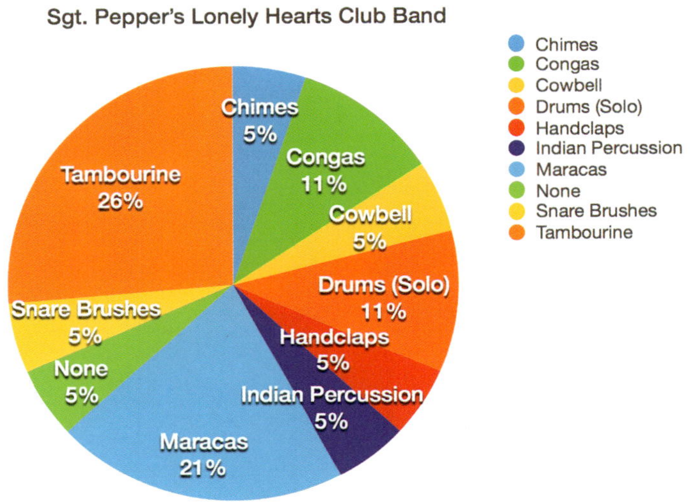

13 Songs

INSTRUMENT	USE
Chimes	1
Congas	2
Cowbell	1
Drums (Solo)	2
Handclaps	1
Indian Percussion	1
Maracas	4
None	1
Snare Brushes	1
Tambourine	5

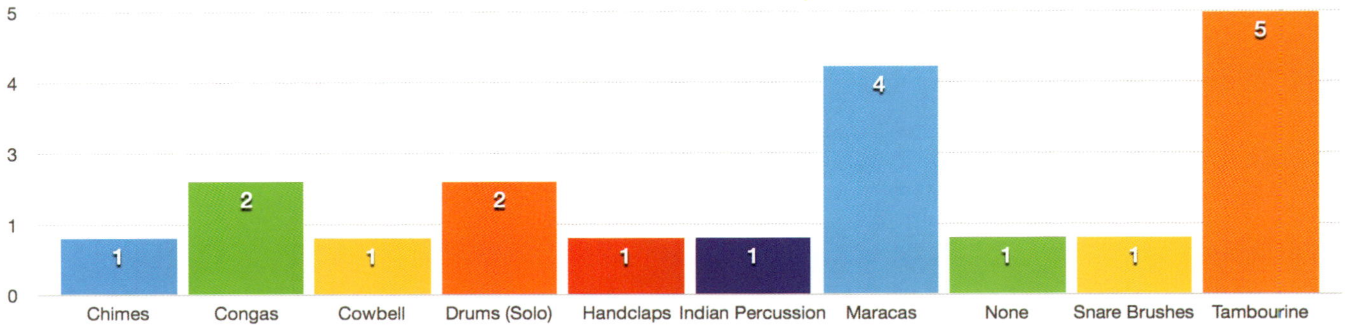

After the disruption of having two tracks of their new album 'pulled' for their next single (*Strawberry Fields Forever* and *Penny Lane*), the Beatles pressed on regardless, their enthusiasm still intact. Ringo's drumming again displayed the evolutionary steps taken throughout their recording careers. Enhancing and tweaking the work on Revolver, most of the engineering techniques in evidence on *Sgt. Pepper's Lonely Hearts Club Band* would become industry standard, overnight everybody HAD to have that sound.

Sgt. Pepper's Lonely Hearts Club Band

Time Signature – 4/4

Recorded – February 1/2, March 3/6, 1967. **Engineer** – *Geoff Emerick*

Drums – *Ringo Starr*

The immediacy of the ponderous groove, eschewing hi-hats or cymbals from the 'off', sets the tone for the album. A stark bass and snare combination is soon joined by floor tom on the first verse, and while this approach in some regards mirrors *Taxman* (the first track of the preceding LP *Revolver*), the execution and feel is relaxed rather than urgent. When added to the removal of the bottom skins of the toms, plus the damping, close miking and heavy compression of Ringo's drums, the resulting sound we are left with is enthralling, the perfect foil for McCartney's shrill guitar stabs and vocal.

Note the 'dotted' quaver in the final bar above, a superb example of Ringo's unique style and technique. Being left-handed yet playing a right handed drum kit, and therefore 'leading' around his drums with his left hand, Ringo instinctively leaves a 'space' as he shifts position to use his left hand first, as opposed to a right-handed drummer effortlessly leading with his right hand. A dotted quaver is essentially 3/4 of a beat, as a quaver (1/8th note) is 1/2 a beat, the addition of a dot (1/4 beat). How different would the Beatles have sounded with a 'conventional' right or left-handed drummer?

Ringo's touch is oh-so deft on the horn section [0.42], it's entirely possible to envisage him being conducted from the orchestra pit. Not heard for some time, his 'swishy' hi-hats are the perfect foil to the incredibly 'heavy' (for the day) guitars of the chorus [0.55]. Trademark fills [1.49] & [1.55] take us to the bridge and Ringo's album showcase, the first in particular mimicking the phonetics of the vocal. What's perhaps most interesting about the title track, is the complete lack of any overdubbed percussion[112]. It had become the norm for Beatles' recordings to be layered in percussive instruments, but with their love of emerging acts such as The Jimi Hendrix Experience, perhaps they felt a harsher, more organic live 'performance' would strike the right note for the new album, or perhaps they were simply attempting to portray a 'live' performance of Sgt. Pepper's Band, somewhat ironic as they had now forsaken live performances?

With A Little Help From My Friends

Time Signature – 4/4
Recorded – March 29/30, 1967. **Engineer** – *Geoff Emerick*
Drums, Tambourine – *Ringo Starr*
Cowbell – *John Lennon*

Ringo's prominence and importance to a new Beatles' album took on a new twist with *Sgt.Pepper*, never before had he been featured so early into an album, nor would he again. As if to reinforce this, his introduction 'in character' as Billy Shears allows him the spotlight, his entrance preceded with '4's' on his snare followed by a brisk roll on timpani [0.04]. His gentle side is on show here, opening his hi-hats where needed, while lazily and deftly tapping his bass drum, a counterpoint alongside McCartney's sometimes 'punchy' bass. Again we have the gentle progression and 'build' of the drum track. Merely tickling the hi-hats from the start (first bar below), Ringo doesn't feel the need to introduce the snare until the second line of the first verse (2nd bar below), followed by the addition of a gentle tambourine and barely audible bass drum at the start of the chorus (bars 3 and 4 below).

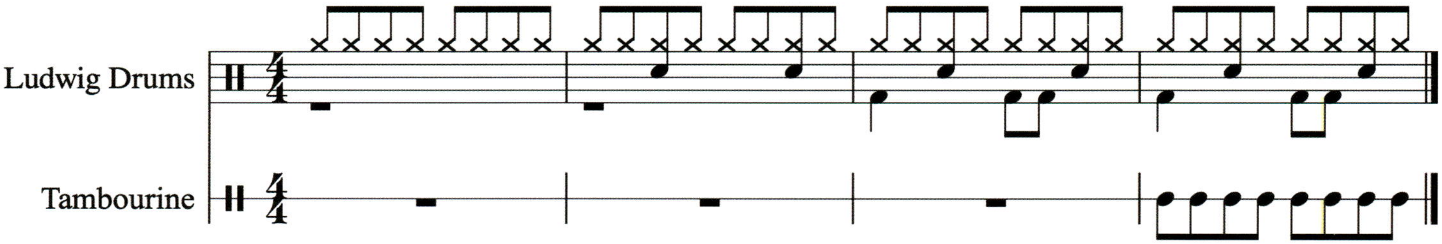

Ringo's signature fill (3rd bar, below), is a lovely two-bar loose and open affair, the feel of which probably had more to do with the (increasingly) late-night recording sessions employed by the band?

Tambourine, heavily mixed throughout, beefs-up the chorus. The working title of *'With A Little Help From My Friends'* was *Badfinger Boogie*, illustrating the 'boogie' feel of the song was foremost on the Beatles' agenda during the song's recording, which also provided forthcoming Apple act *Badfinger* with their name.

Lucy In The Sky With Diamonds

Time Signature – 3/4, 4/4
Recorded – February 28, March 1/2, 1967. **Engineer** – *Geoff Emerick*
Drums, Maracas- *Ringo Starr*

A feature of John Lennon's songwriting (and especially true of his work around the time of Sgt. Pepper) was his use of different time signatures within a single song. As we have seen previously, it was not an intentional ploy, the process came entirely naturally to him, the more extreme examples simply to make lyrics fit the framework of the song. On *Lucy In The Sky With Diamonds,* he employs a basic structure of 3/4 on the verses, switching to 4/4 on the chorus. The movement towards this is achieved by utilising vocals to slip back to the 4/4, following three basic, jarring beats on the tom.

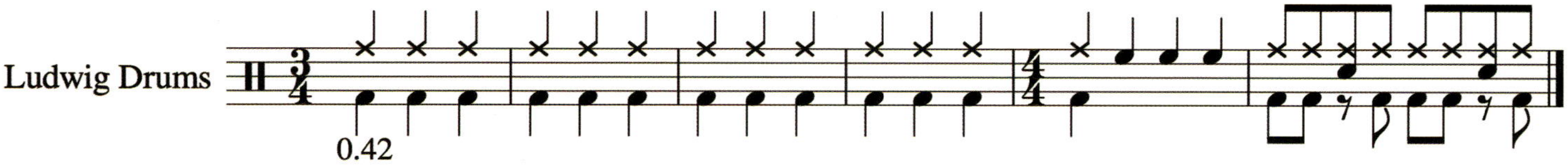

Ringo's handling of the 3/4 meter is particularly marked by the use of brushes on increasingly busy open hi-hats and ride cymbal that echo and compliment Harrison's dreamlike tambura. McCartney's bass again provides much of the urgency, while Ringo enlivens (perhaps through boredom) the final 4/4 section with extra eighth note tom and snare strokes at [2.42 & 2.56], the latter illustrated below.

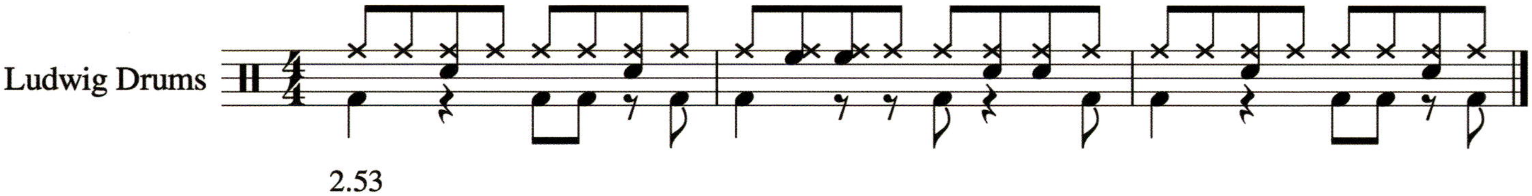

Getting Better

Time Signature – 4/4
Recorded – March 9/10/21/23, 1967. **Engineers** – *Malcolm Addey, Ken Townsend, Peter Vince*
Drums, Congas, Handclaps – *Ringo Starr*
Handclaps – *Paul McCartney, George Harrison, John Lennon*

With Geoff Emerick enjoying a well-earned night off due to enduring one too many late-night Beatle sessions, engineering duties fell to Malcolm Addey and Ken Townsend. As a result, the drums possess a more open sound than Emerick's recent recordings. Peter Vince engineered the last (vocal) session for the track. Beginning with harsh, forceful, choppy, guitar strokes, the emphasis here is on perceived shifting rhythms. The guitar is joined by electric piano in creating unity as off-beat rhythms are employed later in the song. As has now become the norm, the song opens with the chorus, Ringo cutting into the last 4 beats of the 3rd bar with simple military style snare beats echoing the vocal phrasing. Swiftly moving on to the first verse (bar 5) he alternates bass and snare on the first 3 beats, with a surprising accented strike of his hi-hat before the 4th beat.

Leaving the last beat lingering on the hi-hat enables the song to apparently shift time into the chorus. The tambura-rich bridge [1.35] displays the typical 'Pepper period' use of percussion – basic '4 in the bar' hi-hats joined by off-beat congas and handclaps -

The final verse sees a simple hi-hat beat tapped out, with the off-beat congas again prominent in the mix. All this in 2 minutes, 48 seconds.

Fixing A Hole

Time Signature – 4/4
Recorded – February 9/21, 1967. **Engineers** – *Adrian Ibbetson, Geoff Emerick*
Drums, Maracas – *Ringo Starr*

Picking up the tempo from George Martin's introductory harpsichord, Ringo provides a functional beat, cleverly alternating between a shuffle and a straight 4/4. A foretaste of things to come, he uses his hi-hats to great effect, allowing them to 'hang' [1.04 & 1.22] before once again swiftly picking up the beat. Maracas are present, although buried in the mix.

As with the previous track (*Getting Better*) the drums sound a little distant, but this time because (save for overdubs), *Fixing A Hole* was the first Beatles track to be recorded away from Abbey Road, which was unavailable at short notice, even for the Beatles. As the EMI Engineers were contracted to work exclusively at Abbey Road, Geoff Emerick was unable to take the trip across town to Regent Sound Studios. The result is a departure from the close mic techniques employed by Emerick on the rest of the album. Hi-hats are prominent, the bass drum lacks punch, while the snare is at times almost imperceptible. In truth, it doesn't sound like Ringo's Ludwig kit – it may possibly have been Regent's 'in-house' set, possibly a Premier, or Gretsch?

She's Leaving Home

Time Signature – 4/4
Recorded – March 17/20, 1967. **Engineer** – *Geoff Emerick*

No drums or percussion, just John & Paul sat around a mic in a moodily-lit Abbey Road. What a great image to conjure up while listening to the song?

Being For The Benefit Of Mr. Kite

Time Signature – 4/4

Recorded – February 17/20, March 28/29/31, 1967. **Engineer** – *Geoff Emerick*

Drums, Tambourine, Maracas/Shaker – *Ringo Starr*

Illustrated in the opening bars above, *Being For The Benefit Of Mr Kite* sees Ringo interpreting the Victorian fairground imagery to perfection. From the opening 2 bars of exposition on dampened toms and bass drum, to providing a platform for the wheezing, foot powered harmonium, the listener is instantly transported to the circus tent. Continuing the theme of simple time keeping by utilising 'choked' hi-hats, not to mention announcing the verses with crush rolls on the snare (bar 3), he takes on the role of the orchestra-pit percussionist, emphasising the high in the mix hi-hats of the 4/4 verse (bar 4).

Below we can see Ringo seamlessly switching to Henry the Horse's 'waltz' (bar 2 below), much in the same vein as *We Can Work It Out,* as is the use of harmonium.

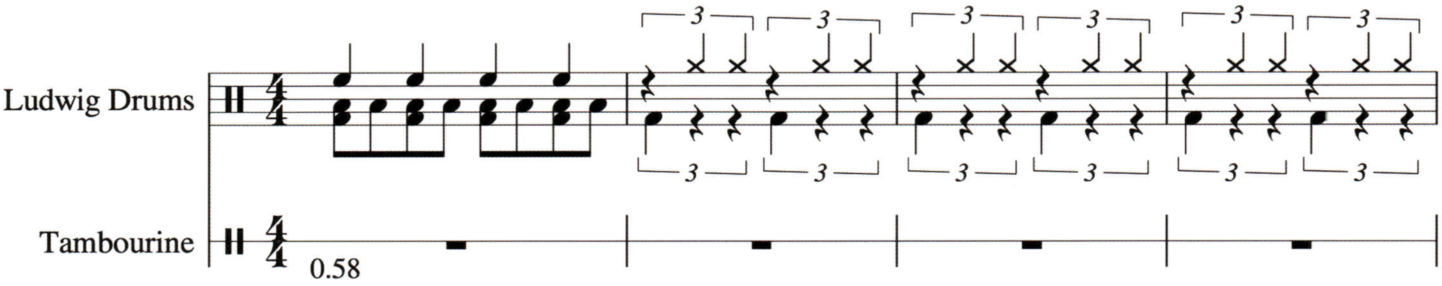

While to the ear this passage appears to be in 3/4 time, it is correct to interpret the meter here as continuing in 4/4 time – essentially 2 sets of triplets within a bar of 4/4. Percussive progression is not evident here, rather the discipline required to knit the various sections together, thus maintaining the fluidity of the song as it progresses. This is aided by the bass drum being tightly locked to McCartney's bass guitar, providing unity and purpose. Tambourine again enters the fray, increasingly prominent, displacing the hi-hats in the mix.

Within You, Without You

Time Signature – 4/4
Recorded – March 15/22, April 3/4, 1967. **Engineer** – *Geoff Emerick*

As is probably to be expected, the absence of Western percussion in *Within You Without You* leads to an extremely fluid arrangement. Indeed, after the instrumental break at [3.40], Harrison can be heard in an ad-hoc fashion counting in the final verse, presumably due to the song being recorded in 3 separate sections. George Martin's score binds the song together, staccato strings moving things along swiftly. Again, Geoff Emerick's close-microphone technique is in evidence, especially apparent on the mono mix.

When I'm Sixty Four

Time Signature – 4/4
Recorded – December 6/8/20/21,1966. **Engineer** – *Geoff Emerick*
Drums, Tubular Bells (Chimes) – *Ringo Starr*

It's back to the orchestra pit once more, with Ringo utilising wire brushes on his closely miked snare, effortlessly emulating the dance-hall style he grew up with. Playful use of the ride cymbal bell [0.57 & 1.48] provides a trade-off with the overdubbed tubular bells. Lovely stuff!

Lovely Rita

Time Signature – 4/4
Recorded – February 23/24, March 7/2, 1967. **Engineer** – *Geoff Emerick*
Drums – *Ringo Starr*
Guiro – *Unknown*

Characteristic drumming from Ringo, with his snare drum sitting gloriously behind the beat, trademark fills are interplayed between snare and toms [0.08, & 1.09], the latter providing a release from the tension of the build-up to the piano solo. The percussive element of the 'chicka-chicka' vocal [0.42], and the similar vocal exertions at the extended coda [2.14 to end] allow Ringo the luxury of providing a steady, almost languid back-beat, embellished [0.24-0.34] with what appears to be an anvil or probably something similar from the Abbey Road FX cupboard.

Always eager to add that little something extra, at [1.49] we have a lovely touch – a guiro coinciding with the lyrics 'wink' and 'think'.

The simple instinctive timekeeping on hi-hat, bass and snare [2.32 to end] became something of a trademark throughout Ringo's remaining Beatles career, probably best exemplified on *Hello Goodbye* and *Don't Let Me Down.*

Good Morning, Good Morning

Time Signature – 3/4, 4/4, 5/4
Recorded – February 8/16, March 18/28/29, 1967. **Engineer** – *Geoff Emerick*
Drums, Tambourine – *Ringo Starr*

'Good Morning, Good Morning' once again displays Lennon's unusual and instinctive sense of timing. While it may have appeared completely natural to him, there must have been some rubbing of hand on head from Ringo? Indeed, on an isolated track, perhaps in order to keep time, he can be faintly heard singing the song as he plays. As we have seen and will see again, the song doesn't possess the same time signature throughout – it has at it's core a 5/4 meter, with 3/4 used to connect the transition between 5/4 and 4/4.

This is illustrated below, and best described as:

5/4 Bar 5 – 'Nothing to do, to save his life'

5/4 Bar 6 – 'call his wife in'

5/4 Bar 7 – 'Nothing to say, but what a day'

3/4 Bar 8 **– '**How's your boy'

4/4 Bar 9 – 'been?'

5/4 Bar 10 – 'Nothing to do it's up to yo-'

4/4 Bar 11 – '-ou, I've got'

3/4 Bar 12 – 'nothing to say'

3/4 Bar 13 – 'but it's ok…good'

4/4 Bar 14 – 'morning, good morning, good morning -a'

Tight, forceful and explosive drumming coupled with the now familiar close-miking techniques enhance the sense of urgency and edginess of Lennon's vocal. Throughout, Ringo plays solidly on snare, bass drum and hi-hat, introducing a triplet feel on hi-hats during the bridge -

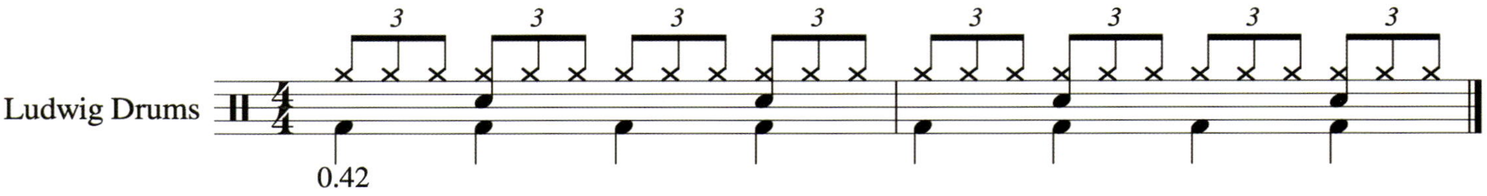

The second incarnation of the bridge (after the guitar solo) features a much busier drum track – Mark Lewisohn in his *Complete Beatles Recording Sessions* states this was achieved by overdubbing two bass drums, or as is perhaps the case, by simply beating a floor-tom or overturned bass drum, pretty believable as this would have been some feat to achieve with just a single pedal!

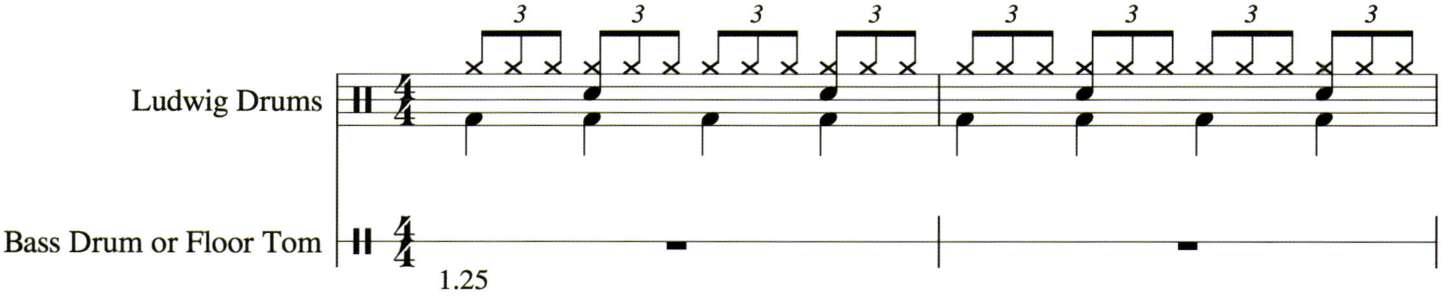

However this was achieved, Ringo turns in a very creditable performance, and anyone who has attempted to play this on *The Beatles Rock Band* will have been left in no doubt of the precision needed to pull off the demands of the song!

Sgt. Pepper's Lonely Hearts Club Band (Reprise)

Time Signature – 4/4
Recorded – April 1, 1967. **Engineer** – *Geoff Emerick*
Drums, Tambourine – *Ringo Starr*

Not so much of a reprise where the drumming is concerned, with Ringo playing a steady 4/4 beat (the first 4 bars, below), as the Beatles play live, huddled in a circle in the middle of the studio. High in the mix maracas sit on the first beat of the bar, increasing urgency. The somewhat clumsy fills [0.26] appear disjointed on the stereo version, however in mono there is a greater degree of unity due to the lack of separation and synergy with the overdubbed maracas.

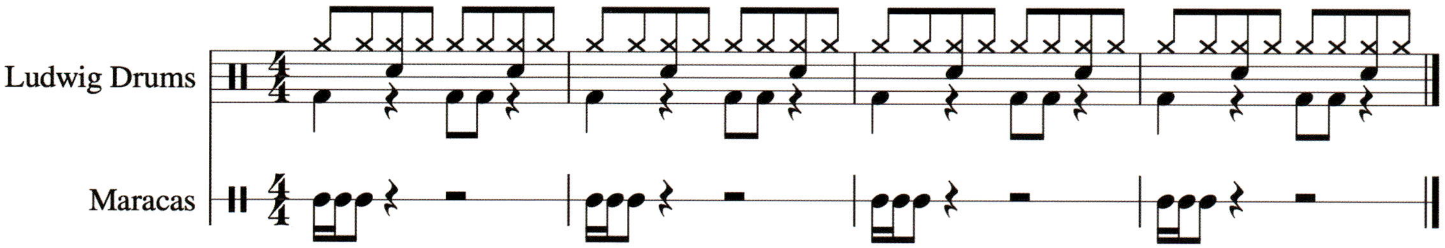

A Day In The Life

Time Signature – 4/4
Recorded – January 19, 20 February 3, 10, 22 1967. **Engineer** – *Geoff Emerick*
Drums, Congas – *Ringo Starr*
Maracas – *George Harrison*
Tambourine – *?*

While *A Day In The Life* is often regarded as Ringo's finest work, his performance is greatly enhanced by Engineer Geoff Emerick's treatment of his drum kit. Having recently and similarly experimented with Ringo's drums on *Tomorrow Never Knows* from *Revolver,* Emerick slackly-tuned the top drum skins, removed the bottom skins, and the front bass drum skin. Microphones were placed deep inside the drum shells, while the snare drum was similarly closely-miked. With heavy compression added to the drum track, Ringo's drums possessed a deeper, 'fatter', more open and powerful sound, lending a sense of drama and weight to the drums which would have been otherwise absent.

A great deal of Ringo's drumming on *Sgt. Pepper's Lonely Hearts Club Band* takes the form of simple time-keeping, and while *A Day In The Life* is no exception, Ringo plays with an empathy and creativity that befits the song. Mimicking the rhythmical nature of the lyrics, he perfectly places his drums alongside both Lennon and McCartney's vocals. With slight variation, his tom fills dominate, occasionally appearing unexpectedly from the shadows, punctuating and driving the song forward.

Following the simple and perhaps unusual combination of gentle '8 in the bar' maracas (played by Harrison) and subtle, low in the mix congas (Starr), Ringo introduces his drums in the second verse to great effect, subliminally referencing the sound of the car crash in the lyrics. Notice how in this first interjection, Ringo also imitates the cadence of the lyric *"He blew his mind out in a car",* a device that continues to be employed throughout.

Picking up the pace with snare that was previously absent in the bars between verses, McCartney's bass provides rhythmic variation. Congas are introduced and mixed at a low level.

From here on in, snare is gradually introduced between the increasingly hurried and tumbling tom fills, providing power and purpose, building towards the climactic orchestral rush. Congas are mixed out by the 5th bar below, maracas rather abruptly by the 6th bar. As this 'link' had yet to be decided upon when the drum track was recorded, Ringo knits the sections together by playing simple '4 in the bar' hi-hat beats, with occasional bass drum and cymbal crashes. 'Roadie' Mal Evans also keeps time by counting aloud, as congas and maracas are swiftly removed from the mix.

1.29

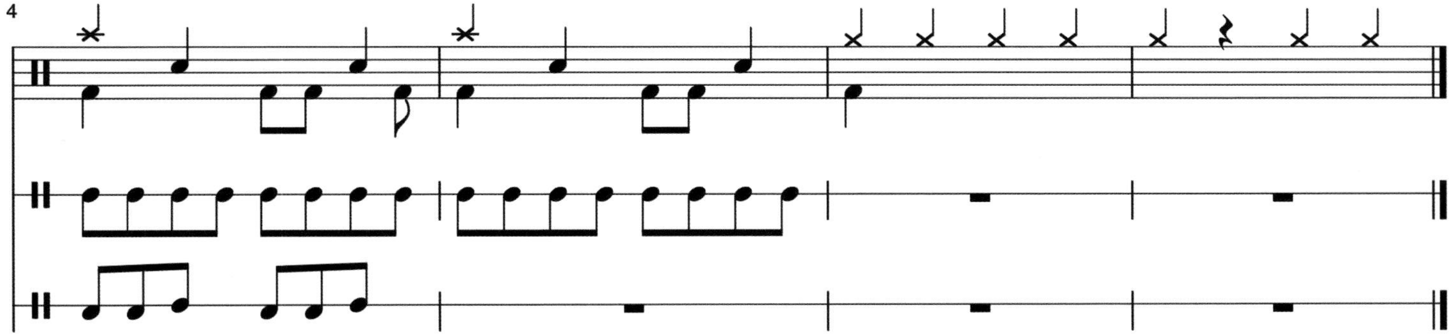

Ringo's in a playful mood on McCartney's jaunty middle section, a heavy '4 in the bar' snare leading us through the change in tempo. Alongside tambourine, swift bars of 2/4 are interjected to emphasise the hurried nature of the lyric.

2.18

By slipping out of the 4 beats of snare into 2 beats per bar, Ringo leads us back into the main body of the song, as if we are indeed drifting off into a dream.

The final verse sees Ringo engaging in a 'call and response' with Lennon's vocal phrasing, sometimes almost matching him consonant for consonant over John's "*Now they know how many holes it takes to fill the Albert Hall*" (bar 2, belɔw), with busking fills to the orchestral finale.

With the benefit of hindsight, *A Day In The Life* (and indeed the whole of *Sgt. Pepper's Lonely Hearts Club Band*) can be viewed as the pinnacle of the Beatles' creativity, with Ringo rising to the challenge magnificently. The other side of the coin is Ringo's recollection of recording the album as an opportunity to learn to play chess – he viewed his contribution as being 'another day in the office', nothing more, nothing less.

Ludwig Drums
Maracas

23. All You Need Is Love / Baby You're A Rich Man

Single – Released July 7 1967

Hot on the heels of *Sgt. Pepper's Lonely Hearts Club Band*, *All You Need Is Love* was released in what was referred to as the 'Summer of Love', even as it was happening – and 'Peace and Love' is still Ringo's mantra even today.[113]

All You Need Is Love
Time Signature – 3/4, 4/4
Recorded – June 14/19/23/24/25, 1967. **Engineers** – *Geoff Emerick, Eddie Kramer*
Drums – *Ringo Starr*
Handclaps, Various Percussion – *Audience*

All You Need Is Love sees Ringo playing live in front of a worldwide TV audience approaching an unprecedented 400 million, a daunting fact which may have inspired him to employ the simplest time-keeping possible. There is a common misconception that *All You Need Is Love* has a time signature of 7/4, however the song consists of alternating bars of 4/4 and 3/4, with the listener once again blissfully unaware as they hum their way through another Beatles classic. To illustrate this, the timings displayed below indicate the introductory bars after Ringo's snare roll [0.08], the first verse [0.26], the second verse [0.44], the chorus [1.01] and the first bar of George's guitar solo [1.19]. We have deliberately omitted the tambourine, as it only features lightly and sparingly between the verses, landing with the snare on the chorus, before being joined on the second chorus by handclaps to the end. Another classic case of using percussion to enhance and build the listening experience. There is also the merest hint of the hi-hat becoming '8 in the bar' along with the introduction of the tambourine, but again, it is so low in the mix and only present in the left channel to be rendered negligible.

Being able to see and count the song through as set out above, it becomes apparent why Ringo kept a simple, disciplined beat throughout. A single bar of 2/4 resolves the chorus, and introduces the guitar solo (sometimes interpreted with the previous 4/4 bar as a bar of 6/4). Quite what the learned members of the orchestra thought of it all, we can only guess.

Baby You're A Rich Man

Time Signature – 4/4
Recorded – May 11, 1967**. Engineers** – *Geoff Emerick, Keith Grant*
Drums, Tambourine, Maracas – *Ringo Starr*
Handclaps – *George Harrison*

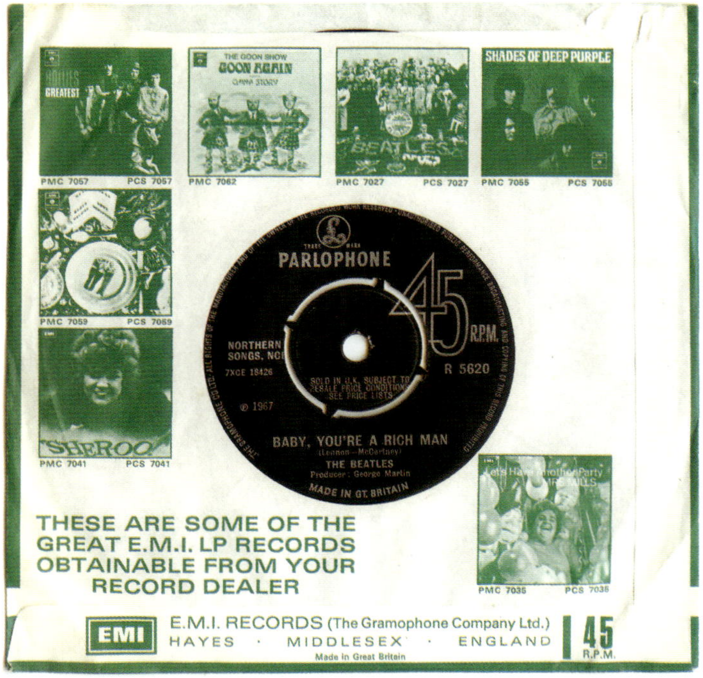

With such a forceful groove, and pre-dating the off-beat piano and driven 'dance music' boom of the late 80's by some 20 years, *Baby You're A Rich Man* was recorded away from Abbey Road at Olympic Studios. Due to this, the track has a different feel to the Beatles output of the time, the drums being no exception. The snare drives this song, there is no mistaking Ringo's distinctive snare work during the chorus – that fabulous 'slap echo' feel, with the cymbals also vibrant. Oddly, his bass drum is largely absent, much of the bottom end unsurprisingly taken up by McCartney's Rickenbacker bass, while Ringo's foot gently delivers.

But it's not just the drums that demand attention here, the Beatles really went to town with percussion on *Baby You're A Rich Man*.[114] Driven by prominent handclaps and tambourine, the ever so slightly 'trippy' rhythm track moves along with purpose. Again we hear Ringo's now trademark 'coming off the hi-hats' motif (bar 4 below, and also at [0.45 & 1.12], followed by some sloppy yet enchanting snare work [0.48 & 2.11]. 'The Boys' are clearly having fun here, one wonders how different their work would have sounded had they moved away from the confines of Abbey Road?

Ludwig Drums
Maracas
Tambourine
Hand Claps
5
Ludwig Drums
Maracas
Tambourine
Hand Claps

24. Hello Goodbye / I Am the Walrus

Single- Released November 24 1967

Hello Goodbye

Time Signature – 4/4
Recorded – October 2/19/25, November 2, 1967. **Engineers –** *Ken Scott, Geoff Emerick*
Drums, Tambourine, Maracas, Handclaps – *Ringo Starr*
Bongos, Congas – *Uncredited*
Handclaps – *Paul McCartney, George Harrison, John Lennon*

Another McCartney 'percussion by numbers' track, *Hello Goodbye* is notable for swift and well executed snare/tom interplay from Ringo, plus expansive use of percussion on the playout. When heard in isolation on an early (Take 1) version, Ringo's performance is extraordinary – chock-full of flams, ruffs, and assorted off the cuff fills, rolls and cymbal/ hi-hat inter-play, picking up a regular beat where the song dictates. It is unfortunate this approach was somewhat reined-in on the selected take, although the final release is nevertheless a lesson in how to play for the song.

Alongside his bandmates, Ringo leaps straight in with a sharp cymbal and bass drum attack (first bar below), the urgency of the impact enhanced by constant '8 in the bar' maracas. Repeated throughout, the open and closed hi-hat phrasing serves a punctuating purpose, filling the gap between the "high" and "low" vocal exchanges at [0.38].

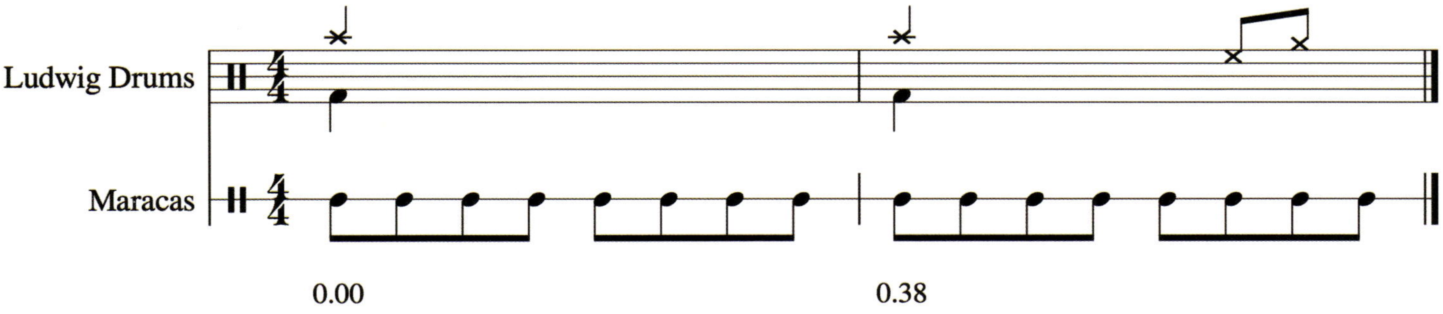

Illustrating that it was not only Lennon who added bars of different timings to resolve lyrics, McCartney inserts a 2/4 bar in the middle of the chorus – notice Ringo enhancing the earlier hi-hat timekeeping with the addition of ride cymbal -

Well – executed off-beat handclaps heighten the perceived pace as they introduce the instrumental break -

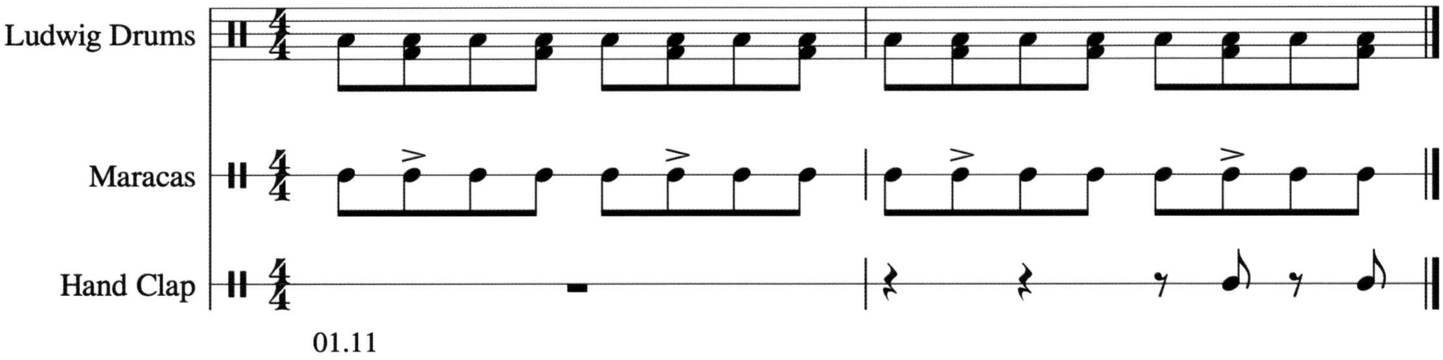

Inspired busking by Ringo follows, loosening up as the song progresses using all available drums and cymbals at his disposal.

The exuberant coda (surely inspired by a similar passage found on the Beach Boys' magnificent *I'm Waiting For The Day* from *Pet Sounds)* features some extravagantly overdubbed percussion, mirroring the conclusion of *Strawberry Fields Forever*. Paul was initially underwhelmed and disappointed by this section, but delighted by the results of added reverb on the drums at the mixing stage.

On a production note, the drums sound remarkably open here, while as a counterpoint the bass drum had never been so prominent on a Beatles' record? Ken Scott can take the credit for this enhancement, as he engineered the backing track session on October 2, with Geoff Emerick later recording Paul McCartney's bass overdubs.

Editing a promo film for the 'Hello Goodbye' single

I Am The Walrus

Time Signature – 4/4
Recorded – September 5/6/27/28/29, 1967. **Engineers –** *Geoff Emerick, Ken Scott*
Drums – *Ringo Starr*
Tambourine – *Paul McCartney*

Recorded in the immediate aftermath of Brian Epstein's untimely death, *I Am The Walrus* apparently saw Ringo having difficulty concentrating on the matter in hand – namely producing the simplest of 4/4 beats to bind the fledgling track together. In stepped McCartney, standing in front of Ringo, offering encouragement by playing tambourine along with the downbeat drummer. The end result is a solid if unspectacular offering, besides the opening fill and the play-out, he is committed to a fairly unadventurous rhythm. But isn't that just what was required – forming the ground upon which such an imaginative and fertile mind such as Lennon's could work it's magic? There *are* touches of flair, witness the bass drum emphasis at [1.34], the snare also enhancing and mimicking the "*jooba-jooba*" vocal at [3.24]. At times, Ringo appears to be literally leaning into his hi-hats as he plays, attempting to inject variety into the beat.

Production wise, Ringo's drums are closely miked on the first half of the song, after the radio intermission [2.11], they are thinner and pushed back in the mix, swapping channels on the stereo version. Again, the mono mix shines, though curiously at [1.17], rather than disappearing for one bar (as per the stereo mix), the drum track is re-introduced late – being clumsily mixed back in mid-way through the next bar – a mistake, a result of the many problematic mixes completed, or another instinctive Lennon curio? Perhaps not, with the original US version possessing an extra bar between the first 2 verses, experimentation and uncertainty seemed the order of the day.

25. Magical Mystery Tour

EP- Released December 8 1967

Engineers – *Geoff Emerick, Malcolm Addey, Ken Scott, Peter Vince, John Timperley*

> "*Magical Mystery Tour* was terribly badly organised and it's amazing anything came out of it."
>
> **- George Martin**[115]

Having basked in the glow of *Sgt. Pepper* and the 'Summer Of Love', the Beatles embarked upon a period of lugubrious and self-indulgent recording, the fruits of which were a mixed-bag. Some efforts were decidedly low-key and uninspired – *You Know My Name (Look Up The Number)* being a prime example. With only the recording of *Your Mother Should Know* having taken place before the untimely death of manager and mentor Brian Epstein, this chaotic state of affairs was understandable. So it was possibly with some relief that Paul McCartney rallied the troops, with a naive approach to film (and soundtrack) creation becoming the next project.

Creatively, we see once again a continuation of the recording techniques of *Sgt. Pepper*, in the absence of Geoff Emerick[116] the engineering duties at Abbey Road were shared amongst the Abbey Road engineers, though chiefly by the emerging Ken Scott. It's worth noting that on these sessions Scott often started work on a half-completed song (*I Am The Walrus*, for example), and the approach was to mimic Emerick's work as closely as possible for purposes of continuity. So again we hear the close miking of Ringo's drums, to some extent enhanced and pushed forward even more in the mix. Listening to *Magical Mystery Tour*, one would have no idea the songs were recorded by multiple engineers.

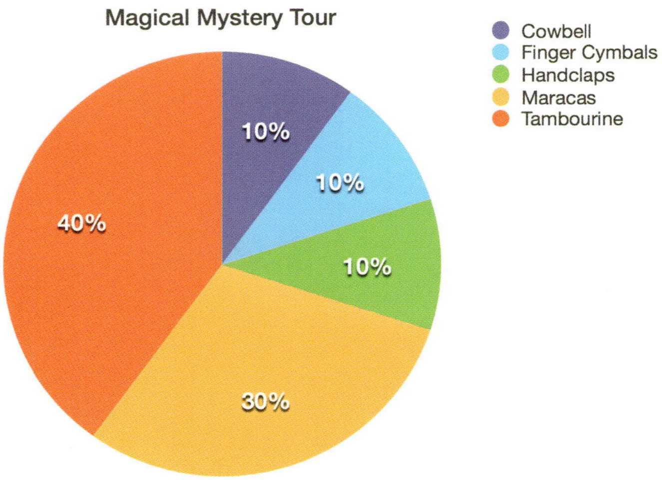

6 Songs

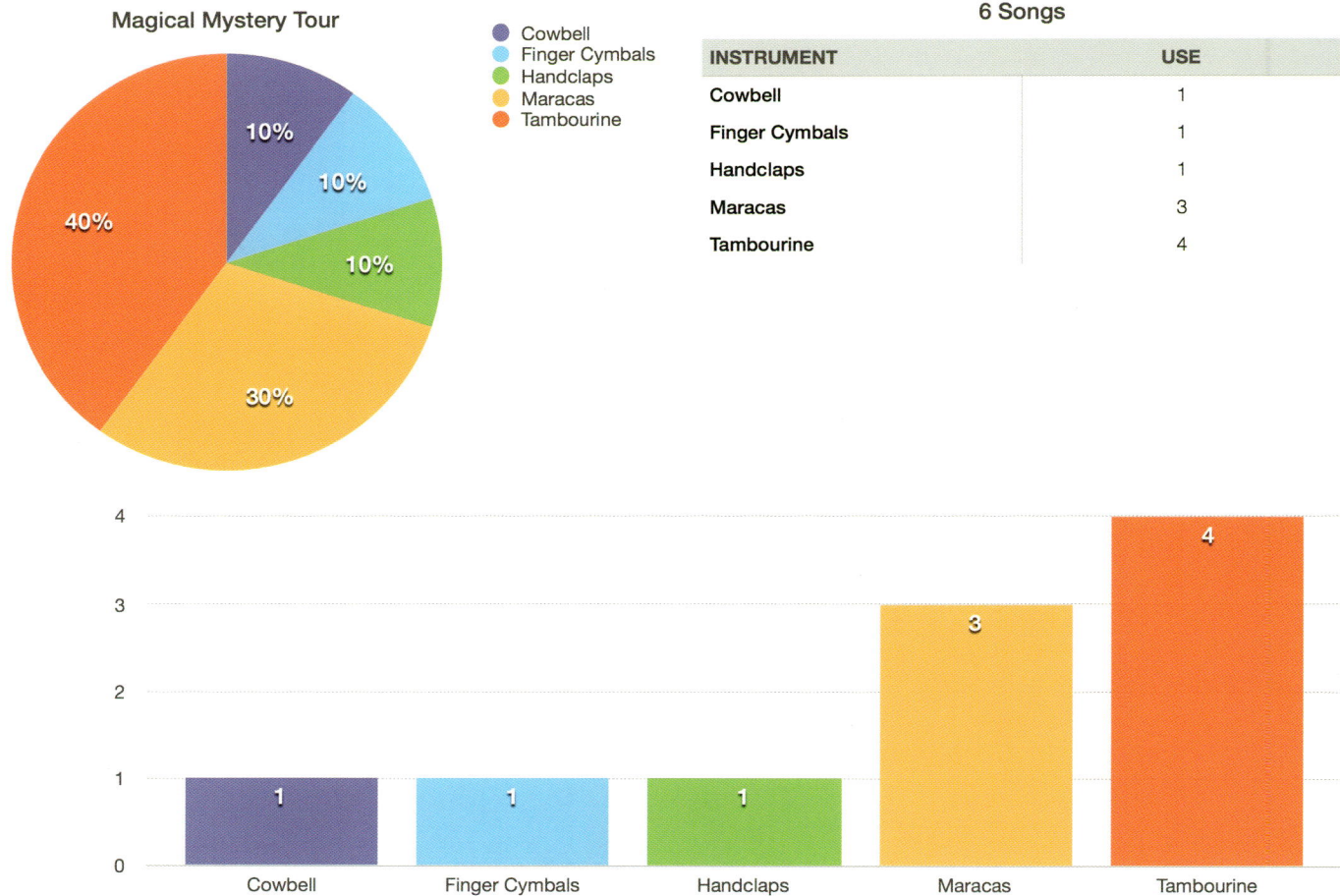

INSTRUMENT	USE
Cowbell	1
Finger Cymbals	1
Handclaps	1
Maracas	3
Tambourine	4

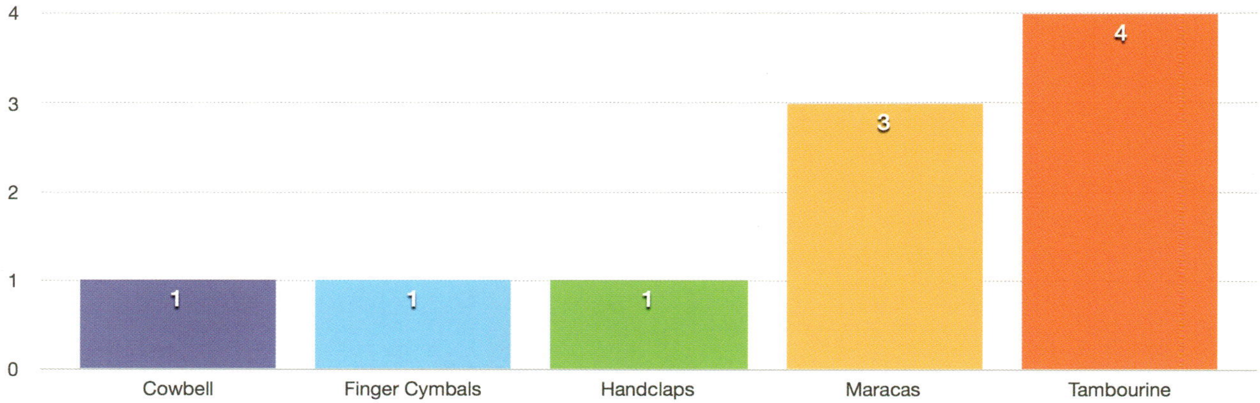

Magical Mystery Tour

Time Signature – 4/4

Recorded – April 25-27, May 3, 1967. **Engineers –** *Geoff Emerick, Malcolm Addey*

Drums – *Ringo Starr*

Maracas, Cowbell, Tambourine, Handclaps, Undocumented Percussion – *Ringo Starr, Paul McCartney, John Lennon, George Harrison, Mal Evans, Neil Aspinall*

A bright, brash opening on sharply-struck cymbal and bass drum, with the emphasis on the first and third beats. After 2 bars, that emphasis shifts to beats two and four, with a prominently mixed drum kit beat and trademark busy McCartney bass line driving the song forward.

One of the features of the song is the shifting structure, witness the transitions throughout [0.32], [0.41], [1.26], especially at [1.56] to end. Starr's job here is to bind the sections together, a job he does with his usual minimum of fuss. He is bizarrely helped along by thunderously panned sound effect of a passing coach, surely the strangest of percussive moments in the Beatles' catalogue? The coda, echoing the instrumental bridge (at 1.12), is once again reminiscent of much of the instrumental work on the Beach Boys' *Pet Sounds*, sprinkled liberally with snare flams and drags, as the song slips into the transition to the first scene of the film.

The Fool On The Hill

Time Signature – 4/4

Recorded – September 25/26/27, October 20 1967. **Engineer –** *Ken Scott*

Drums, Maracas, Finger Cymbals – *Ringo Starr*

Early takes (as heard on *Anthology 2*) see Ringo employing brushes on snare and hi-hat on the instrumental bridge, along with a steady 'one in the bar' bass drum beat, much in the fashion of his earlier work on *Rubber Soul*. For whatever reason, McCartney eschewed this approach for a more subtle percussive arrangement, the tempo reined back to a more sedate pace. Finger cymbals and maracas enhance the verses [0.27], [1.06], providing an ethereal atmosphere, echoing the confused mind of the Fool.[117] Brushes on snare make a welcome reappearance on the instrumental bridge [1.23], [2.03], as does the single stroke bass drum and an open & closed hi-hat. A tender, gentle treatment then, McCartney's change of heart another case of instinctively knowing what is required for the song.

Flying

Time Signature – 4/4

Recorded – September 8/28, 1967. **Engineer –** *Geoff Emerick, Ken Scott*

Drums, Maracas, Undocumented Percussion – *Ringo Starr*

Ringo's second songwriting credit (after *Rubber Soul's What Goes On*) is a purely instrumental affair, with the oh-so sweet engineering of the drums, again closely miked and prominent in the the mix. Boosted by high compression, the dominant snare drives the song, the floating dreamlike feel provided by the ambient ride cymbal. What appears to be yet again a simple, unimaginative work-out is nothing of the sort. Listen for the introduction of the guitar in the left channel, as it is soon joined by a deftly-stroked bass drum or tom-tom. Such a touch is imperceptible, but bolsters the effect of the guitar, as the drum echo's it's phrasing. Maracas are used sparingly, initially falling with the snare, building throughout.

Blue Jay Way
Time Signature – 4/4
Recorded – September 6/7, October 6, 1967. **Engineer –** *Geoff Emerick, Peter Vince.*
Drums – *Ringo Starr*
Tambourine – *John Lennon*

Another Ringo tour de force provides an interesting approach, dampened bass drum and floor tom enhancing the droning bass line of the dark, eerie intro, mimicking the mystery of the swirling fog. Before long (in the second verse) Ringo switches to a shuffle feel on ride cymbal, snare and bass drum. Progressively, the drums are drenched with ADT and flanging[118] – put simply the feeding of the track back into the mix, coupled with the vocal being treated by a Leslie speaker (a speaker that rotates within it's cabinet) creating a 'swirling' effect as the sound is bounced around.

This passage at [2.14] is indicative of the drumming as a whole – a dreamy shuffle, interrupted by great use of 16th note patterns, before resuming the 'floating' ride cymbal feel. Note the use of a bar of 2/4, extending the vocal -

Of further note is the interplay of Ringo's fills with the vocal [2.50] to end , embellished by tambourine to great effect. To complete the experimentation, a backwards drum track is expertly mixed in and out throughout, adding to the already crowded percussive mix. As an aside, we feel the mono version of *Blue Jay Way* is superior to the stereo – as is often the case, the mono mix provides a unity to the drum track – the flow of the song is more pronounced, adding a greater sense of urgency to proceedings when necessary.

Your Mother Should Know

Time Signature – 4/4
Recorded – August 22/23, September 16/29, 1967. **Engineer –** *John Timperley, Ken Scott*
Drums, Tambourine – *Ringo Starr*

With McCartney in full-on Vaudeville mode, *Your Mother Should Know* sees Ringo on auto-pilot, which is a surprising contrast to the earlier version of the song, evidenced on *Anthology II*. Initially recorded at Chappell Studios (Abbey Road was already booked), a remake was attempted featuring a military style snare roll on the verses, with opening hi-hat introduced on the 4th beat -

Finally, we see the introduction of the shuffle beat that made it to the final release (bars 3 & 4 below)

This was embellished with what typically may be a packing case or similar? The version we hear today is the original Chappell version plus overdubs – complete with a Ringo signature, turning what is in effect the laid-back shuffle (above), introduced at [0.25], and aided by tambourine.

I Am The Walrus

Time Signature – 4/4
Recorded – September 5/6/27/28/29, 1967. **Engineer –** *Geoff Emerick, Ken Scott*
Drums – *Ringo Starr*
Tambourine – *Paul McCartney*

Released 2 weeks previously as the B-Side to *Hello Goodbye*, *I Am The Walrus* is arguably the stand-out track from the *Magical Mystery Tour* EP. We are fortunate to see Ringo performing (or rather, miming) the song as featured in the TV movie – his Ludwig kit in all it's glorious 60's colour.

26. Lady Madonna / The Inner Light

Single – Released March 15 1968

Lady Madonna

Time Signature – 4/4
Recorded – February 3/6, 1968. **Engineer –** *Ken Scott*
Drums, Handclaps – *Ringo Starr*
Handclaps – *Paul McCartney, George Harrison, John Lennon*
Tambourine – *Paul McCartney*

Moving into 1968, McCartney continued to be the driving force behind the Beatles' output. With his band mates seemingly content to 'go with the flow', another single was on the cards. As on *Good Day Sunshine*, we again have Paul's multi-layered percussive approach to the Beatles recordings, with two separate and distinct drum patterns at play. From the start, Ringo lays down a drum track with a silky solo snare beat on brushes, placed on the left channel of the stereo mix. On the right channel, after 4 bars, we have a jauntily overdubbed bass drum and snare beat.

The beat takes a twist with the replacement of the snare and bass drum with eighth note hi-hats, opened on the 2nd and 4th beats of the bar.

Handclaps are introduced over the sax solo, the bridges to the chorus and solo punctuated with brushes on cymbal. Tambourine (very low in the right channel) is evident, the overall effect a little jarring on the stereo mix, with the mono version possessing the usual solid, unified feel.

The Inner Light

The Inner Light Single

Time Signature – 4/4

Recorded – January 12, February 6/8, 1967. **Engineer –** *J.P. Sen, S. N. Gupta*

The backing track recorded by George in Bombay while completing his *Wonderwall Music* soundtrack, *The Inner Light* features India's finest session musicians laying down a hybrid of Eastern instruments to a Western beat. The result produces a sympathetic backing to a quite beautiful melody.

27. Hey Jude / Revolution

Single – Released August 30 1968

1968 saw the hippie Utopian dream collapse – with violent student riots in Paris, the peaceful Czech uprising brutally suppressed by the Soviet Union, the Vietnamese Tet offensive and Mai Lai massacre by American troops turning public opinion against the war, the assassination of Martin Luther King and the ensuing riots, plus MP Enoch Powell's 'Rivers Of Blood' speech – all stoking the activist fire within John Lennon. The resulting blistering version of *Revolution* released as the B-Side of *Hey Jude* stands as that rare thing – a cleverly conceived and brilliantly executed snapshot of it's time. Amidst this chaos, the Beatles set up Apple records, and still found time to produce a double LP (The Beatles), two singles, and contribute material to the *Yellow Submarine* cartoon.

Hey Jude

Time Signature – 4/4
Recorded – July 29/30/31, August 1, 1968. **Engineer** – *Ken Scott*
Drums , Tambourine – *Ringo Starr*

With *Hey Jude*, the Beatles spent a painstaking amount of studio time seeking perfection. Two days of recorded rehearsal at Abbey Road culminated in a session at Trident Studios, specifically to take advantage of Trident's 8-track recorder, as such technology was still absent from EMI's 'flagship' studios.

For such an epic track, Ringo takes his usual empathetic, laid-back approach, utilising a plodding beat, helped along by the earlier introduced '2 in the bar' tambourine and added emphasis of his ride cymbal bell at [1.33]. The tambourine switches to a 16's feel which is deployed effectively and constantly lifts the choruses, aided by multiple handclaps. Punctuated by sometimes repetitive fills, Ringo either adds colour between lines [1.07], or reflects the phonetics of the vocals, illustrated by the second half of the introductory fill over "And anytime you feel the pain" [0.53], and later throughout the lengthy play-out.

Recording wise, Ringo's drums are once again deadened by tea-towels, presented here in perhaps their most muted form. As an aside, Ringo almost missed his cue – unbeknownst to his band-mates he had taken a toilet-break, and just managed to slink back behind his kit in time.

Revolution

Time Signature – 4/4
Recorded – July 9/10/11/12, 1968. **Engineer** – *Geoff Emerick*
Drums – *Ringo Starr*
Handclaps – *Ringo Starr, Paul McCartney, George Harrison, John Lennon*

With a prototype Glam Rock beat, Ringo is in a minimalist mood, his bass drum powering the rhythm track, with powerful matched strokes on his snare and floor tom neatly linking verses. A foretaste of the stark nature of *The Beatles* LP, *Revolution* sees the Beatles 'going for it' like never before – Ringo's heavily compressed drums and cymbals fighting for air against the tremendously distorted guitars and forthright bass. While the guitarists played directly into the consoles in the control room of Studio 2, Ringo performed in splendid isolation in Studio 3. Again we have a 2/4 bar inserted in order to resolve the vocal delivery.

However, perhaps the best moments are the forceful and dramatic cymbal/drum trade-offs (shown below) and the subtleties of the snatched moments of snare work [1.22], [2.06] & [3.10]. Lennon emphasises the repetitive beat with his vocal during the guitar and electric piano solo.

"Ringo got a bit carried away, officer.."

Recording a promotional film for Revolution at Twickenham Studios. Photos by kind permission of Bill Minto

28. The Beatles

LP – Released November 22, 1968

Engineers – *Geoff Emerick, Ken Scott, Barry Sheffield, Peter Bown*

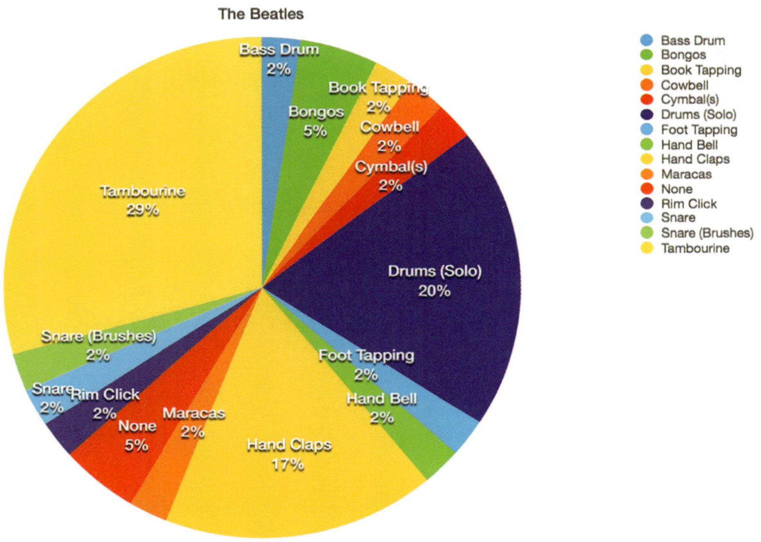

30 Songs

INSTRUMENT	USE
Bass Drum	1
Bongos	2
Book Tapping	1
Cowbell	1
Cymbal(s)	1
Drums (Solo)	8
Foot Tapping	1
Hand Bell	1
Hand Claps	7
Maracas	1
None	2
Rim Click	1
Snare	1
Snare (Brushes)	1
Tambourine	12

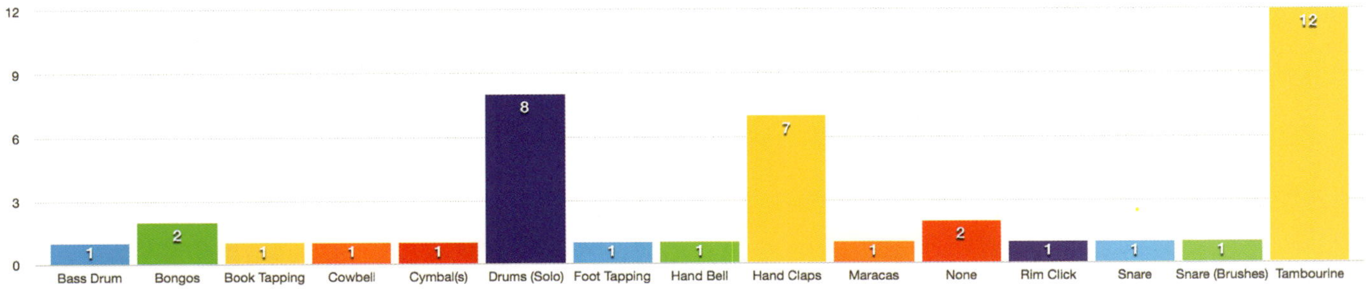

In many ways, *The Beatles* LP proved a turning point in the band's career. The loss of Brian Epstein, leading to the malaise and lack of direction since *Magical Mystery Tour*, coupled with the distraction of their fledgling Apple project, led to a haphazard approach to recording their new album. The group were beginning to mature as individuals, developing their own styles and becoming less dependent upon each other. The sessions for what we all refer to as the *White*

Album began in earnest in May 1968, each Beatle essentially acting as each other's session musicians. Tensions amongst the Group and the EMI staff grew. Having less of a creative influence, George Martin took the opportunity to take a holiday in the middle of the albums sessions, leaving his assistant, Chris Thomas, to supervise. Geoff Emerick, such a technical influence upon their post-*Revolver* sound, found the sessions similarly disheartening and stressful, departing with a request never to work with the Beatles again. Ken Scott took over the engineering duties, and from a different perspective flourished, despite the perceived fractious nature of the sessions.

Technically, the *The Beatles* finally saw the introduction of 8-track recording to EMI, albeit somewhat subversively. Having enjoyed 8-track recordings at Trident Studios (*Dear Prudence* and *Hey Jude* cases in point), when they discovered EMI had such a machine under wraps they insisted upon it's use on the sessions for their new album. There was however a problem – strict rules stated new equipment had to undergo the rigours of thorough technical testing before studio deployment. Beatles being Beatles, Ken Scott and David Harries were sent to liberate the machine, and installed it post-haste.

As far as Ringo was concerned, most of his time was taken up in the Abbey Road reception, reading magazines while waiting to be called upon by whichever Beatle felt the need for drums on his new recording. By 22nd August, riled by McCartney's dictatorial style while relaying the drum part he desired for *Back In The USSR,* Ringo had had enough. Fed-up with 'just being the drummer' he quit the band and left the country for a well-earned holiday. It took the other three Beatles two weeks of persuasion for Ringo to return to the fold, his first session back at Abbey Road famous for Harrison's decoration of his Ludwig kit with an exuberant floral arrangement. Starr's remaining time on the album must have been a happy one, as he has consistently referred to the album as being memorable for the Beatles playing together as a band again. Despite this notion being somewhat against the nature of the album's recording sessions, Ringo's recollections do have some merit, as we will see with tracks such as *Yer Blues*. With *The Beatles* containing so many diverse styles and genres, whether it be Rock 'n' Roll, Blues, Country and Western, Dance Band, gentle ballads or Folk, Ringo once again proved he was up to the task, and then some.

Back In The U.S.S.R.

Time Signature – 4/4
Recorded – August 22/23, 1968. **Engineer –** *Ken Scott*
Drums – *Paul McCartney, George Harrison, John Lennon*
Percussion – *Paul McCartney, George Harrison, John Lennon*
Snare Drum – *Paul McCartney, George Harrison, John Lennon*
Handclaps- *Paul McCartney, George Harrison, John Lennon*

With a thoroughly despondent Ringo having left the group during the recording of *Back In The USSR,* it's no surprise McCartney saw fit to take up the drumming duties on this track and also Lennon's *Dear Prudence*. How many of us instinctively believed it was Ringo playing on the first two tracks of the *White Album*?

Such was the desire for a seamless percussive feel in Ringo's absence, McCartney's drum track was further enhanced with snare overdubs by both Harrison and Lennon. The layered effect of these multiple snare drums (McCartney's drums on one channel, Lennon and Harrison's snares on the other) appears disjointed on the stereo mix, especially when joined by multiple handclaps. The effect of these dislocated overdubs is lessened on the mono mix, the overall impression is one of solidity and continuity.

As for the main drum track, Paul lays down a forthright and powerful backing, creating a Ringo-esque performance by playing ever so slightly *behind* the beat. *Back In The USSR* also displays McCartney's penchant for hurried closed hi-hat time-keeping between lines and verse and chorus. Note the slightly off-beat matched-stroke snare/tom fills [2.14] and handclaps throughout, a percussive style we would become familiar with in his drumming on the *McCartney* and *Band On The Run* solo albums.

Dear Prudence

Time Signature – 4/4
Recorded – August 28/29/30, 1968. **Engineer –** *Barry Sheffield*
Drums, Tambourine, Cowbell, Handclaps – *Paul McCartney*
Handclaps – *George Harrison, Jackie Lomax, Mal Evans, John McCartney (Paul's Cousin)*

Recorded away from Abbey Road at Trident Studios, Paul again picks up the sticks in the wake of Ringo's departure, once more showing us his versatility and talent by providing a nicely constructed drum part. There *are* errors and misjudgements, but it would be harsh of us to pick over the bones of such a performance. Perhaps trying to compensate for their drummer's absence, we hear different patterns for each section of the song. The introduction has a solitary tambourine echoing the first bass note of each line of the verse, maintaining this pattern on subsequent verses. Unusually, the first verse [0.44] sees busy if somewhat 'stiff' and robotic '16 to the bar' hi-hats, perhaps giving the game away as Starr is always incredibly fluid with his hi-hat work. Paul gets a bit more forceful on the bridge [1.48], cutting the intensity in half by playing '8's' on his floor tom, the tambourine compensating by providing the sense of urgency normally provided by the hi-hat.

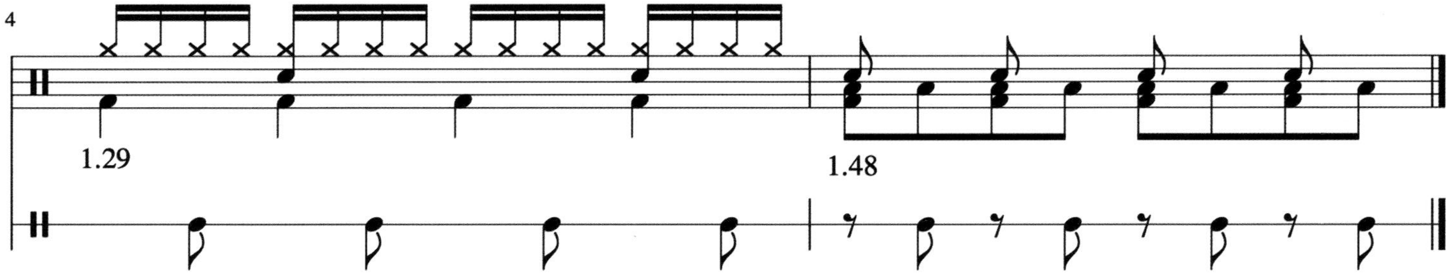

Moving on, we can see the use of handclaps superseded by tambourine, the snare doubling-up towards the songs resolution [3.19].

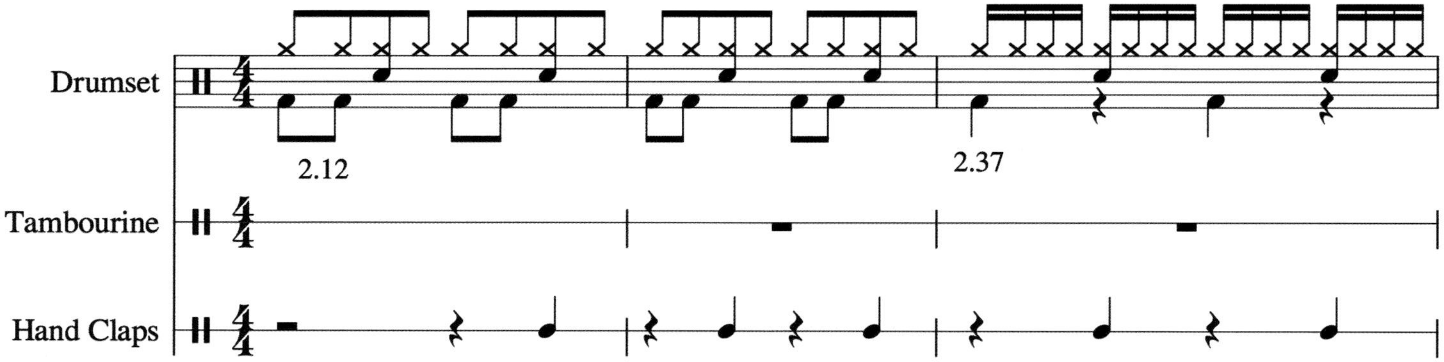

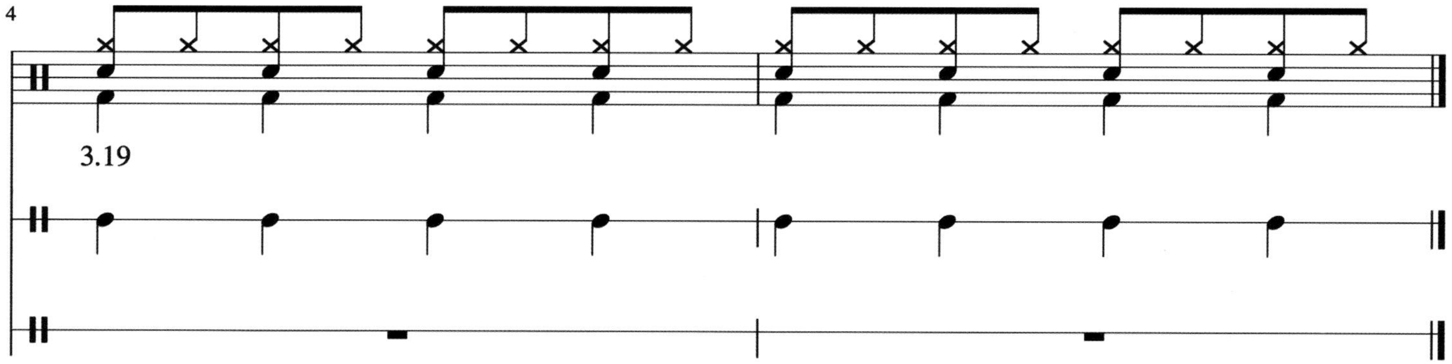

Turning in an overly fussy performance by making full use of the kit, Paul lets loose for 10 bars, before the solid beat 5 bar resolution. Or is it Paul after all? It is quite possible this end piece was performed by Ringo at Abbey Road upon his return to the fold, the production does appear slightly different than the preceding performance, and it does bear all the hallmarks of Ringo's drumming, if perhaps a little too sloppy. Despite this possibility, for all those years how many of us thought the *whole song* was played by Ringo?

Glass Onion

Time Signature – 4/4
Recorded – September 11/12/13, October 10, 1968. **Engineer –** *Ken Scott*
Drums, Tambourine – *Ringo Starr*

After two competent but occasionally erratic contributions by Paul, Ringo kicks off his presence on the album with his usual solidity and fluidity. Signature matched strokes played simultaneously on snare and floor tom open the song, repeated with overdubbed snare at the start and end of each verse, coupled with some funky snare work on the James Bond-esque bridge [1.01]. Tambourine enhances the last line of each verse before the chorus, providing support to the snare and hi-hat. Back in the saddle!

Ob-La-Di, Ob-La-Da

Time Signature – 4/4
Recorded – July 3/4/5/8/9/11/15, 1968. **Engineer** – *Geoff Emerick*
Drums, Tambourine, Bongos, Maracas, Handclaps – *Ringo Starr*
Handclaps – *Paul McCartney, George Harrison, John Lennon*

> "They'd do it (Ob-La-Di, Ob-La-Da) one night and you'd think 'that's it'. But then they'd come in the next day and do it again…. Poor Ringo would be playing from about three in the afternoon until one in the morning, with few breaks in between, and then have to do it all over again the next night".
>
> **- Richard Lush, 2nd Engineer[119].**

A track that created much friction within the group, caused by McCartney's constant reworking of the song, and as a result tensions started to rise. The weariness and uncertainty of the constant re-workings of the song is evidenced by the multiple percussive overdubs throughout. Closely-miked handclaps introduce the song proper, with the overall style mimicking the popular Ska recordings of the day. The snare is prominent in the mix, providing the one point of solidity and purpose. The liberal and sometimes unsubtle [1.07] overdubs of bongos, maraca, tom, and bottles pervade, the 'clicks' and '*chicka-chackas*' of the vocals giving the track a heavily percussive, exotic feel. How did such a tortuous set of recordings turn into such a joyous offering, and provide Scottish group *Marmalade* with a number 1 hit single.

Wild Honey Pie

Time Signature – 4/4
Recorded – August 20, 1968. **Engineer –** *Ken Scott*
Drums – *Paul McCartney*

Paul again played drums on this short, spontaneous and largely inconsequential ditty. A strident bass drum (playing '4's') and what sounds like the back of an acoustic guitar drives the song along. He plays slight variations on this theme using either a snare with the strainer off or a dry sounding top tom, in fact anything that gave him the sound he was looking for, natural reverb is dominant. A clue of what to expect on his self-titled solo albums.

The Continuing Story of Bungalow Bill

Time Signature – 4/4
Recorded – October 8, 1968. **Engineer –** *Ken Scott*
Drums, Tambourine – *Ringo Starr*

Making a welcome return we have brushes on snare, providing an off-beat playful presence throughout. This brushes on snare pattern would soon re-surface as rim clicks on the following track, *While My Guitar Gently Weeps* (below), and perhaps more recognisably on *Get Back* . With deliberately bold bass drum preceding the singalong chorus, ubiquitous tambourine alongside accented snare is doubled-up on the last chorus. The song was originally intended to fade-out, illustrated by the drums ending before the mellotron coda.

While My Guitar Gently Weeps

Time Signature – 4/4
Recorded – July 25, August 16, September 3/5/6, 1968. **Engineer –** *Ken Scott*
Drums, Tambourine, Drum Rim – *Ringo Starr*

While My Guitar Gently Weeps marked Ringo's return to the group, and again he keeps things simple, with overdubbed percussion taking centre stage. The opening and closing (or 'choking') of the hi-hats of the introduction are a feature here (1st bar above), opening the song and heralding his movement around the kit. Perhaps conscious of letting Eric Clapton's superb guitar work dominate, his fills are perfectly timed to complement the opening solo, returning to the snare rather

than ending on a cymbal crash (2nd bar above), drumming that is sympathetic and appreciative of the emotions of the song. Overdubbed rim-clicks, (3rd bar above, and not castanets as suggested by some) drive the song along on the left channel of the stereo mix, trading places with tambourine throughout. Hi-hats are introduced on the first appearance of the bridge (1st bar below), it is entirely possible his drum track was originally devoid of hi-hat work, as hi-hats appear to have been overdubbed and introduced throughout. This is best evidenced prior to the solo – at [1.57] as we hear their somewhat clumsy introduction in the stereo right channel. Accented tambourine playing '16 in the bar' picks up the pace mid-way through the solo (2nd bar below), settling on the 3rd beat in the bar (bar 3 below), before moving to the 2nd beat (bar 4 below).

While My Guitar Gently Weeps sees the blossoming George Harrison prove there was more than one Beatle capable of producing an imaginative and cohesive drum track to one of his songs.

Happiness Is A Warm Gun

Time Signature – 2/4, 4/4, 9/8, 10/8, 12/8
Recorded – September 23/24/25, 1968. **Engineer –** *Ken Scott*
Drums, Tambourine – *Ringo Starr*

One of Ringo's most complex pieces of timekeeping, due to the time-shifting brilliance of this Lennon piece. Taking upwards of 70 takes to complete, the Beatles were especially proud of this track, presumably due to the complexity of the structure and the tightness of their playing? There is a degree of debate as to the exact time signatures at play here, especially in the hemiolic "*Mother Superior*" section. (A hemiola is the playing of 3 beats in the time normally taken by 2, e.g. 3/2 – a great example being *America* by Leonard Bernstein). Do we hear 9/8 and 10/8, or is it 6/8 and 3/4, and does it really matter?

What does matter is Ringo is at his best, negotiating the time-shifts with ease, ensuring the song flows perfectly, allowing the vocals and guitar the room to breathe and provide purpose.

0.00 – **(4/4 & 2/4)** With a count in 'on the 4th beat' – from *"She's not a girl …* – we have 5 bars of 4/4 (drums introduced mid-way through the 4th bar) to

0.14 – **(4/4 & 2/4)** A bar of 4/4, followed by a single 2/4 bar to accommodate the lyrics (Ringo's fill at [0.21]), returning to 4/4

Having seen the insertion of a 2/4 bar, we soon see no less than 4 consecutive different time signatures in succession – 5/4 – 4/4 – 9/8 – 10/8.

0.45 – **(9/8 & 12/8)** Wisely keeping things simple, Ringo plays with restraint – allied to the gentle organ, the harsh guitar provides fluidity.

1.13 – **(9/8 & 10/8)** *'Mother Superior jump the gun'* – 2 bars of 9/8 & 10/8 repeated three times. Ringo picks up the pace with 16th notes on bass and snare, urgency later provided with similarly busy 16th note hi-hats.

1.34 – **(4/4)** 'Happiness is a warm gun' – Ringo effortlessly leads the group from 10/8 into 4 bars of 4/4, any hint of a harsh transition well hidden from the listener.

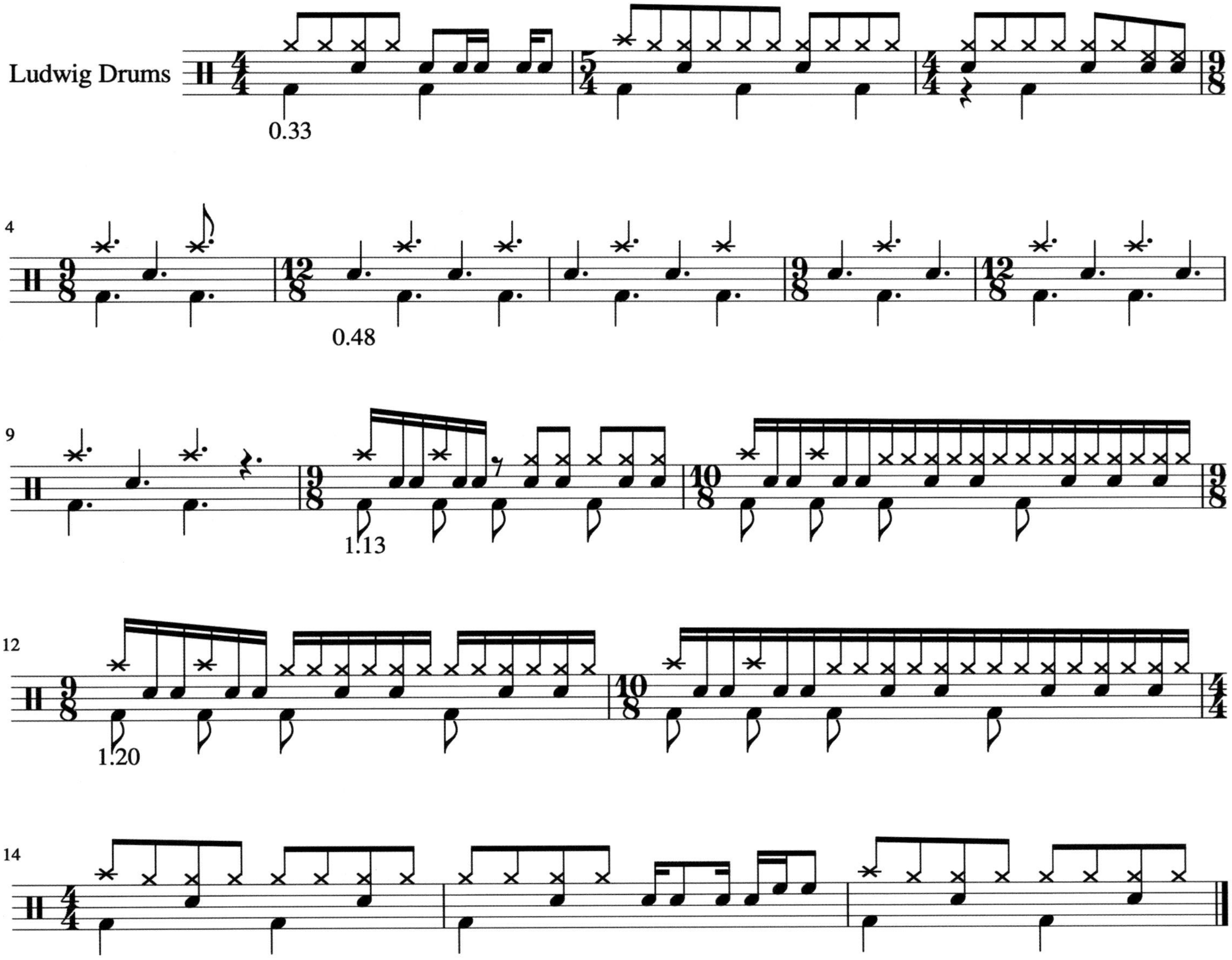

1.48 – **[12/8 & 4/4]** *'When I Hold You In My Arms'* – 3 bars of 12/8. Being incredibly easy to become sidetracked by listening to the meter of the vocal, this is a 'heads down and keep counting passage' for the drummer!

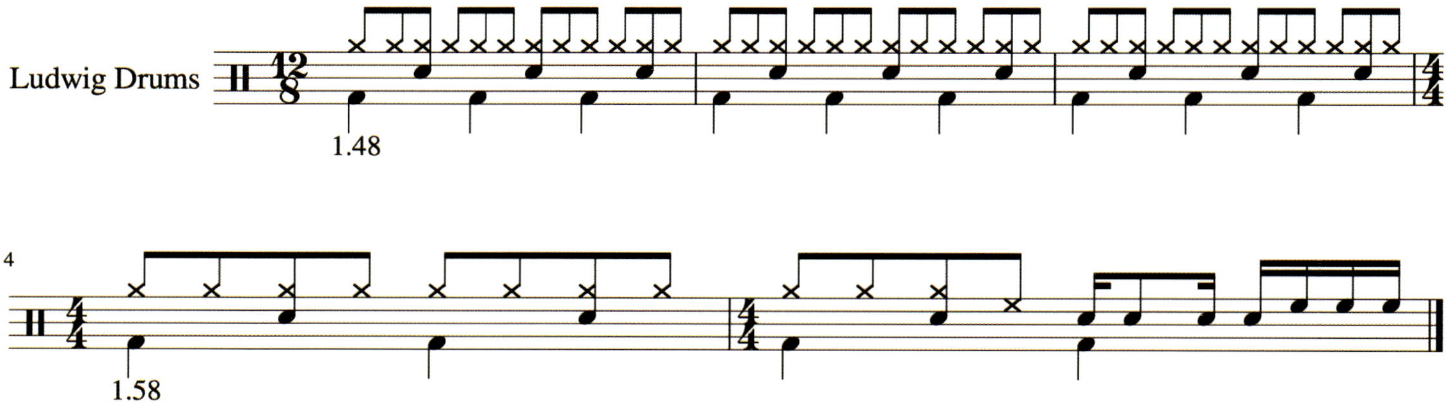

The last bar above contains a fantastic example of a typical Ringo fill, utilising just the two drums, he manages to once again play perfectly for the song by providing a simple resolution to the passage.

Aside from the deliberate stitching together of four different song ideas, writing six different time signatures was obviously not a conscious decision by Lennon. As we have seen before, his sometimes erratic style must have felt completely natural to himself, and Ringo must have rolled his eyes when he heard the rambling time signatures as the song was presented. Unlike the majority of the songs on the album, *Happiness Is A Warm Gun* was a collaborative effort – a true Beatles record. The performances here are superb, with Ringo particularly deserving of mention. Despite their recent trends of liberal percussion overdubs, save for tambourine (which has all the hallmarks of a McCartney performance) on the *"Mother Superior"* section [1.16-1.32], all we have are drums played with precision and poise. Note how Ringo plays essentially the same pattern [0.21],[0.35] & [1.34], [2.07], [2.27], & [2.34] – ending the song on a typical familiar fill – we don't notice because everything he plays around these fills is so exquisitely performed. Who else could get away with that?

Martha My Dear

Time Signature – 4/4
Recorded – October 4/5, 1968. **Engineer –** *Barry Sheffield*
Drums, Handclaps – *Paul McCartney*

Back at Trident, and apparently a solo effort (save for horns and strings), on evidence here is McCartney's penchant for layering his songs with instruments as the bars progress. A catchy and ingenious intro from Paul on piano with a 3/4 bar followed by a 2/4 which is repeated throughout. More prominent on the mono mix, the drums playfully appear at

[0.59] into the song (we have already had a whole verse, piano introduction, another verse, and an extended bridge), disappearing in the mix and overtaken by '2 in the 4' handclaps on the brass instrumental [1.19], before resurfacing (albeit low in the mix) at [1.39], ending before the final flourish [2.02]. Playfully executed with minimum of fuss, Ringo couldn't have done any better.

I'm So Tired

Time Signature – 4/4
Recorded – October 8, 1968. **Engineer –** Ken Scott
Drums – *Ringo Starr*

Deliberately recorded as a live performance, on the stereo version we can hear Ringo's drums in the left channel, his overdubs panned centre. As a result, we can hear overspill from Ringo's drums in the right channel, providing the open sound John was after in the first place. Thankfully, this effect carried over to the mono version well. Languid drumming from Ringo, matching the subject matter and Paul's comatose bass. Purpose is provided by the overdubbed bass, snare and floor tom [0.47], joined by busy 8's on the overdubbed snare [1.28] as the protagonist's frustration increases. As evidenced by the *Anthology* version, Ringo repeats his fills, possibly under instruction from Lennon?

Blackbird

Time Signature – 4/4
Recorded – June 11, 1968. **Engineer** – *Geoff Emerick*
Foot-Tapping – *Paul McCartney*

No drums or percussion, save for McCartney's John Lee Hooker-esque foot-tapping timekeeping.

Piggies

Time Signature – 4/4
Recorded – September 19/20, October 10, 1968. **Engineer –** *Ken Scott*
Tambourine – *Ringo Starr*

Deliberate animal title song sequencing also sees minimal percussive input once again – a solitary tambourine shake throughout, generally settling on the 3rd beat of the bar. Prompt and punchy, the bass guitar takes the place of bass drum, although there is the hint of the latter over the vocal *"eat their bacon"* [1.39].

Rocky Racoon

Time Signature – 4/4
Recorded – August 15, 1968. **Engineer –** Ken Scott
Drums – *Ringo Starr*

Playful treatment from Ringo, perfectly adding to this folk pastiche by limiting his playing, allowing the narrative to speak for itself. Simple, busking hi-hat taps and shuffles build from the second verse, joined by snare on the 3rd, and bass on the 4th and subsequent verses. Bass drum and hi-hat pedal embellish the singalong vocal busking section [1.55], opening out to bass, snare and closed hi-hat on the repeat at [3.06]. A solitary heavily struck snare mimics the pistol shot [1.48].

Don't Pass Me By

Time Signature – 4/4
Recorded – June 5/6,12/22, July 1968. **Engineers** – *Geoff Emerick, Ken Scott*
Drums, Tambourine, Sleigh Bells – *Ringo Starr*

With the track listing providing continuity from the previous song, and with a song he'd toyed with for some years finally coming to fruition, we see Ringo again wearing his Country & Western clothes. What initially seems a naive and playful drum track is brought to the fore by the earlier version found on *Anthology 3* – imaginative overdubbed bass drum and tom patterns abound – trading off against snare and hi-hat. It's worth listening to this earlier take, as it provides us with an idea of what does and doesn't work for the song, the final version here benefits greatly from the more restrained feel. Now where's my *Rutles* album?

Why Don't We Do It In The Road?

Time Signature – 4/4
Recorded – October 9/10, 1968. **Engineer –** *Ken Scott*
Drums, **Handclaps** – *Ringo Starr*
Handclaps – *Paul McCartney*

It's back to Paul's percussive layering – and typical of the sessions for the album. After beginning to record the track solo, while George and John were busying themselves on overdubbing *Piggies*, he grabbed Ringo and recorded this 'Cock-Rock' pastiche. The track begins with simple '4 in the bar' tapping on the back of his acoustic guitar, before moving on to a snare and bass introduction, with prominent handclaps (almost imperceptible in mono) soon following. It appears the drum introduction is (at the mixing stage) faded in and out of the song – placing the emphasis on the introduction of the handclaps at [0.02]. Simple but effective blues fills on the snare 'top and tail' verses (or are they choruses?). A bass and hi-hat (with possibly a light touch on a crash cymbal) bring an abrupt halt to proceedings.

I Will

Time Signature – 4/4
Recorded – September 16/17, 1968. **Engineer –** *Ken Scott*
Bongos – *Ringo Starr*
Cymbals, Maracas – *John Lennon*

Here Lennon plays a nondescript percussion instrument[120], along with a deftly played ride cymbal, all of which sits quite quite high in the mix. Starr provides bongos and a discernible tom fill at [1.32]. Single beat maracas enter at [0.40] and provide energy on the final flourish. Notice the bass-heavy vocal/percussive performance from Paul. Lovely stuff!

Julia

Time Signature – 4/4
Recorded – October 13, 1968. **Engineer –** *Ken Scott*

A stark contrast to the preceding track, no drums or percussion are present, a deliberate ploy to enhance the morose feel?

Birthday

Time Signature – 4/4
Recorded – September 18, 1968. **Engineer –** *Ken Scott*
Drums, Tambourine, Handclaps – *Ringo Starr*
Maracas – *Undocumented*
Handclaps – John Lennon, George Harrison, Paul McCartney, Patti Harrison, Mal Evans, Yoko Ono.

Inspired and energised by a mid-afternoon recording session TV viewing of the 50's rock'n'roll movie *The Girl Can't Help It, Birthday* sees the Beatles in blistering form. Driven by a dual-guitar riff underpinned by Ringo's forthright beat and George's 6-string bass, the song motors along its ridiculously short 2 minutes and 45 seconds with gusto. Despite its frantic nature, the song is well thought out, especially in terms of percussion, and again bears all the hallmarks of a McCartney production. Introduced by Starr's one bar snare/tom fill on the 3rd beat, the song then sets the pattern of a 4/4 rocker. The first 3 bars show the frenetic nature of the song apparent by the use of 3 separate drum patterns within the first 10 seconds -

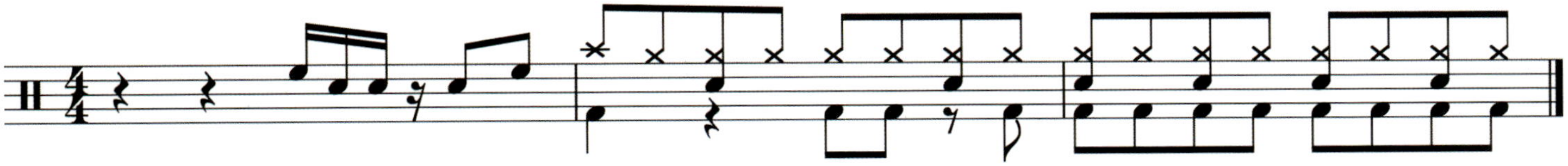

After the first chorus we have 8 bars of raucous drums and tambourine (counted by an exuberant McCartney), enhancing the party mood. The repetition here serves to heighten tension, the release of which is heightened by the frantic movement (bar 8) to the next passage -

The following bridge sees handclaps introduced, building the tension to the chorus -

The instrumental break [1.26] features hastily shaken maracas, as does the final flourish towards the song's conclusion. As Ringo is documented as playing tambourine, maracas were probably played by another Beatle.

Yer Blues

Time Signature – 12/8, 6/8
Recorded – August 13/14/20, 1968. **Engineer –** *Ken Scott*
Drums – *Ringo Starr*

Along with the preceding *Birthday*, *Yer Blues* sees another true 'band' performance of a super blues feel, reinforcing Ringo's fond memories of the *White Album* sessions as the moment the Beatles returned to playing together as a group again. A departure from the recording norm and continuing their studio experimentation, Lennon had the group perform the song live, in the tiny (for a four piece band with drums, amps etc) side room within the Control Room of Abbey Road's Studio 2. The intimacy of the situation certainly adds to the performance, especially as it affects the final product in terms of acoustics. Ringo's 'open' drums (especially his ride cymbal) add an edge that may have been lost by the more traditional recording approach.

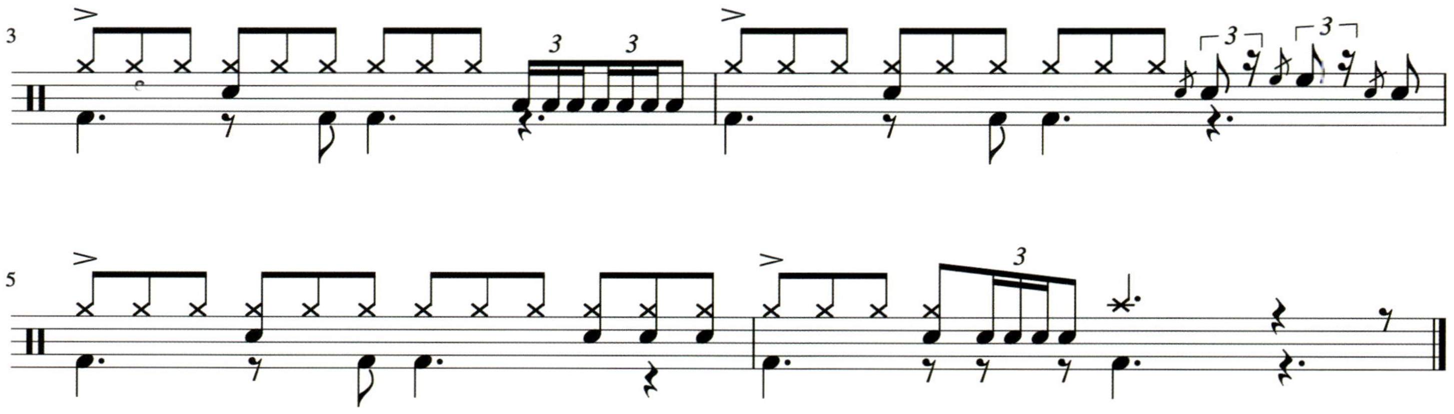

As for the song itself, we have a traditional 12/8 blues beat admirably punctuated at relevant moments by snare/tom fills and patterns, as illustrated by the first 6 bars of the song above. Effortlessly slipping into 4/4 for the solo at [2.06], for some reason best known to Lennon, we have an overdubbed snare introduced at 2.24 for the twin guitar solo passages. Master of the shuffle, Ringo's right at home here. At [3.16] we are rudely interrupted by a jarring and perhaps deliberately clumsy edit, taking us back into the main (12/8) body of the song.

Mother Nature's Son

Time Signature – 4/4
Recorded – August 9/20, 1968. **Engineer –** *Ken Scott*
Bass Drum, Book Tapping- *Paul McCartney*

Typically, this under-rated gentle acoustic classic is punctuated by McCartney's inventive and intuitive percussive effects to wonderful effect. The tender guitar intro is abruptly and rudely brought to a halt by three beats on the bass drum, which is closely miked and clumsily placed, perhaps intended as a musical joke? This device is repeated at the end of the second bridge, more of which later… Percussive layering had become a feature of McCartney's solo Beatles recordings, and *Mother Nature's Son* is no exception. Besides the stark bass drum after the introduction, it is not until we are half way through the 2nd verse [0.58] that he introduces a percussive element – this time showing an imaginative and experimental approach by tapping a book on his lap. This effect continues over the introduction of a single bass drum beat on the 1st (singalong) bridge, becoming increasingly random until it slips out of the mix completely. The bass drum (given it's loose, natural reverb effect by being closely recorded in an un-carpeted corridor at Abbey Road) is played on the 1st and 3rd beats, before taking the tempo down by relegating the beat to just the 1st of the bar. The second bridge sees a repeat of the first, erratic tapping to the fore, with the abrupt bass drum pattern making a re-appearance at [2.14].

Everybody's Got Something To Hide Except Me and My Monkey

Time Signature – 4/4, 3/4
Recorded – June 26/27, July 1/23, 1968. **Engineer** – *Geoff Emerick*
Drums, Handclaps – *Ringo Starr*
Handclaps, Percussion – John Lennon, George Harrison, Paul McCartney
Hand Bell – George Harrison

Another Lennon 'time-slipping' song, cunningly shifting from 4/4 to 3/4, with separate, disjointed sections. As with all things Beatle, what appears to be random or thrown together is nothing of the sort, the song is a veritable whirlwind of percussive meter and busy effects, cleverly constructed and executed. First off, we have the dislocated 4 bar exposition of the introduction, with handclaps mimicking the bass drum pattern, accompanied by somewhat frantic 16's on a fire bell salvaged from the effects cupboard.

At the resolution of the chorus, we have the typical Lennon device of inserting bars of alternate meter to accommodate lyrical content.

The bell is dropped (figuratively) in subsequent verses in favour of shakers but reappears at [1.19] and during the playout. Randomly mixed off-beat handclaps appear with fantastic energy throughout.

Sexy Sadie

Time Signature – 4/4
Recorded – July 19/24, August 13/21, 1968. **Engineer –** *Ken Scott*
Drums, Tambourine – *Ringo Starr*

Recorded a month prior to his temporary departure, Ringo delivers an uninspiring performance, typified by his bass drum patterns [0.13] and fills. A great deal of what we have here has a semblance of 'going through the motions', however despite this the final product is yet again perfect for the song, it is difficult to imagine another performance in it's place. Part of the problem lies with the production – the drums are closely miked and prominent, perhaps a more ambient sound as on *I'm So Tired* would have lifted the malaise? Ringo moves from familiar fills on the 4/4 chorus, replacing the hi-hat with single floor-tom strokes on the bridges [0.54]. We hear accented hi-hats on the play-out, adding a modicum of interest to proceedings [2.16]. Tambourine is present over the piano introduction (once on the mono mix, twice on the stereo!), but oddly disappearing until [2.26]. Perhaps wary of the sparse arrangement, Lennon smothers almost everything except bass and his ADT vocals in flanging, though thankfully not on the scale of *Blue Jay Way*.

Helter Skelter

Time Signature – 4/4
Recorded – July 18, September 9/10, 1968. **Engineer –** *Ken Scott*
Drums – *Ringo Starr*

In an attempt by McCartney to 'out-do the Who[121]', we have probably the most raucous self-penned Beatle track committed to tape, although performance-wise *I'm Down* and production-wise *Revolution* take some beating. Strange then, that Paul and Ringo opt for an annoyingly simple drum track, leaving the vocal, guitars and overly busy bass to do the damage. That's not to say Ringo doesn't play hard – he does acquire those infamous blisters after all……

In a response to fans who had noticed subtle differences between mono and stereo mixes of Beatles records, McCartney spent a great deal of time with Engineer Ken Scott creating significantly different versions of tracks on *The Beatles*, most noticeably *Helter Skelter*. Disjointed in the inferior stereo version by being panned to the right channel, Ringo's playing appears more coherent and forceful in the mono mix, largely due to his kit (his snare in particular) being smothered in echo and by (somewhat contradictory) being buried deep in the mono mix. By being some 50 seconds shorter and therefore lacking one of the two false endings, the drumming also appears more concise and straight-forward. A pity then, that McCartney saw fit to exclude Ringo's *"I've got blisters on my fingers"* from the mono mix. Drumming wise, Ringo nails his colours to the mast with a snare/tom buildup before settling into a driving heavy beat utilising heavy-handed '4 in the bar' strokes on cymbal or half opened hi-hats. He keeps his fills simple with just small variations. A real shame.

Long, Long, Long

Time Signature – 6/8, 3/8
Recorded – October 7/8/9, 1968. **Engineer –** *Ken Scott*
Drums – *Ringo Starr*

A welcome semblance of calm from the mayhem of the previous track, Ringo soon shatters the illusion of peace, punctuating the mellow harmonies of the ballad with seemingly irrelevant heavy-handed and echo layered fills before gently picking up the pace of the beat. Predominately played in 6/8, there are some interesting 3/8 bars as further fills flesh-out the gaps, bringing drama to this under-rated and dramatic Harrison track. The bars below illustrate the impact drumming, and are typical of the style employed here, gainfully striking out in the bars between George's vocal.

A clumsy snare roll [2.39] sits on top of a happy accident, whereby a knocked-over bottle was recorded spinning on top of a (internally rotating) Leslie speaker cabinet, thus providing an eerie ending to the song.

Revolution 1

Time Signature – 4/4, 2/4
Recorded – May 30/31, June 4/21, 1968. **Engineers** – *Geoff Emerick, Peter Bown*
Drums – *Ringo Starr*

The first version of *Revolution* to be recorded sees Ringo turn in a workman-like and functional performance, laying down a solid shuffle feel, notable for deft touches on the closely-miked snare. This is coupled with opposable heavy snare/bass drum crashes on the bridges to the (hook of) the chorus. The drums sit differently in the mono mix, buried deeper but still delivering punch.

Timing wise, the song is essentially in 4/4, with the usual bars of 2/4 to accommodate lyrics, this time the *"we-ell, you know"*… of the chorus, before the adoption of a 'pushing' and punctuating 3/8 beat at [3.24] over the *"shoop-bee-dooh-wop"* play out.

Honey Pie

Time Signature – 4/4
Recorded – October 1/2/4, 1968. **Engineer –** *Barry Sheffield*
Drums – *Ringo Starr*

Another Trident recording, with Ringo once again dusting off his brushes and showing that he can swing with the best of them, Starr's performance perfectly compliments this 1920's pastiche. As on *When I'm 64,* he again recalls the feel of the dance hall music of his Parents. Hi-hat and accented snare [1.18] expertly top and tail phrases, especially over Lennon's superb guitar solo.

Savoy Truffle

Time Signature – 4/4, 6/8, 7/8
Recorded – October 3/5/11/14, 1968. **Engineers –** *Barry Sheffield, Ken Scott*
Drums, Tambourine – *Ringo Starr*

With recording initially at Trident and overdubs at Abbey Road, *Savoy Truffle* possesses a closely-miked drum track, largely at odds with the rest of the album. The effect exacerbated by added delay and suspiciously tea-towelled drums, the production adds to the claustrophobic overly heavy compression of the track. With *Savoy Truffle*, George proves he's not the only Beatle averse to alternating time-changes, Ringo's intricate, accented starting fill brings us into a 4/4 bar followed by a 7/8 then a 6/8 bar, before resuming in 4/4, the cycle beginning again.

Playing similar tom fills to other songs on the LP, note how the production techniques employed deliberately alters and lessens their impact. Almost an after-thought, random tambourine embellishes the latter stages.

Cry Baby Cry

Time Signature – 4/4, 2/4
Recorded – July 15/16/18, 1968. **Engineers –** *Geoff Emerick, Ken Scott*
Drums, Tambourine – *Ringo Starr*

The session that saw off Geoff Emerick, and his replacement by Ken Scott, *Cry Baby Cry* is perhaps Ringo's greatest performance on *The Beatles*, as we hear fantastic rolling and tumbling fills around a largely accented rhythm track. Tambourine enhances the tension over a simple introductory beat [0.28] before the inventive fills interject. While similar, no two patterns are exactly the same, possibly the best examples occurring while moving from open hi-hats to snare at [1.24] and [1.55], where Ringo resolves the urgency and tension of his ride cymbal work [1.40] and on, below. Worthy of note is a sloppily mistimed tambourine (bar 5 below), unusually prominent and disjointed in the stereo mix, but buried in the mono version.

Illustrated above, we have a bar of 2/4 appended to each line of the verses, for example -

2 Bars of 4/4 – *"Queen was in the parlour, playing piano for the children of the King."*
1 Bar of 2/4 -
5 bars of 4/4 – *"Cry, baby cry…make your mother sigh, she's old enough to know better, so cry, baby cry."*
1 Bar of 2/4 -

The un-credited coda (commonly referred to as *Can You Take Me Back*) is a left-over fragment of a longer improvisation from the *I Will* session, and sees McCartney enhancing the track with maracas and single tom strokes.

Revolution 9

Recorded – 6/10/11/20/21, June 1968. **Engineer** – *Geoff Emerick*

Somewhat surprisingly, this avant-garde montage possesses a great deal of percussive intent, the emphasis of pace created by tape edits, with fader movements being used to great effect.

Good Night

Time Signature – 4/4

Recorded – June 28, 2/22, July 1968. **Engineers** – *Geoff Emerick, Peter Bown*

Lush strings on this touching melody, and the only Ringo vocal track without drums or percussion, or his band-mates for that matter. Nevertheless, with this tender treatment, it's arguably his finest vocal contribution.

29. Yellow Submarine

LP – Released January 17 1969

Engineers – *Geoff Emerick, Eddie Kramer, Ken Scott, Dave Siddle*

Yellow Submarine

With *Yellow Submarine* and *All You Need Is Love* not exclusive to this release, we have not included these songs in the data for the *Yellow Submarine* LP.

Cowbell	1
Finger Cymbals	1
Handclaps	2
Maracas	1
Tambourine	2

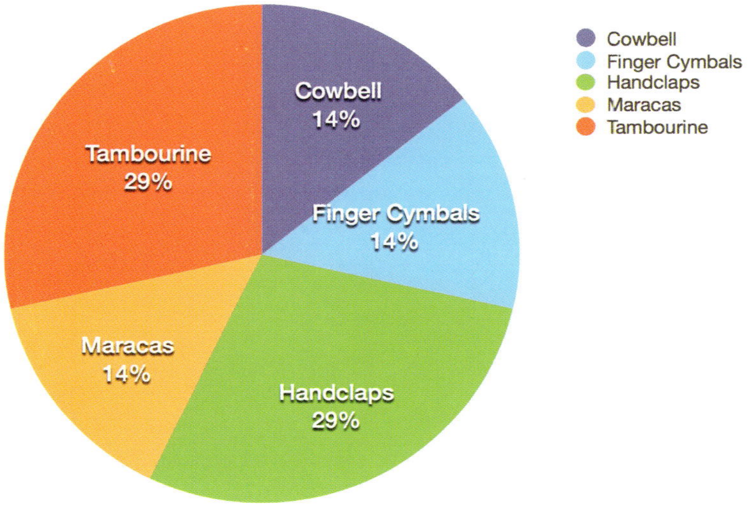

With *The Beatles* double-LP released only a matter of months previously, and the Christmas festivities still fresh in the memory, it's no wonder this lightweight soundtrack LP failed to make top spot. With only 4 new songs on the album, and two of those dating from the *Sgt. Pepper* era, the *Yellow Submarine* soundtrack would have made a terrific EP release, and may well have made the top of the charts?

Lennon's commitment to the 'Yellow Submarine' project was never in doubt

Yellow Submarine

Time Signature – 4/4
Recorded – May 26, June 1, 1966. **Engineer** – *Geoff Emerick*
Drums – *Ringo Starr*
Bass Drum – *Mal Evans*

The title track of the film illustrates just how much the Beatles had moved on since it's original release two years previously.

Only A Northern Song

Time Signature – 4/4
Recorded – February 13/14, April 20, 1967. **Engineer** – *Geoff Emerick*
Drums, Finger Cymbals, Handclaps – *Ringo Starr*

Considered too weak for inclusion on *Sgt. Pepper*, Ringo does his best to lift this sloppily languid George Harrison offering, for once over-egging the opportunity for fills. With the obligatory introductory snare/tom fill [0.07] Ringo (and his band-mates) amble along in second gear. Strange then how well the song translated to the big screen when coupled with expansive psychedelia, the Beatles' magic dust sprinkled liberally.

All Together Now

Time Signature – 4/4
Recorded – May 12, 1967. **Engineer –** *Geoff Emerick*
Drums, Handclaps – *Ringo Starr*
Handclaps – *Paul McCartney, George Harrison, John Lennon, studio attendees*
Triangle, Sleigh Bells, Tambourine, Maracas – *Uncredited*

The first song donated to the film, *All Together Now* dates from mid 1967, and sees Beatles and bystanders picking up all manner of percussion instruments, building progressively. Sounding like an out-take from *The Beach Boys Party,* the first bridge sees the introduction of drums and overdubbed tom (or is it bass drum?), swiftly followed by maracas, tambourine, bells, triangle, sleigh bells, maracas, handclaps, and possibly more.

Hey Bulldog

Time Signature – 4/4
Recorded – February 11, 1968. **Engineers –** *Geoff Emerick, Ken Scott*
Drums – *Ringo Starr*
Tambourine – *Paul McCartney*

By a stroke of good fortune, in 2009 we were treated to newly-unearthed rare footage of the group at work in the studio. The session that produced *Hey Bulldog* was slated to shoot a promo film for the Beatles' next single release, *Lady Madonna*. By the time the film crew arrived, the recording of *Lady Madonna* had been completed, the group now working on *Hey Bulldog*. As a result we have a documented insight into the Beatles' recording process, Ringo's drums dampened with tea-towels, Paul simultaneously laying down tambourine as Ringo records the drum track.

With the nature of the riff-driven guitar track, it's no surprise Ringo plays essentially the same pattern, echoing the stabbing guitar track perfectly, the fills resolved with tambourine.

Overdubbed snare with added reverb is introduced, filling out the bridges prior to the solo and the play-out [0.52 & 1.52].

Tambourine(s) played by Paul busk over the fade.

It's All Too Much

Time Signature – 4/4
Recorded – May 25/26, June 2, 1967. **Engineer** – *Dave Siddle*
Drums – *Ringo Starr*
Tambourine – *John Lennon*
Maracas – *George Harrison*
Cowbell – *Paul McCartney*

Another pre-recorded track from 1967, and the greater of the two offerings on the album from Harrison. Recorded at De Lane Lea studios, *It's All Too Much* is notable for a radically different drum sound to the recent Abbey Road recordings, due to a different engineering approach and of course, room acoustics. Instead we hear a more distant Ringo, with prominent 'high in the mix' overdubbed handclaps, tambourine, cowbell and hi-hat. With Ringo turning in another creditable performance, the strong snare backbeat takes centre stage. Here we have a typically "trippy" mood, a simple forthright beat backed up by strong ADT soaked handclaps, with cowbell maintaining the constant. Managing to both enliven the drum track with copious fills around his kit, he produces a coherent piece of timekeeping, which is somewhat lacking in Harrison's *Only A Northern Song*.

During quieter passages, replacing the heavily overdubbed handclap back-beat, we hear cleverly arranged off-beat hi-hat and tambourine.

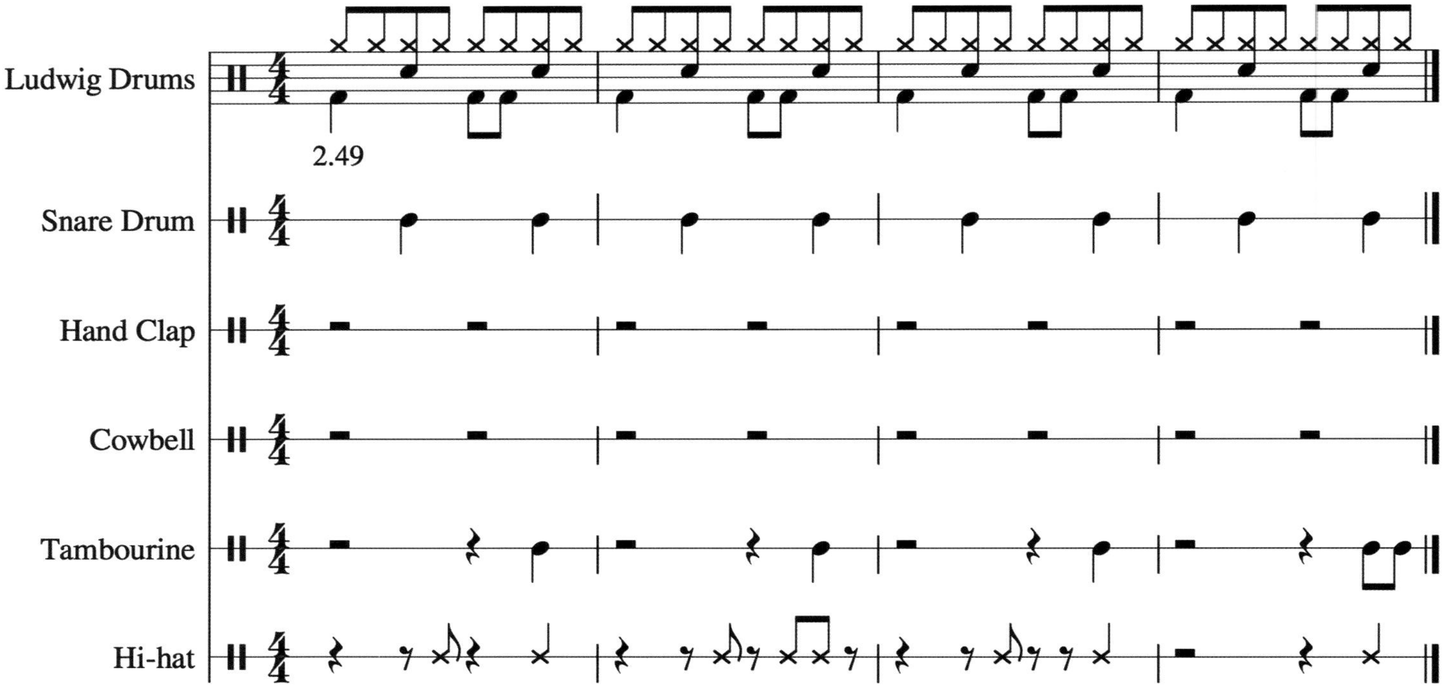

Tambourine and cowbell pick up the pace during the chorus (3.06), the tambourine less busier 4 bars later, where it's previous urgency is heightened by placement along with snare, cowbell, and opened hi-hats on the 2nd and 4th beats of the bar [3.15].

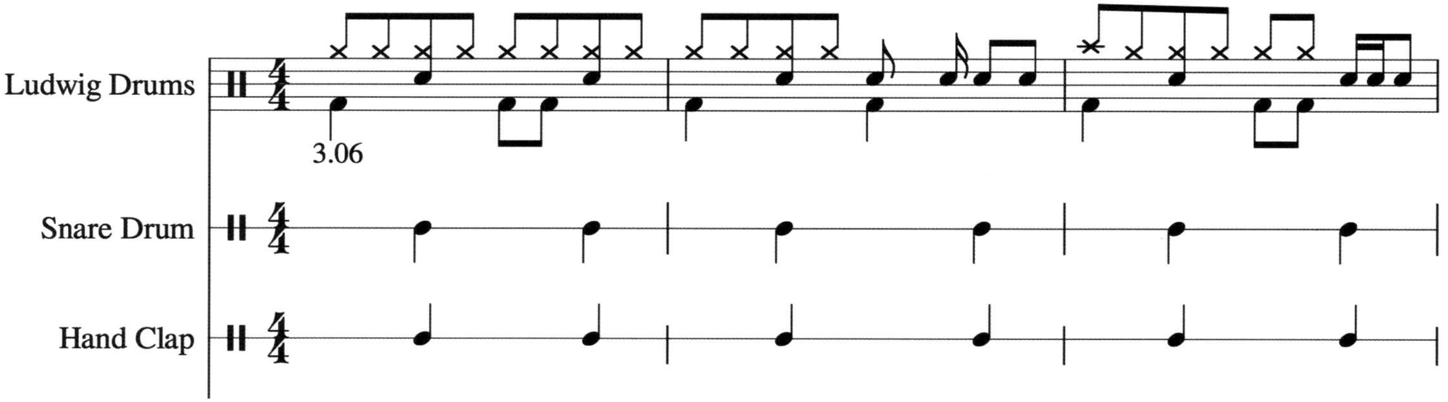

The play-out is nothing but a percussive free for-all, with drums, tambourine, maracas and cowbell prominent. The whole effect is one of psychedelia for sure, but the guitar possesses a sound both The Edge and Jimi Hendrix would have been proud of, and an inventive use of percussion that with an increased tempo wouldn't have been out of place in a nightclub of the late 1980's / early 90's.

All You Need Is Love
Time Signature – 4/4, 3/4
Recorded – June 14/19/23/24/25, 1967. **Engineers** – *Geoff Emerick, Eddie Kramer*
Drums – *Ringo Starr*
Handclaps, Various Percussion – *Audience*

Previously released in the summer of 1967, and included here as the showpiece finale of the movie.

Listening to a playback at Apple Studios.

30. Get Back / Don't Let Me Down

Single – Released April 11 1969
Engineer – *Glyn Johns*

Get Back

Time Signature – 4/4
Recorded – January 23/27/28/30, February 5 1969
Drums – *Ringo Starr*

Having enjoyed performing in front of an audience while shooting the *Hey Jude* promotional film, the Beatles re-grouped in January 1969 with a new direction – a 'back to basics' approach to their new project. As a result, the ensuing *Get Back* single saw no percussion overdubbing – it must have been tempting to at least add the ubiquitous tambourine, but the group stuck to their guns. This wasn't the only new direction the group were taking – the sessions were to be recorded at the newly installed Apple Studios in the basement of their HQ at Savile Row.

Technically, this smaller environment produced a 'tighter', more modern sound than Abbey Road could offer. Ringo's drums benefit here from close-miking and are once again dampened with tea-towels, making his cymbal interjections all the more brighter and refreshing. Dampening drums in this way can prove counter – productive, you may achieve the sound you are looking for, but at the expense of less bounce – back from the drum skin. A heavier touch is required, in turn affecting the sound of the drum. Ringo negotiates this perfectly, a less experienced drummer may be tempted to eschew this simple yet effective approach and overplay.

Early rehearsals saw Ringo employing a straight 4/4 '8 in the bar' hi-hat beat, while the finished product sees Starr in a wonderfully forthright mood, the bulk of the song taken up with a simple snare-driven pattern. The introduction sees Ringo and band shuffling their way to the first verse by way of accented cymbal crashes which punctuate throughout, bolstering the lyrics with more weight and substance.

There are percussive elements coming at us from every direction, Harrison's underrated and excellent rhythm guitar working in tandem with Ringo's superb snare/bass drum combination. Providing a notion of variety and respite from the relentless snare beat, Billy Preston's electric piano solo is underpinned by a shift to a straightforward floor tom/snare/bass drum beat (the final bar below), punctuated with cymbal strikes replicated on the tagged-on play-out, preceded by Ringo's snare to tom fill.

Don't Let Me Down
Time Signature – 4/4, 5/4
Recorded – January 22/28/30, 1969
Drums – *Ringo Starr*

A perfect companion piece to *Get Back*, Lennon's superb 'weepy' *Don't Let Me Down* has Ringo once again at the top of his game. The 'back to basics' dictat ensured the song was recorded live – we can clearly hear his 'buzzing' snare wires vibrating over the introduction. From the opening bass drum/crash cymbal, we have a great example of Ringo utilising the dynamics of his drum kit to match the emotions of the song, particularly the vocal delivery. His triplet emphasis during Lennon's embittered cry of the song title (bar 4 below) provide thrusting impetus, the fairly sparse drumming allowing the song to breathe, thus preventing it becoming cluttered.

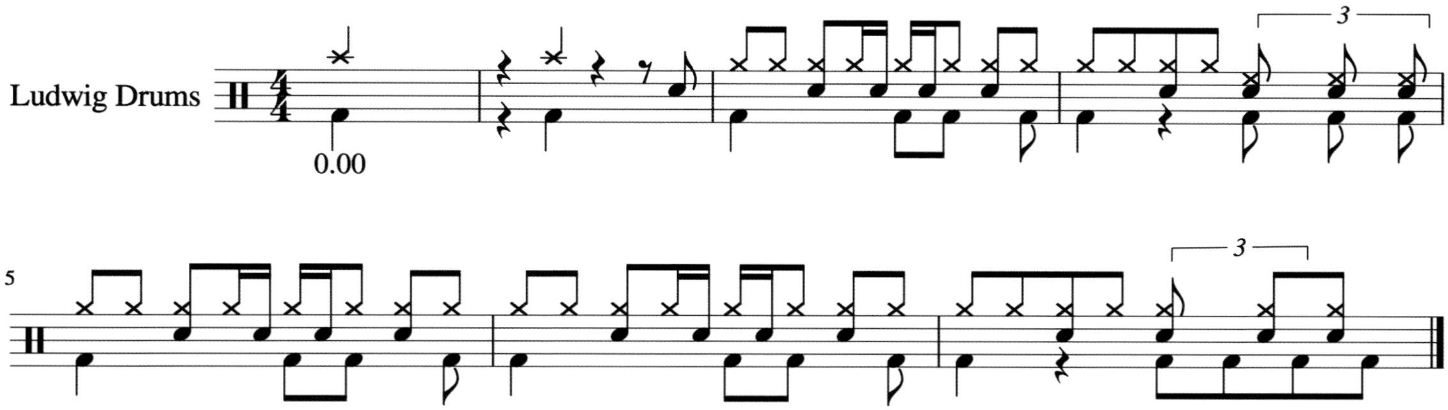

The bridge [0.41] and [2.10] sees John's usual playing with time – we have a 5/4 bar of vocal only, before returning to 4/4. This provides the listener with the effect of a dream – like state of mind, one could almost argue the swirling mind of one being in love?

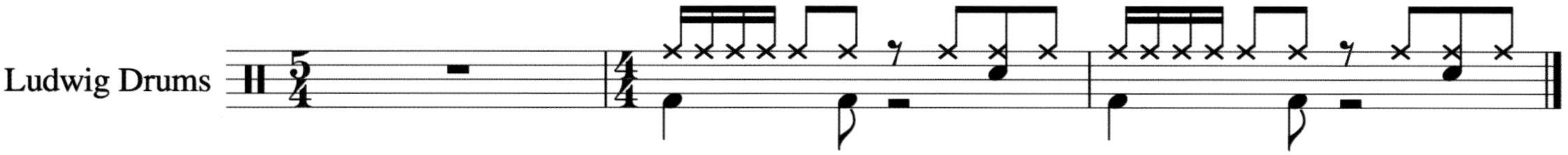

Elsewhere, Ringo's busking style from [3.05] allows Billy Preston's keyboard to take centre stage, the inspiring open hi-hat work helping to push the song forward.

31. The Ballad Of John And Yoko / Old Brown Shoe

(**Single** – Released May 30 1969)

The Ballad Of John And Yoko

Time Signature – 4/4, 2/4
Recorded – April 14, 1969. **Engineer –** *Geoff Emerick*
Drums, Maracas, Handclaps – *Paul McCartney*
Guitar Body Taps, Handclaps – *John Lennon*

With Ringo and George both absent overseas, John and Paul took the opportunity to record a new track, destined to be the new Beatles single. Once again picking up sticks, McCartney delivers an admirable if unspectacular job, busying himself with a repetitive beat, enlivened with off-beat snare strokes to counterpoint the vocals. Another cheeky 2/4 bar with urgent 8th note snare (bar 5 below) punctuates the lyrical 'joke' and heralds busy maracas. Perhaps mindful of Ringo's absence and eager to utilise any object to obtain the sound they had in their minds, Lennon enthusiastically bolsters the snare beat by slapping the back of his acoustic guitar, further enhanced by added handclaps evident in the left channel of the mix. The otherwise busy mix (the first Beatles stereo UK single release) is nonetheless pleasing on the ear, perhaps due to the laid – back feel of the repetitive beat.

Old Brown Shoe

Time Signature – 4/4
Recorded – April 16/18, 1969. **Engineer –** *Jeff Jarratt*
Drums – *Ringo Starr*

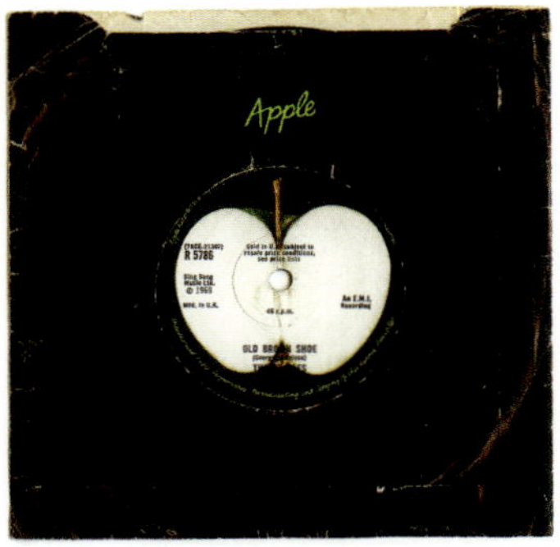

Something of a hidden gem in the Beatles' catalogue, *Old Brown Shoe* sees Ringo performing a very different kind of Beatle beat – a tight off-beat 'Texan Blues' style shuffle on the 1st and 3rd beats (bar 4 below). With subtle rim clicks in evidence, Ringo seamlessly breaks into an orthodox 4/4 beat either side of the guitar solo (bars 1 & 2), with some incredibly forceful matched-stroke fills on snare and floor tom at pertinent points throughout, the best occurring in the 3rd bar below. It's a powerhouse performance from Ringo, one of his very best.

32. Abbey Road

LP – Released September 26 1969

Engineers – *Geoff Emerick, Phil McDonald, Jeff Jarratt, Glyn Johns, Tony Clark, Barry Sheffield*

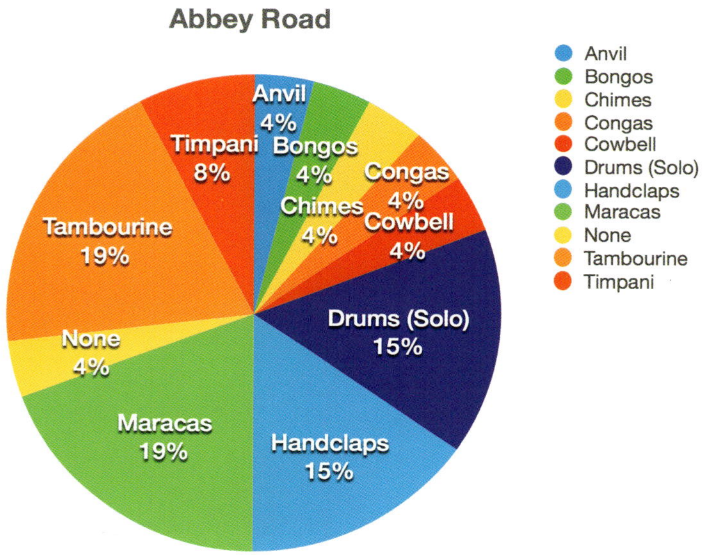

On what would prove to be the band's swan-song, we hear a warmer, smoother Beatles – thanks largely to the replacement of the old valve (tube) mixing desk with a more modern transistorised desk at Abbey Road. Crucially, each channel had its own limiter/compressor and equalisation, meaning each instrument could have these treatments applied in isolation, rather than being grouped together. Having 8 tracks also enabled the drums to be recorded in stereo, the result of these advancements is a cleaner more defined sound, with the drums arguably the most to benefit.

17 Songs

INSTRUMENT	USE
Anvil	1
Bongos	1
Chimes	1
Congas	1
Cowbell	1
Drums (Solo)	4
Handclaps	4
Maracas	5
None	1
Tambourine	5
Timpani	2

The first Beatles album to be exclusively mixed in stereo, the resulting mix largely sees the drum track still routinely panned to one side, the addition of extra tracks to play with however lessens the effect of the earlier, more stark stereo mixes of preceding albums.

Come Together

Time Signature – 4/4
Recorded – July 21/22/23/25/29/30, 1969. **Engineers –** *Geoff Emerick, Phil McDonald*
Drums, Maracas – *Ringo Starr*
Handclaps – *John Lennon*

Perhaps the Beatles song most recognisable by the drums alone, *Come Together* is also an obvious fan-favourite of Ringo's drumming, featuring clearly defined and distinctive drum patterns. On the terrifically quirky and lengthy (for the day) introduction, Starr plays an incredibly tight, yet fluid 'around-the kit' movement from hi-hats to toms.

Or does he? In 2008 Ringo stated that because he leads with his left hand, he plays his floor tom first, followed by mounted tom(s). However, perhaps due to his toms being closely tuned, it does appear as if he is moving around his drums from left to right. If this was indeed the case, it is likely Ringo is playing a pattern that is conducive to his unique style of leading with his left hand, as notated here –

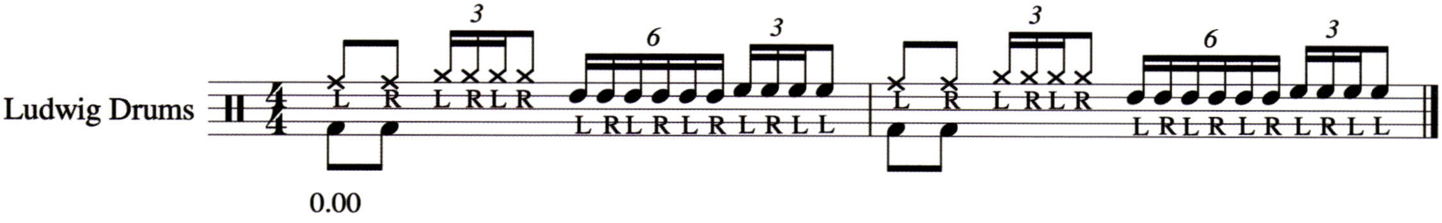

Moving on we hear the solidity of the verses, played on bass and toms, the bridge to the chorus cunningly featuring just the bass drum -

The short chorus is kept simple on bass and snare – the snare benefitting from the induced vibrating snares on the bottom skin, adding a dash of room ambience to the track.

Each pattern is punctuated either side by surprisingly gentle use of his crash/ride cymbal, the play-out seeing liberal and powerful 'edge of the cymbal' use. Ringo's drums and performance underpin and set the tone for the rest of the album that follows.

Something

Time Signature – 4/4
Recorded – April 16, May 2/5, July 11/16, August 15, 1969. **Engineers**- *Jeff Jarratt, Glyn Johns, Phil McDonald*
Drums, Handclaps – *Ringo Starr*

Featuring the full expanse of Ringo's new 5 piece drum kit, the range of playing here is stark – from gentle cymbal strokes to thunderous fills, Ringo plays for the emotions of the song. Taking a cue from the previous track, Ringo brings in the song with simplistic tom fills, repeated throughout the song. Again, as in *Come Together*, Ringo then declines the opportunity to pad the song out with a straight hi-hat heavy 4/4 beat. Instead we have only snare and bass, with fills appropriately placed between the vocal.

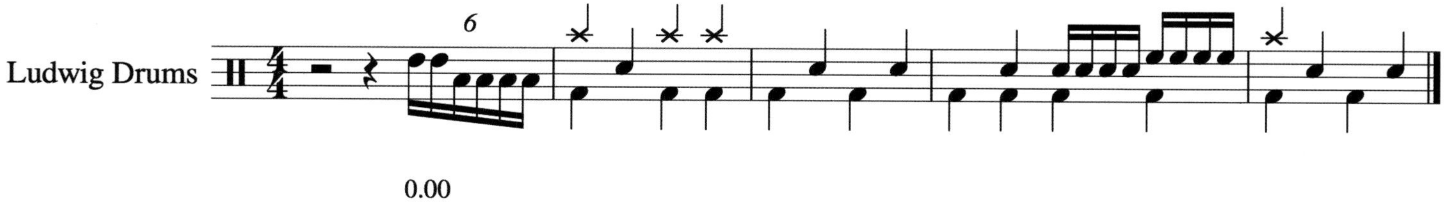

Ringo ‘ups the ante’ with some forceful and anguished drumming for three bars on the bridge to the guitar solo [1.14] which sees perhaps his busiest and most inventive drum patterns – before releasing the tension (bars 4 & 5 below). Such a busy, intrusive drum track to the tender love song either side of it, however the anguish of the vocal is greatly enhanced by solid tom-tom work.

The pattern played here may feel fussy and too much for one drummer – was it perhaps recorded in one pass, or were the toms recorded first with the hi – hat overdubbed later? There is evidence that a percussion track was “bounced – down” to accommodate 2 tracks for the orchestral overdub, but this appears to have simply contained the cymbal (perhaps played with timpani sticks) that links the verses and this passage. As was the case with the rest of the album, if there had been additional overdubs they would surely have been panned either left or right into one channel of the stereo mix? Presented below is an example of the possible overdubbed hi-hat.

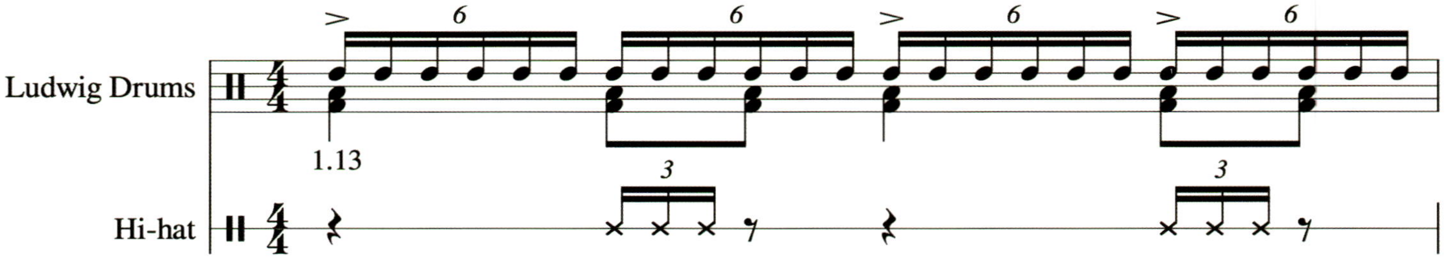

We hear the only perceptible straight 4/4 hi-hat beat only later in the song – in this case the last lines of the vocal [2.35]. It's this device that moves us along towards the song's climax – the effect is one of suddenly being carried along by an escalator. Having previously walked the length of the song, the resolving fill coming off the hi-hats at [2.47] the moment your feet land on the floor once again.

Maxwell's Silver Hammer

Time Signature – 4/4
Recorded – July 9/10/11, August 6, 1969. **Engineers. –** *Phil McDonald, Tony Clark*
Drums, Anvil – *Ringo Starr*

A McCartney leftover from the *Let It Be* sessions (and derided by his bandmates, particularly Lennon), this annoyingly simplistic, yet dark 'nursery crime' sees Ringo plodding along, like his colleagues, seemingly under duress. Workmanlike and simplistic, the naive nature of the playing (on bass drum and open and closed hi-hats) lends the song the intended sinister feel.

First seen on the *Get Back* sessions, the 'hired for the day' anvil (whatever the Beatles wanted, they got) proved too much for Ringo (he was unable to lift the hammer and thus strike it with sufficient force, bless him…), so duties were passed to gentle giant Mal Evans, who expertly provided the wallop on the first two beats of the bar of the chorus. However, it is believed Ringo was able to muster the strength to tackle anvil duties on this *Abbey Road* version.

Oh! Darling

Time Signature – 12/8
Recorded – April 20/26, July 17/18/22, August 11, 1969. **Engineers –** *Jeff Jarratt, Phil McDonald, Geoff Emerick*
Drums – *Ringo Starr*

Classic Ringo – seemingly loosely played yet with all the precision of a guided missile. Employing a 'Blues/Doo-Wop' 12/8 discipline, his triplet fills recall those on *Come Together*, however this time played as a hi-hat/bass/snare beat. Heavily dampened drums make his overplayed snare work (in particular at [1.04] & [2.11]) appear simplistic and sometimes clumsy and at odds with the simple feel of the song. A little reverb applied to the drum track may have improved matters?

Octopus's Garden

Time Signature – 4/4
Recorded – April 26/29, July 17/18, 1969. **Engineers –** *Jeff Jarratt, Phil McDonald*
Drums – *Ringo Starr*

A return to the Ringo album-cameo of old, the self-penned *Octopus's Garden* once again sees Ringo in a playful Country & Western mood. Possessing the panache and gravitas of being recorded while simultaneously singing and playing drums,

Ringo's patterns here compliment the simple nature of the song, as does his uncanny knack of knowing just what portions of his kit to play, and when. Perhaps as an afterthought, tom overdubs were deemed necessary.

I Want You (She's So Heavy)

Time Signature – 6/8, 4/4, 2/4

Recorded – February 22, April 18/20, August 8/11, 1969. **Engineers –** *Barry Sheffield, Jeff Jarratt, Phil McDonald, Geoff Emerick*

Drums, Congas – *Ringo Starr*

Topping and tailing the song in 6/8 time, we are soon in familiar Lennon territory – with a short and sparse (compared to the end!) 6/8 introduction ……

Ludwig Drums

……soon followed by 4 bars in 4/4, and in typical Lennon fashion, an additional bar of 2/4 which then takes us into the verse proper.

Ludwig Drums

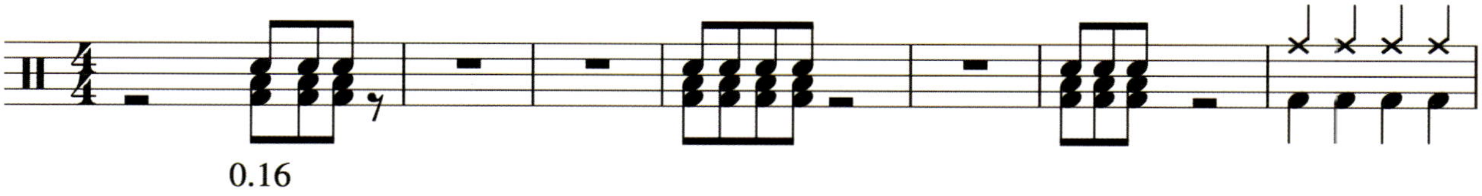

The stop/start nature of the song is smoothed over by the use of open ride and crash/ride cymbals, negotiating the slipping in of a 2/4 bar -

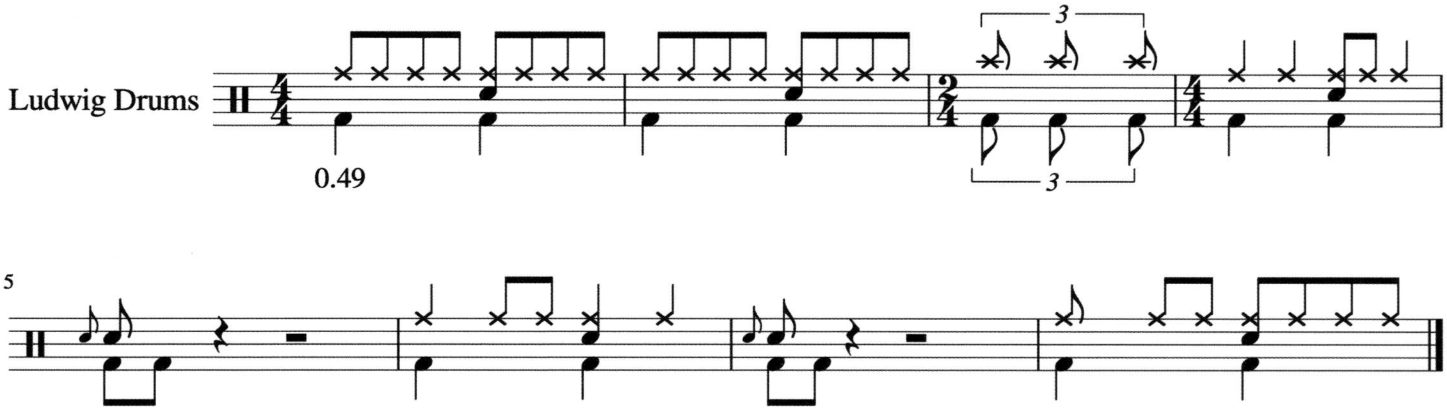

A variation on the bossa-nova beat (not heard since the "Help!" album), gives the song a "lounge" feel, also due in part to the liberal use of ride cymbal and overdubbed congas.

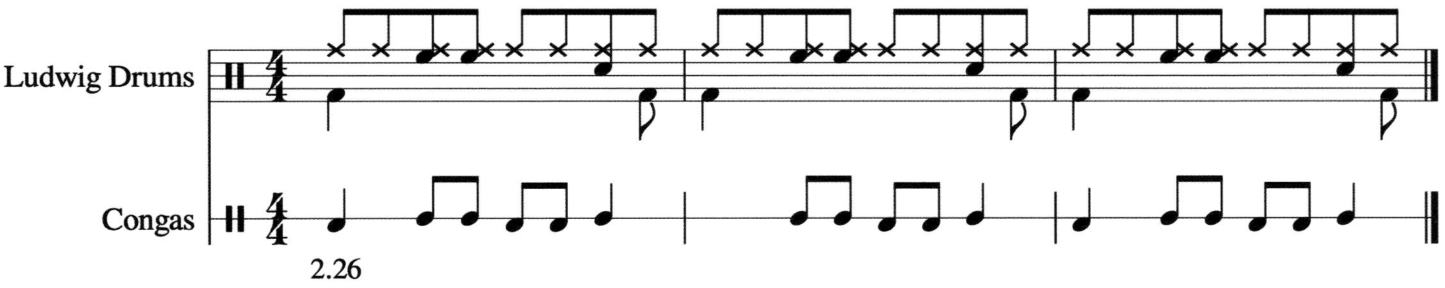

With plenty of improvisation on the final repetitive passage, especially from multi tracked guitars and the busy bass, Ringo reinforced his drum track, overdubbing snare and tom to bind the performance together. Things are kept simple yet there's still power present, it's almost as if his performance has been waiting for the tom roll at [6.26], and when it arrives, it's at just the right moment.

Here Comes The Sun

Time Signature – 4/4, 2/4, 3/8, 5/8
Recorded – July 7/8/16, August 6/15/19, 1969. **Engineers** – *Phil McDonald, Tony Clark, Geoff Emerick*
Drums , Handclaps – *Ringo Starr*
Handclaps – *George Harrison, Paul McCartney*

> *"Ringo's tom fills really make the song, but funnily enough, he hated doing them because he could never remember what he did one take to the next. I think that's why his fills are so spectacular – he felt that he would never reproduce them, so he'd better get 'em right".*
>
> **Geoff Emerick**[122]
>
> *"He'd (Harrison) been to India or something, and he says to me "I've got this song, it's like ….."7 & 1/2 time" …he might as well have talked to me in Arabic…"*
>
> *(Plays fill on thighs) "And that's how I do it. I had to find some way…that I could physically do it, and do it every time..so that it came off 'on the time'….. That's one of those Indian tricks, I had no way of going ' 1,2,3,4,5,6….7 – that's not how my brain works."*
>
> **Ringo Starr – *George Harrison – Living In The Material World.***

Another excellent example of Ringo's ability to cope with unusual time signatures, *Here Comes The Sun* is also notable for a fantastically laid-back groove. The opening bars have a hint of what is to follow, with a delightful double-fill into the first verse -

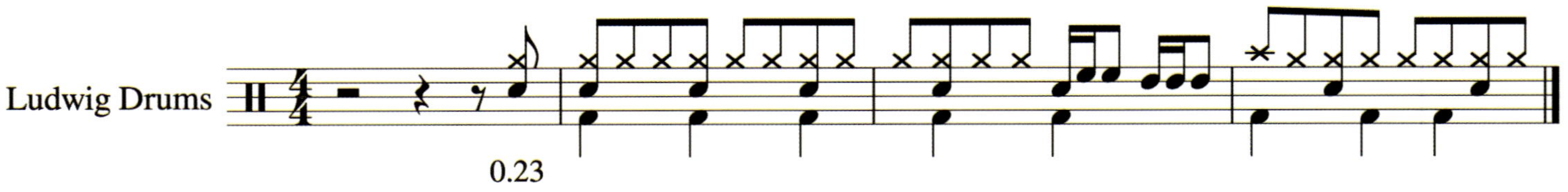

The numerous time changes within the song, first occur on the bridge. This section sees a 2/4 before alternating between 3/8, 5/8, 4/4, a 2/4, and finally 3/8 that returns to 4/4. Ringo draws upon his 'Indian trick' – using his experiences of Indian music time-keeping rather than counting out the time in the usual Western fashion.

Sharp and snappy handclaps hasten the end of the bridge, cleverly used to great effect. The complexities of 3 people (George, Ringo & Paul) together, negotiating such a minefield of shifting time signatures becomes apparent in the bars below. Ringo also provides a wonderful moment across a bar of 2/4 and 3/8 (bars 2 & 3 below), returning to the snare when half-way through rather than taking the easy option of staying on the tom.

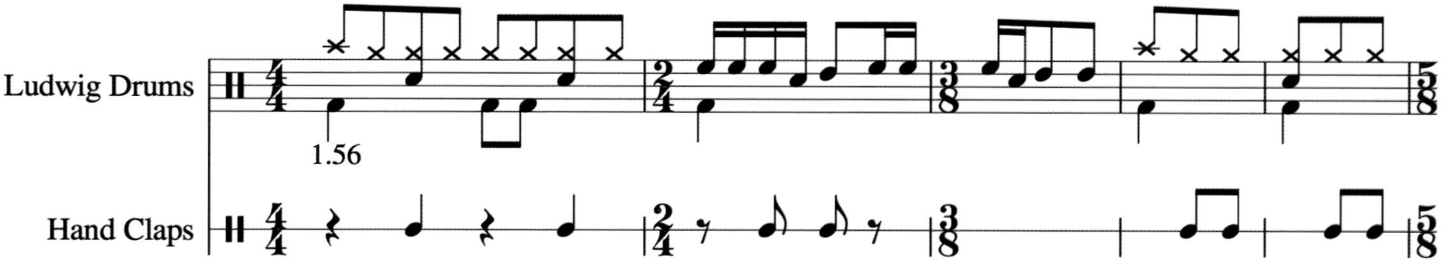

Ringo's drums sound fantastic here, benefitting greatly from the new technology of the mixing desk and new skins. The snare and hi – hats sound crisp and tight, with the drums having a punch not previously heard on Beatles' recordings.

Because

Time Signature – 4/4
Recorded – August 1/4/5, 1969. **Engineer –** *Phil McDonald, Geoff Emerick*

No drums or percussion, simply gorgeous harmonies to rival their Californian contemporaries.

You Never Give Me Your Money

Time Signature – 4/4
Recorded – May 6, July 1/15/30/31, August 5, 1969. **Engineers –** *Glyn Johns, Phil McDonald, Geoff Emerick*
Drums, Tambourine – *Ringo Starr*
Chimes – *Paul McCartney*

Another 'section by section' composition, Ringo's drums are tacit during the melancholic piano intro, appearing as deft cymbal touches at the start of the second verse [0.48]. Ringo enters with a typically tumbling fill around the toms (below) swiftly moving into gear to a choked hi-hat swinging boogie feel, with fills matching the phrasing of the piano [1.18 & 1.29].

A gear change down [1.32] takes us into a straight 4/4 hi-hat beat with liberal use of his ride cymbal bell, matching the 'chiming' nature of the guitar track. A simple inventive double-stroke on his tom [1.48] trades-off with the lyrics. A funky arrangement punctuated with fills between snare and toms [2.11] fills the gaps between the guitar phrases. Notice how Paul slips a 2/4 bar into the song [2.47] to accommodate the "*came true*" lyrical section. A typically languid feel takes us to the end of the track, with copious fills along the way. Chimes (played by Paul) make their second and final appearance in the Beatles' repertoire, *When I'm 64* being the other occasion.

Sun King

Time Signature – 4/4
Recorded – July 24/25/29, 1969. **Engineers –** *Phil McDonald, Geoff Emerick*
Drums, Tambourine, Cymbals, Congas – *Ringo Starr*
Maracas – *John Lennon*

Utilising timpani sticks, Ringo taps-out a measured beat on his tea towel dampened floor-tom. Maintaining the constant, hi-hats provide steady timekeeping on the second and fourth beats. Maracas and cymbal swashes fill the gaps, with congas subtly introduced at [1.50], enhancing the play-out.

Mean Mr. Mustard

Time Signature – 4/4, 12/8
Recorded – July 24/25/29, 1969. **Engineers –** *Phil McDonald, Geoff Emerick*
Drums, Tambourine – *Ringo Starr*
Maracas – *John Lennon*

After his tight opening fill, Ringo's bass drum sits solidly in the groove alongside Paul's bass, the bottom-end bass sound enhanced throughout. Tambourine (playing '16's') is introduced after 3 bars, further beefing up the track. Slightly before the rather abrupt ending, there are 2 bars of 12/8 finishing with a final tom flourish, segueing nicely into *Polythene Pam*. Traces of erratic time-keeping are evident, one wonders if the drum track was added as an afterthought?

Polythene Pam

Time Signature – 4/4
Recorded – July 25/28/30, 1969. **Engineers –** *Phil McDonald, Geoff Emericks*
Drums, Tambourine, Cowbell, Maracas – *Ringo Starr*
Handclaps – *John Lennon*

With the impatient Lennon reputably unhappy with the drum track laid down live, Ringo begrudgingly overdubbed the recurring tom patterns that became such a feature of this song. Workmanlike, yet effective and precise, Ringo's tom work (accented and landing with snare on the 4th beat of the bar) keeps the track motoring along. Making full use of his toms, the busy percussion track builds progressively, tambourine introduced with cowbell and maracas, doubling up [1.11] towards the climax of the lead-in to….

She Came In Through The Bathroom Window

Time Signature – 4/4
Recorded – July 25/28/30, 1969. **Engineers –** *Phil McDonald, Geoff Emerick*
Drums, Tambourine – *Ringo Starr*

Recorded as one track with *Polythene Pam*, from John's overly Scouse "*Oh! Lookout!* " followed by Ringo's fill [0.07] and groove, you know this is going to be a real mover. With '8 in the bar' hi-hats prominent, the song moves along at a pace slower than it actually feels. Plentiful, sympathetic fills (the best of which are heard typically coming off the open hi-hat) are bolstered by the introduction of tambourine at [0.29]. Mimicking the feel of *Polythene Pam*, we again hear the snare landing on the '3 and' beat, this time enhanced by reverb, producing an effective 'slap echo'.

Golden Slumbers

Time Signature – 4/4
Recorded – July 2/3/4/30/31, August 15, 1969. **Engineers** – *Phil McDonald, Geoff Emerick*
Drums, Timpani- *Ringo Starr*

After the melodic piano and vocal from Paul, a mighty tom fill [0.33] serves to introduce the searing change in the vocal. There's plenty of light and shade here, with bars of powerful accents in the chorus, and slight, delicate strokes on the cymbal enhancing the second verse, joined at [1.20] with the interplay of the tom. Another forceful fill, virtually identical to that which announced *Golden Slumbers*, takes us into…

Carry That Weight

Time Signature – 4/4
Recorded – July 4/23/30/31, August 15, 1969. **Engineers** – *Phil McDonald, Geoff Emerick*
Drums, Timpani- *Ringo Starr*

With Ringo's drum track evident in the left channel, overdubbed snare, bass, and possibly floor tom are present in the right channel. The result is a heavy drum sound, carrying the weight of the song, so to speak. Ringo gets his teeth into proceedings – the four bars below show his tom work and use of 'space' on the "*I never give you my pillow*" section that follows the guitar solo [0.44] -

The best of the fills that follow [1.11] sees him coming off the snare with a roll onto his toms, very much in the Motown style. Gentle cymbal accents and toms follow George Martin's score, before strident snare, bass drum and toms kick in on the final chorus [1.36].

The End

Time Signature – 4/4

Recorded – July 23, August 5/7/8/15/18, 1969. **Engineers –** *Phil McDonald, Geoff Emerick*

Drums – *Ringo Starr*

Ringo's showpiece drum solo very nearly didn't happen – dead-set against drum solos, it took a lot of encouragement from his bandmates (and engineers), plus their agreement to halve the allotted time of the solo before he would step behind his kit. Doesn't he pull it off? – and then some! The use of his drums (where space is used as an instrument between fills) – is underscored with a powerful bass drum playing 'eight in the bar'. At [0.29] we hear a slight breath from Ringo, and an even slighter increase in tempo on the bass drum prior to his last tom fill – as sign of relief at completing his solo?

Ringo's drums on *The End* benefitted from two improvements, namely the fitting of new calf skin heads and the ability for them to be recorded in stereo for the first and only time. Looking at earlier photographs of Ringo's drums, both in the studio and at live performances, his drum skins are well-used, the dirt and grime clearly embedded in the skins, which are markedly worn away.

As we have seen, the introduction of an eight-track recording machine allowed the use of more tracks, therefore more mikes were deployed and most importantly, the kit could be recorded in stereo. As drummers will be aware, listening to stereo mixes can be a little disconcerting, as the listening experience from in front of the speakers is from the perspective of the audience, rather than the performer. By simply switching the channels around, or even easier changing headphones over, we can hear Ringo's perspective as he played, top tom to the left, middle toms to the centre, floor tom to the right. The quality of the recording (especially on the 2009 version released by Apple on USB stick, or the 'Mastered for iTunes' version) certainly helps in this respect.

Her Majesty

Time Signature – 4/4
Recorded – July 2, 1969. **Engineer –** *Phil McDonald*
Drums -

An accident at the mastering stage, *'Her Majesty'* was intended to be placed in the Medley on Side 2 (between 'Mean Mr. Mustard' & 'Polythene Pam'), but was removed and placed at the end of the master tape. True to form, upon hearing it, Paul insisted on leaving it in, another imperfection to prove they were human after all.

★

Something / Come Together

Single – Released October 31 1969.
Engineers – *Jeff Jarratt, Glyn Johns, Phil McDonald (Something) / Geoff Emerick, Phil McDonald (Come Together).*

This superb single incredibly failed to make the top spot in the UK, reaching a ridiculously low number 4 for such a quality release. This was possibly due to a radio ban by the BBC stifling it's promotion, plus the fact the single features the first 2 tracks from the Beatles new LP, released some 4 weeks previously.

33. Let It Be / You Know My Name (Look Up The Number)

Single – Released March 6 1970

Let It Be

Time Signature – 4/4
Recorded – January 25/26/31, April 30 1969, January 4, 1970. **Engineers –** *Glyn Johns, Jeff Jarratt, Phil McDonald*
Drums – *Ringo Starr*
Maracas – *Paul McCartney*

This, the George Martin produced 7" version of *Let It Be,* is a more sedate affair than it's corresponding LP Phil Spector incarnation. Besides organ and strings, drums (with the possible exception of the ride cymbal) are mixed lower, lending the ballad a more sympathetic feel. With echo applied evenly, we hear a clearly defined single hi-hat beat on the second verse, as opposed to the repeat echo favoured by Phil Spector on the LP version, which has a sloppy leakage of echo prior to the guitar solo at [1.50]. Bereft of high in the mix maracas, the overdubbed tom fills are driven only by the single hi-hat beat.

Each version of *Let It Be* has it's own merits – but matters were complicated further with the release of *Let It Be – Naked* in 2003. Here we have a drier version, more faithful to the sound of the original *Get Back* sessions. Most notably McCartney removed the overdubbed toms [2.40], the song benefitting from the less fussy drum track, the simple 4/4 beat allowing the song to breath, becoming more soulful in the process. Which has to beg the question – why were the overdubbed toms considered and recorded in the first place?

You Know My Name (Look Up The Number)

Time Signature – 4/4
Recorded – May 17, June 7/8 1967, April 30, 1969 **Engineers –** *Geoff Emerick, Jeff Jarratt*
Drums, Bongos – *Ringo Starr*
Maracas – *John Lennon*
Handclaps, Cowbell – *Uncredited*

Recorded way back in 1967, *You Know My Name (Look Up The Number)* sees the Beatles perfectly parody their former Northern nightclub haunts[123], in the style of their current inspiration *The Bonzo Dog Dooh-Dah Band*[124]. Issued at Lennon's insistence as a 'pants down moment' flip-side counterpoint to McCartney's A-Side, the track does however feature some interesting drumming. Opening with a beat surely inspired by Motown, and featuring a wonderfully tight snare with slap-echo, this makes way [0.47] for a rhumba-style beat heavily layered with maracas, cowbell and congas. A snare drum with slackened snares is liberally and erratically played throughout, lending a great 'Latin' flavour. Random conga and tom strikes then follow [2.17], before making way [03.05] for a 'ring-a-ding' hi-hat feel on brushes, again played with that inimitable 'Social Club' feel. Marimbas and comb, plus Rolling Stone Brian Jones on saxophone bring an end to the madness. A long way from *Love Me Do*.

34. Let It Be

LP – Released November 6 1970

Producer – *Phil Spector*

Engineers – *Glyn Johns, Martin Benge, Ken Scott, Geoff Emerick, Phil McDonald, Peter Bown, Jeff Jarratt*

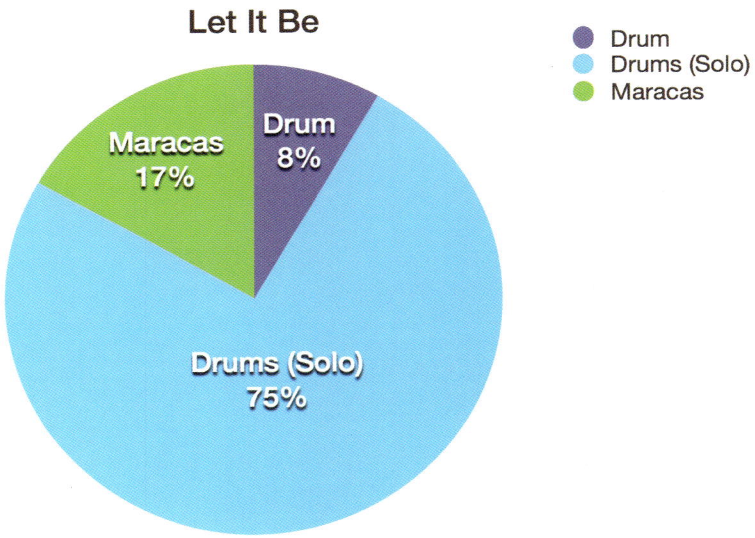

12 Songs

INSTRUMENT	USE
Drum	1
Drums (Solo)	9
Maracas	2

"I just recently got a message from Donald Fagen…he was listening to 'Let It Be…Naked' and said, "Oh my God, were these guys ever influenced by The Band?"

Robbie Robertson (The Band), 'Uncut', August 2013.

After the disorganised sessions of the Beatles, the group re-assembled under McCartney's tutelage to document the recording of their next album project – reflecting Ringo's late *White Album* mood of getting 'back to basics'. While it appeared to lead to disinterest amongst 3/4 of the group, Ringo at least rose above the malaise to perform some of his best work. In particular, the precision shuffle of *Get Back*, and in general his penchant for 'feel' as typified by *Dig A Pony* and *Don't Let Me Down*.

By 1969, the Rock world was changing rapidly, with the likes of Led Zeppelin and The Band coming to the fore. Central to the sound of these two bands were drummers John Bonham and Levon Helm, their differing approach and styles united by both being exponents of 'feel', something Ringo had long been held in regard for. Perhaps with this in mind, the sessions saw the introduction of a newly acquired (from Drum City, Shaftesbury Avenue) Ludwig kit – a Superclassic Thermo-Gloss Natural Maple set – crucially with the addition of a third tom, thus providing an extra dimension to Ringo's drumming style. Out with the old, and in with the new.

Ringo's new Ludwig Hollywood kit led to a more expansive and experimental approach

Two Of Us

Time Signature – 4/4, 2/4
Recorded – January 24/25/31, 1969. **Engineer –** *Glyn Johns*
Drums – *Ringo Starr*

Originally rehearsed and recorded as a straight rocker at Twickenham Studios, by the time the Beatles came to record it at their Apple Studios, it had morphed into its familiar folk-rock style with un-natural meter. What appear to be (and indeed are) simplistic drumming patterns, are as usual perfectly executed by Ringo, performed with precision and discipline. A dampened floor-tom provides a chugging groove, with simplistic 'building' single snare beats on the bridges. Essentially in 4/4, there are additions of 2/4 time to accommodate lyrics – [1.01] "*letters*", [1.11] "*latches*" and on… and 3/4 [1.18] "*on our way home*".

Hi-hat punctuation [1.31] leads to a return of the dampened tom fill, bringing us back into the verse and ultimately the layout.

The percussion track appears to have been supplemented by overdubbed acoustic guitar body tapping and/or our old friend thigh slaps.

Dig A Pony

Time Signature – 4/4, 2/4, 3/4

Recorded – January 22/24/28/30, February 5, 1969. **Engineer –** *Glyn Johns*

Drums – *Ringo Starr*

Not one of Lennon's personal favourites[125], this 3/4 laid-back rocker does however feature some of Ringo's most inventive and overlooked drumming, giving the track plenty of colour and space to 'breathe'.

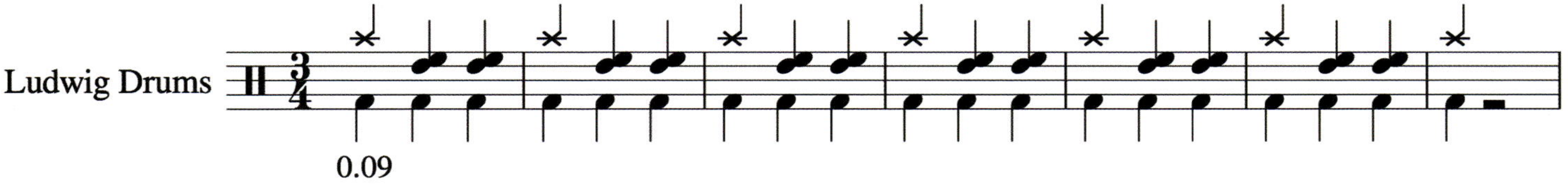

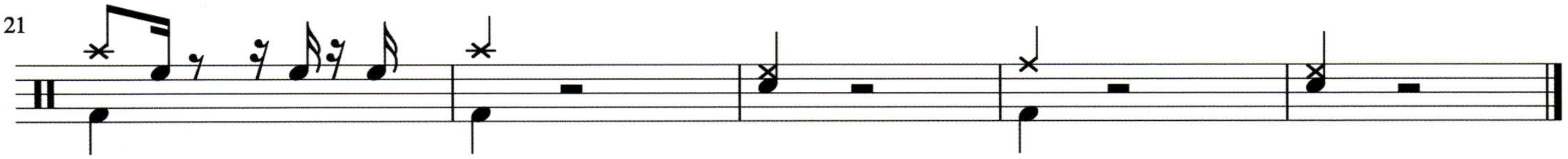

Topping and tailing the song with primitive single-strokes on his new twin-tom set up, the rest of his performance sees Ringo (surely taking inspiration from the playing style of Levon Helm of The Band) acutely aware of his timing – we don't actually hear what can be described as a typically 'straight' bass/snare/hi-hat pattern until half-way through the second verse (at 1.30), and indeed just under half-way through the song itself. Instead Ringo offers us a simultaneous bass/cymbal followed by snare/hi-hat pattern, pausing only to punctuate and mimic the guitar and vocal phrasing (1.46).

The sublimity and placement of his fill introducing the guitar solo at [2.01] is 'feel' personified, as is just about everything else the song has to offer. The 'choked' hi-hat and snare over the solo [2.26] coincides perfectly with George's guitar.

Across The Universe

Time Signature – 2/4, 3/4, 4/4, 5/4
Recorded – February 4,8, 1968. **Engineers –** *Martin Benge, Ken Scott, Geoff Emerick*
Drums, Maracas – *Ringo Starr*

Another Lennon 'time-changer', *Across The Universe* is essentially in 4/4, and despite the simplest of drum parts (single strokes on one tom tom, gently nudging the song along) is worthy of exploration. Due to the monotonous delivery of the lyrics, the time signatures that allow this are set out below -

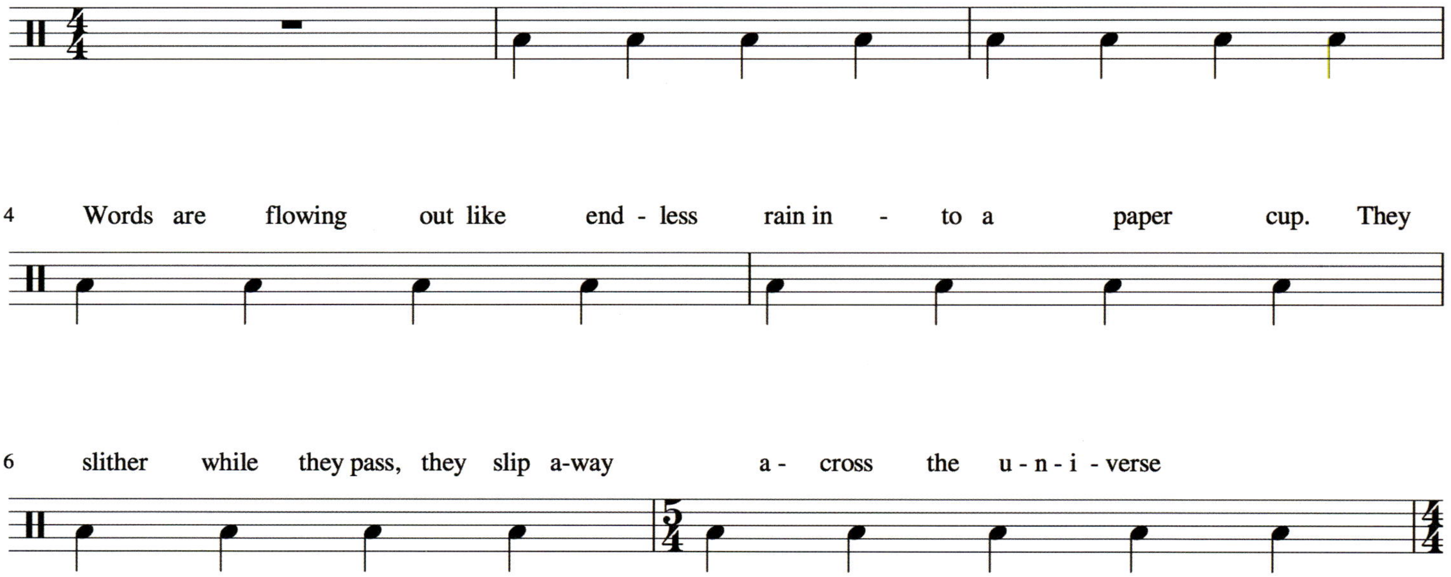
4 Words are flowing out like end - less rain in - to a paper cup. They
6 slither while they pass, they slip a-way a - cross the u - n - i - verse

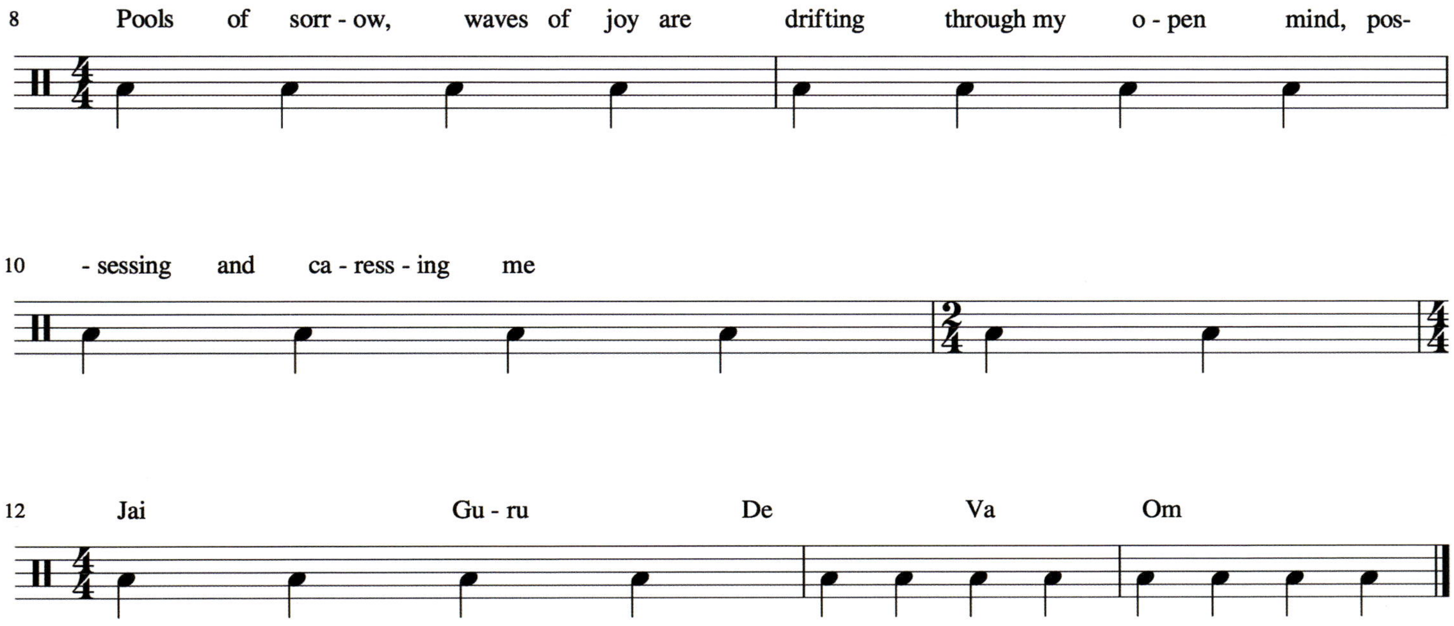
8 Pools of sorr - ow, waves of joy are drifting through my o - pen mind, pos-
10 - sessing and ca - ress - ing me
12 Jai Gu - ru De Va Om

As for the percussive side of things, we have a simple single-stroke on either bass drum or tom-tom. Maracas enhance the "nothing's gonna change my world" sections.

I Me Mine

Time Signature – 6/8, 12/16
Recorded – January 3, April 1/2/3, 1970. **Engineer –** *Phil McDonald*
Drums – *Ringo Starr*

Holding the distinction of being the 'final' Beatles recording (until the *Anthology* 'reunion'), Paul, Ringo and George expertly negotiate the shifting 6/8 and 12/16 meters, the song flowing impeccably. Taken in isolation, Ringo's hi-hat driven shuffle is truly metronomic -

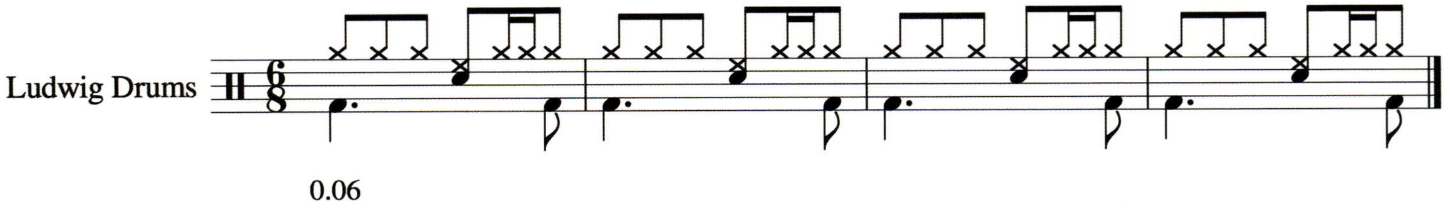
Ludwig Drums
0.06

Displaying his usual solidity, even the use of matched-stroke fills [0.40] and [0.48], bars 4 & 6 below, fails to break up the song's progress -

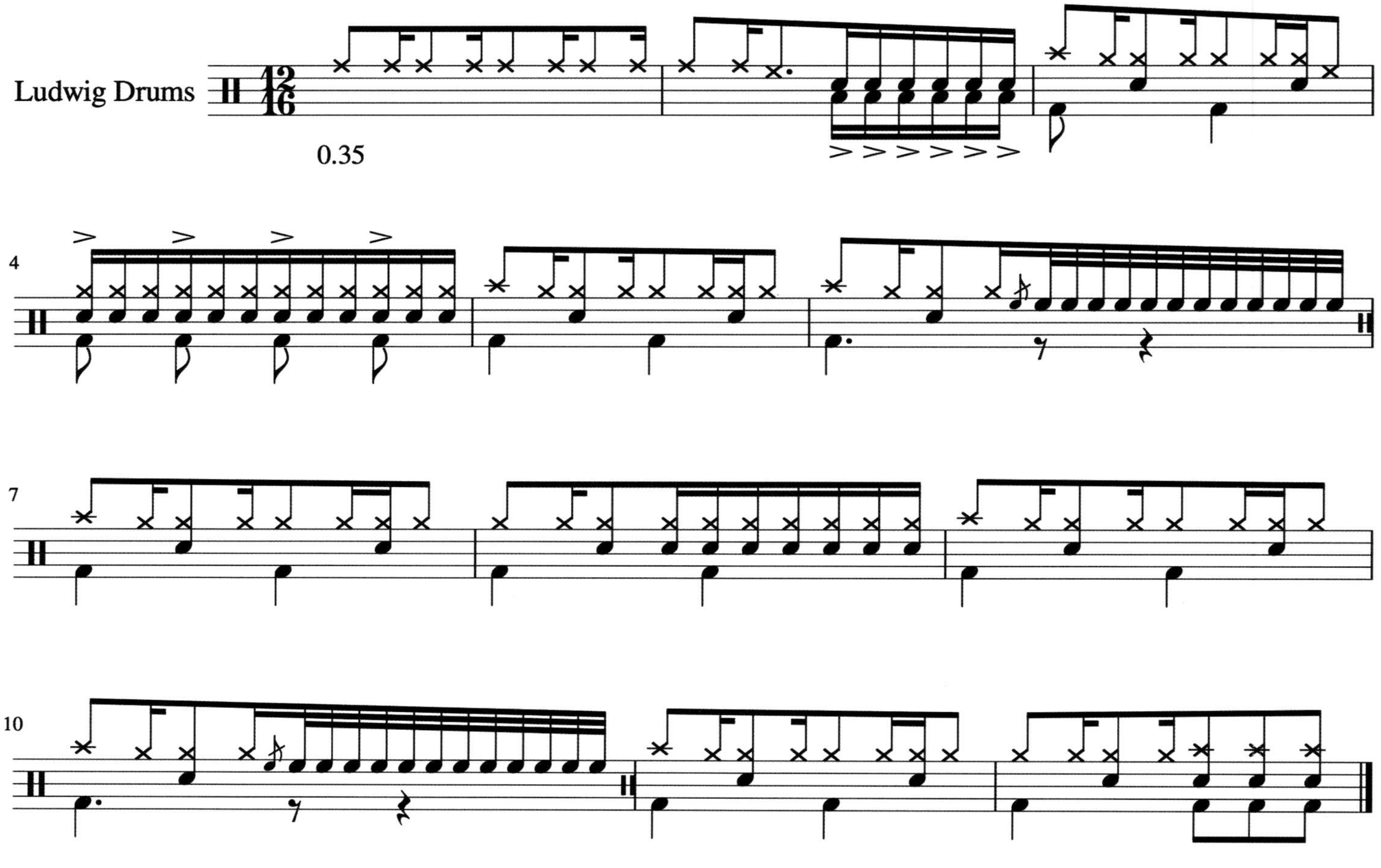

Coming out of the 12/16 passage into the 6/8 groove, we have a bar reminiscent of the return to the verse in *We Can Work It Out,* this time without the aid of a tambourine -

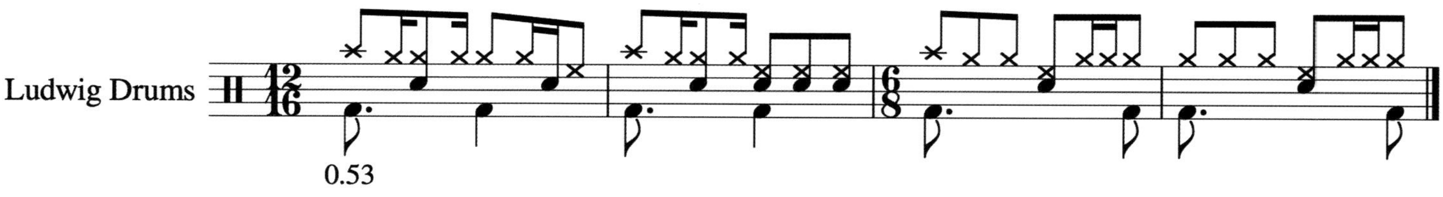

Ringo's finest moment here is reserved for the tension relieving fills at [1.04] & [1.54] – the song originally running at a terse [1.34], Phil Spector repeated this passage, therefore extending the song by some 50 seconds. If you're going to repeat yourself, make sure you use the right device and get it right first time!

Dig It

Time Signature – 3/4
Recorded – January 24/26, 1969. **Engineer** – *Glyn Johns*
Drums – *Ringo Starr*

A snippet of a rambling Blues 'jam', Phil Spector chose the only section that just about possessed a coherent beat. Busking snare dominates this 3/4 shuffle.

Let It Be

Time Signature – 4/4
Recorded – January 25/26/31, April 30, 1969, January 4, 1970. **Engineers** – *Glyn Johns, Jeff Jarratt, Phil McDonald*
Drums – *Ringo Starr*
Maracas – *Paul McCartney*

The album version of *Let It Be* sees Ringo perfectly translating McCartney's percussive vision for the song he hoped would rival *Yesterday*. Ringo's drums are more prominent on this version (as are the keyboards and guitar). With syncopated and reverberated hi-hats from the second verse, Ringo soon picks up the pace, a swift snare to tom fill leading to the second chorus. Sympathetic accented tom fills punctuate, before '16 in the bar' hi-hats enhance Harrison's scintillating solo. Ride cymbal then dominates the chorus, before at [2.40] simple movement around his kit (with prominent overdubbed maracas) drive the last verse. Essentially, we have Ringo expertly shifting between six different passages and patterns of drumming, without the listener being acutely aware. Making full use of his ride cymbal bell, Ringo then reins in the tempo with simple fills around his kit, bringing the song to its conclusion.

Maggie Mae

Time Signature – 4/4
Recorded – January 24, 1969. **Engineer** – *Glyn Johns*
Drums – *Ringo Starr*

Simple playful busking again, as the group do their best 'Dusty Road Ramblers' impersonation (look them up!) on this traditional Liverpool sea shanty sung in a thick Scouse accent.

I've Got A Feeling

Time Signature – 4/4
Recorded – January 22/24/27/28/30, February 5, 1969. **Engineer** – *Glyn Johns*
Drums – *Ringo Starr*

Some pretty inventive punctuation on the opening bars, Ringo starts gently with accented cymbals and syncopated bass drum before ripping in with powerful tom and crash cymbals followed by intuitive, funky, bluesy drumming throughout. The final bars mimick his corresponding passages on *Dig A Pony*. The fluidity of his fills provide the perfect bridge between the alternating sections of the song, especially at [1.02] & [1.15]. Making a welcome return are the tea-towelled dampened snare and toms.

One After 909

Time Signature – 4/4
Recorded – January 28/29/30, 1969. **Engineer** – *Glyn Johns*
Drums – *Ringo Starr*

Returning to an old self-penned rocker, the beat is taken up a notch from the original. Swishy (half open) hi-hat cymbals provide simple but effective choppy '4's', driving this Hamburg and Cavern fan favourite rocker along.

The Long And Winding Road

Time Signature – 4/4
Recorded – January 26/31, 1969, April 1, 1970. **Engineers** – *Glyn Johns, Peter Bown*
Drums – *Ringo Starr*

On the original release, Phil Spector's production buries the drum track, however the 2015 *1* remix of *The Long And Winding Road* has greater separation of the orchestral overdubs from the original performance, thereby greatly enhancing Ringo's drum track. Early versions of *The Long And Winding Road* see Ringo chiefly playing on the bell of a cymbal with sensitivity and a light touch, discovering what works for the song. This approach was carried through to the final version, taking care not to dominate, we hear sympathetic, deftly played snare, cymbal, and hi-hat. Perhaps also mindful and wary of John's plodding bass playing (Paul was on piano), simple time keeping is the order of the day here.

For You Blue

Time Signature – 4/4
Recorded – January 25, 1969. **Engineer –** *Glyn Johns*
Drums – *Ringo Starr*

A simple and forceful brushes on snare and bass drum shuffle throughout, the band not only sound tight, but surprisingly for the mood of these sessions, it seems as if they are having a really good time driving the 12 bar blues along at a purposeful pace.

Get Back

Time Signature – 4/4
Recorded – January 23/27/28/30, February 5 1969. **Engineer –** *Glyn Johns*
Drums – *Ringo Starr*

A 'live' version of the single release from the previous year, this time without the tagged-on drum introduced coda.

PART NINE

Appendix

THE BEATLES

PAST MASTERS

PAST MASTERS

The 1987 CD release of the Beatles' catalogue took the British LP's, added the US LP version of *Magical Mystery Tour*, and collected the remaining non-LP singles and EP releases on two CD's, christened *Past Masters Volumes 1 & 2*. In 2009, the catalogue was again issued, this time in a remastered form. *Past Masters Volumes 1 & 2* were this time released as a double CD rather than two individual discs, and are presented here, omitting the German language versions of *I Want To Hold Your Hand* (*Komm, Gib Mir Deine Hand*) and *She Loves You* (*Sie Liebt Dich*).

Love Me Do

Time Signature – 4/4
Recorded – *September 4 1962*
Drums, Handclaps – *Ringo Starr*
Handclaps – *Paul McCartney, George Harrison, John Lennon*

Despite all the 'hoo-ha' of who-played-what on *Love Me Do,* Ringo definitely performs on the gentler tambourine-less single version. It may not contain the punch of the Andy White album version, but it undeniably possesses more charm.

Premier Drums

A snapshot of time, the nervousness and trepidation (especially from Paul's faltering vocal) creeps from the speakers. Ringo sounds like he is feeling his way through the song – his confidence increasing with every bar. *Love Me Do* still possesses a hangover from the Pete Best EMI audition version – Lennon can't help but get carried away during the last few bars of the harmonica solo – Ringo doing his best to keep the tempo in check. A taster of things to come – to add urgency and depth, handclaps are introduced over the solo, conservatively placed on the 2nd and 4th beats of the bar.

From Me To You

Time Signature – 4/4
Recorded – March 5 1963
Drums – *Ringo Starr*

From Me To You is notable for some hurried snare and tom fills, Ringo enjoying a new found sense of freedom and expression in the studio absent from his earlier performances. Despite this, he keeps his bass drum tightly in sync with McCartney's booming bass. Tightly shut high-hats pin down the middle 8, loosening up on the build-up to the snare-fill resolution.

Thank You Girl

Time Signature – 4/4
Recorded – March 5 1963
Drums – *Ringo Starr*

Ringo plays in much the same style on the flip-side of this single with controlled, tight drumming, especially on his drum fills at the end of the song [1.44] and [1.51]. *Thank You Girl* was a work in progress and as evidenced on *The Beatles Bootleg Recordings 1963,* Ringo hadn't quite mastered or developed these fills. As a consequence, the end sequence [1.37] was re-recorded and edited on to the best available complete take. Taking six takes to complete, the tagged-on ending of *Thank You Girl* displays tight snare (and the second time around) tom movements.

She Loves You

Time Signature – 4/4
Recorded – July 1 1963
Drums – *Ringo Starr*

With *She Loves You,* the Beatles (and no doubt George Martin) had clearly thought through the drum patterns, they possess a structure and power that demands attention, Starr executing his moves to perfection. Recorded at a session rudely interrupted by screaming fans rushing into Abbey Road, the excitement and energy created translated to the performance and positively leaps at the listener, grabbing attention and demanding to be heard. Has there been a greater attention-grabbing opening few bars than this? Kicking off with the simple but effective floor tom fill – illustrating purpose and intent -

Swiftly moving on to floor tom/snare/bass drum on the introduction (and subsequent choruses), we soon hear those famous 'swishy' hi-hats dominate[126], swaying comfortably above the pounding bass drum. If anything, the busy patterns *look* impressive when performed live – so much energy adding appeal to the Beatles' live performances.

I'll Get You

Time Signature – 4/4
Recorded – July 1 1963
Drums, Handclaps – *Ringo Starr*
Handclaps – *Paul McCartney, George Harrison, John Lennon*

With the bulk of their 5 hour session devoted to *She Loves You*, the B-Side was afforded little time. As befits a 'rush job', *I'll Get You* features a workmanlike performance by Ringo, he's driving the bus here, no more, no less. He does however attempt to liven things up with a bit of inventive bass drum playing now and then. Off-beat handclaps feature on the opening bars as the only overdub on the track.

Due to the more sedate pace and volume, the drums appear more closely miked than *She Loves You*, and while hi-hats dominate, the snare and bass drum have a depth not usually heard on early Beatles recordings. Despite previously having recorded Ludwig drums, perhaps the engineers were familiarising themselves with Ringo's handling of his new kit, achieving the right balance with the rest of the group's instruments?

I Want To Hold Your Hand

Time Signature – 4/4
Recorded – October 17 1963
Drums, Handclaps – *Ringo Starr*
Handclaps – *Paul McCartney, George Harrison, John Lennon*

I Want To Hold Your Hand – the song that seduced America, and again we have well defined rhythmical patterns, simply oozing diversity and panache. The stark nature of the opening bars demands attention, open hi-hats dominating.

Having seen fit to embellish *I'll Get You* and most of *With The Beatles* with off-beat handclaps, they again feature heavily. Prominently mixed, the handclaps form an integral part of the song's success – providing a hook in which to reel-in the listening public.

The bridge [0.50] features tightly closed hi-hats, heightening their impact when open again at [1.02], raucously leading into the chorus. Era-defining matched-stroke fills again feature on snare/tom/floor tom [0.20], saving the best for last at [2.06]. Having earlier played them straight, they take us by surprise, occurring ever so slightly behind the beat – splendid stuff!

This Boy

Time Signature – 12/8
Recorded – October 17 1963
Drums – *Ringo Starr*

This Boy is unusual in that it features Ringo on brushes – he briskly busks on his hi-hats, filling out the introduction and verses with variations on this theme -

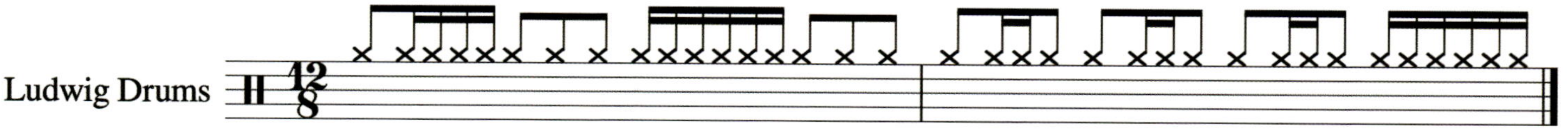

On the lead-in to the middle 8, Ringo accents the hi-hats before moving into normal bass/snare/hi-hat territory, a solid structure underscoring Lennon's impassioned vocal. Accented hi-hats again lead-up to the fade [1.52]. A very novel, innovative approach.

Long Tall Sally

Time Signature – 4/4
Recorded – March 1 1964
Drums – *Ringo Starr*

A simply astonishing track, even more so as the Beatles' version of Little Richard's *Long Tall Sally* was recorded in one take – thereby equalling their feat on *Twist And Shout*. They didn't even bother with a second attempt, they knew they'd got it in one. It's a blistering performance from all concerned – Paul's vocal, John and George's twin guitar solos, even

George Martin on piano puts in a great turn. As for Ringo, he never lets up from his forthright and solid beat, his punctuation on snare and bass drum tight and precise. Ringo treads that narrow path between a shuffle and straight '8's' as he saves his best for last – terrific triplet movements[127] between snare, tom and cymbal. The sample presented here is a sample from [1.40] onwards -

I Call Your Name

Time Signature – 4/4
Recorded – March 1 1964
Drums, Cowbell – *Ringo Starr*

A workmanlike 4/4 beat from Ringo, enlivened by seamlessly moving in and out of a great shuffle beat on the (for the day) experimental swinging 'ska' section at [1.08]. The emphasis on the tightly tuned snare, with the cowbell cleverly dropping out of the mix, notice how the perceived tempo change is achieved by the switch from eighth to accented quarter note (opening) hi-hats. Four-in-the-bar snare beats (bar 3) ease the transition.

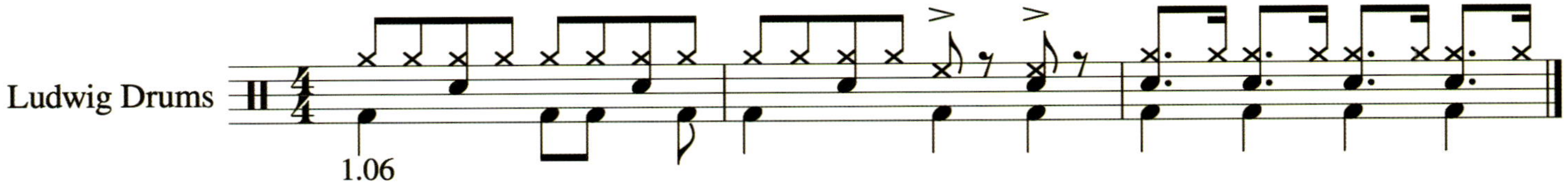

The return to a straight 4/4 almost a mirror image of the move into the ska section – an unexpected but welcome variation from the norm.

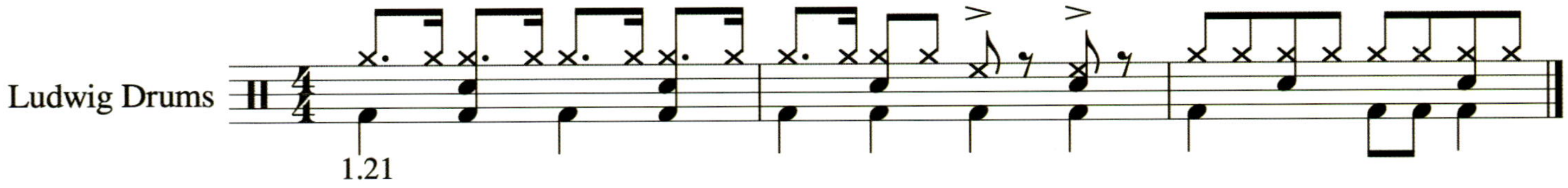

Slow Down
Time Signature – 4/4
Recorded – June 1 1964
Drums – *Ringo Starr*

As with all the tracks on the EP, a great open drum sound sees Ringo with his head down, ploughing-through on swishy hi-hats.

Machine-gun snare and tom fills at relevant points between verse and chorus, the best utilising quadruplets on snare, then tom at [2.26] -

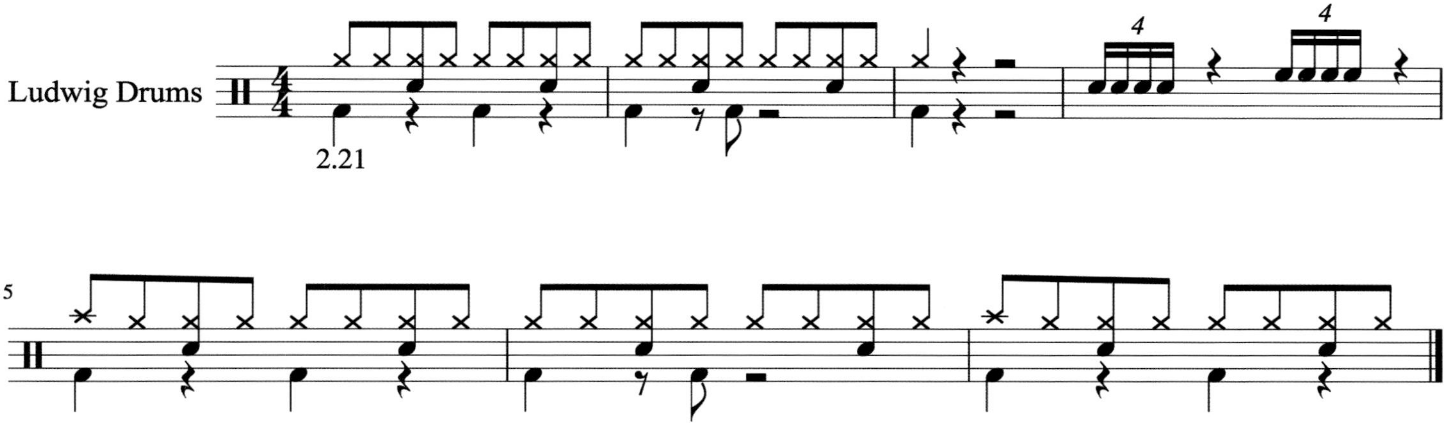

and playing ‘against the beat’ with triplets at [2.43] -

Matchbox

Time Signature – 4/4
Recorded – June 1 1964
Drums – *Ringo Starr*

With the song's composer and performer Carl Perkins present at the session, Ringo must surely have been apprehensive about his performance here. If he was it doesn't show as he leads us through a Rockabilly shuffle with perfection. Playing constantly on bass drum, snare and ride cymbal without interruption (save for the ending), perhaps to create a smoother transition from the guitar introduction, the Beatles saw fit to overdub 4-in the bar handclaps.

I Feel Fine

Time Signature – 4/4
Recorded – October 18 1964
Drums – *Ringo Starr*

> *"The drumming is basically what we used to think of as What'd I'd Say* (by Ray Charles) *drumming. There was a style of drumming on What'd I Say which is a sort of Latin R&B that Ray Charles's drummer Milt Turner played on the original record and we used to love it. One of the big clinching factors about Ringo as the drummer in the band was that he could really play that so well."*
>
> **Paul McCartney**[128]

As we move to the end of 1964, we see more studio experimentation from the group. *I Feel Fine* possesses the (in)famous opening bars of guitar feedback – yet it's the prominence of the drum pattern that's arguably the striking feature here.

By late 1964, the Beatles were afforded more time to develop their songs in the studio – from basic strumming/working-out to final product. The drum parts were no different – they would evolve. Utilising his snare more freely than usual, takes 1-6 see Ringo developing his drum part, feeling his way, getting to learn what is best to play for the song. Take 6 is not vastly different than take 1, but it is played with more purpose and confidence. Crucially though, it wasn't 'right' for the song. That's why the drum pattern changed (probably from Paul's suggestion) to what we know and love today, with the movement from tom to cross-stick snare and interplay between drums and ride cymbal bell. This was not a massive shift from the earlier takes, as Ringo is essentially playing the same pattern, but with greater fluidity than the 'stuttering' pattern of simply staying on the snare, allowing time to trade-off (and be more inventive with) the bell of the ride cymbal.

Perhaps to extend the song further, the guitar solo is extended with a 4 bar guitar break, Ringo re-introducing the song with an offbeat feel between snare and a combination of bass drum and floor tom -

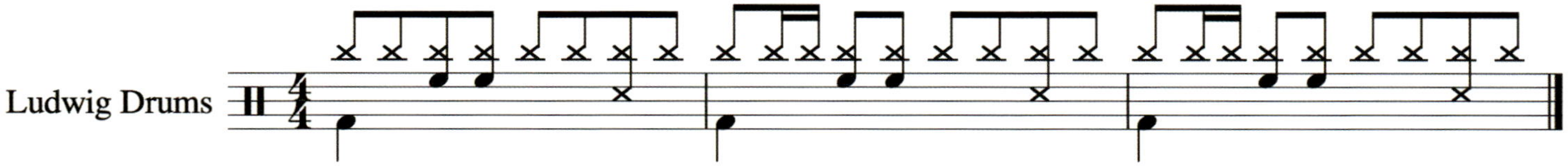

As for live performances, probably due to having to play harder to make the drums heard, Ringo made subtle changes to his drum part, simplifying the pattern and occasionally substituting the cross-stick snare for a full-bodied stroke.

She's A Woman

Time Signature – 4/4
Recorded – October 8 1964
Drums, Chocalho – *Ringo Starr*

She's A Woman is distinctive in that although it possesses an incredibly sparse arrangement, this remains hidden by a strong drum and percussion track. With a chocalho (a type of 'shaker' hailing from Portugal) to the fore, providing a harsher sound than maracas, the hi-hats are somewhat buried in the mix. With Lennon's chopping rhythm guitar placed on top of the snare, no backing vocals, no Harrison present until his overdubbed guitar, and only the addition of piano to come, the emphasis falls on Ringo to provide purpose and drive – he has to bring the components together by providing unity. This is achieved with busy 8th note hi-hats in the verses, open '8's' hi-hats on choruses, and a no-nonsense yet lively bass drum pattern.

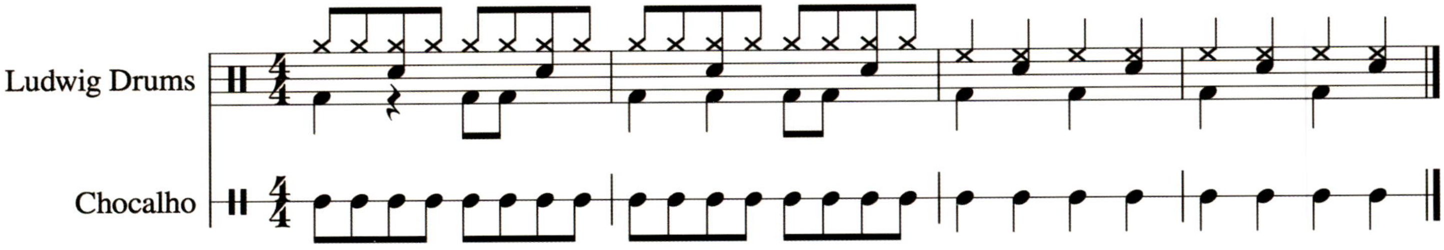

1.12

McCartney's rolling bass provides much of the rhythmic variety here, along with the '8-in the bar' chocalho, although Ringo does his best by using the bass drum to mimic the phonetics of the vocal throughout.

It is also worth noting that the "choppy" guitar slashes at the start of the track are placed on the 2nd and 4th beats in the bar, not as usual on the 1st and 3rd beats. If the drummer doesn't hear the guitarist's count-in (if he bothers to do one!), the drums would most probably enter at the wrong time, creating much mirth and merriment amongst band members, a red-faced drummer, and confusion amongst the audience! Interesting then, that when performed live, Ringo joined the introductory bars of guitar with the following -

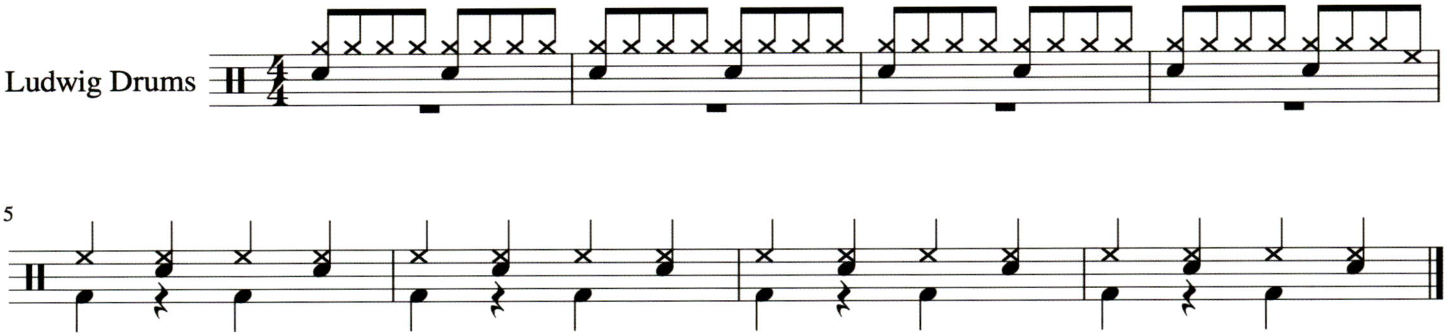

Bad Boy

Time Signature – 4/4
Recorded – May 10 1965
Drums, Tambourine – *Ringo Starr*

Requiring two more songs for a new US Capitol LP, *Bad Boy* was hastily committed to tape at the same session as another Larry Williams cover[129] (*Dizzy Miss Lizzy*), but remained unreleased in the UK until it's inclusion on the following year's LP *A Collection Of Beatles Oldies…But Goldies,* surely serving as an enticement for completists only.

The track itself? A workmanlike run through of an old favourite, notable for some nifty 'tommy-gun' style snare work. While Ringo's cymbal shines, the tambourine perhaps sits too high in the mix?

Yes It Is

Time Signature – 12/8
Recorded – February 16 1965
Drums, Tambourine – *Ringo Starr*

In contrast to its 'busy' A-Side, the 12/8 time *Yes It Is* sees Lennon in a tender mood. Drawing on the earlier *This Boy*, this time Ringo is less busy, opting instead for a laid-back approach, with gently struck hi-hat and bass drum buried behind the prominent overdubbed choked hi-hats, which coincide with cross-stick snare.

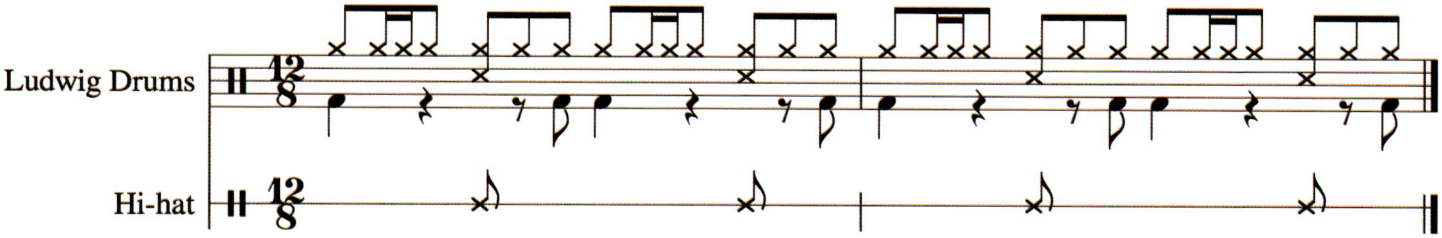

Much of the rhythmic urgency is provided by John's busily strummed acoustic guitar, George once again 'pushing the envelope' by providing a dreamy counterpoint with his innovative volume/tone pedal, enhancing the pervading somnambulistic air.

I'm Down

Time Signature – 4/4
Recorded – June 14 1965
Drums, Bongos – *Ringo Starr*

The B-Side of *Help!*, *I'm Down* features sharp snare punctuations and cymbal-grabs from Starr, with some wonderful Motown-style snare/tom/snare rolls thrown in for good measure. The open sound of his kit is a joy, adding to the excitement of the recording, especially Take 1 found on *Anthology 2*. Mixed progressively louder, busy bongos keep the chorus's moving along, becoming almost dominant over the drums. On the play out, the bongos mimic the vocal intonation. Regarding the raucous vocal, it's incredible to think McCartney recorded *Yesterday* after this!

Day Tripper

Time Signature – 4/4
Recorded – October 16 1965
Drums, Tambourine – *Ringo Starr*

One half of a great double A-Side single, *Day Tripper* is notable for predictable yet well executed single-tom rolls, and some quite inventive snare work from Ringo. Driven by high in the mix tambourine, the repetitive drum pattern of the chorus is broken-up and enlivened by some lovely touches on the snare that are sneaked-in to the beat at [0.40] and [2.11], as illustrated below.

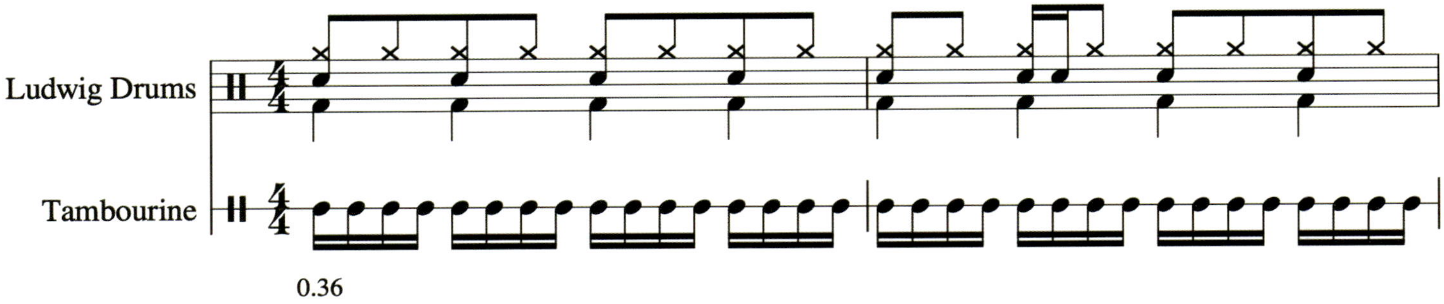

Tambourine creates tension ahead of the tom-rolls that herald each verse. The play-out is a joy, Ringo revelling in the chance to disrupt the flow [2.34] and [2.41], alternating with the resurrected tom rolls from earlier, the best of which is saved from the obscurity of the fade-out [2.47].

We Can Work It Out

Time Signature – 4/4
Recorded – October 20/29 1965
Drums – *Ringo Starr*
Tambourine – *George Harrison or Ringo Starr*[130]

We Can Work It Out has the distinction of possessing one of the most striking pieces of time-altering trickery only the Beatles could unwittingly conjure up. The perceived change in meter of the bridge occurs without the listener being aware of such a change – all without a hiccup. Utilising triplets, the song slips seamlessly into a 3/4 feel contained within a 4/4 structure[131], rather than moving to a strict, jarring change from 4/4 to 3/4. Once underway, the triplets (a bass drum/cymbal crash combination followed by two tambourine beats), are reminiscent of Bavarian oompah, tumbling towards a sharp return to the 4/4 feel, bringing the protagonist's views back into focus. A device aided by Starr's reading and handling of the situation.

346

Ludwig Drums
0.37
Tambourine

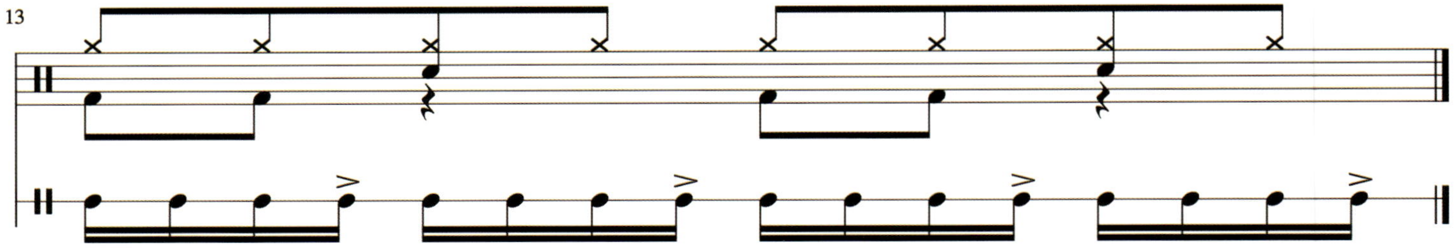

Paperback Writer

Time Signature – 4/4
Recorded – April 13/14 1965
Drums, Tambourine – *Ringo Starr*

The 4 bars above provide a snapshot of the drum track, illustrating the busy, repetitive tambourine (echoing the overdubbed hi-hat work of *You Won't See Me)* plus snare and tom fills that reintroduce the verses. We hear Ringo in forthright mood, providing the platform for Paul's pumped up bass part. In more ways than one, this is *Day Tripper* Pt 2 – yet *Paperback Writer* benefits from a heavier, more modern sounding drum kit, particularly the heavier bass drum. The bass guitar in particular provides much of the rhythmical quality, the drum track providing a repetitively solid bass. Perhaps Ringo was saving himself for the B-Side?

Rain

Time Signature – 4/4
Recorded – April 14/16 1966
Drums, Tambourine – *Ringo Starr*

> *"I think I just played amazing. I was into the snare and the hi-hat. I think it was the first time I used this trick of starting a break by hitting the hi-hat first instead of going directly to a drum off the hi-hat."*
>
> ***Ringo Starr*** [132]

To achieve the 'trippy' feel required, *Rain* was performed at a quicker tempo, the tape consequently slowed down on playback. There also appears to have been a degree of tomfoolery regarding the control of the tape varispeed – the song appears to speed-up and slow down throughout, although as we will see this may not have all been due to surreptitious knob twiddling. Ringo's performance here is quite unique and remarkable, busily attacking his kit from the get-go, with fills every few bars as the pleasure takes. Prominent tambourine (simultaneously overdubbed with the backing vocals), plays on the 4 beats of the introduction, then beats 2 and 4 until the final 2 verses, thus keeping a constant focal point around which the drums move. The 17 bars below represent the first 32 seconds of the song, introduced by the sharp attention-grabbing sixteenth note snare pattern, setting the tone for what follows. Everything here is purely instinctive – of particular note throughout is the movement between hi-hat and snare, (exemplified at [0.16] – bar 9 below), rather than moving from snare to tom as he had moments before.

Near the end of the second verse, we return to the subject of erratic time keeping[133] alluded to earlier – namely the insertion of a 'cheeky' 2/4 bar at 0.44. Whether this was by accident or design we'll probably never know, but it certainly adds a twist to proceedings. Coupled with John's elongated vocal, we are transported through a passage of uncertainty, with Ringo doing his best to navigate us safely.

The much lauded interaction between bass guitar and drums at [2.24] below, is truly innovative, as is the dramatically syncopated fill and melodious bass that bring it cascading back in wonderfully.

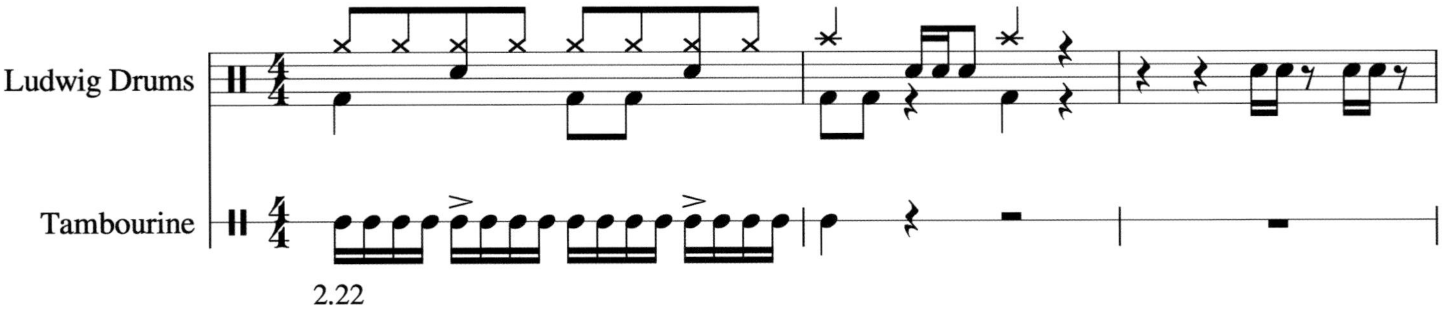

So, yet another fantastic single release, and a foretaste of what was to shortly follow on *Revolver*.

Lady Madonna

Time Signature – 4/4
Recorded – February 3/6, 1968. **Engineer –** *Ken Scott*
Drums, Handclaps – *Ringo Starr*
Handclaps – *Paul McCartney, George Harrison, John Lennon*
Tambourine – *Paul McCartney*

Moving into 1968, McCartney continued to be the driving force behind the Beatles' output. With his band mates seemingly content to 'go with the flow', another single was on the cards. As on *Good Day Sunshine*, we again have Paul's multi-layered percussive approach to the Beatles recordings, with two separate and distinct drum patterns at play. From the start, Ringo lays down a drum track with a silky solo snare beat on brushes, placed on the left channel of the stereo mix. On the right channel, after 4 bars, we have a jauntily overdubbed bass drum and snare beat.

The beat takes a twist with the replacement of the snare and bass drum with eighth note hi-hats, opened on the 2nd and 4th beats of the bar.

Handclaps are introduced over the sax solo, the bridges to the chorus and solo punctuated with brushes on cymbal. Tambourine (very low in the right channel) is evident, the overall effect a little jarring on the stereo mix, with the mono version possessing the usual solid, unified feel.

The Inner Light

Time Signature – 4/4

Recorded – January 12, February 6/8, 1967. **Engineer –** *J.P. Sen, S. N. Gupta*

The backing track recorded by George in Bombay while completing his *Wonderwall Music* soundtrack, *The Inner Light* features India's finest session musicians laying down a hybrid of Eastern instruments to a Western beat. The result produces a sympathetic backing to a quite beautiful melody.

Hey Jude

Time Signature – 4/4
Recorded – July 29/30/31, August 1, 1968. **Engineer** – *Ken Scott*
Drums , Tambourine – *Ringo Starr*

With *Hey Jude*, the Beatles spent a painstaking amount of studio time seeking perfection. Two days of recorded rehearsal at Abbey Road culminated in a session at Trident Studios, specifically to take advantage of Trident's 8-track recorder, as such technology was still absent from EMI's 'flagship' studios.

For such an epic track, Ringo takes his usual empathetic, laid-back approach, utilising a plodding beat, helped along by the earlier introduced '2 in the bar' tambourine and added emphasis of his ride cymbal bell at [1.33]. The tambourine switches to a 16's feel which is deployed effectively and constantly lifts the choruses, aided by multiple handclaps. Punctuated by sometimes repetitive fills, Ringo either adds colour between lines [1.07], or reflects the phonetics of the vocals, illustrated by the second half of the introductory fill over "And anytime you feel the pain" [0.53], and later throughout the lengthy play-out.

Recording wise, Ringo's drums are once again deadened by tea-towels, presented here in perhaps their most muted form.

As an aside, Ringo almost missed his cue – unbeknownst to his band-mates he had taken a toilet-break, and just managed to slink back behind his kit in time.

Revolution

Time Signature – 4/4
Recorded – July 9/10/11/12, 1968. **Engineer** – *Geoff Emerick*
Drums – *Ringo Starr*
Handclaps – *Ringo Starr, Paul McCartney, George Harrison, John Lennon*

With a prototype Glam Rock beat, Ringo is in a minimalist mood, his bass drum powering the rhythm track, with powerful matched strokes on his snare and floor tom neatly linking verses. A foretaste of the stark nature of *The Beatles* LP, *Revolution* sees the Beatles 'going for it' like never before – Ringo's heavily compressed drums and cymbals fighting for air against the tremendously distorted guitars and forthright bass. While the guitarists played directly into the consoles in the control room of Studio 2, Ringo performed in splendid isolation in Studio 3. Again we have a 2/4 bar inserted in order to resolve the vocal delivery.

However, perhaps the best moments are the forceful and dramatic cymbal/drum trade-offs (shown below) and the subtleties of the snatched moments of snare work [1.22], [2.06] & [3.10]. Lennon emphasises the repetitive beat with his vocal during the guitar and electric piano solo.

Get Back

Time Signature – 4/4
Recorded – January 23/27/28/30, February 5 1969
Drums – *Ringo Starr*

Having enjoyed performing in front of an audience while shooting the *Hey Jude* promotional film, the Beatles re-grouped in January 1969 with a new direction – a 'back to basics' approach to their new project. As a result, the ensuing *Get Back* single saw no percussion overdubbing – it must have been tempting to at least add the ubiquitous tambourine, but the group stuck to their guns. This wasn't the only new direction the group were taking – the sessions were to be recorded at the newly installed Apple Studios in the basement of their HQ at Savile Row.

Technically, this smaller environment produced a 'tighter', more modern sound than Abbey Road could offer. Ringo's drums benefit here from close-miking and are once again dampened with tea-towels, making his cymbal interjections all the more brighter and refreshing. Dampening drums in this way can prove counter – productive, you may achieve the sound you are looking for, but at the expense of less bounce – back from the drum skin. A heavier touch is required, in turn affecting the sound of the drum. Ringo negotiates this perfectly, a less experienced drummer may be tempted to eschew this simple yet effective approach and overplay.

Early rehearsals saw Ringo employing a straight 4/4 '8 in the bar' hi-hat beat, while the finished product sees Starr in a wonderfully forthright mood, the bulk of the song taken up with a simple snare-driven pattern. The introduction sees Ringo and band shuffling their way to the first verse by way of accented cymbal crashes which punctuate throughout, bolstering the lyrics with more weight and substance.

There are percussive elements coming at us from every direction, Harrison's underrated and excellent rhythm guitar working in tandem with Ringo's superb snare/bass drum combination. Providing a notion of variety and respite from the relentless snare beat, Billy Preston's electric piano solo is underpinned by a shift to a straightforward floor tom/snare/bass drum beat (the final bar below), punctuated with cymbal strikes replicated on the tagged-on play-out, preceded by Ringo's snare to tom fill.

Don't Let Me Down

Time Signature – 4/4, 5/4
Recorded – January 22/28/30, 1969
Drums – *Ringo Starr*

A perfect companion piece to *Get Back*, Lennon's superb 'weepy' *Don't Let Me Down* has Ringo once again at the top of his game. The 'back to basics' dictat ensured the song was recorded live – we can clearly hear his 'buzzing' snare wires vibrating over the introduction. From the opening bass drum/crash cymbal, we have a great example of Ringo utilising the dynamics of his drum kit to match the emotions of the song, particularly the vocal delivery. His triplet emphasis during Lennon's embittered cry of the song title (bar 4 below) provide thrusting impetus, the fairly sparse drumming allowing the song to breathe, thus preventing it becoming cluttered.

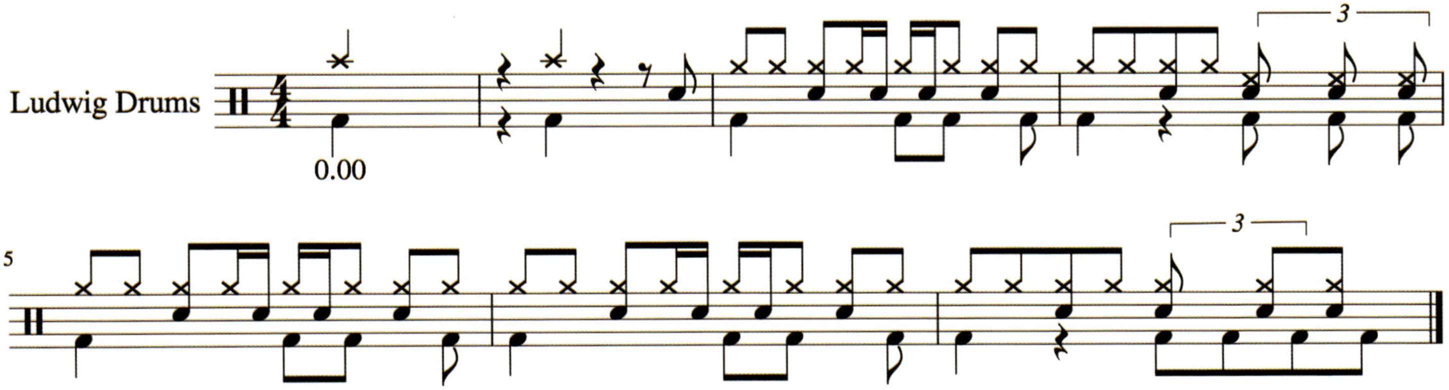

The bridge [0.41] and [2.10] sees John's usual playing with time – we have a 5/4 bar of vocal only, before returning to 4/4. This provides the listener with the effect of a dream – like state of mind, one could almost argue the swirling mind of one being in love?

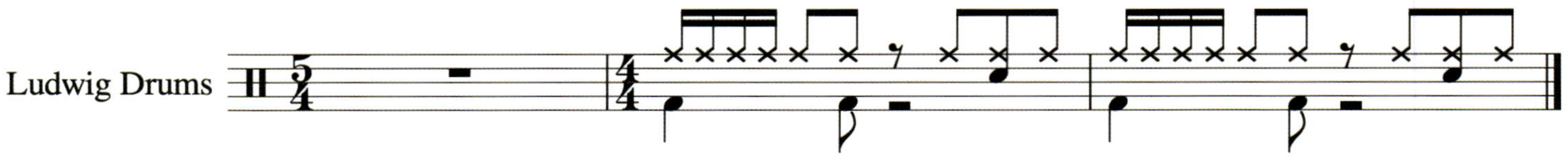

Elsewhere, Ringo's busking style from [3.05] allows Billy Preston's keyboard to take centre stage, the inspiring open hi-hat work helping to push the song forward.

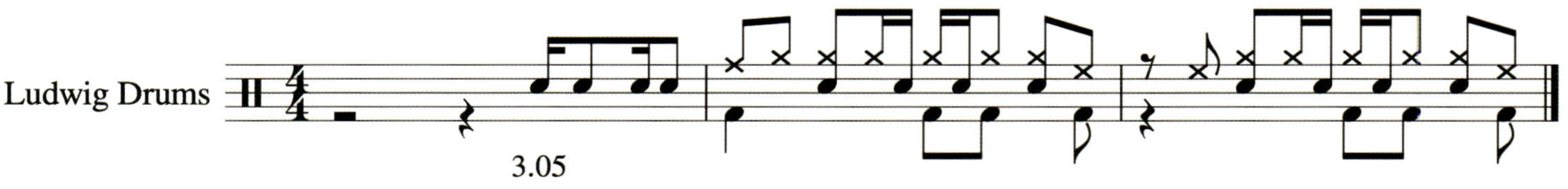

The Ballad Of John And Yoko

Time Signature – 4/4, 2/4
Recorded – April 14, 1969. **Engineer –** *Geoff Emerick*
Drums, Maracas, Handclaps – *Paul McCartney*
Guitar Body Taps, Handclaps – *John Lennon*

With Ringo and George both absent overseas, John and Paul took the opportunity to record a new track, destined to be the new Beatles single. Once again picking up sticks, McCartney delivers an admirable if unspectacular job, busying himself with a repetitive beat, enlivened with off-beat snare strokes to counterpoint the vocals. Another cheeky 2/4 bar with urgent 8th note snare (bar 5 below) punctuates the lyrical 'joke' and heralds busy maracas. Perhaps mindful of Ringo's absence and eager to utilise any object to obtain the sound they had in their minds, Lennon enthusiastically bolsters the snare beat by slapping the back of his acoustic guitar, further enhanced by added handclaps evident in the left channel of the mix. The otherwise busy mix (the first Beatles stereo UK single release) is nonetheless pleasing on the ear, perhaps due to the laid – back feel of the repetitive beat.

Ludwig Drums
1.36
Slap
Maracas
Hand Clap
5
Ludwig Drums
Slap
Maracas
Hand Clap

Old Brown Shoe

Time Signature – 4/4

Recorded – April 16/18, 1969. **Engineer –** *Jeff Jarratt*

Drums – *Ringo Starr*

Something of a hidden gem in the Beatles' catalogue, *Old Brown Shoe* sees Ringo performing a very different kind of Beatle beat – a tight off-beat 'Texan Blues' style shuffle on the 1st and 3rd beats (bar 4 below). With subtle rim clicks in evidence, Ringo seamlessly breaks into an orthodox 4/4 beat either side of the guitar solo (bars 1 & 2), with some incredibly forceful matched-stroke fills on snare and floor tom at pertinent points throughout, the best occurring in the 3rd bar below. It's a powerhouse performance from Ringo, one of his very best.

Across The Universe

Time Signature – 2/4, 3/4, 4/4, 5/4

Recorded – February 4,8, 1968. **Engineers –** *Martin Benge, Ken Scott, Geoff Emerick*

Drums, Maracas – *Ringo Starr*

Another Lennon 'time-changer', *Across The Universe* is essentially in 4/4, and despite the simplest of drum parts (single strokes on one tom tom, gently nudging the song along) is worthy of exploration. Due to the monotonous delivery of the lyrics, the time signatures that allow this are set out below -

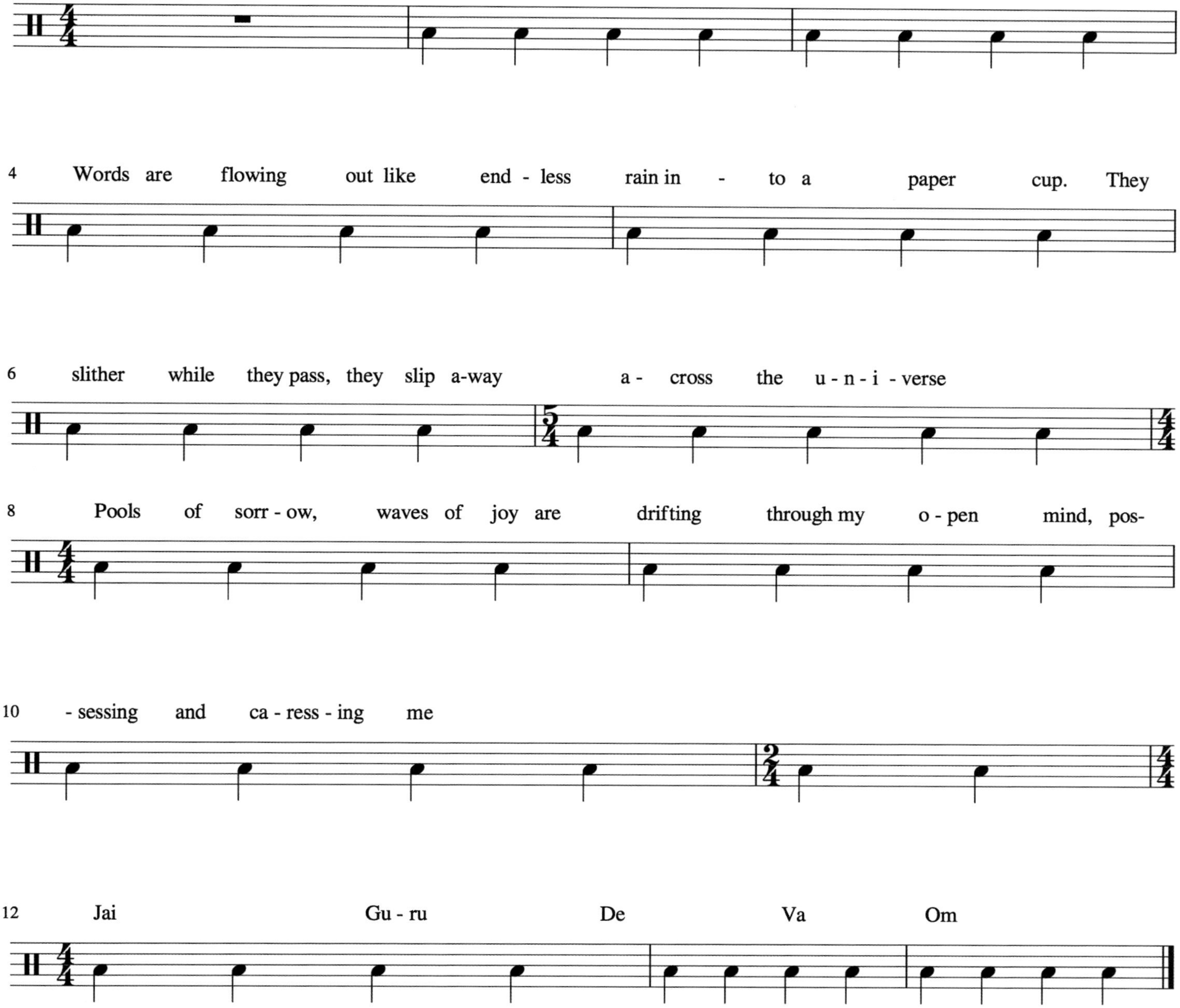
4 Words are flowing out like end - less rain in - to a paper cup. They
6 slither while they pass, they slip a-way a - cross the u - n - i - verse
8 Pools of sorr - ow, waves of joy are drifting through my o - pen mind, pos-
10 - sessing and ca - ress - ing me
12 Jai Gu - ru De Va Om

As for the percussive side of things, we have a simple single-stroke on either bass drum or tom-tom. Maracas enhance the "nothing's gonna change my world" sections.

Let It Be

Time Signature – 4/4
Recorded – January 25/26/31, April 30 1969, January 4, 1970. **Engineers –** *Glyn Johns, Jeff Jarratt, Phil McDonald*
Drums – *Ringo Starr*
Maracas – *Paul McCartney*

This, the George Martin produced 7" version of *Let It Be,* is a more sedate affair than it's corresponding LP Phil Spector incarnation. Besides organ and strings, drums (with the possible exception of the ride cymbal) are mixed lower, lending the ballad a more sympathetic feel. With echo applied evenly, we hear a clearly defined single hi-hat beat on the second verse, as opposed to the repeat echo favoured by Phil Spector on the LP version, which has a sloppy leakage of echo prior to the guitar solo at [1.50]. Bereft of high in the mix maracas, the overdubbed tom fills are driven only by the single hi-hat beat.

Each version of *Let It Be* has it's own merits – but matters were complicated further with the release of *Let It Be – Naked* in 2003. Here we have a drier version, more faithful to the sound of the original *Get Back* sessions. Most notably McCartney removed the overdubbed toms [2.40], the song benefitting from the less fussy drum track, the simple 4/4 beat allowing the song to breath, becoming more soulful in the process. Which has to beg the question – why were the overdubbed toms considered and recorded in the first place?

You Know My Name (Look Up The Number)

Time Signature – 4/4
Recorded – May 17, June 7/8 1967, April 30, 1969 **Engineers –** *Geoff Emerick, Jeff Jarratt*
Drums, Bongos – *Ringo Starr*
Maracas – *John Lennon*
Handclaps, Cowbell – *Uncredited*

Recorded way back in 1967, *You Know My Name (Look Up The Number)* sees the Beatles perfectly parody their former Northern nightclub haunts[134], in the style of their current inspiration *The Bonzo Dog Dooh-Dah Band*[135]. Issued at Lennon's insistence as a 'pants down moment' flip-side counterpoint to McCartney's A-Side, the track does however feature some interesting drumming. Opening with a beat surely inspired by Motown, and featuring a wonderfully tight snare with slap-echo, this makes way [0.47] for a rhumba-style beat heavily layered with maracas, cowbell and congas. A snare drum with slackened snares is liberally and erratically played throughout, lending a great 'Latin' flavour. Random conga and tom strikes then follow [2.17], before making way [03.05] for a 'ring-a-ding' hi-hat feel on brushes, again played with that inimitable 'Social Club' feel. Marimbas and comb, plus Rolling Stone Brian Jones on saxophone bring an end to the madness. A long way from *Love Me D*

ACKNOWLEDGEMENTS

This book has been an incredible journey, and we would like to thank the following kind people and organisations, without whom this book would be half the book it is, and the past four and a half years would have felt more like forty!

David Bedford, for his encouragement, help and support.
Sandi Anne Borowsky, for her Ringo concert photos.
Iain Bradshaw, for his invaluable skills and advice.
Viv Ellis, for his advice and passion for vintage drums.
Bill Harry, for his Merseybeat clipping.
David Hobbs, for the photos of Ringo's Ludwig Oyster Black Pearl drum kit.
Anthony Hogan, for his memories of Tommy Moore. We can thoroughly recommend Ant's book about Ringo's former band and leader, Rory Storm – "From A Storm To A Hurricane".
Frieda Kelly, for her photo with Ringo and Barbara, and her encouragement.
Billy Kinsley, for his memories of the Beatles rehearsing and recording.
Sam Leach, for his photo of Rory Storm and the Hurricanes.
Mark Lewisohn, for the Beatles/Country Four ticket.
Michael McCartney, for his drumming reminiscences.
Bill Minto, for his photos of the Beatles Revolution shoot.
The Lord Mayor of Liverpool, Councillor Gary Millar, and
Francis McEntegart LL.B (Hons) (www.mclegal.co.uk) for their invaluable advice.
Don Powell, for his contribution and kind words.
Birkenhead Transport Museum, for the use of their bus and conductor!
DIG Vinyl, Bold Street, Liverpool.
Premier Drums, Leicester.
SAE Institute, Liverpool.
The Beatles Story Café, Liverpool, for the endless supply of tea and coffee.

Thanks folks,
Alex & Terry

DRUMMING GLOSSARY

<u>Bass Drum</u>: The largest, lowest pitched drum of the kit, it sits on the floor and is struck by a 'beater' attached to a bass drum pedal.

<u>Bongos</u>: A small pair of (single) top-skinned drums joined together, and usually played with the hands while seated. As seen being played by Ringo on *You're Going To Lose That Girl'* in the film *Help!*

<u>Brushes</u>: A bunch of wires that fan out from a stick, allowing a softer touch than a traditional drumstick. Also used in a 'sweeping' motion to fill-out the song, such as in *A Taste Of Honey* . Widely used by jazz and big-band drummers, many more varieties and weights of brushes are available today than in the 50's and 60's.

<u>Cabasa</u>: A Latin percussion instrument, originally a gourd filled with dried seeds, nowadays consisting of a cylinder on a handle, which when rotated causes a steel ball chain to produce a soft, metallic grating sound.

<u>Chimes (or Tubular Bells)</u>: Long metal tubes that are struck with a mallet. Featured on *When I'm Sixty-Four*.

<u>Claves</u>: A pair of cylindrical hardwood sticks, which when beaten together produce a 'click'. Featured on *Don't Bother Me,* and *And I Love Her.*

<u>Congas</u>: Similar to bongos, but larger and usually played standing up, these barrel shaped single-headed drums feature on *Getting Better*.

<u>Cowbell</u>: Struck with a drumstick and sometimes mounted on the bass drum, a cowbell features prominently on *You Can't Do That* and *I Call Your Name.*

<u>Crash Cymbal</u>: Less heavy and often smaller than the ride cymbal, the crash cymbal is used (usually in conjunction with the bass drum) to emphasise or accentuate a beat. A fabulous example of this is the chorus of *No Reply.*

<u>Finger Cymbals</u>: A pair of tiny cymbals, which are attached to the fingers and struck together, producing a high-pitched 'ting'. Finger cymbals feature on *The Fool On The Hill.*

Floor-Tom: The deepest tom, the floor-tom is mounted on legs, normally parallel with the snare drum, on the other side of the drummers' bass drum leg.

Hi-Hats: Operated by the foot, hi-hats are the two cymbals on a stand that open and close together. Normally struck when closed together, Ringo gave early Beatles recordings a distinctive sound by opening the cymbals slightly, enveloping the songs with a 'swishy' sound. By briefly opening and sharply closing the cymbals, hi-hats can also be used to produce a 'choked' sound, A good example of this technique can be heard on *Being For The Benefit Of Mr. Kite*.

Maracas: A hollowed-out wooden body held by a stick, traditionally filled with seeds, grain, or sand. Shaken to produce a distinctive rattle sound.

Ride Cymbal: A large, heavy cymbal, usually played with the tip of the stick, replicating the patterns normally associated with hi-hats.

Rim – Shot: The deliberate, simultaneous striking with a stick of the snare skin and rim (the metal hoop of the drum that holds the skin in place). The resulting sound can produce a louder 'crack' than the conventional strike.

Shaker: Similar to maracas, a generic term to describe any (seed filled) instrument that can be shaken to produce a sound.

Sizzle Cymbal: A cymbal with a series of rivets positioned within holes around the cymbal edge, lending a sizzle effect when struck.

Snare Drum: With it's roots as a military drum, the snare sits between the drummers legs, and is distinguished by the use of a series of metal wires (originally animal gut or string) strung across the bottom skin, giving the snare either a 'buzz' when a roll is played, or a 'crack' when a single stroke is applied.

Timpani (or Kettle-Drum): A large orchestral drum played with mallets, featured on *Every Little Thing.*

Tom-Tom (or 'Top', 'Mounted' or 'Rack' Tom): Usually the smallest drum of the kit and mounted on the bass drum, the tom-tom is also used as bridge between the snare and floor-tom. Ringo graduated to using two of these drums towards the end of his Beatles career.

DRUM RUDIMENTS

Drum Rudiments are the building blocks of all drumming. They are the exercises that all drummers should learn if they are to achieve their creative potential and in turn develop their own style. Ringo's initial playing was limited to an extent, because he had no formal training as a drummer. Typical of the day, once he had a drum he just got on with it. Nowadays, children go to a drum tutor as a matter of course, and in the process learn in five weeks what previously took five years to learn. Or of course, they just go to *Youtube* where they can watch – and learn – the most amazing things.

Rudiments originally evolved from the military, where marching or battlefield orders were delivered from a snare drum hanging from the waist at an angle from a sling or belt. Because of this angle, the drum had to be addressed using the 'orthodox' grip where the left hand holds the stick in the cradle of thumb and forefinger (and gripped between second and third fingers) as opposed to a matching grip where both hands hold the sticks as if cracking a whip. In modern 'kit' drumming, drums can be positioned where they feel ergonomically 'correct' for the drummer, so using one grip or another is not an issue. There are always discussions about which grip is 'right or wrong', both have their plus and minus points, however it comes down to what feels best for you. Why not become skilled in both?

Many are the tales of where and how marching drums developed, one of which mentions the troops at the battle of Waterloo, where the drummers joined in with the pipers of a Scottish regiment as they marched into battle. A sort of 'jam session' in the middle of blood-letting and mayhem. Marching bands now seem to be more popular than ever, and what a great nursery in which to learn how to play 'properly[136]'.

Despite there being many rudiments, we need concern ourselves with just a few, as Ringo's playing style (at least in the early days) was a simple yet effective one.

Flam: A quieter beat delivered with one hand just before a louder one using the other hand. This creates a much fatter note than one single strike.

Drag: Very like a flam but with two quiet beats played with one hand followed by a louder beat using the other hand.

Roll: Rolls are very challenging for the beginner and can take a long time to learn. For our purposes, they are usually divided up into single stroke [played LRLRLRLRLRLR…..), double stroke (played LLRRLLRRLLRR…..) and crush (or press) rolls. They are executed mainly by a combination of finger and wrist movement which involves bouncing the stick on the drum head in either single or double strokes with each hand. In the case of a crush roll, the drummer will 'dig in' in order to get that powerful, continuous, exciting sound. Think of the circus drummer and the clown falling over – or perhaps the introductory bars of *All You Need Is Love.*

Triplets: Basically three notes played in the space of two. An easy way to pick out a triplet is to say the word *'EVENLY',* emphasising the three syllables like so – 'EV-EN-LY'. Ringo plays more than a few of these. For example at the start of *Something,* Ringo plays two triplets on his toms which provides the launchpad for the atmospheric melody of the song. A simple yet effective exposition device.

Paradiddle: The word is onomatopoeic, a big word which just means it sounds like it is said. Again, just say the word *'Pa-Ra-Di-Ddle'* and there you have it. Just four beats played LRLL or RLRR – playing the last two beats with one hand can allow the drummer to move his free hand around the kit, for instance to strike a cymbal. This rudiment can be used in many places for example between snare and cymbal bell or tom fills etc. Paradiddles can be powerful and emotive – disparate examples being Buddy Holly's *Peggy Sue* and Ravel's *Bolero*, where the paradiddle drives the melodies much like an express train running over the tracks.

Matched beats (or strokes): Two drumsticks striking a drum or drums simultaneously. This is something that Ringo used many times, to great effect. It isn't really a recognised rudiment, but worth mentioning because of the number of times it was used in Beatles recordings.

Drum Fill: While not a rudiment as such, a drum fill is a description you will notice occurring with regularity throughout the book. Essentially, a fill is the playing of a drum or drums between regular beats, very often 'around the kit', before returning to the consistent beat of the song. A fill can contain rudiments, and be played in a variety of ways, for example the simplistic fills occurring in *Something* can be played with one hand or two. It is possible any of these may contain paradiddles or single or double-stroke rudiments.

The lesson here is not to get too hung up on the terminology or the notation, just enjoy the music. Better still, buy yourself a pair of sticks, a drum (or even a practice pad) and beat seven bells out of it – you will feel better and, it won't hit back!

AUDIO AND RECORDING GLOSSARY

With particular relevance to the Beatles' recordings, here you can find the major terminology and explanations of audio recording chiefly used in this book.

Artificial Double-Tracking (ADT): Invented by EMI Engineer Ken Townsend during the Revolver sessions, ADT takes the original recording of a vocal part and duplicates it onto a second tape machine which has a variable speed control. The manipulation of the speed of the second machine during playback introduces a delay between the original vocal and the second recording of it, giving the effect of double tracking without having to sing the part twice, much to the relief of John Lennon who apparently despised the laborious process, but loved the effect produced.

Ambience: The sound of the performance that naturally reverberates around the recording room.

Amplifier: A device that amplifies or boosts the signal of an instrument (or voice) through a loudspeaker.

Backwards Tape: A technique (claimed by John Lennon to be his invention!) by which audio tape was fed through a tape machine backwards. Upon playback, the resulting recording was naturally heard backwards. This technique was first used on a popular music release anywhere on John's vocal on *Rain*, swiftly followed by George's guitar on *I'm Only Sleeping*, and Ringo's cymbals and drums on *Strawberry Fields Forever'*.

Balance: The relative level of two or more recordings (of instruments, or voices) in a mix. Also the relative levels of the 2 channels of a stereo mix.

Channel: The left or right side of a stereo (2 channel) recording, or one signal path from an input to output of a mixing desk.

Chorus: The section of a song that repeats the same melody and lyrics throughout.

Close Miking: The positioning of a microphone as near as possible to the instrument, in order to eliminate background room ambience as much as possible. A technique used to great effect on Ringo's drums by Engineer Geoff Emerick. (See also '*Distant Miking*').

Compression: The reduction (or narrowing) of the dynamic range (the difference between the loudest and quietest passages) of an audio signal.

Compressor: A device that produces compression of an audio signal as it passes through.

Direct Injection (or 'D.I.'): The injecting (or feeding) of an electronic instrument directly into the mixing desk (via a signal convertor box), rather than recording the signal with a microphone placed in front of an amplifier. The resulting sound produced is much clearer, cleaner and crisper, as it eliminates room ambience and electronic 'hum' from the speaker. Direct Injection was an innovative approach to recording in the 1960's, and although already in use in the US by Motown's studio staff, was developed independently by Ken Townsend at Abbey Road. Used extensively (especially on Paul McCartney's bass guitar) from the *Sgt. Pepper* sessions onwards, and most notably on guitars (and bass guitar) on *Revolution*.

Distant Miking: The deliberate placement of a microphone further away from the norm, in order to pick-up more room ambience, and therefore more instrument decay. Deliberately employed by Norman Smith on the *Please Please Me* album, in order to capture the essence of a live performance. (See also 'Close Miking).

Distortion: The overloading of an audio signal, either before or during its journey through the mixing desk, producing a loud, 'fuzzy' sound, again used to superb effect on *Revolution*. When EMI sent the tape of *Revolution* to their counterparts at their American label Capitol, the US engineers marked their test sheet as *'DISTORTION DELIBERATE'*, presumably after a swift transatlantic phone call to EMI.

Double-Tracking: To record a second track, with a second performance that closely matches the first. Beloved of John Lennon, who would double-track his vocal until the introduction of Artificial Double-Tracking (ADT) rendered this painstaking process redundant.

Drop-Out: A short absence or loss of signal caused by a fault or dirt on the recording tape.

Drum Booth: An isolation booth consisting of large acoustically treated panels, employed to prevent overspill of the drum kit onto the other instrument microphones.

Echo Chamber: A room possessing hard surfaces, which is equipped with a speaker and a microphone. 'Dry' sound is played through the speaker from the control room, the resulting 'echo' is picked up by the microphone and mixed with the original sound, producing a natural sounding echo, or reverberation.

Editing: The splicing of recording tape to alter the sequencing of that recording.

Engineer: The technician who operates, sets up recording equipment, and monitors the recordings session. Usually assisted by the 2nd engineer (tape operator).

Equalisation (EQ): The increase or decrease in amplitude of a certain band of frequencies of an audio signal in relation to other frequencies.

Fade: The gradual reduction of an audio signal.

Fader: A physical control (a 'knob' or more commonly a 'slider') that increases or decreases the level of an audio signal, for our purposes usually on a mixing desk.

Feedback: the reception (or pick-up) of a signal out of a channel by its input, creating a loop or whistling/ howling sound as the signal is fed back into itself. Famously used to great effect at the start of *I Feel Fine*.

Frequency: the number of cycles of a waveform occurring in a second.

Gate: A device that turns a channel down or off when the signal drops below a certain level.

Input: The physical connection, where a mixing desk receives the signal from an instrument.

Leakage: Sound from other instruments or voices that were not intended to be picked up by a microphone.

Level: The amount, or strength of a signal.

Live Recording: A recording session where all of the musicians play together at the same time, without overdubs. This formed the basis of a great deal of early Beatles recordings. The natural reverberation of instruments was picked up by the various microphones.

Loop: The splicing of a section of recording tape to effect a constant repetition. Please refer to '*Feedback*' for an explanation of an audio signal loop.

Mic: An abbreviation of microphone.

Miking: The use of a microphone or microphones.

Mix/Mixing: The blending of audio tracks (signals) together to produce a coherent and balanced product.

Mix-down: The recording of a mix onto tape.

Mixer: A console that accepts and blends audio signals together and outputs that signal.

Mono: A single sound source, or a signal that possesses a single source.

Multi-Track Recording: The recording of separate instruments on different sections of recording tape in time with each other, allowing a more creative approach to recording. The Beatles began with 2-track recording, and ended their recordings with 8 track.

Out of Phase: Being similar to another signal in amplitude, frequency and wave shape but being offset in time by part of a cycle. Used to great effect in Psychedelic Rock music, giving the appearance of a 'swooshing' effect.

Overdubbing: The adding of further instrument recordings onto multi-track tape. Here, we are primarily concerned with the overdubbing of percussion instruments onto tape which already contains the main performance.

Overload: See **Distortion**.

Phase: The measurement of the time difference between two similar waveforms. See Out Of Phase.

Producer: The person in charge of the recording sessions, usually responsible for the budget, quality and sound of the entire project.

Reverb/Reverberation: The persistence of a sound after the source stops emitting it.

Stereo: A recording of at least two channels where positioning of instrument sounds left to right can be perceived.

Tempo: Measured in Beats Per Minute (BPM), how many steady, even pulses there are in the music per minute.

Timbre: The unique sound of an instrument, that sounds like that instrument and no other.

Track: An audio recording made on one portion of tape.

THE BEATLES UK DISCOGRAPHY

Love Me Do / P.S. I Love You – (Parlophone – October 5, 1962)

Please Please Me / Ask Me Why – (Parlophone – January 11, 1963)

Please Please Me – (Parlophone – March 22, 1963)
I Saw Her Standing There
Misery
Anna (Go To Him)
Chains
Boys
Ask Me Why
Please Please Me

Love Me Do
P.S. I Love You
Baby It's You
Do You Want To Know A Secret
A Taste Of Honey
There's A Place
Twist and Shout

From Me To You / Thank You Girl – (Parlophone – April 12, 1963)

She Loves You / I'll Get You – (Parlophone – August 28, 1963)

With The Beatles – (Parlophone – November 22, 1963)
It Won't Be Long
All I've Got To Do
All My Loving

Don't Bother Me
Little Child
Till There Was You
Please Mr. Postman

Roll Over Beethoven
Hold Me Tight
You Really Got A Hold On Me
I Wanna Be Your Man
Devil In Her Heart
Not A Second Time
Money

I Want To Hold Your Hand / This Boy – (Parlophone – November 29, 1963)

Can't Buy Me Love / You Can't Do That – (Parlophone – March 16, 1964)

Long Tall Sally – Parlophone – June 19, 1964
Long Tall Sally
I Call Your Name
Slow Down
Matchbox

A Hard Day's Night / Things We Said Today – (Parlophone – July 10, 1964)

A Hard Day's Night – (Parlophone – July 10, 1964)
A Hard Day's Night
I Should Have Known Better
If I Fell
I'm Happy Just To Dance With You
And I Love Her
Tell Me Why
Can't Buy Me Love

Any Time At All
I'll Cry Instead

Things We Said Today
When I Get Home
You Can't Do That
I'll Be Back

I Feel Fine / She's A Woman – (Parlophone – November 23, 1964)

Beatles For Sale – (Parlophone – December 4, 1964)
No Reply
I'm A Loser
Baby's In Black
Rock And Roll Music
I'll Follow The Sun
Mr. Moonlight
Kansas City/Hey Hey Hey Hey

Eight Days A Week
Words Of Love
Honey Don't
Every Little Thing
I Don't Want To Spoil The Party
What You're Doing
Everybody's Trying To Be My Baby

Ticket To Ride / Yes It Is – (Parlophone -April 9, 1965)

Help / I'm Down – (Parlophone – July 19, 1965)

Help! – (Parlophone – August 6, 1965)
Help!
The Night Before
You've Got To Hide Your Love Away
I Need You
Another Girl
You're Going To Lose That Girl
Ticket To Ride

Act Naturally
It's Only Love
You Like Me Too Much
Tell Me What You See
I've Just Seen A Face
Yesterday
Dizzy Miss Lizzy

Day Tripper / We Can Work It Out – (Parlophone – December 3, 1965)

Rubber Soul – (Parlophone – December 3, 1965)
Drive My Car
Norwegian Wood (This Bird Has Flown)
You Won't See Me
Nowhere Man
Think For Yourself
The Word
Michelle

What Goes On
Girl
I'm Looking Through You
In My Life
Wait
If I Needed Someone
Run For Your Life

Paperback Writer / Rain – (Parlophone – May 30, 1966)

Eleanor Rigby / Yellow Submarine – (Parlophone -August 5, 1966)

Revolver – (Parlophone – August 5, 1966)
Taxman
Eleanor Rigby
I'm Only Sleeping
Love You To

Here, There and Everywhere
Yellow Submarine
She Said, She Said

Good Day Sunshine
And Your Bird Can Sing
For No One
Dr. Robert
I Want To Tell You
Got To Get You Into My Life
Tomorrow Never Knows

A Collection of Beatles Oldies – (Parlophone – Dec 10, 1966)
Bad Boy

Strawberry Fields Forever / Penny Lane – (Parlophone – February 17, 1967)

Sgt. Pepper's Lonely Hearts Club Band – (Parlophone -June 1, 1967)
Sgt. Pepper's Lonely Hearts Club Band
With A Little Help From My Friends
Lucy In The Sky With Diamonds
Getting Better
Fixing A Hole
She's Leaving Home
Being For The Benefit Of Mr. Kite

Within You, Without You
When I'm Sixty Four
Lovely Rita
Good Morning, Good Morning
Sgt. Pepper's Lonely Hearts Club Band (Reprise)
A Day In The Life

All You Need Is Love / Baby You're A Rich Man – (Parlophone – July 7, 1967)

Hello Goodbye / I Am The Walrus – (Parlophone – November 24, 1967)

Magical Mystery Tour- (Parlophone – December 8, 1967)
Magical Mystery Tour
Your Mother Should Know
I Am The Walrus
The Fool On The Hill
Flying
Blue Jay Way

Lady Madonna / The Inner Light – (Parlophone – March 15, 1968)

Hey Jude /Revolution – (Apple – August 30, 1968)

The Beatles – (Apple – November 22, 1968)
Back In The U.S.S.R.
Dear Prudence
Glass Onion
Ob-La-Di, Ob-La-Da
Wild Honey Pie
The Continuing Story of Bungalow Bill
While My Guitar Gently Weeps
Happiness Is A Warm Gun

Martha My Dear
I'm So Tired
Blackbird
Piggies
Rocky Racoon
Don't Pass Me By
Why Don't We Do It In The Road?
I Will
Julia

Birthday
Yer Blues
Mother Nature's Son
Everybody's Got Something To Hide Except Me and My Monkey

Sexy Sadie
Helter Skelter
Long, Long, Long

Revolution 1
Honey Pie
Savoy Truffle
Cry Baby Cry
Can You Take Me Back
Revolution 9
Good Night

Get Back / Don't Let Me Down – (Apple – April 11, 1969)

The Ballad Of John And Yoko / Old Brown Shoe – (Apple – May 30, 1969)

Abbey Road – September 26, 1969
Come Together
Something
Maxwell's Silver Hammer
Oh! Darling
Octopus's Garden
I Want You (She's So Heavy)

Here Comes The Sun
Because
You Never Give Me Your Money
Sun King
Mean Mr. Mustard
Polythene Pam
She Came In Through The Bathroom Window
Golden Slumbers
Carry That Weight
The End
Her Majesty

Something / Come Together – (Apple – October 6, 1969)

Let It Be / You Know My Name (Look Up The Number) – (Apple – March 6, 1970)

Let It Be – (Apple – May 8, 1970 with book / November 6, 1970 without book)

Two Of Us
Dig A Pony
Across The Universe
I Me Mine
Dig It
Let It Be
Maggie Mae

I've Got A Feeling
One After 909
The Long And Winding Road
For You Blue
Get Back

BIBLIOGRAPHY

Beatles, T. and Roylance, B. (2000). ***The Beatles Anthology***. London: Weidenfeld & Nicolson.

Emerick, G., Massey, H. and Costello, E. (2007). ***Here, There and Everywhere: My Life Recording the Music of the Beatles.*** New York: Penguin Group (USA).

Leigh, S. (1998). ***Drummed Out!: the sacking of Pete Best.*** United Kingdom: Northdown Publishing Ltd

Lewisohn, M. (1996). ***The Complete Beatles Chronicle***. New Ed. London: Chancellor Press.

Lewisohn, M. (2013). ***The Beatles – All These Years: Volume One: Tune in.*** **(Extended Edition)** 1st ed. London: Little, Brown & Company.

MacDonald, I. (1994). ***Revolution in the Head: 'Beatles' Records and the Sixties***. London: Fourth Estate.

Kevin Ryan & Brian Kehew. (2006). ***Recording the Beatles.*** S.l.: Curvebender Publishing.

McCartney, M. (1982). ***Thank U Very Much: Mike McCartney's Family Album***. London: HarperCollins Distribution Services.

Miles, B. and McCartney, P. (1997). ***Paul McCartney: Many Years From Now***. London: Martin Secker & Warburg.

Scott, K. and Owsinski, B. (2012). ***Abbey Road to Ziggy Stardust: Off the Record with the Beatles, Bowie, Elton & So Much More.*** Los Angeles: Alfred Publishing Co Inc.,U.S.

NOTES

Preface Notes

1 Although sharing a love and repertoire of Carl Perkins and Buddy Holly songs, being a clean-cut country & western outfit, the Country Four were less than enamoured by the leather-clad and frankly dishevelled Beatles. Probably their first engagement after the departure of Sonny Webb (Kenny Johnson), the Country Four (with Brian Newman stepping up to fill the void) performed with the Beatles at St.Paul's Church Youth Club in Birkenhead on Saturday 10th March, 1962.

2 The same can't be said of their contemporaries - listen to almost anything from the same period, and the percussion on show is either too fussy, poorly mixed, or seems to have been added for the sake of it. The Beatles would never have released anything as shoddy as the Rolling Stones did with *I'm Free* - it's one thing to have a performance that is intentionally 'loose', but to release a recording so lacking in basic timekeeping regarding both the drums AND percussion is truly shocking.
In that respect, the Beatles were fortunate to have seasoned Producer George Martin overseeing their work - the Rolling Stones had their business-minded manager Andrew Loog Oldham.

3 This supposed quote probably took hold as if you have ever visited Merseyside, you will know that acidic, playful comments like this are delivered daily among friends and workmates - and to get the best effect - within earshot of the recipient who bears it stoically, knowing that eventually his turn will come.

4 To this can be added Ringo's portrayal as the dead-pan clown of the group in the Beatles' films, an image he seemingly felt comfortable with and did little to challenge until his final years as a Beatle.

5 The Simpsons - *Brush With Greatness* (Episode 31 - April 11 1991)

6 Famously, when asked his opinion of Ringo, Buddy snapped back - "adequate".

7 *Early Days* from the album *New*. Lyrics by Paul McCartney. Published by MPL Communications Inc. Copyright 2013 MPL Communications Inc.

8 The late actor Lewis Collins, himself a drummer with Merseybeat group the Mojos, referred to Terry as the "creme de la creme of Liverpool drummers".

9 Terry's room had in fact previously been a voice-over booth.

10 The Dynatron radiogram was purchased from the Epstein family store NEMS as a 21st birthday present for

11 How It's quite possible Ringo's missing kit was due to an episode of sabotage, as the Beatles' equipment was still stored at the Best's Casbah Club home in West Derby, an occurrence that continued on through 1963, until the Beatles moved themselves, and their equipment to London.

Main Notes

1 One such exception is the inclusion of *Bad Boy* as part of the US release Beatles VI, (Chapter 15 of Part 2).

2 From the excellent "Abbey Road To Ziggy Stardust" by Ken Scott and Bobby Owsinski.

3 Transistor radios (still single-speaker), enabling music to be truly portable for the first time, were still in their infancy. Batteries were expensive and had short life expectancy.

4 Later released as the *Let It Be* LP in 1970.

5 Witness his snare work on *Drive My Car* from *Rubber Soul.*

6 In a display of 'one-upmanship', four retired Yorkshireman relate to each other with increasing absurdity, how poor and deprived their formative years were.

7 Brian Farrell, a friend of ours, whose sister dated Paul McCartney, recalled the moment he arrived home to find Macca on his hands and knees, holding the Echo across the front of the fire in order to increase the draught in order to get the fire started.

8 As a child, Alex can remember his Nan possessing "SMOG Masks", which she would don on her way to work at her kiosk at Mann Island, by the Pier Head. The nearby blackened buildings (including the Royal Liver, featured in the film, *Yellow Submarine)* were testament to the pollution breathed in by generations of Liverpudlians.

9 This experience was still the case up to the 1980's, we both have similar recollections of our childhood Sundays, even the best part of a quarter of a century apart!

10 Dettol is the trade name for a line of antiseptic hygiene products popular in Britain since the post-war years.

11 This exit was however not accessible to the audience, who were unaware of it's existence.

12 Another 'Beatle myth' since proven to be unsubstantiated.

13 Derived from the first letter of their christian names – JaPaGe

14 Author interview with Mike McCartney, July 2015.

15 Ant is the author of the excellent *Merseyside At War*, published by Amberley Publishing – ISBN 978 1445637600

16 Common in use among Liverpudlians, 'skitting' or 'giving skits' is the (constant) and often sarcastic, barbed criticism and taunting of an individual.

17 Probably the Jacaranda in Slater Street. Known as "The Jac", this cafe by day, club by night was run by an early mentor of the group, Allan Williams. A larger than life and affable character, Williams was instrumental in furthering the Beatles' early career. The Silver Beatles would rehearse downstairs in the Jacaranda.

18 Facebook post November 9 2015.

19 The Pillar Club shut it's door in 1966, and reportedly remains untouched since.

20 Interview by Paul Drew, US Radio, April 1975, and quoted in *The Beatles Tune In (Extended Edition*) by Mark Lewisohn. Published by Little, Brown Book Group, 2013.

21 From the *Beatles Book* magazine, issue 3 (October 1963) and quoted in *The Beatles Tune In (Extended Edition)* by Mark Lewisohn. Published by Little, Brown Book Group, 2013.

22 This section became known as Pete's 'skip-beat' and was abandoned soon after this session.

23 And this is a quote from a non-drummer. "Drummed Out! The Sacking Of Pete Best", Spencer Leigh, Northdown Publishing 1998.

24 The Beatles Tune In (Extended Edition) by Mark Lewisohn. Published by Little, Brown Book Group, 2013.

25 Known as the 'Exies' (from existential) the Beatles soon developed friendships with young 'art-house' students, and often were guests at their new friends homes, taking the chance to bathe, feed and rest. Pete was rarely a visitor, although the charms of a nightclub stripper girlfriend may just have had an influence upon his decision making.

26 The Beatles Tune In (Extended Edition) by Mark Lewisohn. Published by Little, Brown Book Group, 2013.

27 Preludin was routinely made available to the Beatles and other Liverpool groups by 'Mama' Rosa, the toilet attendant at the Top Ten Club. Just about every Hamburg club had it's own lady who kept the toilets clean, and sold combs, toothpaste and other such 'stuff' from her little table. Every time you went paid a visit, you would drop a few pfennigs into her little dish. Terry also remembers Rosa supplying another "upper" Captogan. Allegedly.

28 *The Beatles Tune In (Extended Edition)* by Mark Lewisohn. Published by Little, Brown Book Group, 2013.

29 The Beatles In Hamburg, Spencer Leigh, Omnibus Press 2011.

30 Over time, The Beatles' relationship with Mona and the Bests was patched up, to the extent that Mona supplied the medals the group sported on the cover of *Sgt. Pepper's Lonely Hearts Club Band.*

31 The Beatles had auditioned for Decca on January 1st 1962, their lacklustre and nervous performance heightened once again by erratic timekeeping.

32 *The Beatles Anthology,* Cassell & Co, 2000.

33 *Photograph* – Ringo Starr, 2013

34 Around this time, Ringo seriously considered emigration to America.

35 *The Beatles Tune In (Extended Edition)* by Mark Lewisohn. 2013.

36 *Off The Record*.HBO.2008.

37 The Beatles' choice of boots were made by Annello and Davide, Terry purchasing a pair from The Toggery in Stockport.

38 To alleviate boredom while recuperating from having his tonsils removed, Ringo took LPs by these artists with him into hospital.

Interview from the DVD *The Beatles From Liverpool To San Francisco*, Eagle Rock Entertainment, 200539

39 Expanding upon the limited range available in the early 60's, the drummer of today is able to choose from a variety of cymbal types with a specific sound in mind. From china and splash cymbals to an expanded range of crashes and rides, even some with areas deliberately cut away to achieve a specific sound.

40 At the time of writing, 18" (and even 16") bass drums are once again proving popular.

41 Considered to be the UK's first bespoke drum shop.

42 Ringo Starr Tells the story of his First Ludwig Drum Kit - Rock and Roll Hall of Fame + Museum youtube feed.

43 As did Clem Burke of Blondie, some 20 years later.

44 It is probable that while recording tracks for Apple artist Jackie Lomax's album *Is This What You Want?* in Los Angeles in late 1968, George was sufficiently inspired by session drummer Hal Blaine's expansive drum kit to expand Ringo's sound with this purchase. Indeed, within weeks Ringo had added his old bass drum to his new kit – although it is open to debate if this experimental arrangement found it's way onto any Beatles recordings.

45 The use of tea-towels to dampen the drums was also a technique deliberately employed to produce a flat, dry, 'dead' sound, in order to match the dynamics of the song.

46 A true story – *Many are the tales of violence offered to over enthusiastic and inexperienced sound guys, a classic one tells of a particular engineer who was unhappy with his drum sound. The engineer, an overbearing chap, said the kit sounded 'awful' and proceeded to completely cover the heads in tape and tissue which totally deadened the sound. This infuriated the drummer so much that when the engineer went back to his control room he ripped all of the stuff off leaving his drums as he had set them up in the first place. After playing the kit, the drummer asked 'How do they sound now?' 'Much better', came the reply.*

47 Such material extended to literally anything that was lying around the studio, including bizarrely, an eight-armed woollen sweater, a legacy of the film *Help!* (originally titled *Eight Arms To Hold You*), which was found lying around the studio.

48 *VH1 online Interview* – http://www.vh1.com/music/tuner/2014-09-16/beatles-engineer-ken-scott-on-mono-vinyl-box-set/

49 The Beatles were contracted to record '4 sides' of 2 single releases. EMI were not obliged to release these singles, rather the contract was designed for EMI's publishing group Ardmore and Beechwood to 'claim' the rights to Lennon & McCartney compositions. Having previously rejected the group out of hand, Martin was forced into a corner by Ardmore and Beechwood's pursuit of the Beatles compositions, plus EMI's top brass being less than enamoured with George Martin's long – term relationship with his secretary becoming known to the stuffy Edwardian executives.

50 Originally referring to a group of New York publishers and composers who dominated early to mid 20th Century music, Tin Pan Alley became known as a generic term to describe such people and practices. Britain's Tin Pan Alley was Denmark Street in London.

51 Ringo interviewed by Elliot Mintz, 1976.

52 The timing of the break in the middle of the chorus was probably what proved problematic – relying upon a degree of 'feel', without the vocal cue to recommence playing, each Beatle may have been milliseconds away from each other. This was probably enough for George Martin to be unhappy with the cohesion between bass guitar and drums.

53 Mark Lewisohn – *The Complete Beatles Recording Sessions*, Hamlyn, 1988.

54 Interview with the Daily Record.

55 Mark Lewisohn – *The Complete Beatles Recording Sessions*, Hamlyn, 1988.

56 The Beatles Anthology.

57 The documentary Andy White's claim surfaced (*Love Me Do, 1962*. BBC, 2012) tended to err on the side of controversy rather than caution, chiefly reinforcing the myth Brian Epstein was able to manipulate *Love Me Do* into the charts by purchasing 10,000 copies of the single for his NEMS record stores. Sales numbers had no bearing upon a 45's chart position from each store, figures were derived from popularity against other releases (ranked from 1 to 30) rather than total sales.

58 *Love Me Do, 1962*. BBC 2012.

59 *Here, There and Everywhere – My life Recording The Music Of The Beatles.* Gotham Books, 2006

60 *Merseybeat*, January 3rd, 1963

61 *Abbey Road: The Story of the World's Most Famous Recording Studios* – Brian Southall, Peter Vince, Allan Rouse 1982

62 According to Lewisohn (*The Complete Beatles Recording Sessions*), Please Please Me was listed as 'takes unknown'. Why were these takes not properly documented?

63 In 2013, to mark the 50th anniversary of the recording of *Please Please Me*, BBC4 commissioned current artists to 're-record' the album in Studio 2 Abbey Road Studios.

Despite utilising the constraints of the original session timescale, the project employed large numbers of artist and musicians and completely missed the point that the original album was played and sung by four nervous and exhausted Beatles (one of whom had a stinking cold), having driven hundreds of miles around the country completing a series of engagements.

64 Notably, both are Lennon songs. John was a big fan of Arthur Alexander, and this drum pattern must have made an impression.

65 Another oddity is an alternate vocal on the stereo vocal track (John's final round of "C'mon's), which adds further to the mystery surrounding the song.

66 One can't but help but wonder how *Twist And Shout* would have sounded with the more powerful Ludwig drums at play?

67 And probably Andy White's Ludwig drums to boot!

68 The bass drum was particularly more powerful from this point on.

69 More noticeable on the 2014 vinyl remaster than the 2009 cd remaster, the hi-hats betray a tape drop-out due to an edit inserted between 1.15 and 1.22.

70 This pattern was also simultaneously employed across the Atlantic as a staple of the burgeoning Surf sound.

71 The overloading of an audio signal, either before or during its journey through the mixing desk, producing a loud, 'fuzzy' sound

72 With long-term use, a drummer can become reliant upon his attachment to his bass drum pedal, the familiarity of the pedal-travel, the bounce-back from the skin, both contributing to the feel and confidence of his playing.

73 Many recordings from the 60's suffer this fate – have a listen to *Needles And Pins* by The Searchers, or how about Led Zeppelin's *Since I've Been Loving You*? Why didn't anyone send out for a can of '3-in-1' oil?

74 Issued on the German Odeon *"Beatles Greatest"* and the World Records *"The Beatles Box",* this introduction should have been edited out by the mastering engineer.

75 Although it has to be noted, this was probably under the direction of George Martin.

76 *Little Child* is possibly inspired by Sonny Boy Williamson's Blues standard, *Good Morning, Little Schoolgirl.*

77 Not content with performing their own songs as a means to stay one step ahead of their Merseybeat rivals, the Beatles would regularly be found scouring Brian Epstein's NEMS record store for that unusual and distinctive song. *Devil In His Heart* was the B-Side of *Bad Boy* – the only release by the Donays.

78 Terry – *'In the early days, The Beatles were adept at picking original songs like this Barrett Strong track. I remember this as being one of their most popular onstage songs played at the Cavern. It was not only down to John's emotive vocal – but to the way they produced such a powerful, stomping beat.'*

79 "That's me doing Wilson Pickett. You know, a cowbell going four in the bar…."

John Lennon

All We Are Saying, David Sheff.

This quote does seem a little odd, as Wilson Pickett had yet to attain prominence at the time of the recording of *You Can't Do That*. However, always on the look-out for new music (especially American R&B), the Beatles regularly drew up lists of new releases they would like to hear.

80 Visually thrilling, a fantastic example can be found during the Beatles' performance of *Long Tall Sally* on the Swedish TV show '*Drop-In*', available in episode 2 of *The Beatles Anthology.*

81 *Here, There and Everywhere* – Geoff Emerick and Howard Massey, Gotham Books, 2006

82 *Paul McCartney – Many Years From Now,* Barry Miles. Secker & Warburg, 1997.

83 *Paul McCartney – Many Years From Now,* Barry Miles. Secker & Warburg, 1997.

84 Terry – *Rock 'n' Roll Music* takes me right back to 1961 and the Cavern. If you want to enjoy that experience, get into a sauna with your clothes on, mop the place out with disinfectant, close your eyes, eat a really bad hot dog, sip from a bottle of warm Pepsi – Cola – and play the music loud!"

85 UK Channel 4 serial drama set in Liverpool.

86 Tying in with Jeremy's story, in a July 2015 interview, Paul McCartney tells how he and John Lennon 'lost' dozens of potential Beatles classics, as they constantly forgot them due to having no means of recording them while away from home or the studio. http://www.theguardian.com/music/2015/jul/31/the-beatles-forgot-dozens-of-songs

87 In an interesting twist, George's excellent 12-string Rickenbacker guitar work on *What You're Doing* pre-dates the Byrds' *Mr.Tambourine Man by a good 6 months* – a track that also featured Hal Blaine on drums.

88 *Dizzy Miss Lizzy,* found it's way onto the upcoming UK *Help* LP.

89 Possibly, besides *Julia* from *The Beatles* and the vocal only *Because* from *Abbey Road* – even *Revolution 9* from *The Beatles* has cymbals!

90 Released in the US on *Beatles VI*, and later on the UK compilation *A Collection Of Beatles Oldies.* See Part 11, Chapter 15.

91 Not dissimilar to the later Beatles release *Get Back*.

92 To be found on the *Plastic Ono Band – Live Peace In Toronto* release.

93 Some sources indicate George Harrison may have played tambourine.

94 Stevie Wonder's hit version of We Can Work It Out eschews this 3/4 feel, opting to continue the solid 4/4 throughout.

95 As a newly discovered 1966 letter by George Harrison to Atlanta DJ and friend Paul Drew reveal, plans were made by The Beatles to record their next album in the Stax studios, with Stax Producer Jim Stewart at the helm. Having booked and cancelled a 2 week stint at Stax, Harrison revealed to Drew – *"P.P.S. Did you hear that we nearly recorded in Memphis with Jim Stuart [sic]. We would all like it a lot, but too many people get insane with money ideas at the mention of the word 'Beatles,"'and so it fell through!"* It's tantalising to imagine just what would have emerged from these sessions, and how different the resulting album (which we know as *Revolver*) would have been.

96 Tambourine was perhaps played by Lennon, as the maracas have the more percussive element, and would probably have been recorded as an overdub with the maracas.

97 The deliberate, simultaneous striking with a stick of the snare skin and rim (the metal hoop of the drum that holds the skin in place). The resulting sound produces a loud "crack" than the conventional strike.

98 111 bars including the fade-out – but who's counting?

99 *Paul McCartney – Many Years From Now,* Barry Miles. Secker & Warburg, 1997.

100 The 2/4 bar addition here in *Rain* is not necessarily associated with time-keeping per-se, but rather "half a bar" of 4/4 thrown in for good measure.

101 Paul ditched his Hofner bass in favour of a Rickenbacker, taking advantage of a 'cleaner' sound afforded by the use of Direct Injection (D.I.). This relatively new invention involved the instrument being plugged directly into the mixing desk, negating the need to place a microphone in front of a speaker in order to record it. This provided a higher quality signal with a deeper, richer, texture, which allowed for more accurate and expansive post-production. Further Innovations such as Artificial Double Tracking (ADT) were also employed. A technique invented by Recording Engineer Ken Townsend, ADT uses tape-delay to simulate the natural doubling of voices or instruments by double tracking. ADT was first used here and throughout the remainder of the Beatles' sessions.

102 The housewife in question was actually Terry's Mum.

103 A brief run-through of the song possesses an eerie vibraphone, with a harsh tambourine on subsequent early takes.

104 It is documented John Lennon played tambourine and maracas, however due to the limitation of available tracks on which to record, it is likely these instruments were played simultaneously by two members of the group.

105 Issued on *Anthology 2* in 1996.

106 At a reported cost of $250,000, *Tomorrow Never Knows* was used at the end of the episode of AMC TV Series Mad Men, Lady Lazarus. Don Draper is told by his young wife Megan to play her copy of *Revolver*, and is instructed to put on T*omorrow Never Knows*, the most artistically radical track the band had produced up to that point. The stodgy, conservative Draper is not impressed by the song and turns it off, underscoring a recurring theme through the season that the character is entirely out of touch with youth culture.

107 While the Beach Boys' influence can be heard on Revolver *(Here, There And Everywhere*), the vast majority of the material had been written and recorded prior to the albums' release in August 1966.

108 *When I'm 64* was spared this fate, making it onto *Sgt. Pepper's Lonely Heart Club Band.*

109 Former 'roadie' turned assistant, trusted and loyal friend of the group.

110 The playing of the hand bell is open to conjecture.

111 Like other instruments on *Penny Lane*, the drums were subjected to limiting whilst also being recorded slower, to be sped-up on replay. This process certainly alters the sound of the drums, leading to an increase in "depth".

112 *She's Leaving Home* being the only other song on the album without percussion, or for that matter, drums.

113 Yet, around the world turbulent events were unfolding. America was having troubles both at home and abroad with peace marches at home and over 475,000 men stationed in Vietnam. The 'Summer of Love' didn't extend to inner cities either – in Detroit riots intensified to the extent that 4,000 paratroops were sent in to restore order and prevent the city being burned to the ground.

114 Was this percussive approach due to insecurity? Away from Abbey Road, were the Beatles feeling unease as they were out of their comfort zone, while also having doubts about the strength of the song?

115 Lewisohn – *The Complete Beatles Recording Sessions.*

116 By all accounts, Geoff was 'burnt-out' as a result of having to shuffle regular day-time studio sessions with the Beatles' erratic and late night sessions.

117 A version released as a bonus item on the iTunes version of the *Love* album contains a prelude to the song, featuring finger cymbals and maracas.

118 **Flanging** – similar to ADT, an effect created when an audio signal is played back alongside a delayed version of itself. Unlike the

constant signal of ADT, with flanging the signal is fed at a variable rate of speed, resulting in the swirling sound we hear on Blue Jay Way. Although the first use of flanging is attributed to guitar and production pioneer Les Paul in the 1940's, the effect first came to prominence on the Small Faces *Itchycoo Park,* notably applied to Kenny Jones' drums to link the verses and choruses. The similar effect of phasing tends to be more subtle and smooth, flanging taking on the mantle of a harsher 'jet plane' sound.

119 Lewisohn – *The Complete Beatles Recording Sessions.*

120 Most likely a muted cowbell.

121 *Helter Skelter* is widely believed to have been inspired by the Who's *I Can See For Miles,* although McCartney's recollection is of reading an article in the music press about the Who recording the "loudest, most raucous song.." (*The McCartney Interview* LP 1980).

122 Interview, Music Radar, September 2009.

123 A hunting ground the Authors can attest to as being accurately portrayed here.

124 The 'Bonzos' feature in *Magical Mystery Tour*, and, under a pseudonym McCartney produced their hit *I'm The Urban Spaceman*.

125 Probably due to the subject matter relating to his then use of heroin.

126 More noticeable on the 2014 vinyl remaster than the 2009 cd remaster, the hi-hats betray a tape drop-out due to an edit inserted between 1.15 and 1.22.

127 Visually thrilling, a fantastic example can be found during the Beatles' performance of *Long Tall Sally* on the Swedish TV show '*Drop-In*', available in episode 2 of *The Beatles Anthology.*

128 *Paul McCartney – Many Years From Now,* Barry Miles. Secker & Warburg, 1997.

129 *Dizzy Miss Lizzy,* found it's way onto the upcoming UK *Help* LP.

130 Some sources indicate George Harrison may have played tambourine.

131 Stevie Wonder's hit version of We Can Work It Out eschews this 3/4 feel, opting to continue the solid 4/4 throughout.

132 *Paul McCartney – Many Years From Now,* Barry Miles. Secker & Warburg, 1997.

133 The 2/4 bar addition here in *Rain* is not necessarily associated with time-keeping per-se, but rather "half a bar" of 4/4 thrown in for good measure.

134 A hunting ground the Authors can attest to as being accurately portrayed here.

135 The 'Bonzos' feature in *Magical Mystery Tour*, and, under a pseudonym McCartney produced their hit *I'm The Urban Spaceman*.

136 Americans, who take marching drumming very seriously have developed over 40 rudiments, although many are just basic examples joined together in different configurations.

INDEX

IMAGE CREDITS

Every effort has been made to correctly acknowledge the source or copyright holder of each illustration and unintentional errors or omissions will be corrected in future editions.

Alex Cain & Terry McCusker - All notation images and data charts.

Drum catalogue images and Beatles singles are from Alex Cain's collection – 63, 65, 71, 72 (left), 73 (left), 74 (left), 75 (left), 76 (top and bottom left), 103, 104, 105, 108, 116, 118, 121, 136, 137, 138, 139, 141, 145, 153, 154, 155, 157, 168, 170, 171, 172, 173, 184, 187, 203, 207, 220, 221, 227, 229, 248, 249, 251, 254, 255, 261, 262, 263, 264, 289, 290, 299, 302, 303, 304, 319, 321, 322, 334

Alamy Stock Photo – XVI, 19, 22, 27, 30, 31, 43 (top right), 44, 46, 66, 68, 73 (right), 79, 97, 120, 180, 298, 323

ANL/Rex/Shutterstock - 132

Sandi Anne Borowsky - 45

Alex Cain – XI, XIV (Top), XV, 32, 38, 39, 40 (left), 41, 43 (top and bottom left)

Corbis Images - 126

Daily Mail/Rex/Shutterstock - 86

Getty Images – 28, 74 (right), 75 (right), 117

Bill Harry – 33

David Hobbs - 72

Frieda Kelly – 45

Sam Leach - 62

Mark Lewisohn – XIV (Bottom)

David Magnus/Rex/Shutterstock - 246

Bill Minto - 266

Terry McCusker – XIX, 23, 43 (bottom right), 61, 69, 76 (right)

Mirrorpix – Front Cover, 1, 11, 20, 21, 37, 40 (right), 42, 47, 50, 55, 63 (top right), 64, 67, 70 (both images), 135, 140, 144, 174, 183, 226, 253, 258, 265, 291, 352

News Syndication – 78, 106

P.A. Images – 48

Rex/Shutterstock – 83

Don Powell – XIII